"Don Sharpes' book makes the argument that the current rancid political atmosphere in this country is in many ways merely an extension of the profound divisions we saw result in catastrophic violence during the Civil War. It should serve as a warning to those who continue to divide us, especially along the lines of race, that if we fail to move forward as one nation we could well descend into another fruitless and bloody conflagration."

Mark Potok
Director, Intelligence Project
Southern Poverty Law Center
Montgomery, Alabama

"In this provocative book, *A House Still Divided: The Rise of U.S. Anti-Government and Radical Movement,* Don Sharpes persuasively demonstrates a persistent pattern of anti-government stridency and powerfully narrates the hostility to authority as emblematic of a culturally conflicted society. The current political dogma of "Movement Conservatives" for a limited government is mired in our historical past and Sharpes forcefully exposes the moral bankruptcy of a sizable segment of the American populace, from the colonial slave owners to the Tea Party radicals, for fiercely exhorting the value of limited government while gaming the system to enrich itself. Sharpes' analysis of antagonisms in American society is forceful, revealing, scholarly, and a must read especially for those who are concerned about the zealotry of Movement Conservatives to destroy the pillars of the Progressive State, so it crashes."

T. Ramakrishna Reddy, Ph. D.
Chair and Professor of Political Science
Weber State University
Ogden, Utah 84408

SELECTED BOOKS BY DON SHARPES

The Education of Allah's Warriors
Handbook of International Studies in Education (Ed.) (Information Age
   Publishing, 2010)
Outcasts and Heretics, Profiles in Independent Thought and Courage
   (Lexington Books, 2007)
*Sacred Bull, Holy Cow, A Cultural Study of Civilization's Most Important
   Animal* (Peter Lang, 2005)
Lords of the Scrolls, Literary Traditions in the Bible and Gospels
   (Peter Lang, 2004)
*Advanced Educational Foundations, The History, Philosophy and Culture
   of Schools* (Routledge, 2002)
Advanced Psychology for Teachers (McGraw Hill, 1999)
International Teacher Education Perspectives (Editor) (Routledge, 1988)
Curriculum Traditions and Practices (Routledge, 1988)
Education and the U.S. Government (St. Martin's Press, 1987)
Improving School Staffs (American Association of School Administrators,
   1974)
Strategies for Differentiated Staffing (McCutchan Publishers, 1974)

OUR DIVIDED HOUSE

Anti-Government and Radical Movements And the Failure of National Unification

Donald K. Sharpes

Vulcan Publishers
2012

ISBN: 13: 979-0615604954

Published by Vulcan
Printed By CreateSpace, A Division of Amazon
2012

TABLE OF CONTENTS

ACKNOWLEDGEMENTS

I am indebted to both individuals and institutions. I owe an enormous debt to the late Dr. Don Bigelow, a former history professor at Brandeis and Columbia and later Director in the U.S. Government from 1961, who hired me into government service in 1968 and who remained a friend and discussant on governmental affairs until his death in 2007. Steve Pappas has been a federal friend for nearly thirty years, and his long-serving public service in the military and government has been an inspiration. Our decades-long intellectual discussions and numerous collaborations involving government programs have always been insightful and beneficial for me.

My personal knowledge of government civil servants, of federal government administration, and graduate university teaching of constitutional principles has prompted me to respond more fully in this study to casual and caustic critics who demean public service and democratic understandings of how government functions.

The eleven million volumes of the library at the University of Cambridge provided me with the needed access to, among other rare, archival volumes, and complete sets of American presidential papers. I always found the books I required at the library at Arizona State University. I am grateful both to the Emeritus College of Arizona State University, and Wolfson College at Cambridge University for support, my academic homes in retirement.

I am also thankful to the Council for International Exchanges of Scholars that sponsors Fulbright programs by honoring me over the past years with four grant awards to Malaysia, Cyprus, Denmark and Indonesia that gave me unique understandings of government foreign policy practices.

PREFACE

The Mississippi River divides the country geographically east and west. Slavery and its supporting states once divided the country north and south. We are not just a nation of two bickering, taunting political parties, only divided over domestic policymaking. We are two co-existing national mentalities, oppositional ideological differences defined by our turbulent history. [1]

The chief political division in the nation today is the rising tide of anti-government sentiment, a sectarianism that has carried over from the days of slavery and the century of segregation after the Civil War. According to former Governor of Massachusetts and presidential candidate Mitt Romney, the greatest threat to economic prosperity is not the budget deficit, the competition with China, the collapse of the housing market and the middle class, out-of-control entitlement programs, or the European debt crisis but "a government that is overbearing, intrusive, and demanding." Anti-government advocates curiously never identify whether this applies to all three branches of government, or just one. The whole of democratic government is broad-brushed with a universal enmity that overlooks the constitutional fact each branch has its own built-in checks and balances.

Anti-government feeling is most visible in what polls use to describe a person's political philosophy as "very conservative" wing of the Republican Party, and not the "somewhat conservative," or "moderate." I will use a variety of descriptions like "radical" and "ultra" to describe this political orientation but basically it identifies primarily the "very conservative" tier of the Republican Party.

Slavery and segregation hung like Spanish moss over the South trying to cover national shame but not resident pride. It's easy to understand an anti-government perspective in North Korea, Cuba, Burma, maybe even Saudi Arabia and Russia, but more difficult in America since so many immigrants come here because of American government freedoms and opportunities. The anti-government movement, of which the Tea Party and anti-tax groups form a part, has morphed from those who once saw government as a problem to now seeing it as an enemy, a dangerous transformation in a democracy.

This study speaks to the anti-government movement as a longstanding American historical phenomenon that manifests itself in today's political debate as if coming from the political Left. In the past the anti-government movement came from the South. Today it is a southern mentality, now existing everywhere, that has become resurgent, polarizing the country. My aim is to show our past national conflict before and after the Civil War and to demonstrate that the same issues that divided us, absent slavery, in previous centuries are now palpably present in our politics. If we substitute today's political Left for yesterday's North, and the South for the far Right, then the contemporary terms fit a similar pattern.

As I have tried to define the broader outlines and debates in American domestic policy I have concluded that the southern mentality has not been converted into American unity. The nation is knitted loosely together with thin strands holding the fabric tenuously. The South has never really broken free from its traditional anti-government attitude. United States history is a litany of compromises and indulgences to this inherent hostility. America cannot continue to exist with this permanent, internal discord, with the last vestiges of a long-ago civil conflict if it wants to achieve competitiveness in the global world. This is not about just a conservative counterbalance to a progressive, liberal agenda but a defined antagonism to a separatist way of life. This study is an exploration of that turbulent history whose results are now fully exposed in our dysfunctional government.

I use the term ultra or radical Republicans to describe far right Republicans who promote this anti-government movement. They favor almost universally corporations and business, decry domestic programs for the less fortunate, block domestic government initiatives and tax increases even for natural disasters. From 2008 to 2012 to be a Republican politician meant you had to have a dogmatic catechism of denouncing Big Government, new taxes, be in favor of cutting federal programs (but without alienating those receiving Medicare or Social Security), and censuring President Obama for instituting a socialist federal health care program, even though it passed Congress. Hating government and being against it, and having no practical solutions for modern problems are not attributes for actually legislating or administering government. Moderate Republicans, like William F. Buckley's and Nelson Rockefeller's brand of pragmatic conservatism, have lost appeal or gone into hiding.

I am not contending that a strong conservative viewpoint is antithetical to American democracy, but that its more radical side is historically a part of a southern politics from an earlier era and its political habits have hardened. And although this is an indictment of sorts against the ultra-conservative bias of the Republican Party, it is not meant to be an implied endorsement of Democrats either. The ambition of both parties to gain power to control their political agendas is the overriding cause of all political activity.

This book is an historical analysis of our bitter racist and segregated history, and a study to demonstrate that that influence still resonates in our national discourse, political campaigns and legislative activities. The separatism that used to run only in the South has thoroughly permeated American society and fractured the political process so that little of electoral or legislative consequence gets accomplished. The principal political action of radical conservatives is to struggle against federal legislation, subvert democratic institutions like unions, belittle public servants, and keep legislation from interfering with business and corporations or from raising taxes. Aggressive antagonism toward government is distorting politics with a resurgent and disquieting historical legacy.

The contemporary oppositional and casual language we use to define ourselves—liberal v. conservative, progressivism v. capitalism, Labor v. Business, New Deal v. Free Markets—masks a long historical tradition of deeper social and political divisions. The North/South chasm has always been the nation's most pronounced distinction, and it contributes yet to our profound political disagreement. We are mired in a political dogmatism that rivals religious fundamentalism as a national characteristic.

The constitutional mistake was to enunciate property as a right, as it once had been in regal England, but then to confound that right by legitimizing institutionalized slavery. When slavery was introduced in the colonies, slaves were legal property like land or any other commodity. The entanglement of a human right—for slaves to be free—and a civil right—to be the property of someone else—was the legal, social and economic American dilemma for over two hundred years. Its racial legacy is still with us politically.

I use the term "national government" and not "federal government" deliberately because I believe it is the more appropriate term. A federal government, that is to say, a union of the states and a unified national partnership agreement between colonial colonies, existed under the *Articles of Confederation* (1774-1787). In a sense, there were many nations existing in North America even prior to the arrival of Europeans. Multiple native nations or tribes, speaking a variety of languages and enjoying various cultural lifestyles, inhabited the continent. Their subdued numbers today are a pale representation of their once flourishing empires.

Since the Constitution created a new form of government where none existed before, the result was not a union of existing states but an entirely new government that superseded states that previously had been British colonies. We still use the term "federal government" because it is older and more traditional. But a national government, "a more perfect union," is what the Constitution created, supplanting a federalized union of states.

There are multiple ways in which we can view divisions in American society and certainly the obvious ones are income equality and social class and ethnic differences. I think that the North/South distinction is subtler and still as divisive as it was centuries ago, which is why I have chosen to illustrate its lingering influence on American life. We cannot fully understand our contemporary social and political dilemmas without examining origins and causes within an historical context.

The American South is different because of its history of engrained bigotry. It is as different as Basque and Catalan are from Spain, Corsica from France, or American Indian culture from urban life. Because the South had been a separatist region evolving a distinct lifestyle prior to and after the Civil War, and through the disastrous period of Reconstruction and throughout the 20th century, it has been unable entirely to shake free from its conflicted past. The nation attempted un-successfully to make civil rights laws for more than two hundred years. For ultra-conservatives seeking a return to the purest form of the Constitution they must accept that the original document condones slavery.

I believe we are still two nations, which is why our political process is handicapped with competing ideologies and an incapacitated and oppositional legislative agenda in Congress and state houses as it was prior to the Civil War.

We are not alone in this fracturing of national unity. Yugoslavia and Czechoslovakia are two examples of former European countries that broke into separatist states. At this writing, Iraq is breaking into ethnic and religious factions, and Belgium into linguistic and ethnic divisions. The *Parti Quebecois* seeks sovereignty for French-speaking citizens in Canada, and the dual language requirement shows the fragility of union between the French and English. America is not in danger of a political rupture but its cultural differences are more divisive than we have been prepared to admit.

The radical right has always existed in the South. But just like the 49 existing Klu Klux Khan groups in 2011, radicalism has migrated all over America. We have a right peaceably to assemble and express our views regardless of how hated or absurd they appear. But it is well carefully to monitor extreme hate groups since from them come militant, violent actions and assassinations based largely on deranged ideas about government. The continued expansion of the radical right's anti-government Patriot groups, nearly doubling in the past few years, is one of the more alarming indexes. [2]

One example of militant extremism is the acceleration of hate groups in the U.S. that topped over one thousand by 2011, a 66% increase since 2000, an issue I discuss in Chapter 14. These groups are fueled by conspiracy theories, changing racial demographics, and the sluggish economy. The shift to conservative extremism also appears in state houses. Birthright citizenship, guaranteed by the 14th Amendment, is under attack by anti-immigrant zealots. Multiple state legislative proposals seek to nullify power and responsibilities from the national government.

The South and its sibling state allies form the core of Republican conservatism posture as if they had a patrician complex. They fight against the national government that seemingly tries to tell them what to do, that uses tax money to fund social services that principally benefit the nation's poor and minorities that they are vehemently opposed to, and resist efforts to modify an immoderate dogmatism. [3]

The anti-government movement is a hand-me-down tradition from the days of slavery when the South was the master of all its ways, and states were self-professed to be sovereign over all their affairs. Radical conservatism is an ideology based on viewing liberalism as a political perversion, and is friendly to industry and free market enterprise as the sacred cow of all social activity. Ultra-Republicans have been so keen to focus on simplistic and obstructionist ideology that they have blinded themselves to the complexities of a global economic life. Health care plans are about saving lives and preserving a healthy society and not about the profits of pharmaceutical companies, for example. Obsessing about less taxes and debt clouds the search for formulas about improving the society, especially in education, to compete globally.

Wrap this philosophy together with a high sense of moral righteousness and you can quickly identify the shift to the far political right that characterizes the obstructionist ideology and prevents meaningful dialogue and agreement on domestic initiatives. The congressional strength of the radical right means that there is no nuanced political dialogue as everything is too imperious, either black or white and without compromise. The conservative agenda is like Samson breaking the pillars of the temple of the progressive state.

Rigid adherence at the temple of orthodox ideology has its own built-in perils. We need look for illustration no farther than America's foreign policy debacles. China's Great Leap Forward and Russia's inflexible belief in Marxism are historical examples of ideological hubris. It will do the country no better if we replace the arrogance of old leaders with the ignorance of new ones.

The political division is partly compounded by economics. Today, America is more divided economically than at any time in its past. From the end of World War II in 1945 and for the next three decades the economy grew at about 3% annually, lifting everyone's financial boat. But in the last three decades significant income growth has been concentrated at the top of the financial heap. In 1976 the top one percent of the U.S. population was garnering 8.9% of all incomes. By 2007, that top one percent was raking in 23.5% of all incomes. During the same period, inflation-adjusted hourly wages fell 7%. This widening of income disparity and inequality has eroded a middle class and deepened those at the lower end of the economic scale making poverty more pronounced.

Wealth disparity has accelerated the historical language and anti-government feelings that previously divided the country. Wrath at government is legendary. Southern anger protected slavery and a self-sufficient plantation economy from government interference. Now that anti-government sentiment is distributed equally throughout the country. Then mix in overt moves to secede and have states declare some government actions unconstitutional and you have a description of the prevailing national mood.

Politicians, political candidates and pundits have inveighed against so-called government takeovers when in fact much of the economic distress has been caused by financial institutions that have gamed the system and recklessly bilked customers and governments alike. America has been luring financial gamers to Wall Street with fat paychecks paid out by banks and lenders who have exposed an ethical bankruptcy in the management of the public's money, and led to the collapse of taxpayer confidence and the erosion of middle class economic stability. The first stranglehold was the invention of credit cards, and America fell in love with them. Smart people knew credit was not real money. Credit cards quickly became a fast road to bankruptcy or insolvency for careless users.

Then came the housing bubble. [4] Adroit manipulation of contracts by banks, lack of government oversight and consumer protection, risky investments, and homeowner gullibility all helped create conditions for a national economic default. The dire financial collapse did not thwart the ultra-right ideological belief. Instead, it calcified far right Republican enmity toward government as if the economic condition did not exist.

Republican congressional extremism during the debt ceiling crisis and funding of the government to continue operations in the summer and fall of 2011 revealed the pattern of anti-government obstructionism that existed prior to the Civil War in the debates about which new territories should be admitted into the union as slave or free states. Radical Republicans, fueled by the Tea Party activists in and out of Congress, clubbed the country over the head with a radical anti-government ideology, purposefully diverting the public's interest in an anti-banking campaign until the clumsy but well-intended Occupy movement revived the misdeeds of financial institutions.

In American democracy there will always be a balance between the government's right to provide welfare to the people, and the people's right to choose life courses without governmental interference. Many liberals lean too far toward the government's role, while Libertarians and many conservatives lean too far toward corporations and individual choices. In these tumultuous times, the extremes are in the ascendancy and much-needed intellectual discourse is often absent.

Our tormented history in the third millennium has created an alarming social and political dysfunction. Our level of political ignorance and petty squabbling is dismaying. American politicians do not play as if they are on one team. Political parties play as if they are in permanent opposition and that obviously lessens the chances of national problem solving. Visceral emotions play a bigger role in political decisions than sober reason. Every few decades zealots and extremists on the right, like McCarthyism, and on the left like the New Dealers—what Richard Hofstadter called the paranoid style in American politics—emerge to imperil rational political discourse. In this era the challenge is from the extremist right with movements like the Tea Party. But I believe its roots lie deeper in our historical narrative, buried in our shame and political compromise with the peculiar institution of slavery. A sizeable proportion of Americans have always been susceptible to blatant demagoguery perhaps because of their attunement over the years to the fiery oratory and delusions of evangelical preachers.

America has a 300-year history of enslavement, which is why I think remnants of racism and xenophobia still run deep in American culture, both in the North and the South, and have recently emerged to taint the politics American citizens mirror. The political spectrum has become a mixture of racist, anti-intellectual, and extremist views. Political life is imitating parody and caricature. Many voters cannot get beyond repeating the mantra on their election signs, and, when asked to explain them, have negligible responses to what they actually mean.

There will always be partisan opposition from the political party out of power to the party in power of either the Congress or the presidency. But the recent trend is toward rancid hostility and not just opposition. We cannot divest ourselves of our divided past any more than we can throw off our ancestry and genetics. The pain and stigma of slavery won't go away, even after a war over 150 years ago that ended it, because the arrogance, language and culture of White supremacy survives buried deep in the population and surfaces periodically in political representation. As Alexis De Tocqueville noted presciently in his classic *Democracy in America* (1835, 1840) "I perceive slavery receding; the prejudice to which it has given birth is unmoving." [5]

It's no longer just Congressman Joe Wilson's incivility and discourteous outburst during the President Obama's State of the Union address in 2008, and (no surprise) solid constituency agreement with his action in South Carolina. It's about active attempts to dismember civil liberties. It's no longer about the Governor of Texas hinting that secession might be necessary, nor the subtext of Strom Thurmond's attempt to form a Dixiecrat political party agreeable to segregation, or former House leader Tom Delay's criminal antics in Texas to use his campaign funds for other political candidates, or his nefarious relationships with criminal lobbyists like Jack Abramoff. [6] It is no longer just that school officials want to deny the first African-American President to speak to children about education, or about embarrassing politicians whose oratory and dialogue doesn't rise above schoolyard yelling arguments.

It's about a people and a history that cannot abide that they were militarily forced to unite with northern, liberal states and cannot stomach a non-white President. This is no longer a fight between the blue and grey and the secession of eleven southern states in 1861, but a lingering acerbic intermission from actual military conflict about whether or not radical Republicans—ideological descendants of the South and its sympathizers—are serious about participating in unity government at all and can ever fully divest themselves of a racist, discriminatory and alienating past. The legislative strategy is not compromise to aid the American public, but cynically to block and prevent the Democratic Party from gaining any political advantage.

Historically, one-half of American society in 1860 was based on the relationships in the lives of husband and wife and parents and children. A separate and unequal society was based on those personal relationships plus on the relation of master and slave. One society cleaved to the social principle of the equality of the races, and the other to the principle that the races are not equal and that only the rights of racial equals, as noted in the *U.S. Constitution*, are entitled to equality. For two hundred years America did have an egalitarian society, but only for Whites, and for another hundred years only for White males.

Since 1787 America was forced to tolerate slavery in order to get the cooperation of slave states to pass the Constitution, and not only to acknowledge its existence in that document but to make repeated concessions to its heinous practices. Eight of the first twelve presidents—Washington, Jefferson, Madison, Monroe, Jackson, Tyler, Polk, and Taylor—were slave owners. Would they have not resisted a national government that attempted to divest them of their human property? Scores of executives and cabinet members from 1790 to 1860 from the South were chosen for government representation in the executive branch to uphold racial inequality between the North and South.

Two distinct and incompatible visions of America, and indeed different civilizations, were allowed to live side by side since the inception of the Republic, and endured multiple governmental compromises to permit its continued existence. But slavery could not be protected forever inside a national government that professed internal unity.

Lincoln challenged slavery as unsustainable in a democracy that professed in favor of human rights. Neither in anthropology, political science, logic or humanitarian decency is it possible to conclude that all traces of White supremacy, cultivated over hundreds of years, can be extinguished in a few generations, despite legislation making discrimination illegal. Southern personal, family and regional histories are too compellingly embedded in a discredited idea of a human hierarchy of supremacy of one people over another. Beliefs in racial inequality still exist and have spread through internal immigration throughout American society. It has emerged again in these times of political debates over issues like immigration, and in election biennial campaign cycles that disparage government and any domestic programs.

No respectable American would dare revive slavery as a method of restarting the economy or preserving a sense of superiority over others. But though slavery as an institutionalized form of labor has been eradicated in the western world, the overt motives of those who oppose immigrant labor are just as vitriolic. Who should wear the badge of an American citizenship identity, and who should be allowed to work in the U.S. is patently obvious in the anti-immigrant political debate.

Contemporary events are a reflection of historical values perpetrated over more than two centuries of social and political division. America has never been thoroughly united, and its political compromises and temporizing over slavery for so many decades has inured generations to the mire of anti-government sentiment that contaminates today's national debates. This book shows America's tormented, dual national history and argues that we are a long way from overcoming our tragic legacy.

Chapter One
The Rise of Anti-Government
And Radical Movements

A house divided against itself cannot stand.
(Abraham Lincoln, April 1858)

A strong sense of individualism courses through the veins of Americans, a trait observed by Alexis de Tocqueville in his classic study *Democracy in America* first published in 1835. That fervent desire to be left to one's own devices without government interference is powerful and self-sustaining. It drives the democratic ideals of democracy in choosing representatives and in resisting legislative, executive or judicial acts people believe are unfair. De Tocqueville discovered that America was a nation filled with contradictions, proclaiming in the *Declaration of Independence* that all men were created equal yet a country filled with racial prejudice. It conformed to majority rule but felt empowered with individualism. Though deeply religious, the nation was materialistic in the extreme.

In this initial chapter I tie economic imperatives to the emergence of a centuries-old southern strategy of faulting national government for intruding on individual liberties and so-called state prerogatives. Stagnation in the economy mirrors the political dysfunction. I argue that the anti-government movement is a centuries-old trend locked into issues of states rights, civil rights and fundamentalist religious beliefs. Those arrogant enough to claim God is calling them to some service, even to run for President, appeals to divine intervention as a pandering sop to the religiously devout.

Radical anti-government conservatives have re-emerged after the economic meltdown beginning in 2008 with an anti-government, anti-domestic government spending, anti-federal regulation, the elimination of agencies, and an anti-tax platform. The South always favors a strong military because, apart from its earliest days of growing cotton and sugar, its principal activity has been a literal and figurative militant war against the North. When a southern asks, "Where y'all from?" it is not an idle question because the answer will determine his view of your allegiances.

Incessant hammering on the national debt—which clearly needs to be reduced over time—and not economic stimulation or job growth, reveals a political motivation to undo Democratic presidential and governmental initiatives.[1] Moreover, government regulations invariably protect public health and safety from abusive corporate interests. So the societal and political choice is usually quite clear—does American society favor public safety over private business profits or not?

Republicans criticized the *Dodd-Frank Act* that added safety factors to the banking system, created the Consumer Protection Agency, and reined in abusive lending practices to prevent another financial crisis. The law's purpose was to protect American consumers so they could get clear, accurate information they needed to shop for mortgages, credit cards, and other financial products, and protect them from hidden fees, abusive terms, and deceptive practices.

Republican chicanery, sophistry and hostage-taking of the economy, and the deceit of blaming President Obama for government's expenditures, were an exercise in unrestrained negativism and parochial ideological partisanship. The political strategy of resisting any proposal the federal government assumes by starving it of resources so it cannot spend money on social welfare or infrastructure programs is as old as the slave South. The earliest blockage of national programs like building roads and canals came from the South because national funding for those infrastructure projects would typically only benefit the North.

Anti-government Republican advocates today seek to place fiscal restrictions on government and demonize alternatives. Republican presidential candidates, in attempts to salve citizen anxieties, offer economic solutions disconnected from reality. Government spending is not the sole cause of the budget deficit, nor is reducing the debt, lowering taxes, or assaulting social programs the sole solution.

Republicans are the political descendants of the Anti-Federalists in the 1770s. One of the principal reasons for the *U.S. Constitution* as a replacement for *The Articles of Confederation* was to solve the new nation's fiscal crisis and give it more flexibility in raising taxes and responding to financial disturbances and common security issues. The Constitution is sparse in its fiscal requirements, allowing for future generations to deal with financial problems with appropriate measures. Radical Republicans are trying to limit future generations with balanced budget amendments, government borrowing restrictions, and anti-tax initiatives. As a percentage of national income, the U.S. collects less income tax, about 25%, than nearly all European countries.

Government obstructionism existed after the Civil War during the disaster that was Reconstruction in the struggle to maintain white supremacy. It reared in ugly head again during the period of civil rights reform in the mid-1960s as southern state intransigence showed how deep-seated was any government interference against the South's bigoted vision, including U.S Supreme Court decisions like *Brown v Board of Education* in 1954.

Far right Republican radicalism, of which the Tea Party movement is just one expression, is taking the country hostage to protect partisan interests. Such radicalism was manifested by eleven southern states that severed the binding cords of the Constitution in 1860 by seceding to protect slavery. Today the radical movement strives to disembowel the government from acting to protect the national interests with a dogmatic ideology that conflict with standard, pragmatic economic and legislative rationales. It symbolically unfurls a Confederate flag as a sign of intolerance for national unity. It is a feast of current government dysfunction, but a revelation of a recurring anti-government strategy that has origins in southern intransigence that protected the caddie carriers for the ideology of White supremacy.

Socialism. Federal Takeover. States Rights. Big Government. Freedom not government control. Unconstitutional laws. Tyrannical presidents. What are the emotionally stormy messages underlying these negative words and code phrases, and why do they have such a resonance among so many?

These political labels are easy to understand and therefore politically palatable to tin-eared and uncritical voters. Explanations of what they actually imply are too complicated for the general public. Superficial but catchy slogans, epithets without arguments, exhaustingly boring when repeated endlessly, and the conflicts embedded in their content have been the cleavage in American politics since the founding of the republic when slavery was condoned and embedded in the Constitution. In the past, voicing such phrases easily passed for campaign rhetoric that got the electorate emotionally agitated but did not constitute policy. No one I have spoken to as background for this study could adequately explain the meanings of such phrases or how they were relevant. Now these sound bites have become a part of a major ideology of obstructionism.

Here is some background and consequences resulting from the rise of radical Republican ideology that espouses no business regulation, limited or no taxes, and less government.

In October 2001, the month after the worst terrorist attack on American soil, the Houston, Texas energy company Enron slid into bankruptcy dragging down with it the Arthur Andersen audit accountancy firm, one of the fifth largest in the world. Enron hid billions in debt and when it failed investors lost $63 billion in assets, the largest company bankruptcy in U.S. history until WorldCom in 2002. President Bush, whose Administration ignored financial regulation, afterwards promised new financial regulations. None ever materialized. The financial debacles of 2007 exposed government neglect that created the worst recession since the Great Depression of the 1930s.

And taxes? Americans were not asked to pay with taxes or make any sacrifices for two simultaneous wars or a new pharmaceutical plan, Medicare Part D. In fact, taxes were cut for the wealthiest Americans. The nation's bills were to be piled on top of the financial mortgage legerdemain that sent the economy into a tailspin. The chaos of the war in Iraq was matched by the financial chaos the government instigated with neglect or collusion with private contractors. The nation was once again soiled by a southern strategy, now thoroughly sown in a radicalized Republican party, of elevating political principles above national interests. These political principles, as we shall see, are the same that were used to sustain a doomed economy of slavery over the last two centuries of American history.

Grover Norquist, a Washington lobbyist and Libertarian ideologue who worked for the Reagan Administration, got conservative politicians to sign a document, the *Taxpayer Protection Pledge* that committed Republicans to oppose any federal effort to raise taxes. By 2012 all presidential candidates (except Jon Huntsman) signed, as did 238 House members, 41 Senators, and 1,200 state legislators. Conservative Republicans pledged their souls to a think tank guru—not to the American people—never to raise taxes which resulted in legislative and national fiscal paralysis. Citizens need to question how a private person could get elected representatives to commit to an agreement that limits congressional debate and decision-making, the essence of legislative activity in a democracy.

It doesn't take a professional historian to conclude that the ideology of anti-regulation, anti-taxation, and keeping government from interfering in the financial sector during a period of two wars, plunged the American economy into a depression the Obama Administration inherited. Radical conservatives revived the same civil rights ideology from southern themes of the 1800s—the bumper-sticker, gut-grabbing slogans of distorted ideas of freedom from government interference, states rights, and strict constitutional constructivism. They use anecdotes to make a point, rarely consult relevant historical facts, make visceral arguments devoid of constitutional muster, and never change the subject. Ideology does not have to answer questions; it just has to keep repeating the same dogmatic message.

Anti-government expressions have a long tradition in American politics and I plan to show the predictable pattern over the years of attacks against the government itself and not just arguments over national policy disagreements. A slightly paranoid side of this movement sees government out to destroy individual liberties. [2] What distinguishes members of this following is not just the absence of verifiable facts supporting the assertions—though they often manufacture conclusions and offer them as facts—but the leap into a fantasy world of conspiracy.

The most conspicuous conspiracy examples in the 20th century were the anti-Semitic radio rants of the Catholic priest, Father C. E. Coughlin (1891-1979) and his Social Justice movement of right-wing discontent. Later, in the 1950s, the Senate hearings of Wisconsin Senator Joseph R. McCarthy and his mass appeal against communism alarmed the nation. These demagogues have been matched by the ravings of TV and radio personalities whose millions of listeners constitute an ultra-conservative bloc of disaffected voters who see the government and the world as Manichean. They preach fear, paranoia, ignorance and conspiracy, and offer no evidence for outlandish claims. Extreme divisiveness has abandoned comity in discourse and civility, and promoted demagoguery and ignorance as norms for topics of national discussion. Analogously, such spokespersons are not porcelain but more like unglazed pottery, suitable for storage of home items but unattractive and unaesthetic.

The themes, ideas and even the phrases used in the early 19th century to maintain slavery, to keep the country separate into free and slave states with their differing economies, ushered in a political vocabulary echoing the sentiments that spawned them. The phrases used nearly two hundred years ago are used today to describe peoples' frustration with government. For example, beginning in 1861 all southerners called Lincoln a tyrant, and called government "impatient, overbearing, dictatorial and intolerant," expressions voiced today by radical conservatives. [3] The bigotry is submerged, like the engine of your vehicle: you can hear it, feel it, but can't see it, but know it is operating under the hood.

Radical Republicans categorize Democratic policies and programs as socialist, liberal, progressive. Is it exclusively a liberal, progressive agenda that allows government to seek to mitigate the toxic influences of contaminated air and water? Or to help build an enviable national transportation system? Or to convert to clean energy? Or to protest fighting interminable and invasive wars abroad? Or to reform the spiraling costs of healthcare? Or to curb the lingering effects of discrimination? The Republican political agenda is to obstruct anything the national government proposes and slash what it funds. It is a centuries-old southern strategy that didn't want plantation economies taxed to pay for northern benefits.

Unquestionably, an ageing population combined with expensive new medical technologies and expanded national health care has made the current welfare model unsustainable over the decades. Social benefit reforms are necessary at all socioeconomic levels to balance budgets. Republicans believe that government cannot nurture economic growth, and that government programs monopolize what private enterprise does. Democrats generally believe that government welfare programs are sustainable but need to be adjusted, or that capital markets on their own cannot generate an economy that does not lead to wealth inequalities. The problem is that partisan political fury makes compromise unrealizable. [4]

Amidst this political polarity, American wealth inequality widened. There will always be some wealth inequality as there is in the dispersal of all human abilities. But in the U.S. that economic gap has been widening over the past thirty years even relative to all other developed countries. The gap is not just the result of reduced economic growth but of a political will for redistribution among consumers and taxpayers. The Republican rich believe that the underclass is unwilling to work hard enough to achieve. The new plantation owners and wealthy aristocrats are reluctant to share the goodies through taxes on their gains to help their slaves and lesser deserving minions survive. That is the real class warfare.

Did I mention that the top 1% of the nation's wealthy (average annual income of $468,000) are 82% White, but that 99% of the national population (average annual income of $50,400) is only 64% White, thus exposing the deepening racial divide? Many conservative Whites are reluctant to have government extend the social welfare benefits they enjoy to a growing segment of the minority population. Politicians exploit this racial, ethnic and class difference, many seeking to cut social security and Medicare and Medicaid for future beneficiaries.

The Bush Administration and the Republican Congress, by cutting taxes for the wealthy, slashing spending on the poor, and ignoring or slashing regulations on corporations, and trying to reduce the power of union to negotiate with employers, have all help create the wealth disparity that now endangers the country's economic health. According to an October 2011 *Time* poll, 79% of Americans believe the gap between the rich and poor is too large, though there are great disparities within the U.S., and to be in the top 1% in Manhattan is not the same as it would be in rural Georgia. And 68% say the rich should pay more in taxes. Extreme concentration of wealth in the pockets of the very few is incompatible with a broad-based consumer market. Moreover, wide income inequalities, hastened by war, famine or natural disasters, are predictors of revolutions. As Teddy Roosevelt noted in a speech in 1910: "Those who oppose all reform will do well to remember that ruin in its worst form is inevitable if our national life brings us nothing better than swollen fortunes for the few and the triumph in both politics and business of a sordid and selfish materialism."

A survey by the Employee Benefit Confidence Research Institute in 2011 noted that 56% of American workers have less than $25,000 in retirement savings, and 29% less than $1,000. In the same year, average cash bonuses for Wall Street workers ran about $130,000. Between 1993 and 2008, the top one percent of Americans took home 52% of all income growth in the U.S. According to Standard and Poor's Index, the chief CEO's received, on average, $11.4 million in compensation, a 23% increase in one year, or 343 times an average worker's pay, up from 42 times an average worker's pay in 1980.

According to the IRS, the bottom 50% of all income earners—those making about $33,000 and below per year—constituted only 13% of all income. The top one percent earned 17% of all income. The rest was distributed more or less equally among three other income groups.

There used to be three principal pillars to reasonable retirement: pensions, savings and social security. Let that old rule about "follow the money" guide you. Corporate, government and business pensions have nearly gone the way of the horse and carriage, eroding the traditional way to save for retirement. For example, the nation's smallest state, Rhode Island, has a massive public employee pension crisis. Its pension fund is not only underfunded but broke. Other states surely will follow this eroding financial base for state and local retirees. Cutting retiree pension benefits is no longer off the table. And this is just for state and local government plans.

The second pillar of personal savings are the financial firms of 401(k)s and 403(b)s under which banks and anonymous portfolio managers control your assets that are invested in equities while the banks take any number of fees for management. President George W. Bush tried to privatize social security, the third retirement pillar, so the government would place the escrow funds in the stock market.

How financially comfortable does this shift toward the financial sector make you feel? The ratio of Wall Street profits in 1980 was 7%. In 2007 it was 41%. And if you still want to believe with former President Reagan that government is the problem then go ahead and buy car insurance from a talking lizard with a British accent, or open an attached Email file that says you are a winner.

The Republican supposition that money somehow trickles down as the rich create jobs is not credible. It is consumers who create jobs, not businesses. The argument that businesses and corporations should not be over-taxed because they are the creators of jobs is not credible either. Businesses hire more people only after sales expand; they do not create jobs without customers buying their products.

The global market engulfed America whose citizens ate debt like candy, and who became as complacent about the future as the little pig that didn't build a brick house. According to Jeffrey Sachs in *The Price of Civilization, Reawakening American Virtue and Prosperity* (2011): "The CEO-friendly environment, the economic effects of globalization, and specific regulatory and tax policy choices made in Washington over the past thirty years have combined to create an inequality in income and wealth unprecedented in American history."

According to the Census Bureau and Bureau of Labor Statistics in 2012, 15 million Americans are unemployed and another 10 million partially employed. Using the standard bell curve as an analogy, Americans in poverty are about twice what is normal during a time of economic stability. More than 11 million households owe more than their homes are worth (23% of all mortgages), and 46 million are without health insurance. The nation is short 360,000 teachers, or about a fourth of those needed. These sad economic realities have been conditioned by policies favoring businesses and by stroking anti-government movements.

Ultra-conservatives are the ideological, if not the biological, descendants of southerners who tolerated slavery in a plantation economy and held a preference for worker order, stability, and efficiency that merits comparison with the personality of authoritarian figures. [5] Plantation owners held a similar kind of domestic and feudal dictatorship. Whites born into this southern economy felt emboldened to command, to dominate others. This southern character trait, as Alexis De Tocqueville would describe him, would be "high-minded, prompt, irascible, violent, ardent in his desires, impatient of obstacles, but easy to discourage if he cannot triumph with the first stroke."

Dogmatic rigidity fueled the quest for money in the South from about 1750 to 1964, even if it meant using slave labor, or, into the first half of the 20th century, legalized state segregation against Blacks. Plantation owners did not need collective bargaining organizations for their workers, or to accept the rights of workers to negotiate for wages or working conditions. So, as a contemporary example, governors and politicians, under the guise of cutting budget deficits and the destruction of unions, appear to be returning to an autocratic period when workers simply complied with the demands of the authorities and had no rights to negotiate for wages, benefits or improved working conditions. [6]

In Michigan in November 2011 a vote on a referendum overturned a Republican initiative to curb union activities 61% to 39%. Ultra-conservatives had sought an ideological agenda curtailing peoples' rights to join a union, restricting a woman's right to control her body, to criminalize immigration by states, and restrict voting rights.

The Texas legislature also restricted voting by reducing the number of districts where minorities could elect representatives. Hispanics sued and a federal court overturned the ruling since the state plan clearly violated Section 2 of the *Voting Rights Act* that explicitly prohibits any action that dilutes the ability of minorities to elect their own representatives.

Try a quick quiz about Republican president and initiatives.
Who was pro-union?
Answer: Eisenhower. Ronald Reagan was the head of a union, The Screen Actors' Guild, a union, prior to becoming Governor of California.
Who raised taxes the most?
Answer: Reagan, both as Governor of California and as President.
And also George H. W. Bush
Who proposed serious national health care reform?
Answer: Nixon.
Who initiated the Individual Mandate for health care?
Answer: The conservative Heritage Foundation and Republican Senators Orrin Hatch and Robert Bennett of Utah, and Charles Grassley and Christopher Bond of Missouri in the *Consumer Choice Health Security Act* (1993).
Who established the Environmental Protection Agency conservatives now seek to abolish?
Answer: Nixon.

The contemporary Republican Party has been jerked so far to the right from its moderate base in the 20th century that it is no longer recognizable from its ideological positions on traditional domestic issues. Republicans now exhibit a bunker mentality, a defensive stance with regimented group-speak thinking against any government interference in, or for, any domestic program. They continue to fight the battles of New Deal liberalism in the 1930s—like the elimination of Social Security (*The Federal Insurance Contribution Act*, or FICA) for some presidential candidates—to cure economic distress.

The language of economic security has changed dramatically. In the year of my birth, 1934, millions were out of work, losing jobs and their homes before there were social safety nets. President F. D. Roosevelt made people and family security the centerpiece of economic stability. Today, in a similar period of economic distress, the centerpiece is not people but the size of government and the budget. How did the conversation turn from the needs of people to the presumed threats of the government? We have shifted priorities from personal compassion to fiscal arithmetic, as if math were one of America's strong suits.

Taxes are also a pivotal issue. Doesn't it make sense that taxes should increase incrementally with the rate of population increase so that there is no diminution of services and the tax burden is distributed evenly over time? When Bush found a government surplus when he came to office in 2001—$5.6 trillion projected over a decade—he initiated two wars, installed a Medicare prescription drug program, and gave two tax refunds to high-earning Americans, all without corresponding budget cuts to pay for them. The Republican-controlled Congress then did not ask for spending cuts elsewhere to pay for these bulging programs.

So it's good to cut taxes when there is a surplus, and also when there is a deficit and two ongoing wars. When Republicans gained a majority in the House in 2011 they found a huge government deficit—$10.4 trillion projected over a decade. Since 2001 the single most significant factor in the enlargement of the deficit has been tax cuts. Tax levels have not been maintained over the past decade to equal or match increases in economic expansion or population growth.

Tax and spending cuts for Republicans are the only solution for any economic situation. Sensible economic remedies upheld by most economists have no influence on that unrelenting, dogmatic position. Polls broadly revealed that most Americans favor raising taxes and cutting spending together rather than never raising taxes to reduce the deficit.

Taxes were the scourge of the Confederacy and southern states after the Civil War too. Taxes were essential to rebuild the totally devastated southern economy and the only taxable commodity was land. Scarlett O'Hara in Margaret Mitchell's *Gone With the Wind* steals her sister's fiancee, shoots a man in the face, and sells wood at exorbitant prices to pay state property taxes on Tara. Southern antipathy toward taxes runs deep in the South. [7]

Because of the corporate tax breaks and a weakened economy, the government took in by 2011 the least in revenue since 1950. Additionally, the canard used to blame a political party for spending is bogus. The shortfall in state and local revenues in a depressed economy is because of the loss of taxes from tourism, services, or business or personal income. [8]

Assume a hypothetical family of four living on the economic margin with less than $30,000 in income, with the average credit card debt of $14,000, and in a house that is worth less than the original mortgage. Suddenly, one of the two children is hospitalized and a large co-payment for hospital services is required. Of course, the family goes a little deeper into debt for the sake of the family member's health. Such is the state of the national economy, that for the sake of the nation's health it may be reluctantly necessary to go slightly deeper into debt to salvage an ailing economy.

The plight of Texas can serve as just one example of right-wing conservatives in several states. Despite the claims of the state's power figures that Texas is a haven for small taxes and a business-friendly environment, its corporate bragging cannot conceal its social services deficits. Texas ranks last in the nation in children's health care access, thirty-eighth in the nation in per-student spending, forty-fifth in SAT score pairings, and fiftieth in the percentage of adults graduating from high school. If only hard work and a supposedly strong family values orientation were enough these days to solve any future problem, Texas could lead the nation in eliminating social services altogether.

Tackling the national debt will demand exceptional courage and require more than cuts in congressional, discretionary spending, the smallest part of government expenditures. Ideally, reform and cutbacks in entitlements—Social Security, Medicare and Medicaid, the largest domestic slices of the American budget other than defense—should accompany tax increases to shorten the time the national debt can be seriously reduced or eliminated. The national debt is exasperated by the high level of household and personal debt the public accumulated and will remain a partial barrier to full economic recovery. In 2011 the average credit card debt per household was $14,750, and there were an average of 3.5 credit cards per customer. [9]

The legislation of a social services program does not mean that the country is becoming socialist. A socialist government is not defined by legislation but by a form of government. Some Americans have been hoodwinked into believing America will become like China or the former USSR because a particular piece of legislation is targeted at those less fortunate.

The South was built largely on a paternalistic plantation economy where worker needs were provided by the landowner. The first major riff between the North and South was over national tariffs that benefitted northern businesses. The plantation economy never had any government interference because the plantation owners independently were both the local and state government and had no need of a national government's interference. This southern economic mentality was a negative reaction to all northern taxation, and to all programs that used tax revenues to benefit non-landowner members of society. This is a dim vision for the future because it is anchored in a discredited past. [10]

After assuming elected offices in 2011 the majority of the bills introduced in both the Republican House Congress and state houses were on immigration, gay marriages, unions, gun rights, abortion restrictions—none of which had anything to do with creating jobs, curtailing governmental debt or reducing inequalities. Repealing and restricting social legislation that largely benefits minorities, and the Republican sense of moral righteousness, were revealed as the naked political reality. This was not just a violation of campaign promises but an exposure of intolerant morality and a rejectionist agenda that offered nothing economically substantive, as persistent levels of economic distress were ignored.

All major religions have created institutions for assisting the poor: schools, medical clinics and social support agencies. Patriarchal owners on a southern plantation provided such services for their laboring poor. Today, antipathy toward the national government and all its social services and safety nets has superseded any religious motivations to assist the poor.

> The just man has a care for the rights of the poor; the wicked man has no such concern. (*Proverbs*, 29:7)

Freedom and liberty for individuals is a good campaign gimmick, except when Congress legislates, as it did in the 2011 and in multiple states, to control abortion, the individual right of a woman to choose, or to dismantle other individual actions for moral reasons.[11] The Republican House took up H.R. 358, the *Protect Life Act*, that sought to amend rules under the *Patient Protection and Affordable Care Act* of 2009 which gives uninsured Americans a tax credit they can use to buy private insurance. In practice, however, no federal dollars may be used to fund an abortion. But this H.R. 358 prohibits women from even purchasing private insurance with tax credits if that plan includes an abortion.

So rather than leave an abortion to the woman's choice and her health car provider, Republicans almost exclusively create new legislation, like Arizona's law to require hospitals to provide confidential information about an abortion to the state's Department of Health Services, thus forcibly intruding government in peoples' freedoms while they simultaneously proclaim individual liberties. Mississippi voters rejected an anti-abortion amendment that would have declared fertilized eggs to be "persons," thereby threatening such procedures as *in vitro* fertilization and the ability of infertile women to raise children. Mississippi legislators apparently did not consider this government intrusion.

The so-called personhood movement, in which laws define a person at the time of conception, used to be a far-right ultra right wing anti-choice movement. It is now Republican mainstream. In the 2010 midterm elections 19 states chose anti-abortion legislatures, and 29 states elected anti-abortion governors. As a result, 474 anti-choice measures were introduced by later fall 2011.

Women who seek abortions are unlikely to vote Republican, or vote at all. Therefore Republicans can target them morally and as minorities by finding loopholes in federal law permitting abortions and by restricting federal health care funding. Republicans have no trouble advocating keeping government out of everyone's wallet but take pains to try to inject government restrictions into women's wombs.

Another primary Republican obsession is the voting right. Southerners denied and placed restrictions on Blacks the right to vote for centuries, so it is not unusual to see the same strategy practiced again, this time against political opponents. Conservative legislatures in state houses have been passing voter-ID laws hoping, they believe, to constrain what they say is voter fraud, a crime that is all but non-existent and therefore is an argument without merit. A federal court in 2011 dismissed a challenge from Shelby County, Alabama that sued to have a part of the *Voting Rights Act* declared unconstitutional. Congress had required the Justice Department to obtain "pre-clearances" to any changes in voting procedures and states believed this was a non-essential federal intrusion. Congress was right to conclude that racism in the voting procedures continues.

Perhaps the most fraudulent case of the voting franchise is related in Greg Palast's, *The Best Democracy Money Can Buy*. He describes how 57,700 mostly Black voters were removed from the voting rolls by Florida Secretary of State Katherine Harris, ordered by Florida Governor Jeb Bush brother of the prospective president, prior to the close 2000 election of George W. Bush. The story was not about hanging chads and non-punched holes in voter cards but about a deliberate Republican theft of the public's right to vote in a presidential election. Al Gore lost Florida by only 537 votes but won the national popular vote. Do Republicans want the good old days back when there was a poll tax and literacy laws, a part of the Jim Crow state laws that essentially disenfranchised African Americas until the 24th Amendment, and women prior to the 19th Amendment? Political party membership reveals the racial divide. In North Carolina, 95% of all Republicans are White and 96% of all Democrats are African American.

Government taxes all citizens to support individuals who are unable to support themselves permanently, because they are veterans, elderly, or temporarily because of health or job-related disabilities. Since the New Deal under President Franklin Roosevelt and the passage of Social Security in 1936, and President Johnson's Medicare and Medicaid in 1964, a safety net has been created for society's less fortunate and former soldiers.

Democrats generally favor these programs, although Republicans also once supported them. Radical conservatives believe that people have a right to keep the money they earn, and that government should not use public funds to support social remedies. The political divide between these two opposing views is widening because conservative activists view tax money spent on others as "unconstitutional," "tyrannical" and "illegitimate." According to some who use the code world "liberty," how much of what one earns should be solely kept by individuals? They describe those who want to use tax money to be shared commonly as "socialists." The terms are used loosely but identify underlying conservative ideology that seems rarely applied to defense funds. [12]

> The goal of the federal constitution was not to destroy the existence of the states, but only to restrict it. [13]

Additionally, this is the time of a huge alienation of a large numbers of Americans who face actual or potential bankruptcy, as do some states and municipalities. These debilitating conditions should unite us in an effort to solve our collective problems. Instead, according to a 2010 USA Today/ Gallup Poll, 72% of Americans used a negative word or term to describe feelings toward the national government, and the most common, specific terms were "too big," "confused," and "corrupt," descriptions that should apply to financial institutions. [14] Only 10% of the responses were positive, and the rest neutral. However, while those polled say they want more limited government they also call Social Security and Medicare very important and want the government to be involved in education, to help reduce poverty and regulate health care and its costs. Americans live with a conflicted view of reality, just as De Tocqueville described this trait.

At the high end, six in ten say the government is too powerful and doing too many things that should be left to the private sector or the states. The inconsistency is that the military is half the size of the national government, and the Departments of Homeland Security, U.S. Postal Service and Veterans Affairs constitute much of the remainder of government services, together with the entitlement programs.

About 16 million children, nearly 25% of that population, live in poverty and their health benefits come from Medicaid. The U.S. spends over $8,000 in health care costs per person annually, according to the OECD's 2009 figures, more than any other developed country.

England had a series of Poor Laws for centuries. Medieval monasteries gave food and drink to the poor. But the earliest statute dates from the reign of Edward III in 1349 after the Black Death, and reformed in 1601 during the rule of Elizabeth I. Food and clothing were given away at the parish level, included aid for the unemployed, and later supplied orphanages from which emerged such fictional characters as Charles Dickens' *Oliver Twist*. Legislated relief for the less fortunate is not simply a democratic party initiative but a cherished value of western civilization.

Medicare constituted over 15% of the federal budget in 2012, a ratio that will expand in coming years, so curtailing its rising costs is a national not just a political party problem. Still, over 52 million Americans are uninsured. Some Medicare reform is indispensable. Either beneficiaries will have to be older to enroll, or federal costs lowered, or both. The ultra-Republican solution is to privatize this program and use vouchers that will only benefit private insurers. This is not a drastic solution but is consistent with a southern strategy to strangle federal social programs.

A New York Times/CBS poll in October 2011 found that there is a deep distrust of government. Only 9% approved of the way Congress is handing its job, and only 10% trusted the government to do what is right most of the time. Whether this refers to the Supreme Court or not is problematic because the survey question is too broad and doesn't specify the branches of government that may or may not be effective. So is Big Government too big?

The size of government is only an issue among Republicans. [15] And yet, according to the Gallup Poll in 2012, two in three Americans (64%) say big government will be the biggest threat to the country, more than twice who say the same about big business (26%). What does the size of government indicate and what do people see as a threat from government?

Is Big Government Overweight?

Fear of government is a Republican political ploy, until and unless Republicans control government and then can use it for a moral agenda.

Once elected to Congress or governorships radical conservatives morph into intrusive, big, autocratic government by squashing individual rights to an abortion (several states), the right to have privacy over their Emails (Wisconsin), to not have states demand they be tested for drugs (Florida), to curtail the right of workers to join unions (Michigan and Wisconsin), etc. Republican campaigns redundantly emphasize "limited government," "leave-me-alone without government," and personal liberties and freedoms. What they deliver once in office is often hypocritically the opposite. Government is only as large as Congress has created laws and agencies to administer them. Government has a right to control for the social order of society, as it does with the Homeland Security agency, as it does protecting individual rights.

Hence, it is not only the amount of money government collects, but also the values projected for redistribution. Domestic social programs benefit veterans, the sick and elderly, the disabled and children. Capitalism that favors a nation built on personal consumption is often at variance with the equitable redistribution of wealth. Cutting government waste is almost always a code phrase that means cutting social services programs.

Although businesses can provide jobs and some benefits that constitute what is known as social justice, they do not provide investments in people. That is government's principal task. Corporate profits do not trickle down to prevent poverty, provide access to education, prevent discrimination in the workplace, see to the nation's health, or provide healthy environments for all citizens. Among the 31 countries of the Organisation for Economic Co-operation and Development (OECD) members, the United States ranks 27th in social justice indicators, slightly above Greece, Chile, Mexico and Turkey. All other developed countries in the union have preferable rates of child and senior poverty levels, pre-primary education, health, and income equality. U.S. policies over the past few decades have not promoted the economic and social well-being of its citizens as have all other major developed countries.

The real economy of the South for more than two hundred years was the plantation that provided all services for its occupants on site. So if Big Government is the problem, why don't opponents propose to dismantle the Department of Defense that employs more than half of all the federal employees? Military pay, retirement and benefits payments total about a third of the Pentagon's costs. Military retirees pay only about a tenth of civilian workers for comparable health coverage. Is it fair that military personnel pay $400+ annually in health care premiums, and other Americans pay more than $4,000 (in 2012 figures)?

The budget of the Department of Education is about $4 billion, less than the cost of operating a Nimitz class aircraft carrier for a year and a half. Where were these voices of recrimination when President Bush created with a compliant Congress the legislation known as *No Child Left Behind* which required schools to conduct annual standardized testing, and expanded the laws of state oversight, greatly expanding federal jurisdiction over local schools? Eliminating the Department of Education does not answer the question of where administrators should oversee that congressional legislation, and others like student loans, that constitutes the Department's activities. Federal agencies administer the laws Congress passes. They do not exist as independent fiefdoms.

FEDERAL GOVERNMENT EMPLOYEES 2012
(4.4 million federal employees, 1% of U.S. population)

Military	1.6 million
Defense Civilian	652,000
Veterans Affairs	280,000
U.S. Post Office	224,665
Homeland Security	171,000
Department of Justice	108,000
Department of State	15,000
Department of Education	4,000

Yet even presidential candidates, many state governors like Governor Rick Perry of Texas—when they forget during presidential debates what agencies they want to eliminate as soon as they become president—throw out such pathetic sops to the public. Throwing red meat to the local audience in South

Carolina in 2012, Perry claimed that his state, Texas, and South Carolina, were at war with the federal government. Really? War? The last one turned out well for the South didn't it?

Nothing could so validate my thesis as this kind of vitriolic behavior from a presidential candidate. Perry also wanted to reduce Congress to half-time members and limited term Supreme Court Justices, although for this latter he would have to change the Constitution which requires that all judges hold offices "during good Behavior," essentially a lifetime appointment. He said that Turkey was not a NATO member when it is.

It's bad enough to wince at candidates whose anti-government posturing outruns good sense and common civic knowledge. It's another emotion entirely to tolerate buffoons running for high office who are ignorant of how their own government actually functions. The laughter heard around the world is becoming deafening.

Oddly, proponents of "Big Government" never complain, at least not loudly, when scores of miners are killed in a mine explosion and both aid and regulation are needed quickly.[16] Nor do conservatives complain when drilling rigs like the Deep Water Horizon run by BP that explode and crash in the Gulf of Mexico, and nearly instantaneous government responses are necessary to protect wildlife, marine life habitats and tourism and fishing industries. But predictably, there is too often a culture of cozy complacency between corporate barons, especially those from the massively secretive petroleum industry, and politicians about safety procedures.

Unquestioning sloganeering during elections masking as political discourse has been vitriolic and delivered with passionate intensity mixed with tinges of racism and bigotry. The results of an extensive report on the website of *Tea Party Nationalism* contravenes the standard political propaganda of this conservative movement about the main issues of less taxes and limited government.[17] The 2010 report found that the ranks of the Tea Party movement were permeated with concerns about race and national identity and not just issues about government spending.

A lively argument about the role of the national government in American life is healthy and perennial. But many who argue against any domestic action government takes—health care reform, immigration, energy, abortion, gay rights—occurs because of a strong attachment to individualism, a robust feeling about limited government, often grounded in misinformation, or gobs of ignorance about the U. S. Constitution. Strict constitutionalists, or constitutional conservatives, believe that the document is something like the Ten Commandments that should be read and followed without interpretation or judicial flexibility.

People may feel a strong sense of community spirit and perceive a threat from the federal government since it appears so far removed from everyone's lives . . . except when the mail is delivered daily, or government disability or unemployment checks arrive on time, or when a family knows its food is safe to eat, or when a family visits a national park, or when natural disasters strike and everyone expects government to intervene. Some may have a grievance suffered from a government bureaucratic sleight, such as denial of a claim, a failure to respond to an inquiry, a perceived wrong from taxation. A few who take up arms and plan rebellion—and therefore demean themselves by resorting only to violence to achieve their aims, or who seek to become a government onto themselves—may have other psychological issues. Ironically, constitutional freedoms extend to all citizens the right to criticize government, but not to subvert it. Yet that is exactly what the southern states did when they seceded.

The survival of rational engagements in debates about government policies depends on an informed citizenry. Political campaign rallies are too often characterized at a minimum as organized shouting matches not grounded in substantive debate, and at the other extreme as militancy. The outcome is more often a hardening of views and not a broadening of perspectives, where the recitation of the Pledge of Allegiance to the flag and the singing of the national anthem are the pinnacle expressions of patriotism, not knowledge about how a modern democracy functions, or actually performing service to the country's needs.

Only a prudent and judicious government and selective intervention policies will help an ailing economy adapt to the needs of this ruthless global marketplace, not an anti-government throwback to former centuries.

Anti-Government Tones Amidst Economic Moans

> We are defending not actually our politics or beliefs or even our way of life, but simply our homogeneity from a federal government to which in simple desperation the rest of this country has had to surrender voluntarily more and more of its personal and private liberty in order to continue to afford the United States. (William Faulkner, *Intruder in the Dust*, 1991, p. 150.)

William Faulkner's (1897–1962) literary expression of anti-government feeling in the quote above typifies southern attitudes and permeates Republican ideology. The rosy view Republicans had in 2006, according to the Gallup Poll in 2006 was wildly different from Independents and Democrats. [18] When America was engaged in two wars from 2001 to 2008, Republicans were economically confident. The Federal Reserve under the chairmanship of Alan Greenspan did nothing to calm the irrational exuberance of the explosive rise of the housing bubble. But according to a 2006 Gallup Poll, they differed radically from the rest of the population in the perception of the status of the country, revealing how widely removed they are from the popular experience.

By 2011 according to a similar Gallup Poll, Republicans said that government spending and power was the issue of greatest political importance to them (38%), followed closely by business and the economy (32%). Notice that "government spending and power," a decidedly negative view of government, is not the same as coping with the economy, the top issue at the time among a majority of Americans. Anti-government ideology means more to some politicians than having government help find economic solutions to a financial crisis Congress permitted banks to pursue without regulatory oversight. While the nation's economic health varies, conservative ideology remains solidly entrenched.

> Touching our person seek we no revenge;
> But we our kingdom's safety must so tender,
> Whose ruin you have sought, that to her laws
> We do deliver you. (*Henry V*, II, 2)

One method of government subversion is to put political loyalists in government leadership positions. Would it appear unseemly and unethical to have a lumber industry executive appointed to run the Forest Service? Should we have an anti-government rancher manage the Bureau of Land Management? Or a coal executive to run the Bureau of Mines? Or a lawyer who fought conservation practices to be Secretary of the Interior? All such appointments occurred during the Reagan and second Bush Administrations where political opponents to programs, and their more than friendly lobbyists, sabotaged, dismantled, rendered ineffective, or attempted to privatize government operations they actually managed.[19] The one defining conservative governance message was the politicization of government.

Government is neither a solution nor a problem. It is a partner with the public, business and other institutions in serving society. Government haters are the real problem. They have oddly transferred their hatred of communism and the USSR during the Cold War to the hatred of a free democracy that protects their liberties.

As politicians howled about the federal deficit, saying that the government needed to balance its checkbook just like consumers, a bipartisan compromise at the end of 2010 legislated an $800 billion dollar tax relief. Ridiculing this hypocrisy is easier than explaining its reasoning. The only possible explanation is that Republicans who controlled the House purse strings were so locked into giving collected monies back to taxpayers that nothing else mattered, certainly not what they said in previous statements about reducing the deficit.

In a story that paralleled in the national economic dilemma, Edward Mangano, Tea Party advocate and Executive of Nassau County in New York, the second richest country in the country in property taxes, entered office in January 2010 and immediately began cutting taxes thus adding to the county deficit. Within months bonds were downgraded and a state agency seized the county's checkbook and credit cards.

Financial markets cannot regulate themselves or deliver sustained prosperity, except to themselves. Those who believed that nostrum, if they are honest, now know that to be untrue. The growth of public and household debt, propelled by an essentially un-regulated financial sector and a massive redistribution of wealth to the richest during the Bush-era tax cuts, created a global economic crisis beginning in 2007. Congress passed tax cuts for the wealthiest Americans shortly after entering office in 2001, and then another tax cut in May 2003. All this was while America was engaged in two wars. What kind of country passes tax cuts so as to avoid paying for wars it has started?

Answer: a radical Republican-run government that is more adhered to corporate toadies that to economic realities.

Politicians turned a blind eye to credit card abuses that allowed homeowners to push debt to new highs. The same unregulated con was perpetrated on the housing market precipitating the economic collapse. When the economy tanked the government had little debate over massively funding the banks in late 2007, and no political will to fund an equally necessary jobs creation bill that would have stabilized unemployment and helped revive the economy.

Government has indeed lived beyond its revenue needs because of the failure to raise taxes to pay for military and social largess. It's impossible to have low taxes, a bloated military and high social safety nets. Europeans fund their social programs generally by means of high income taxes and large petroleum taxes. American politicians, beholden to the petroleum industry, shy from such a sensible way of paying for domestic programs even while gas prices rise and everyone moans while the Chevrons, Shells and ExxonMobils of the world rake in excessive profits and pay taxes overseas, a condition documented in Antonia Juhasz's *The Tyranny of Oil* (2008).

Big Corporations—including Big Oil, Big Pharma, and Piggy Banks—not Big Government, are the true masters of people's financial lives, and rulers of the money universe. Follow the money from family wallets to corporate coffers, and from there to politicians' campaign accounts, if you want to know what "Big" means. Then wonder why, America, you have been stupefied by the twisting of deceitful advertisements and propaganda away from criticizing those with the greatest concentration of wealth in history, to criticizing the government of the people. Big Oil companies should never have been permitted to merge by the Federal Trade Commission as they created giant market consolidation and power centers lobbying Congress with even larger campaign contributions. BP grabbed Amoco and Arco; Exxon and Mobil merged; Chevron gobbled up Texaco and Unocal; Conoco and Phillips combined; and Shell and Pennzoil. The nation's anti-trust laws were systematically dismembered to permit this.

As an historical parallel, the first brazen southern response to a national revenue tax began in 1832 when South Carolina decided to secede, an event known as nullification, rather than pay what the state thought was an unconstitutional tax. (See Chapter Seven) Secession was averted when President Jackson threatened military action and agreed to reduce the legislated revenue. Few realized by 1861 when the South did secede that for the Confederate States to be independent blood would have to be shed and money raised. Direct taxation was highly unpopular in the Confederate Congress and was never resorted to. Blood was indeed shed, and confederate currency became exceedingly inflated and eventually worthless.

Many believe that since they perceive government is broken that a new revolution overthrowing the tyranny of government that actually sheds blood is inevitable. Those who propose a revolution against the government may not realize that they already have a constitutional First Amendment right to "petition the government for a redress of grievances." In other words, if they believe they have been wronged they can bring a lawsuit against government, a special act of freedom unavailable in most other countries.

To these revolutionary supporters, government is always too big, but businesses and financial monopolies cannot be big enough. It is an era Klein calls "disaster capitalism." [20] A president who criticizes BP Petroleum for its disastrous oil spill in the Gulf of Mexico is "un-American," according to Rand Paul, Republican Senator from Kentucky in 2010. Conservatives castigate government, but never corporations for fraud, mismanagement and threats to public safety.

Why was there no outcry over the sole-source, non-competitive grant from taxpayer funds to the conglomerate Halliburton and its subsidiary KBR that squandered government funds on un-necessary logistics supporting the war in Iraq? Dick Cheney, former CEO of Halliburton and Vice President of the United States, continued to receive deferred payment from Halliburton while in public office. There may indeed be some government waste and fraud. But conservatives never seem to cry foul when non-competitive grants with corporations associated with a vice president conduct operations the military used to perform. By 2011 private contractors in Iraq and Afghanistan equaled or exceeded military personnel.

The late 1960s witnessed the far left revolution sponsored by groups such as the Weathermen Underground and the Black Panthers. Today, the social revolution is that of the far right and its history is much earlier. In 1963 extremism focused on repealing the income tax; deriding fluoridation in the drinking water; that communists still flourished in the U.S. propagated by Robert Welch and the John Birch Society; that scripture proves that God ordained segregation; that Black Muslims need to establish their own country. [21] Today, anti-tax extremists still abound, people are drinking other kinds of toxins in the water, and groups espousing anti-communism can't be found because Marxism is dead. But racism and bigotry have not disappeared.

Government grows because the population grows and more people seek protective and social services. America's decline in the past three decades is because there has been a disproportionate investment in human capital and infrastructure. America needs to invest in skills, technology and infrastructure and quit bickering over taxes, states rights and debt. The economic model needs to be converted to the production model. Just as important, Americans need to build trust in government, not animosity. Harping incessantly on government spending cuts is a misdirected and a negative response to the nation's problems, but an historically derived southern trait.

No amount of tax cuts to businesses or industry will return the loss of manufacturing jobs that have migrated overseas. The U.S. cannot operate as if it's in a stand-alone economy. The favorite Republican canard that tax cuts go to businesses that then hire U.S. workers is bunko. American industries are increasingly investing in jobs in China, India, Brazil, South Korea and Mexico where their factories are located. Businesses, unions, and workers are frozen in a manufacturing world that doesn't exist anymore. Between 2001 and 2010 the U.S. lost a third of its factories, over 42,000. And the southern style of the tax-cutting, government-hating, union-busting ideology toward governance isn't a strategy that will work in gaining competitive advantage in a global economy.

Civil Rights, the Core Objection

The biggest legislative change in the 20th century brought about by the federal government was not in social security, education or health care. It was the *Civil Rights Act of 1964*, a landmark legislation that should have been written into the *U.S. Constitution*. Civil Rights legislation changed the face of America after two hundred years of discrimination in southern states. While African American, Asian and Hispanic communities have broadened the diversity of America, the majority of the Republican Party remains essentially White. Its members can't seem to stomach a black president, a former female Speaker of the House, an admittedly gay chair of a congressional committee, or an Hispanic woman on the U.S. Supreme Court. Since 1935 Republicans have elected only three African American members of Congress.

Our historical legacy still defines us and its unhealthy aftereffects are evident in our politics. For example, Alabama's Attorney General in 2011, prompted by an Alabama law checking the immigration status of schoolchildren, and with an unusual bluster unassociated with the position, challenged the U.S. Department of Justice's authority to investigate civil rights abuses. The U.S. Supreme Court ruled in *Plyer v Doe* in 1982 that a child has a right to an education regardless of the status on its parents. Hence, the Justice Department had sued Alabama over its law and requested that the state's 39 superintendents forward data on affected students, citing its authority from Title IV of the *Civil Rights Act*. But the fact that Alabama is even challenging federal authority is indicative of its history of not acknowledging federal authority when it believes state interests prevail.

The division in America has always proved a problem for presidential candidates because in order to get elected they must appeal to southern biases or be southerners. The first setback for civil rights began in the Nixon Administration, a president who courted the worst prejudices of the South, unleashed his Vice President, Spiro Agnew (later convicted of taking bribes) who preyed on racial fears. Nixon lowered his priorities for social programs and tried to roll back minority rights. [22] (See Chapter Thirteen)

The states aren't as united as we would like because too many are still fighting the "war between the states," the euphemist phrase that ignored a Constitution that united them. If it was a war just between states why did southern states feel the need to create a Constitution of the Confederacy? They believed that states could go their own way without national government, as they did when they were colonial enclaves, or under *The Articles of Confederation*.

Segregation still existed in Ohio and Michigan in 1956, two years after the Supreme Court decision of *Brown v Board of Education*. The cities of Dearborn,

Wyandotte and Royal Oak, Michigan prohibited Negroes from living in the city limits. Cairo, Illinois had a statue prohibiting segregation in public schools since 1874 but it was systematically ignored for over 78 years. [23]

There is an interesting period in American history when the Continental Congress, not the Congress of the Constitution, passed a resolution giving certain slaves freedom. During 1779 at the height of the Revolutionary War, British troops invaded South Carolina. South Carolinians could not muster a militia because they believed they had to stay at home to prevent slave rebellions. Southerners justifiably feared the British would free or capture the slaves. From the *Journals of the Continental Congress* of May 29, 1779 we read: "(South Carolina) is unable to make any effectual efforts with militia, by reason of the great proportion of citizens necessary to remain at home to prevent insurrections among the negroes, and to prevent the desertion of them to the enemy."

Delegates of South Carolina to the Congress suggested that a force be raised from "among the negroes." Congress further authorized that these recruits be fed and clothed at government expense and "that every negro who shall well and faithfully serve as a soldier to the end of the present war, and shall then return his arms, be emancipated and receive the sum of fifty dollars."

The federal government in 1779 was recruiting slaves to fight the British on the home soil, and that at the end of their service they would receive $50 dollars and be emancipated, and that their owners would receive $1,000 for lost property. The necessity of war dictated the freedom of slaves, and not the economics or consciences of southern plantation owners. [24]

America freed the country from subjugation, only to find itself embroiled in guerrilla warfare. Economic and political dislocation followed the ultimate military withdrawal after independence. The war ended with over 4,000 troops killed. The attempt at nation-building failed and both sides slipped back into previous social and political divisions.

If this sounds painfully contemporary, applicable to foreign wars, it is actually the situation when America entered the defeated South in 1865. A similar series of miscalculations and misjudgments occurred when assassinations of black political aspirants and white idealists forced a political concession under the Grant administration, and the total withdrawal of northern troops sent to maintain order under President Hayes.

President Johnson from Tennessee, who rejected the idea that Blacks have the same rights of other persons and able to hold property as whites, vetoed the Freedman's Bureau Bill, saying it bloated the size of government, and the first 1866 *Civil Rights Bill.* Congress overrode both vetoes.

Congress passed the first *Military Reconstruction Act* in 1867 that treated southern states as conquered territories, each state governed by a Union general. Each state had to agree to ratify the 13th and 14th Amendment granting Blacks citizenship in order to be readmitted to the Union. All southern state legislatures, except Tennessee, voted against it, in some cases unanimously. The South simply then ignored most of the reconstruction laws passed by Congress.

The scalawags—a term for worthless livestock—described southerners who cooperated with federalists during reconstruction, and carpetbaggers described northerners who went south to help Blacks. Once federal troops left the South for good in 1877—because President Hays did not want federal troops providing order and said that states should provide their own security—states reneged on Black suffrage. The southern leadership, the so-called Redeemers, regained the power base and essentially disenfranchised Blacks from civil and political liberties. Southern paramilitary organizations flourished in the South and the KKK terrorist organization gained members.

Southerners, many Grant had faced in battle in a war that cost over 620,000 lives, were ready to use force to reverse the outcome of the war. The weary and often vengeful North gradually backed away from enforcing its own laws and allowed the South to subjugate Blacks again with discriminatory *Jim Crow* laws. The passage of the *Amnesty Act* of 1872 in effect absolved all but the most hardened of those who espoused treason. It took another hundred years, the civil rights movement and a series of laws before the South was reluctantly integrated legally into the union, but not united socially or culturally. [25]

States Without Rights

> Under the proposed Constitution, the federal acts will take effect without the necessary intervention of the several states. They will depend merely on the majority of votes in the federal legislature . . .
> (James Madison, #54 of *The Federalist Papers*)

Riding a tsunami of national anger, radical Republicans are re-proposing the sovereignty of states' rights. The issue had lain like a coiled poisonous snake in the national closet for over a hundred and fifty years. It was first proposed in the 1830s to protect slavery. So-called state sovereignty, secession and inter-governmental squabbling are the prevailing antidotes for solving the nation's problems.

Radical Republicans, uninformed about many of the specific facts and the context of U.S. history, continue to think of our national government as a union between the states, and thereby assert the concept of "states' rights" as if state sovereignty were somehow equal to the sovereignty of the national government. The Civil War repudiated that false idea while the 13th Amendment eliminated slavery that was used to defend the rights of states to do as they pleased, even to secede from the Union. The South was, and in some ways still is, as divided as any other religious or ethnic division in the world inhabiting the same country—Protestants and Catholics in Northern Ireland, Turkish and Greeks on Cyprus, Christians and Muslims in Lebanon, Palestinians and Israelis in that disputed landscape.

"States' rights" is a false slogan voiced first in the 1830s before the Confederacy to claim non-existent state legal powers. Under the U.S. Constitution, only people have rights. States have residual powers. States have no "sovereign" rights since *The Articles of Confederation*, and they certainly do not have powers that supersede congressional laws or U.S. Supreme Court decisions. The states did agree to the *Articles*. But the people, not just states, ratified the *U.S. Constitution* in 1791 that the framers proposed. Ironically, the people of the South were never given a chance to ratify the *Confederate Constitution* in 1861.

There have been multiple, sometimes amusing instances of this misdirected agenda. Because of frustration with Arizona's anti-government legislation, a former Chair of the Arizona Democratic Party and some associates petitioned Pima Country residents, where Tucson is the county capitol, to decide whether or not to secede from Arizona and petition the Congress for admission as the nation's 51st state of Baja Arizona.

A few state legislatures are acting like South Carolina in 1838 or 1860. Kentucky in 2011 sought to be a sanctuary state from the power of the Environmental Protection Agency. Arizona passed a bill that exempted all products made and consumed within the state exempt from federal interstate commerce laws. Montana was considering a bill to nullify federal laws protecting endangered species. Georgia was considering legislation that would override federal monetary regulations. Governors and state legislatures in South Dakota, Wyoming, Utah, Texas, Oklahoma signed into state law or issued resolutions that assault or abrogated federal authority. Alabama, Tennessee and Washington State are considering similar resolutions.

Arizona mangled the 14th Amendment in a way no federal court or Congress ever has, and showed a disdain for existing law. [26] A bill that would deny citizenship to children born in Arizona to undocumented mothers, require hospitals to check patients' citizenship status, and require proof of children's citizenship for attending school are all clearly unconstitutional. Other bills would criminalize driving by illegal immigrants, and evict them from public housing. The U.S. Supreme Court ruled in *Plyler v Doe* (1982) that children of illegal immigrants, who are not responsible for the illegality of their parents, have a right to education, and that states that withhold funds from local school districts for such children violate the equal protection clause. These challenges to federal authority are the same tactics used by southern states to secede.

Would it be acceptable, under the Constitution, to let states have their own so-called rights so they could enslave people again? The question is never asked because under the Constitution slavery was condoned. And since radical fundamentalists are so fond of quoting Jefferson and Madison—never Chief Justice John Marshall who defined the Constitution and the powers of the national government—they should also recall that many of the largest slave owners in America in the 18th century signed the Constitution. So why aren't the actions and behaviors of slave owners, not just what they write and say to the public and for public consumption, held in the same high esteem? No one among these radicals seems to want to discuss "freedom" and "liberty" and "individual rights" for the slaves of Washington, Jefferson and Madison and other representatives of slave states.

By 2010 lawmakers in Idaho, Utah, Arizona, Oklahoma, Louisiana, Missouri, Mississippi, Alabama, Tennessee and Virginia had passed measures that nullified federal health care reform. Additionally, 24 state legislatures passed laws declaring themselves sovereign, but only seven governors actually signed those laws. [27] The States' Rights movement is located in the Tenth Amendment to the Constitution that reverts power to the states or the people (See Chapter Seven). Ignoring other parts of the Constitution and U.S. Supreme Court decisions that legally interpret what the Constitution means, these radical know-nothings have simplistically employed one amendment to justify their mission to dismantle federal programs. [28] Followers believe that everything the national government does is unconstitutional and full of "executive excesses."

Here is a typical argument for states' rights advocates.

> Against the will of the people, Congress passed a massive health-care bill that displaces individual choice and responsibility with sweeping government mandates. But liberty-loving Arizonians can do something to protect personal autonomy in our state. The Health Care Freedom Act will forbid government from forcing individuals or employers from participating in a government-approved health care system. [29]

In this quote are two principal legal contradictions. The first error is that when Congress passes legislation that the President signs, that somehow that action is against the "will of the people." America is a representative democracy. There is no imperative that directs Congress or the U.S. Supreme Court to poll public opinion before voting. If constituents do not like a representative's vote, they can vote him or her out of office, but cannot negate the vote. If public opinion does not like a U.S Supreme Court's decision, as states did not in 1954 when it ordered the desegregation of public schools, the public can protest but not pretend the decision is illegal or unconstitutional. The second inconsistency in this passage is ignorance of Article VI (2) of the *U.S. Constitution* that clearly indicates the priority of Congress over any state legislation.

> This Constitution, and the laws of the United States which shall be made in pursuance thereof; and all the treaties made, or which shall be made, under the authority of the United States, shall be the supreme law of the land; and the Judges in every state shall be bound thereby, anything in the Constitution or laws of any State to the contrary notwithstanding.

It's difficult to misread the intent of Article VI, Section 2 as somehow conferring a preference of state over federal control. Yet somehow, libertarians and fundamentalist Republicans ignore or are unaware of this constitutional provision, and insist that the 10th Amendment is an obligation for states to assert an authority they had under *The Articles of Confederation*, but do not have since the ratification *by the people* in 1791 and adoption of the *U.S. Constitution*.

Science vs. Salesmanship

The Tea Party and its allies created a movement around the strident politics of anti-government, anti-elite and anti-science beliefs. Historical rejection of initiatives by the national government particularly in the South, a general fear of change, the changing multiracial demographics of America, a fundamentalist religious perspective, and heavy energy company and financial sector campaign contributions to politicians have combined to create hostile and oppositional political voices.

But the exposure of radical Republican anti-science claims against the general consensus of scientists is the antithesis of the universal goals of education. And yet it is the campaign tactic of serious presidential contenders. Crass campaign appeals to willful ignorance and popular prejudices are the new cynical faces and litmus test for success in American politics. The anti-government, anti-science movement is incessantly strident, diversionary, ideologically driven, moralistic, and an historically typical southern strategy.

One example of this appeal to anti-intellectualism is the casual dismissal of the scientific evidence for global warming. Disbelief about global warming—or its Republican euphemism climate change, a result of what planetary warming does—is conspicuous indication of the dismissal of science and the reliance on religion for understandings about the natural world. Global warming does not mean that locales just might be hotter. The warming refers to greenhouse gases like carbon dioxide and nitrous oxide that rise in the atmosphere and then trap the sun's heat and light from escaping. The heated oceans warm and alter the earth's weather patterns like the 2011 tornadoes in the South and floods along the Mississippi, and hurricanes and storms along the east coast. The majority of Republicans in the 112th House and 75% of the Senate in 2012 are on record as skeptics, denying that global warming is attributable to humans.

Far-right fundamentalists believe that God created the earth with enough minerals and goods for humans to enjoy. So belief is based on un-named scriptural passages, and incredibly on conservative radio personalities who believe that accepting any agreement on world climate policy is to impose a world government with a loss of national sovereignty. These naysayers have selective amnesia because President George H.W. Bush first proposed a so-called "cap and trade" policy for controlling acid rain.

The world's economy is built on energy needed for home heating, vehicles, airplanes, industrial plants, farms, etc. Energy comes almost exclusively from fossil fuels and primarily coal. All fossil fuels produce carbon dioxide, the principal ingredient in the atmosphere that traps heat. The more carbon dioxide and monoxide in the atmosphere, the warmer the planet that results in the melting of polar ice, rising seas, flooding of low-lying coastal towns and regions, alteration of the earth's temperature to produce more storms, droughts and heat waves, and hence the depletion of plant and some animal species and disruptions in the human food supply chain. [30]

Science has the accumulated evidence as compelling as that reported by the National Aeronautics and Space Administration (NASA).

• The current level of atmospheric carbon dioxide (CO_2) is 390 parts per million. It was only 280 parts per million in 1950.

- Oceanic acidity has been increasing because of the input of carbon dioxide since 1750 when records were first kept, and the rate is currently an additional 2 billion tons per year, a 30% increase.

- Global sea levels rose 6.7 inches in the last century, double that of the previous century.

- The 20 warmest years in history have occurred since 1981, and the ten warmest years in the past 12 years.

- The Greenland and Antarctic ice sheets have decreased in mass, by 36 to 60 cubic mils per years since 2002. Moreover, glaciers are retreating everywhere in the world.

- Since 1950 in the United States the record number of high temperatures has been increasing and the number of record low temperatures decreasing.

A scientific team from the University of York found that many species have moved at twice the predicted rate to higher altitudes where the earth has warmed the most. [31]

These scientific studies come from the most respected international journals, like *Nature*, *Science*, publications of the National Research Council and the National Academy Press, *Journal of Climate*, *Geophysical Research Letters*, *Bulletin of the American Meteorological Society*, NASA, among many others. The general public does not ordinarily subscribe to these scientific publications. But by denying these well-known findings they reduce all scientific and expert evidence to superstition, fiction and a denial ideology.

Skepticism about climate change is an article of faith among radical conservatives. This disbelief is representative of anti-intellectualism in the population. The most recent evidence comes from a 2011 congressionally-mandated report, *America's Climate Choices* of the National Research Council, a part of the National Academy of Sciences. It declares unequivocally that greenhouse gases are responsible for global warming trends. Rep. Joe Barton of Texas, who had been seeking further deregulation of carbon emissions, blithely dismissed the report. Former presidential candidate and Texas Governor Rick Perry similarly dismissed climate change. Big Oil doesn't want scientific evidence to halt or curtail its air pollution.

Senator James Inhofe of Oklahoma introduced legislation to prohibit the Environmental Protection Agency (EPA) from using its powers under the *Clean Air Act* to reduce greenhouse gases. Inhofe claimed that the super cold winter of 2010 proves that theories about global warming are a fraud. No one has explained to him that it is the oceans that have warmed causing changes in the atmosphere that result in extreme variable weather patterns. What is clear is that by 2010 Inhofe had received $457,550 in campaign contributions from oil and gas companies, more than any other contributor. [32]

Republican environmental opponents, if they can't eliminate the EPA, want to legislate against the regulation of carbon emissions. The EPA regulated carbon emissions because the Congress has mandated it under the *Clean Air Act*. The U.S Supreme Court has said that the EPA must decide when greenhouse gases endanger public health.

Unlike Europeans, or new policies in China, India and Brazil, Americans gambol on oblivious to global warming, still buying big cars, valuing personal freedom and not collective good sense or scientific evidence, distrustful of government intervention and dismissing climate change as an event that only happens in the Arctic, unconscious that they are the biggest global contributors to the problem. According to a Pew poll, over 70% of Chinese, Indians and South Koreans are willing to pay more in taxes to offset the effects of climate change. In the U.S. that number is only 38%, a low ratio partly because of Republican denials about a serious climatic problem.

Yet 6,000 years ago the Sahara was full of vegetation prior to an upheaval in climate that did not bring needed rains and created major drought conditions that essentially created a desert roughly the size of the United States. [33]

Today, and notwithstanding understandings of the earth's climatic history, global agreements on reducing carbon emissions are almost impossible to achieve, even within any industrialized country. The greatest accomplishment thus far from conferences convened to deal with this issue is disillusionment.

Moreover, politicians are becoming the public relations spokespersons for corporate America, which does not bode well even for public safety and health. They contribute to the negation of commonsense about the weight of scientific evidence. American secondary school students have one of the lowest rankings among developed countries in science, and now we have Republican politicians repudiating globally accepted scientific findings.

This scientific debunking is also a testimony to the strength of the energy conglomerates that produce much of the world's energy products, and to the developing countries that believe that it is their responsibility to provide abundant fossil energy to their citizens. These countries gather from time to time to discuss the earth's distress but never reach agreement on how much to reduce carbon emissions.

On May 5, 2011 the Republican-controlled House passed three bills that required the Department of the Interior Department to accelerate permits for drilling without legislatively required environmental or engineering reviews. Such bills would not reduce the price of gasoline, satisfy the general public about environmental safety, or lessen taxpayer subsidies to the petroleum industry. Greater auto efficiency, a raft of alternative fuels and improved mass transit would help reduce America's reliance on fossil fuels. However, energy saving measures would not continue to line the pockets of the energy industries or fill the campaign coffers of Republican backers from the energy companies for such folly.

It is intellectually dishonest that conservatives cling to a rigid orthodoxy when faced with an abundance of scientific evidence. Should the American public trust least those who know the most and are experts? Apparently not in moonshine America where everyone has become an expert, and experts have become elitists, as were the Founding Fathers conservatives claim to worship. The world needs purposeful unity, some wisdom and lots of farsightedness in combating threats to everyone's way of life, not denial rationalizations to solve global environmental problems. [34] But today the majority of the people are mentally inert, but aggressive in demands, a few militantly assertive, suspicious of whomsoever they view as elitist.

The aim of radical Republicans is the same as used by corporations and governments to disparage the public about what it is selling. The tobacco industry conducted a campaign of skepticism against cancer research about cigarette smoking for decades. A constant media bombardment against scientific procedures—and the media today is largely outlets for political parties—and a parade of pseudo-scientists is enough to overcome actual scientific evidence. This is true of tobacco companies, stem cell research debunking, or the lack of adequate regulation of corporate pharmaceutical, petroleum and financial excesses.

The shaping of public opinion has been occurring since John Watson developed behaviorism and the cultivation of human needs in the 1920s that applied as much to schooling as advertising. Slick advertising and incessant propaganda pitches have convinced the American public to take a pill for every physical inconvenience, to seek medical attention for every cold, to buy expensive health care insurance, to purchase the latest huge truck or SUV (formerly known as a sedan), to eat fatty foods and then seek weight loss programs, to believe that oil companies are really in the business of conservation, and then to think that government and its regulations are the source of all their money problems.

The conservative right adores the founding fathers and romanticizes their invention of a new national government that replaced the unworkable *Articles of Confederation*, a weak union of states. But they had displaced that conservatism for the narrow interests of moneyed groups like the financial sector, banking, insurance, pharmaceutical and petroleum companies from which they receive generous contributions. [35] The concept of stewardship, where business acts together with government to produce an improved quality of life for all citizens, is missing. Radical conservatism has emerged as a movement of no taxes, limited government, and a sorry list of slogans that offers negligible solutions to the complexities of the global marketplace. Its appeal is to the hardcore conservative, the semi-brain dead, and the naïve, greedy, credit-addicted consumer who is as much to blame as any institution for the economic meltdown.

The idealism of a perpetual Union has been ceaselessly romanticized as the compromise of the fragile unity with slavery that was inherent from the beginning of the republic and today still permeates our political system. The South was transformed as industry and infrastructure expanded after World War II. Its anti-government and discriminatory mentality, however, did not disappear but migrated to all parts of the country. The American creed, the glorification of patriotism, the land of liberty and opportunity, the home of democracy, of equality, the guarantor of life, liberty and property and human freedoms, is still a house divided.

The image of Col. Reb, a caricature of an antebellum plantation owner, had been the unofficial mascot of "Ole Miss," the University of Mississippi team until 2010 when it was abandoned. However, Col. Reb still survives as a mascot at Mississippi's segregated Carroll Academy, in part supported by the Council of Conservative Citizens, a white supremacist group. [36]

It isn't difficult to see how the tradition of what the South was now survives into a modern age when multicultural and diversity interests define American society and the developed world. And yet in the South political party identification has often been closely associated with race. According to 2008 exit polls, 96% of self-identified Republicans in Mississippi were White, and nearly 75% of Democrats were Black. [37] The political divisions reflect deep social conditions and define us, as they have throughout our history.

President Reagan began the process of dismantling government's role in managing the economy and in undermining its salubrious influence in promoting the general welfare. A large segment of the body politic still believes vehemently in his discredited strategy. Republican politicians consistently try to implement Reagan's failed policies. All this leads to political stagnation as the nation slips further behind in international competitiveness. The unbalanced emphasis on wealth and corporations to drive the economy leads to an erosion of the social contract among citizens to help government reinvest in its children and future prosperity. Even if they purchase Tee shirts for local youth soccer players, businesses do not have social responsibilities as their primary mission.

Our national economy cannot be built only on the pursuit and attainment of wealth. It needs, at a minimum, quality education, solid infrastructure, consistent and clean energy sources, and environmental sustainability. Fair taxes provide for these services, but only government can dispense the taxes it collects from Americans, who are according to the OECD the least taxed people in the industrialized world except for Australia. America spends the least of all industrialized countries on public social spending as a percentage of GDP. [38] Only government, not corporations or businesses, are charged with stewardship, of protecting the rights of the present and future generations.

If there is one conclusion I have drawn from about half a century of research it is that it is never just one variable either in personal health or the economy cause system breakdowns. Therefore, the debt, the loss of manufacturing jobs, the failure to invest proportionately in our crumbing infrastructure, increased risk to speculate to account for a decrease in revenue, the trade imbalance, the whole global competitiveness—all these and other invisible hands have a bearing on the health of the economy. Claiming the government is at fault is a false message and voice from a failed southern past.

I will continue to counter this anti-government message in the following chapters to show how it permeates our dialogue but is detrimental to our future.

Cannons at Shiloh

Chapter Two
The New Know Nothings

In general, only simple conceptions take hold of the minds of the people. A
false idea, but one clear and precise, will always have more power in the world
than a true, but complex idea.

(Alexis de Tocqueville, *Democracy in America*, p. 155)

There are cycles in American political history when party advocates believe that
their views are transformative because a new electoral majority has emerged in
the presidency or Congress. The record suggests that this phenomenon appears
about every quarter century. However, believing in the historical inevitability of
any historical cycle is a seductive dream.

Richard Nixon, Ronald Reagan, Bill Clinton, Newt Gingrich, and the Tea
Party thought their political ascendency was pivotal in representing the national
mood. Yet the dogmatic adherence to a simple but fixed ideology—like that
described in the quote above by De Tocqueville—and in some cases ignorance
and gobs of misinformation, has blinded elected leaders to the nation's
problems. The social and political chasm in politics, and simulated fear among
the public, is about the role of national government in the lives of its citizens, as
it has been since independence from Britain and constitutional inception.

It is instructive in this chapter to review this trend toward radicalization that
has generated a polarized public and led to legislative dysfunction. So this story
is not just about presidential candidates or any one election. It is about a shifting
cultural current that is a reversion to our dysfunctional past, a sordid history of
our division we can't seem to overcome.

The Original Know Nothings

Citizen anger because of a disintegrating economy and the slow erosion of
quality of life standards finds government an easy target for animosity. This is
partly because of historical anti-government feelings left over from the days of
actual slavery, and partly because anger is stroked by radical conservatives—
with more bravado than brio, more clannishness than clarity—who seek to keep
government from funding any domestic programs. Latent bigotry has combined
with legitimate vexation over financial distress to create an unprecedented
swelling of social and political discontent.

There are historical parallels. In the northern states in the 1840s and 1850s,
a political group known as the Know Nothings—so designated by the New York
journalist Horace Greeley because they would not reveal their anti-immigrant,
anti-Catholic sentiments—flourished in Ohio and Massachusetts. They were
largely composed of working class citizens. By 1854 the party had burgeoned
into a national political influence, winning nine governorships in the 1850s and
electing 104 of 234 members to the House of Representatives. It named itself the
American Party but refused to take a stand on the slavery issue. By 1860 its

influence waned and its remaining members eventually split on the slavery issue. Members became assimilated into the two major political parties.

Like the balance of powers in the Constitution between the three branches, the two political parties provide a balance between competing ideologies. As I noted, on one side of the Democratic Party is the Liberal Left largely in favor of domestic spending programs that aid all citizens and is suspicious of corporations and big businesses. Moderates and centrists within the Democratic Party typically favor the financial sector, the military, and law and order issues. The Republican Party, on the other hand, favors a reduction in federal spending, less taxes, free enterprise for businesses, and limited government. A radical conservative and libertarian movement has emerged within the Republican Party that seeks to eliminate the Internal Revenue Service—notwithstanding the Constitution's Amendment XVI, "The Congress shall have power to lay and collect taxes on incomes"—and eliminate, reduce or privatize federal programs like Medicare, Medicaid, and Social Security.

Today's extreme conservative movement has shifted the power base among more moderate Republicans who believe they must include the radical movement under their political tent. It has alienated Democrats who believe its members are out of touch with reality. To its advocates, the movement has energized a largely forgotten base of White and angry citizens hard hit by a financial crisis. Virulent radicals are challenging the national social safety net programs that benefit lower income Americans. Economic principles are pushing out the virtues of compassion and fairness.

The Tea Party's use of the analogy of the American Revolution, and not the Civil War when the country was in revolt with itself, is more than just a political blind spot in its argument for recognition. It is an attempt to return to the foreign enemy—not the enemy within, the proponents of slavery and those opposed to civil rights—and to religious fundamentalism as a pretext for injecting their version of God into politics. Christianity was strongest in both devotion and hypocrisy in the South during the centuries of slavery.

This anger and resentment will not abate any time soon. And as I attempt to demonstrate, ire has always been a subtext in the American psyche, an integral part of our divided house. It is not a new phenomenon but a traditional antipathy toward government intrusion and against personal liberty, an emotional response to any curtailment of the freedom to act without social or governmental interference. But although individuals can choose, they cannot choose to ignore laws established to protect the rights of others. The stout liberties of the individual cannot always be at the antipodes of the Leviathan of the national government that has to regulate disputes between it, and other states, and protect the liberties of all.

There is little or no antipathy toward states that compel individuals to purchase car insurance, but there is, according to radical conservatives, toward the national government that seeks to compel individuals, for example, to purchase health insurance. Compared to Britain, Canada, France and Germany, the U.S. spends more than double on average for similar surgeries, according to the International Federation of Health Plans. Rising medical costs are breaking individual piggy banks and the government's. Yet a Republican-controlled House lets free enterprise, private health care providers do whatever they please, and keep government from doing anything to control costs.

Far right radical freedom means, without equivocation, freedom from taxes and national government regulation. This ideology became political gospel in Ayn Rand's novel *Atlas Shrugged*, (See Chapter Three) the principal scripture of Alan Greenspan, former Chair of the Federal Reserve, and libertarian politicians like Ron Paul and son Rand Paul.

> I saw the tax-collecting vermin that had grown for centuries like mildew . . . draining us by no right that anyone could name—I saw the government regulations passed to cripple me, because I was successful, and to help my competitors . . . I saw the labor unions who won every claim against me, by reason of my ability to make their livelihood possible . . . (*Atlas Shrugged*, 1999, p. 766.)

The anti-government wing of the Republican Party is celebrating the dismantling of state services too. For example, Arizona is broke primarily because of ill-advised actions pushed through the state legislature yearly since 1993 that cost the state an estimated $3 billion in lost revenue. The legislature refused to raise any taxes to offset these losses. Worse, it borrowed money to finance short-term expenses, while it drastically cut social services including day-care centers. Estimates for anticipated revenue were wildly optimistic and the debt payment begins in 2013. The Arizona Department of Revenue receives in 2012 less funding than it did in 1984, adjusted for inflation, when the state had half the present population. Right wing radicals believe the government is the problem.

THE CENTER CANNOT HOLD

Vote Ratings from Conservative Groups Showing Movement Toward More Conservative Positions in Congress, 1999-2009 (100 = most conservative)

	1999	2009
American Conservative Union	81	89
National Journal	72	80
Navral Pro-Choice America		
(most anti-abortion)	85	97
Gun Owners of America	2.5	3.5
	(4.3 = most pro-gun)	

Sources: Project Vote Smart, National Journal, Gun Owners of America

Republicans in Congress have also drifted from centrist political positions toward more conservative positions in the decade from 1999 to 2009. The issue is not the positive or negative value of conservatism but that conservative politicians are moving from the moderate political center. As a result, legislative government has become less efficient. The Table demonstrates this shift.

The fact that congressional Republicans are edging toward more demonstrable conservatism is a sign that the country is moving in that direction too. For more than a decade polls have shown that about 35% of the electorate is conservative, about 33% moderate, and about 20% liberal.

Anti-government activities include congressional hearings and legislative bills that seek to restrict regulations of the Environment Protection Agency (EPA) on emissions, or the Department of Agriculture's regulations on food safety, the abolition of Planned Parenthood, the National Endowment of the Arts, and National Public Radio. [1]

Let's just look at one glaring example of the illogic of this argument about suppressing taxes. The Big Oil companies—ExxonMobil, Chevron, BP, Shell, ConocoPhillips (which also owns Circle K convenience stores), Marathon, Valero (the blended names are because of mergers; Chevron acquired Texaco but did not keep the name) are the main contributors to Congress to prevent government regulation from affecting their environmentally destructive business. Big Oil is not rebuilding bridges or national highways, funding improved public transportation, investing in more fuel-efficient vehicles, developing meaningful alternative energy sources, or keeping gasoline prices lower for the consumer. Let's acknowledge that demand also spurs higher prices, yet still negligible taxing of Big Oil's is only increasing profits more liberally spent to lobby politicians to reduce regulations.

George W. Bush worked as an oil executive. Dick Cheney, prior to becoming Vice President, spent six years as CEO of Halliburton, one of the largest oil services industries in the world. Condoleezza Rice served on Chevron's Board of Directors, and head of its policy committee. The Bush Administration was loaded with oil executives, especially in the Department of Interior. Big Oil was included in task force recommendations within the first ten days of the Administration. None of these energy task forces ever resulted in proposed legislation for the nation's needs, only for advances to the energy industries. Big Oil was in the planning with the Administration from the beginning of the Iraq war, and positioned their officials in charge of Iraq petroleum reserves during the war so Iraqi laws would be friendly to them. The Bush Administration married Big Oil with government.

Lest anyone forget, it was Reagan who in 1981 ended price regulations (*The Crude Oil Entitlement Program*) that allowed large petroleum companies to merge, driving out smaller competitors, and allowing them to determine the price of gasoline. According to data collected by the Center for Responsive Politics, over a hundred lawmakers have hired former industrial lobbyists to help draft new legislation favoring industries.

And just to be satirically sure, let us rid ourselves of those pesky regulations that keep food companies from introducing contaminated products, or those redundant regulations that force pharmaceutical companies to rigorously test pill products before introducing them to the public that might temporarily mitigate a particular disability while introducing a secondary, possibly more dangerous effect. While we are at it, while not allow companies to introduce as much waste into our water supply system as they like, and pollute the air all they want with toxins. After all, regulations hurt job growth. Of course at the same time the lack of regulations might just as easily kill off some taxpayers, as we discovered was true of the tobacco industry.

The progressive argument is that regulations protect consumers and clients and public safety. No commodity market trader, business executive, or hedge fund manager is obligated to do anything more than seek the highest profit for the company and the stockholders. Federal regulations are designed to protect the public and consumers from price gouging. Neither the public nor government can rely solely on the self-interest of industries to police themselves. The Enron scandal, and the 2010 BP (Deepwater Horizon) oil spill in the Gulf of Mexico and the ensuing costs to public safety, health and welfare, is proof enough of that principle.

On another note, the wrath of conservative voters turned a more militant tone when the Secret Service in late 2009 reported an exponential rise in the number of death threats against President Obama. At the same time there was a corresponding rise in hate groups and anti-government fervor. By 2010 there were over a thousand identified hate groups in the U.S., a near doubling of such groups in the decade. [2] The President and the government became the country's scapegoat egged on by TV and radio demagogues who encouraged hateful speech. [3] But perhaps the most ridiculous and borderline racist attacks were by those who questioned President Obama's birth.

Born in the USA

> But where are the clowns?
> Quick, send in the clowns.
> Don't bother, they're here. (Stephen Sondheim, 1973)

The most ludicrous political movement in American politics was the so-called "birther," or "nativist" movement that began during the early days of the Obama Administration. Half of Republicans believed that Barack Obama was not born in the United States, and only 28% thought he was. Depending on the particular poll as late as 2011, about 40% of Americans believed Obama was born in another country. About 16% to 22% were unsure what to believe. Additionally, 31% to 46% believed he was a Muslim. Republican strategists and propagandists were shaping the debate to invalidate the person and presidency of President Obama to the detriment of American imagery in the eyes of the world.

Historically in the U.S. birthright identity has always been about racial identity, beginning with the Supreme Court *Dred Scott* decision in 1858. The 14th Amendment finally gave citizenship to all in the U.S., a condition that had been only a state prerogative in order to prevent slaves from becoming citizens. [4] Until very recently, Blacks on the streets at night were always asked to show their papers, and if they could not prove their identity would spend time in jail. Whites demanding Blacks to show "identity papers" is an ugly reminder of our racist and bigoted past.

Ten states passed legislation requiring presidential candidates to document their birth in the United States after a similar bill died in Congress in 2009. Hawaii had consistently mailed out responses to requests for copies of Obama's birth certificate. Furthermore, it isn't even necessary to be born in the U.S. to be an American citizen. My son was born in Japan. John McCain, Senator from Arizona and once presidential candidate, was born in Panama, yet no one asked for his birth certificate as a presidential candidate. You are a U.S. citizen if born of an American mother. The "birther" movement was a patent expression of bigotry.

Alarmingly, 32% in 2010 believed President Obama was born in Kenya where he father was from, offering no proof for such a claim and despite conclusive evidence to the contrary. Obama was born on August 4, 1961 in Honolulu, Hawaii, and the two major Hawaiian newspapers, the *Honolulu Advertiser* (on August 13th) and the *Honolulu Star-Bulletin* (on August 14th), reported his birth. Nevertheless, "birthers" insisted that he produce his birth certificate though it was available on the Internet and at the *Los Angeles Times* website.

Among these sad, venomous celebrities fueling this inanity was Donald Trump whose primary business was engaging in multiple bankruptcies in order to avoid paying rightful debts, and posing as a presidential candidate. The unchecked Ego of Donald Trump fed this "birther" insanity, egged on by conspiracy theorists. In the spring of 2011 he topped the list of all viable Republican candidates, nearly 20% of the population, a ratio that likely approximates the bigoted generation.

Trump sought notoriety by appealing to the basest political gimmick of the birthers, lied about his involvement (saying he sent investigators to Hawaii when he didn't), and stroking the resentment of the most uninformed, intolerant, bigoted, and racist elements in American society. He became a caricature and poster comb-over symbol of all those people.

At the time the birther movement was at its peak, Neil Abercrombie, later to be elected Governor, was a congressman from Hawaii but no one in Congress asked him about Obama's birth certificate, which indicated to him that the whole affair was a coded message to smear the president as somehow un-American. For the "birthers" facts do not speak for themselves, and a rumor of a conspiracy is enough to satisfy a bias. Presidential hopeful, Fox News TV host and former Governor of Arkansas Mike Huckabee, shamelessly pandered to this movement's followers and lied when he said, erroneously on a radio show, that he would "Love to know more about where Obama was born" and his life in Kenya, where Obama never lived.

The White House released President Obama's birth certificate on April 27, 2011 and the President commented that the country needed to get behind the "sideshows and carnival barker atmosphere" distracting the country from its serious financial and domestic issues. Again, the historical context comes into play. The South once paid money for kidnapped African Blacks whom they did not acknowledge as persons, never gave them state citizenship, balked at recognizing the 14th Amendment, even as a concession for re-entering he Union. Fear of foreign-born Blacks, or even whether or not Blacks were citizens, began in the South and now runs through the psyche of Americans who have inherited this paranoid mentality and fear of Black legitimacy, even of an elected president.

We have to remember American history from the days of the Constitution— a document frequently waved in front of crowds as if it was sacred—that the Constitution did not recognize Blacks or women as citizens with voting privileges. It recognized only men of property, just like in aristocratic England.

Like lemmings following close behind the "birthers" are the other "birthers," those conservative legislators and their allies who want to obviate the 14th Amendment—"All persons born or naturalized in the United States . . . are citizens of the United States and of the State wherein they reside"—and refuse citizenship to children born of illegal immigrants. State Legislators for Legal Immigration, composed of legislators from 14 states, are behind this unconstitutional silliness. Are children supposed to suffer the sins of their fathers? [5]

In 2007 there were 144 nativist or anti-immigrant groups in the United States, some of whom were cadres of radical extremists. By 2010 there were 319 such groups documented, a nearly three-fold increase. [6] The purpose of the 14th Amendment, as we shall see in a later chapter, was meant to grant citizenship to slaves who were not citizens of the state in which they resided or of the United States. Steven King, Chair of the House Judiciary Sub-Committee on Immigration, introduced such a bill to eliminate citizenship for children when both parents were illegal immigrants. [7] Unless he was consciously pandering to his biased constituency, he was totally misinformed or dismissive about the present constitutional right of children born in the U.S. to be citizens, unconscionably for a lawmaker.

The 14th Amendment was universally resisted by southern states at the conclusion of the Civil War because it legitimized Blacks as citizens, something plantation owners and southern states never would have done on their own initiative. Those opposed to the 14th Amendment's application to immigrants are painting those felt to be alien with the same tainted brush. This movement is just another illustration that contemporary conservative Republicans are reviving the same strategy southerners used to protect slavery.

The "birther" movement was ludicrous but not the most politically insane. Tennessee undertook a study on whether it should create its own currency in case the Federal Reserve collapsed, something specifically prohibited by the Constitution in Article I, Section 10: "No State shall . . . coin money . . ." Texas made it a state crime to hire an undocumented worker. Excepted were nannies, landscapers and housekeepers, convenient for homeowners but not job creators like restaurants or construction companies. Kentucky created a coal company "sanctuary" exempt from federal laws. Montana declared that global warming was good for the business climate. South Dakota, harkening back to its lawless days, required every adult to own a gun. And these actions are just those of the nation's misinformed lawmakers, not what ordinary citizens may have thought about how American democracy actually works, and what the Constitution allows or prohibits.

On the Fringe

> You see, Dr. Stadler, people don't want to think. And the deeper they get into trouble, the less they want to think . . . So they'll bless and follow anyone who gives them a justification for not thinking . . .
>
> (Ayn Rand, *Atlas Shrugged*, 1999, p. 346.)

It's difficult to categorize fringe conservatives as if it were a New Age religion, or palmistry or advocates of toe readings. But a safe bet is that they cannot come to grips with the reality of an African-American president, and were stuck on ways of disenfranchising or debunking his electoral legitimacy. According to a New York Times/CBS Poll, 93% of the Tea Party members felt the country was drifting toward socialism, though it is unlikely few could articulate what that form of governance actually means. Isn't it socialism when taxpayers tax themselves inordinately, while they lay off teachers, to pay for football stadiums they can't afford, or invite casinos in their communities so taxes can be kept low? Mitt Romney spoke about Americans devolving into a "European style of socialism," in an Obama Administration as if that were a bear trap. The implication and political slur is that somehow anything foreign in unacceptable.

In practice, socialism means a tax and welfare system that benefits citizens that exists today throughout Western Europe and the developed world, and not necessarily a political system that is dictatorial or communistic. Is it socialism to readily give health care benefits and even special hospitals to certain groups of citizens, like veterans, but deny those privileges to other citizens?

The changing convictions of the Tea Party movement, even from 2010 during congressional elections to 2011, indicated its ephemeral nature. When asked by Pew pollsters how many were "angry with the federal government," 43% of Tea Party members agreed in 2010, but only 28% did so in 2011. When asked how many "trusted the government in Washington to do what is right just about always or most of the time," only 7% agreed in 2010 but 14% in 2011. These are significant swings in opinion in just one year among the most radical, but apparently volatile, conservative group. They cannot seem to make up their minds about their level of governmental mistrust.

But besides the volatility in government sentiment, the misinformation about government is stunning. Michele Bachmann, Republican Congresswoman from Minnesota, air-brushed American history. In a speech in January 2011 she opined how "once we got here we were treated all the same." The founding fathers, she said, "worked tirelessly to end slavery," ignoring, or unaware that most of them owned slaves. Historical facts do matter. Michele Bachman and her ilk, whether politicians or not, create a distortion of reality that confuses voters, dishonors teachers who must have taught her some history, and makes

America a laughing stock in the educated world community. Her idealism for the founders overpowers inconvenient facts. Her publicity stunts resemble comedians rather than practical politicians, and her entertainment appeal says as much about the lack of Republican thoughtfulness as it does about Bachmann's caustic rhetoric.

Tea Partiers and radical Republicans fear government because it offers change. Fear of change undermines people's reasoning and makes them appeal to the national founding fathers that gave a sense of continuity with a glorious past that offers comfort to a scary present. I am reminded of those laughable singing tractor drivers from Soviet propaganda films of the 1930s and 1940s, supposedly glorifying the communist worker ideal.

Defeated Tea Party Nevada senatorial candidate in 2010 Sharron Angle wanted to repeal the 16th Amendment giving Congress the power to collect income tax. Congressman Reid Ribble from Wisconsin wanted to do away with social security. Several other candidates like Jesse Kelly of Arizona wanted to privatize it. Mike Lee of Utah thought the 17th Amendment, giving the people the choice to directly elect senators, was a mistake. Senator Rand Paul of Kentucky wanted to repeal the 14th Amendment that gave everyone, including freed slaves, U.S. citizenship and made states conform to due process and equal protection of the laws. He was also opposed to mine safety standards.

Republicans believed that the people had given them a mandate to bring about substantive reform according to their agenda—to privatize social security and diminish the impact of Medicare. The people's vote in 2010 was anger and disillusionment about the economy. And so when Republican House congressional votes turned to gradually privatizing Medicare, voter response not surprisingly was largely in favor of keeping the social safety nets. Republicans had read the wrong political tealeaves but had unfolded their ideological ideas anyway.

After the Tea Partiers gained over 700 legislative seats in state houses in 2011, they systematically began eviscerating benefits and bargaining rights of public employees and limiting voter turnout. Kansas Governor Sam Brownback signed a law that required voters to have a photo ID at polling places. A few states sought to return to the gold standard, to crack down on illegal immigration, to bar the use of Islamic *sharia* law in state courts, and to require presidential candidates to have a valid birth certificate to declare for presidency in the state. These ridiculous ideas were presumably supposed to get the country "back on track."

Each generation seeks to define itself in the society where it resides. And it seems to be inbred in our nature that we fight over social status, money—that we equate with power—control, usually expressed as personal liberties, and our love lives. Compulsion for some or all of these attributes means that we value ourselves more if there is a permanent underclass from which we can feel superior. For over three hundred years that was the social identity of the South. Today, those who feel abandoned by government are rising up to threaten what they perceive as the big, bad, intrusive government establishment. But they are missing the real big, global picture—the stupefying dumbing down of America.

The Big Global Picture: The Dumbing of America

> Don't know much about history
> Don't know much biology
> Don't know much about a science book
> Don't know much about the French I took
> (Sam Cooke, *Wonderful World*)

We praise and revere education but disrespect the intellectual values it inculcates. Once America's intellectual values declined in the third millennium so did everything else. As I outline, and as you can discover in any number of reports, America's 15-year olds rank 17th in the world in science, and 25th in math. We rank 12th among developed countries in college graduation, and 79th in elementary school enrollment. Our infrastructure is a low 32nd among major advanced nations. America is 27th in the world in life expectancy. We're generally considered number one in having the most guns, and rank near the top in accumulated debt. In 2010 the American student Scholastic Aptitude Test (SAT) scores dropped to the lowest levels ever in reading, writing, math, and science.

America is losing its competitive edge in the global marketplace, and the intellectual deterioration, partly because of unyielding ignorance and lack of scientific acceptance, is apparent in all educational sectors. The World Economic Forum ranks the American school system as 26th in the world. Of 100 students who enter high school, 25 will drop out, only 50 will continue on to college, and only 22 of those graduate from college.

This dose of educational reality that impacts the economy has not been a part of the national dialogue among competing candidates for congressional office since they are too busy castigating opponents or arguing about the role of government and frightening the public with questionable and sometimes deceitful, but always blustery, opinions. Meanwhile, when parents haven't left public schools for private ones, the state is outsourcing its system to charter schools reducing effective public schooling.

Among 32 developed nations, according to the Organization for Economic Cooperation and Development (OECD), the U.S. ranks at the bottom in science (31st), near average in reading (15th), and next to the bottom in math (23rd). America's global competitiveness and formerly high academic standards are sliding away while we pontificate about the role of government in our lives. We are unable to solve our weakening national problems, like energy, health care and education, because we are absorbed in trying to refashion a centuries-old debate that originally divided us. International rankings tell the tale of our misguided focus.

In spite of these poor rankings and the persistent declines in our international educational achievement scores, it's a persistent belief that the best U.S. students can rank with anyone in the world on international scores. That myth and false comfort has been shattered by a comparison of international test scores. Eric Hanushek and associates at Stanford University used the math results of the Programme for International Student Assessment (PISA) administered to 15-year olds from 60 countries every three years. He compared country scores with scores of individual American states to see how the best students in each state compared with the best in the world in math. Only 6% of all American students scored at the advanced level in math proficiency compared to 19% in the top ten countries. Students in the top ten countries on average scored three times as high in math proficiency as America's top math students. The U.S. ranked 30th among all countries, or about average among the 60 countries. The highest scoring state was Massachusetts, but it only ranked 17th among developing countries.

Assuming that academic ability is scattered more or less evenly throughout the world, the only conclusion from consistently poor U.S. test scores is that students are not receiving the best schooling has to offer, and that most other countries offer more rigorous academic standards. [8]

AMERICA'S GLOBAL COMPETIVENESS

Global Innovation	6th
Rate of Change	40th
Fraction of 25-34 year-olds graduated from high school	11th
College Completion Rate	16th
Broadband Internet Access	22nd
Life Expectancy at Birth	24th
Proportion of College Graduates in science or engineering	27th
Quality of K-12 math & science schooling	48th

Source: 2010 National Academies Report,
Rising Above the Gathering Storm Revisited

There is a systematic weakness in the combined curricula and in the teaching of math and science that becomes magnified over a student's time in school. We can no longer pretend that our national or local school programs match anyone else's in the global marketplace. Our schools, like our former dominance in automobiles, are lumbering along like defunct Edsels, as if there were no serious global competition. The average time spent reading on a weekend day for 15-to19 year–olds declined from 16 minutes in 2007 to 5 minutes in 2009. Playing a video game increased from 46.8 o 61.2 minutes. [9]

In a survey of nearly 350,000 military applicants, about one-quarter failed the entrance exam, according to a report by the Education Trust. [10] The Armed Services Vocational Aptitude Battery (ASVAB) is a standardized test administered to all service applicants and becomes a part of the Armed Services Qualifying Test that determines whether or not an applicant is qualified to serve and in what particular occupational specialties. A score of 31 out of 99 on the three-hour test is the minimum for the army, 32 is the minimum for marines, 35 for the navy, 40 for the air force, and 45 for the Coast Guard. The ASVAB tests basic understanding of arithmetic, rudimentary science and reading comprehension. A high school diploma has lost its meaning and does not mean a young person is ready to serve in the military as an occupational option, or is even prepared for collegiate education. Neither the military nor citizens want the armed services to be a dumping ground for unprepared high school graduates. If applicants are unprepared for the military they likely are unprepared for the civilian work force.

Put these distressing statistics in the context of the national disgrace about the appalling American ignorance of U.S. history. The Intercollegiate Studies Institute, an organization committed to furthering American education, has administered a civil literacy test since 2006. Results are beyond disappointment. 71% of test-takers failed the basic quiz whose questions came from the test for naturalization exams for new citizens. As if that were not bad enough, 49% could not name the three branches of government. Thus, it's easy for politicians to pander to the least knowledgeable of citizens because they are the majority.

Research on 2,300 college students found that 45% "did not demonstrate any significant improvement in learning" during their first two college years, and that 36% demonstrated no improvement over four years. [11] College students appear to be drifting through college without any clear purpose, negligent rigor, and not much commitment to the value of higher education.

> Many students come to college not only poorly prepared by prior schooling for highly demanding academic tasks that ideally lie in front of them—more troubling still—they enter college with attitudes, norms, values, and behaviors that are often at odds with academic commitment. [12]

American students' pitiable knowledge of subjects necessary to compete in the global marketplace is already handicapping the next generation of laborers. But just as distressingly, today's adult citizens are astonishingly ignorant of the very constitutional liberties and principles that define our democracy and political system. Ignorance of basic civic understanding and what the Constitution really means is now fashionable but broadcasts a national disgrace. Politicians regrettably appeal to this pitiable, limited civic understanding with vapid clichés and attacks on opponents, hoping the superficiality of their ideas will win approval and disarm public skepticism. Shrinking government and "reckless spending," and reducing debt is unresponsive to how America is supposed to compete in a global economy and how it is to provide for its citizens, to protect them, and to be a leader to the world community.

The 2006 report of the National Assessment of Educational Progress (NAEP) of civic achievement, in a national survey of twelfth graders, showed that 66% had a basic level, 27% had a proficient level, and only two percent an advanced level. [13] The high school student civics achievement level in the U.S. remained stable from 1998. Politics may be the meat and potatoes of political discussions, but the level of understanding of how representative democracy works in America is inadequate, even for the average high school graduate.

American high school seniors in 2006 scored at or about the same nationally in civics education as they did in 1988. No ethnic group showed any improvement at the high school level. The civics test measures:

1) Civic knowledge including politics and government;
2) Civic skills such as describing, explaining analyzing a political position;
3) Civic disposition, or taking part in exercises that assume citizenship responsibilities, like participation in civic affairs and promoting democracy.

Basic Knowledge means partial mastery. A Proficiency score means reasonable achievement, and Advanced means superior performance. Understandably, the higher the educational level of parents, the higher the civics score of students. [14] This lack of elementary civics is only the foundation of a deeper lack of understanding of the political philosophy of candidates running for political office. The diminution of academic achievement has shown up in adult voters. In a democracy the common man prevails, as in television the commonest, often the most vulgar taste rules. The media caters to the lowest public appetite for entertainment, and the voting public selects the least offensive candidate who will not appeal too strongly to their diminished intelligence but rather to slogans that lubricate their emotions.

American adult understanding of democratic, constitutional government is poor. Only about two-thirds of American adults have a minimum understanding of civil society, constitutional government and politics. They understand the principal forms of government and the functions of political parties and some limited international understandings. Only 27% scored at or above the Proficient level. Proficiency means that they have a good understanding of how constitutions can limit the power of government and support the rule of law. They cannot adequately describe similarities and differences between the branches of government or the structures of government. American thinking about constitutional democracy is muddled, including among politicians, political and clearly presidential candidates, not just the general public.

Finally, the globalized marketplace will cause further dislocations in educational readiness. America will always need an educated and informed public, if only to understand how our democracy works. Having a college education may not cause incomes of the middle class to rise because a college education will not guarantee a good paying job in the future. Here's the downside: the manufacturing and low-paying jobs have already migrated offshore, and, because of America's systematic educational decline, the high paying jobs will also go overseas to more highly educated workers.

Growing numbers of students are sent to college at increasingly higher costs, but for a large proportion of them the gains in critical thinking, complex reasoning and written communication are either exceedingly small or empirically nonexistent . . . They might graduate, but they are failing to develop the higher-order cognitive skills that is widely assumed college students should master. [15]

Let's be blunt. The pervasive conservative agenda of slashing educational budgets, the failure to make necessary tax increase investments in schooling, the increases in class size, the freezing of teacher salaries, the attempt to abolish teacher unions, the manipulation of local and state test scores to please parents, the misguided attempts to abolish federal participation in education, among other causes, have had, and will have, deleterious consequences. Even college graduates in the next generation emerging from school with staggering debt will be unable to find a decent job in the global occupational arena.

State tests are misleading and consistently watered down to please parents. Our schools have become laboratories for social engineering, with too many pom-poms, dances and social and athletic events and not enough academic focus. It's time to put aside the feel-good belief in our inadequate schools and tighten the scholastic rigor. Think of it as going on an educational diet of only sound scholastic nutrition. We can no longer pretend that our national or local school programs match anyone else's in the global marketplace. Our schools, like our former dominance in automobiles, are lumbering along as if there were no serious global competition.

Finally, the diminution of educational standards has resulted in a poorly informed electorate too quickly swayed by hucksterism interests, as they are by associative advertising, and are rooted in a low-level political understanding of political traps into which corporate America and a compliant Congress strides. It is not just that the ultra-Republican agenda tenets are unworthy but that they are dogmatic. And whether in religion, science or politics, dogmatism is anti-intellectual, a biased complacency America cannot afford.

As if the American educational level is not enough to get citizens depressed, our advanced technology, geared almost exclusively toward entertainment and trivia, is helping define our intellectual life downward. Our societal decline has influenced our educational decline and resonates throughout our politics. We are unequal in talent and abilities, as the educational achievement levels demonstrate, but we are all politically equal—which is what "all men are created equal" in the *Declaration of Independence* means—so our votes are equal with other votes.

Ethics has been at the core of western civilization and the centerpiece of a liberal arts education. Its erosion has now convulsed America with scandals in journalism, the financial sector, athletic departments, university students, and sadly even presidential candidates. This isn't about just unprincipled politics or economics anymore. It is a rescue for a lost national and cultural identity where the principal occupations are games, social electronics, sports, the cult of the body, and of making light of the value of intellectuals and scientists and ultimately despising them.

Tea Party Members, Sympathizers and Sponsors

> A zeal for different opinions concerning religion, concerning government . . .
> an attachment to different leaders ambitiously contending for leadership and
> power, or to persons of other descriptions whose fortunes have been interesting
> to the human passions, have, in turn, divided mankind into parties, inflamed
> them with mutual animosity and rendered them much more disposed to vex and
> oppress each other than to cooperate for the common good.
>
> (James Madison, *The Federalist Papers*, No. 10).

George Glenville, a former Treasurer of the Navy, First Lord of the Admiralty, Chancellor of the Exchequer, and Prime Minister, was head of British colonial governance. From 1763 to 1766 he was Leader of the House of Commons and pushed through the *Stamp Act* of 1765 that was later repealed. The King dismissed Glenville that same year. But the House of Commons continued to insist that it had the legitimate right to supervise the colonies and tax them. [16] It's also instructive to recall that the British beheaded a king, Charles I in 1649, for usurping powers the people thought were their prerogatives. This royal beheading was followed by a civil war among English Royalists, who favored a monarchy, and Parliamentarians led by Cromwell, inaugurating a real revolution that trumps dumping tea in Boston harbor as a sign of civil discontent against taxes.

Moreover, during the French Revolution the Jacobins, under the ruse of the French standard for liberty and freedom, behaved like cannibals, enslaving the French and murdering the opposition. Both the French and English have more heinous revolutions than the relatively tame American Revolution. Slavery advocates used the same analogy to begin the Civil War, as *The Charleston Mercury* noted on December 17, 1860: "The tea has been thrown overboard, the revolution of 1860 has been initiated." [17] The South's revolution and secession was to void its constitutional compact so it could retain slaves. All other arguments proposed by southern advocates are bogus.

Supporters of the Tea Party believe in the Constitution as the supreme law, stand for limited government, for free enterprise and capitalism, fiscal responsibility, border security, and state sovereignty. The modern Tea Party movement was an angry protest against government and the federal deficit, acting as if it were still fighting against the British Parliament and King George III. It is a cause mostly with clarity about reducing government, the deficit and not raising taxes, but obscure and incoherent about the complexities of accomplishing those objectives. Yet three-quarters of all Americans, and half of all Republicans, according to a New York Times/CBS poll, believe that any deficit reduction plan should include tax increases which indicates how outside the mainstream are ultra-conservatives.

One of the movement's early leaders was Sarah Palin, former half-time Governor of Alaska whose antics created a coterie of enthusiastic disciples. She spoke with conviction and employed tart slogans to explain deftly, but with abundant ignorance, economically complicated aspects of American political life and foreign policy. Palin packaged her appeal in frontier self-assurance and glib righteousness. But when asked in public could not answer what readings inspired her, or which Supreme Court decisions were relevant in modifying American life. She was aided by her uncommon beauty, the glossy appeal of popular television, and the media's limited ability to conduct comprehensive analysis of constitutional principles.

The Tea Party movement succeeded in garnering increased representation in Congress in the 2010 election cycle but symbolized anti-intellectualism and anti-government persuasions. It's appeal is political smoke and theater, smacks of gobs of ignorance, and stomach-churning platitudes. It signifies voter frustration, has taints of racism, and disillusionment with the economy. But deep down it is a social class difference in society, resistant to wealth and power, elites and elitism, intellectuals and ordinary people, differences that always play well in politics. The term "liberal media" is a code phrase for intellectuals. What is different in the world now is a higher level of the global superrich who are scornful of government, taxes and everyone else. [18]

The resurrection of the Tea Party movement can be traced to a live broadcast on CNBC on February 19, 2009 when a business news editor, Rick Santelli, ranted about a stimulus bill pushed through Congress that gave relief to troubled homeowners. General Motors had already received loan monies and this came quickly after the huge bank loans (mislabeled as bailouts) of over $700 billion known as *The Troubled Asset Relief Program* (TARP) passed in the last days of the Bush Administration. [19] The subsequent bill was known as the Obama Administration's *Homeowner Affordability and Stability Plan* that was intended to provide aid to delinquent homeowners. But instead of requiring banks to modify mortgages, the Treasury Department lent more money to banks to become financially stable. Lending money to banks did not increase the economic recovery nor substantially relieve homeowners in arrears.

Disaffected taxpayers, already suffering from a powerful recession, wanted to know why taxpayers were subsidizing mortgages of financially reckless neighbors who should not have purchased a house they couldn't afford. Economically, subsidies to the improvident are unrewarding. Anger directed at banks evaporated quickly but intensified at government, but generally for the wrong reasons. For example, few criticized the consistent Republican efforts to eliminate or curtail government regulation over banks and financial institutions. Whatever terrifies banks, like regulations, also terrifies Republicans.

As it happened, money spent on distressed mortgages ended in foreclosures anyway, and a subsequent scandal among the banking industry for not reading documents on foreclosures further stained the industry. Citizens who spent wisely were asked to subsidize those who spent unwisely. This argument grew into a rant and then into a movement against the impudence of government, but oddly not a strong reaction against banks. Dick Armey, former majority leader in the House of Representatives, had as his Number One axiom this pithy phrase: "The market is rational and the government is dumb." [20]

Like most political reactions, the Tea Party was a foot stomping, slam-the-door, screaming kind of response to the Obama Administration, the heir, not the instigator, of the budget crisis. Like all angry reactions, it attracted attention and gathered crowds, not unlike the outrageous costumes, comic relief and on-stage absurdities of rock stars and some football fans. Their alarmist conjuring of conspiracies and socialist and apocalyptic government actions bespeak a chronic desperation. Tea Party followers have an astounding and idiosyncratic ignorance, not just superficial, compared to that of a high school student who needs to enroll in a civic course. Some compare the state of America to Nazi death camps, just one example of the level of reckless and moronic thought in public discourse.

It was estimated in 2010 that the core of the Tea Party constituted about 24% of the population, and was composed mainly of White constituents who objected to federal money distributed to the poor, often minorities. The population of the U.S. is about 12% African American. But Tea Party membership is only one percent Black and one percent Hispanic, which shows how unrepresentative of America it is. However, it would have been representative of the South during slavery. A corollary belief of this group is that favoring the poor encourages the poor to remain poor, a typical Republican talking point that may have racial overtones.

Somehow in this combustible mix, the idea of liberalism has been confused with government expansion, an idea that had no conservative resonance during the George W. Bush Administration when the country went to war against two countries and abrogated government regulation of the financial sector. Adam Smith in *The Wealth of Nations* had something to say about taxes, war, and debt. "The taxes upon the necessaries of life, therefore, may be no impeachment of the wisdom of that republic which, in order to acquire and to maintain its independency, has, in spite of its great frugality, been involved in such expensive wars as have obliged it to contract great debt." [21] President Bush recklessly never cut government spending to pay for the wars in Afghanistan or Iraq, nor asked the people to sacrifice as the nation's surplus fell into deep deficit. Though Republicans said nothing at the time about this slick three-card monte scheme with the public's money, they vociferously insisted that President Obama cut anything from the federal budget before adding new services.

In one noticeable contradiction, Tea Party members agreed that Bush caused the economic deficit but still viewed him favorably by 57%. The 2011 report of the *Financial Crisis Inquiry Commission* found that the financial debacle beginning in 2007 was avoidable, and faulted the supervision of the Federal Reserve, shoddy mortgage lending, and the excessive packaging and sale of risky loans and securities by the banking and credit industries. As is true so often in airplane crashes, the financial debacle was due to human error, mixed in with large doses of fraud and deception. [22]

Financial services and banking deregulation advocates want drastically to cut federal spending, but were surprisingly silent when the deficit was significantly increased during the Bush Administration from 2000 to 2008, and government regulation of industries and banking were largely absent. Not to say that the deficit and financial crisis aren't real and begging for solutions. But this deregulation movement offered nothing but sympathetic frustration and fear for people with limited insight into American constitutional history, the complexities of federal spending, or even representative democracy, a balance between competing national interests. Some proponents are the very people the founding fathers didn't even want voting on important issues, like for senators, a process they left to state legislatures (changed by the 17th Amendment in 1913), or the President, a decision left to delegates from the Electoral College.

There is a difference between a short-term problem in a banking crisis, especially if it is a government loan and some of the money is refunded as it was from General Motors, and a long-term problem of deficits. Even during the Roosevelt Administration under the New Deal, sensible politicians believed in a benevolent partnership between business and government that maintained capitalists with their power and status intact. [23]

But equally important economically is that spending government money during a deficit can assist a limping economy recover, and this is the message of non-ultra conservative economists who are not held in bondage by ideology and not facts or historical evidence. Massive deficit spending in England, as it regrouped to build its military in a war with Hitler's Germany in 1939, made the economy boom. It was exactly what the Cambridge economist John Maynard Keynes had predicted in 1936 in *The General Theory of Employment, Interest and Money*, a major study never rarely if ever cited by conservative economists because it refutes their distorted ideas about the economy. [24] On the other hand, war does change the economic equation and satisfies an employment shortage (11 million Americans were in the military in World War II, and 16 million worked in defense plants) but encourages inflation and debt.

SEEKING POLITICAL SOLUTIONS			
	More important To stick to beliefs	Neutral	More Important to compromise
All US adults	28%	21%	51%
Republicans	37%	27%	26%
Independents	27%	20%	52%
Democrats	20%	17%	62%
Tea Party Supporters	45%	23%	31%
Tea Party Opponents	16%	16%	69%

Source: Gallup Poll, September 8-11, 2011

Tea Partiers are frustrated citizens who want revolutionary change that they are unwilling, or more likely unable, to spell out what that means. And they have focused on the peripheral issues, like government and taxes, when it is the collective failures of most of the public and private institutions in society, from banks and schools, to corporations and industry, from local and state governments, from financial and corporate fraud to individual corruption and personal debt that have failed to improve the quality of life.

Moreover, they generally insist on adhering to a fixed orthodoxy rather than compromise their beliefs to reach pragmatic solutions, according to a Gallup Poll. The table above shows the wide disparity between political groups and how uncompromising by comparison the Republicans and Tea Party members are in seeking compromise on workable government solutions.

The Institute for Liberty is an advocacy group that is committed to combating what it characterizes as "petty tyrannies" of government that legislates regulations, like the Occupational Safety and Health Administration (OSHA) and the Environmental Protection Agency (EPA), that it believe infringes on personal liberties. The Institute is one of those pro-business, anti-regulatory organizations sponsored by large corporations posing as grassroots associations close to the goals of the Tea Party advocates.

As a comparable revolutionary movement, the Protestant Reformation inaugurated by Martin Luther started in part because individuals wanted to interpret the Bible as they chose and did not want the Pope or clerics telling them what it meant. As an analogy, there are multiple interpretations of select constitutional passages of what the framers meant. But in most cases the U.S. Supreme Court has adjudicated interpretations of constitutional legalities. This means that no other interpretations can be appealed. Political discourse from the far radical political right never cites court decisions, and extrapolates their own meaning as worthy of any other just like early biblical interpreters who eventually formed separate Protestant denominations.

Let the 2010 election year serve as an example of fudging one's political credibility. The former Republican candidate for the U.S. Senate from Delaware, Christine O'Donnell, had a greatly enhanced but largely fictional biography about her educational background, thus deceiving the public about who she was, had difficulty finding a job, holding onto a home and paying her taxes. In a debate with her opponent she could not respond to one U.S. Supreme Court decision she knew about. In no other country, at no other time, could blatant ignorance about U.S. history, the Constitution that everyone professes to love and few actually understand, allow anyone to stand as a candidate for high national office. In a televised debate she badly stated what the First Amendment was, or even an acceptable interpretation of it bolstered by a Supreme Court decision. She was totally ignorant of its widely accepted meaning of a separation of church and state. Her misinformed views are likely typical of the poorly informed general population.

Richard Blumenthal, a Senate candidate in Connecticut in 2010, repeatedly implied he had fought in Vietnam when he hadn't. Mark Kirk, senate candidate in Illinois, inflated his military history and bragged about a non-existent teaching career. Joe Walsh was campaigning for a House seat in a district outside Chicago when even his top staffers resigned after it was disclosed that he had a home foreclosed, was accused of bouncing checks, of failing to pay taxes and driving with a suspended license. Rich Iott in Ohio for years dressed up as a Nazi SS officer in weekends for reenactments. Such are the kind of "ordinary" Americans the Tea Party movement endorsed as political leaders.

A former alcoholic, drug user, high school graduate who did not attend college, Glenn Beck, who got a new religion, Mormonism, became the favorite chalkboard history teacher on TV followed by over two million viewers daily. He used no notes and talked from a kind of stream of consciousness that portrays an extremely superficial knowledge of American history paired with extreme political opinions. He appeared sincere, which is why so many identified with him, as they would a preacher and not a history or economics buff. He started Glenn Beck University online that advertises—together with all the merchandising accompanying membership—courses in Faith, Hope and Charity, 101 through 103, taught by conservative professors.

His recommended books became best sellers. But the books are ultra-conservative texts that espouse long since discredited ideas. Frederic Bastiat's book, *The Law*, was first published in 1850. It claimed that taxing people to pay for roads and canals was government-sanctioned theft, an idea that surfaced in the 1830s by southerners who did not want to pay for improvements to northern transportation. It was an idea that was favorable to the American South that argued for limited government so southern states could protect slavery.

W. Cleon Skousen (1913-2006), an anti-government crusader and advocate of the John Birch Society, a Mormon and former Salt Lake City police chief, whose book *The 5000 Year Leap* self-published in 1981, argued that under no circumstances should the federal government become involved in public welfare. Clousen thought that state government should promote religion and that public schools should be used for religious study and encourage Bible reading, typical of the attitudes of most Mormons toward religion and against government. His understanding of the Constitution, constitutional law and history are limited and disquieting. Even libraries separate fiction from non-fiction.

All these books usually emphasize that there is a divine purpose in their movement, and that the Obama Administration is socialist, though few define what that means or how it is applicable in a democracy. In general, these books reveal a profound ignorance of U.S. history, or of Enlightenment ideas grounded in the Constitution, and expert opinions in opposition to their extreme views. Populist ideology feeds into an angry clientele disgruntled with a bad economy, and into a resurgent reliance on fundamentalist religion to be injected into the public domain. Outrage has become media profitable, which has led to political idiocy. One of its favorite comparisons of the political opposition is to Nazis. If most people attest to it, as most southerners did slavery, or many religious people favor creationism, than reputedly there is truth in it and it must be correct.

Leaders and followers exhibit a socially determined form of group consciousness that approximates a southern mentality existing since the beginning of slavery, and have never been fully converted to understanding America as a multiracial society. President Obama was compared to Hitler, the Nazi invasion of Poland, and accused of treason. He was cited for his Kenyan ancestry, the Black Africa where slaves in the South originated. The decades have achieved the end of legal segregation but the cultural landscape has not changed.

Tea Party members may pretend familiarity and identification with the founding fathers, but their words and actions more closely resemble the leaders of the Confederacy. The flag they symbolically rally around is the Stars and Bars, not the Stars and Stripes. The phrase in a Republican Party platform statement that government is "an arrogant and out-of-touch government of self-appointed elites," mimics the sarcasm direct at the British crown in the *Declaration of Independence*. It insidiously equates American democracy and representative government with British royal administration prior to the revolution and the Constitution. Tea Party advocates deride intellectuals and elites while adoring the Founding Fathers, who of course were elites—lawyers, constitutional experts, international travelers, linguists and scholars, the very kind of contemporary liberals they hold in disdain.

The disappearance of multiple newspapers, and the decimation of investigative journalism that once kept a skeptical public informed, have been a disservice to political knowledge. The gross amount of money spent on political advertising has been the chief source of political knowledge. Campaign commercials drive elections because they only emphasize the self-interest of the wealthy and corporations, specifically the big three—the financial services, energy, and the health insurance and pharmaceutical industries. [25] Campaign advertising chooses the topics for debate, usually negative comments about the opposition, and omits serious debates about the issues sponsors do not want discussed. Since the public gets most of its political knowledge from campaign ads during an election cycle, and lacks the will or ability to seek a critical scrutiny of candidates, the voting public sadly buys into the political slant of corporate sponsors as a cheap option. Elections results favor the candidates who, once elected, lap up campaign monies from the same sponsors. Democracy is the worse for it.

The American south had a landed aristocracy, just as England still does today. Most of southern ancestors originated from England, whose colonial occupants owned much of the land and the wealth—cotton, rice, tobacco, indigo—it produced. This was the caste that lived in a sheltered cultural existence. But the South also had a class system of Blacks and landless Whites. The poor whites felt psychologically related to the wealthy Whites in a way poor and wealthy do not in other societies because both classes had a Black underclass that they could subordinate and feel superior to. Neither laws nor judicial decisions can change economic or social class differences. Even after the defeat of Reconstruction in 1877 the South was able to revive its White power structure and continue to deprive Blacks of privileges and opportunities.

Contemporary conservative and libertarian advocates want to pay no taxes as if they were still under British dominion and to subordinate minorities by cutting if not eliminating social programs. They also want no regulation by government, no organized labor unions, and no handouts to the unemployed, poor, sick or elderly. Generally, they favor the abolition of Social Security,

Medicaid, federal regulatory agencies, and welfare payments. Conservatism has many sides but dismantling government safety nets for the less fortunate is an extreme agenda with a growing number of followers. All they need is more burning incense to stupefy their innumerable admirers. The names of the individual movements over time may change names, but the face and identity of the ideology will remain the same.

The American public is suckered into accepting lies and distortions as truth, and polls reveal this growing ignorance. Americans bemoan the state of schooling achievement, but their own appalling ignorance, lack of critical thinking and search for answers is just as deplorable. These are the people that believed that home prices would rise forever and so galloped to the bankers' trough to take out home equity loans, a total of $2.3 trillion, to spend on consumer goods and run up credit card debt. Misguided government regulation and financial avarice accelerated the economic crisis. But the greedy American homeowner provided the oxygen that fueled the financial meltdown and now wants to blame government for self-inflicted financial folly.

The middle class can never regain its income losses. It is easy to blame government for the country's woes, as agitated movements do. But the country is in a global recession where labor costs, robotic mechanisms, instant communication, the glacial slowness of new job creation, cheap goods produced abroad, and higher educational standards in Asia and the developed world all factor into the economic equation. But for the rich to hold on to the bulk of the income that is saved, and does not put it back into the American economy, is fiscally unhealthy. In some way, absent a King and aristocracy, the economic climate mimics the days prior to the French Revolution in 1789.

Americans have lost their inquisitive nature, and eagerness to develop and forge new alliances at home and abroad. They are forgetful of American history, if they ever knew it, and afraid of future economic insecurities they helped create. Instead they have dissipated energies in fruitless rallies about the role of government, as if the country still had kings in governance, as it did in colonial times. Many spout vague revolutionary phrases whose implications they clearly have not thought through, appealing to the most coarse and vulgar sentiments. The anger is palpable and misdirected. But the economic crisis is real, deep, and will be long-lasting.

We are witnessing a national decadence, the result of consistently poor educational standards now extended quite thoroughly into the adult population, paltry personal aims based on self-gratification, the belief in consumerism based on monetary housing speculation, a lack of public spiritedness, petulance at perceived wrongs, blaming government because it is a convenient target, and all this with large doses of ignorance and a willingness to believe political demagogues uncritically.

It may not be possible to mediate successfully between love of freedom, both in its abstract sense of individual liberties and in recognized constitutional protections, or to reconcile historical differences between the freedoms won from colonial oppressions and the lack of those freedoms among descendants of slaves. Americans stand for a unity of differences, but they seemed to have gravitated toward a uniformity of distrust and animosity toward the constitutional government forged to be the guardian of those freedoms so enthusiastically extolled. A vociferous group has hijacked an enduring sense of national unity among diverse voices. They have rushed to a public pulpit to preach a sermon of disharmony.

One pertinent issue that defines the far political right is property rights, a social problem that dates from the time of slavery because slaves were legal property. So ingrained and intertwined in the culture and economy of the South was slavery and slave laborers that every economic and political stratagem was used to maintain its status. Hence, governmental incursions on any topic of private property—slaves in particular but in recent times any business interests––that many former southerners and sympathizers have become libertarians. The Libertarian political party (discussed in the following chapter) was founded in 1971 and ostensibly offers members "the natural right of sole dominion over their lives, liberty and property."

Tea Partiers favor property over individual rights, individual choice, a favorable outcome of democracy, and champion individual freedom of choice for businesses. Consequently, they find every means to deregulate government rules for controlling, in the public's interest, corporations and businesses that use any ruse to fix any price for any product they produce or service they offer, often without regard for public safety or interference from public inspection.

Phil and Wendy Gramm are prime examples of deregulation. Texas Senator Phil Gramm was Chairman of the Senate Banking Committee from 1995 to 2000. He was the chief cheerleader and instigator of deregulation of the banking industry. He repealed the *Glass-Steagall Act* (1933) that separated commercial banks from investors and speculators. Gramm exempted derivatives like credit default swaps from regulation by the Commodity Futures Trading Commission that his wife chaired (1988-1993). Then Gramm and his ultra-conservative associates passed the *Commodity Futures Modernization Act* (2000) that deregulated banks and allowed any kind of financial institution to merge. In effect, this led to the same economic conditions the Great Depression sought to avoid.

Then Wendy Gramm, Phil's wife, as Chair of the Commodity Futures Trading Commission, exempted Enron's energy-swap operation from oversight. After totally gutting the government agency she had sworn to uphold, she then resigned to join Enron's Board of Directors. During the Reagan Administration, this was not seen as a conflict of interest. Enron contributed over $100,000 to the Gramm campaign fund. The financial sector added another $4.6 million over about a decade. The result of this massive deregulation initiative directly led to Enron's bankruptcy and the nation's financial collapse in 2008. Phil Gramm retired from the Senate in 2002 and became Vice President of UBS Bank. [26]

We can, indeed, put faces as to who contributed to our national debt. Phil Gramm, born in Georgia but living his adult life in Texas was a purebred champion of the southern cause of limited government and used his public position to benefit industry, and, while as a public servant, profiting from it with his wife for personal gain.

President George W. Bush is another who soiled the relationship between Big Business and government. Congress established a Council on Environmental Quality in the Office of the President in 1969 to advise the president on environmental concerns. Bush appointed James Connaughton, a former lobbyist for ARCO (now a part of BP) as head of this agency. Then Bush appointed Philip Cooney as chief of staff. Cooney was a lobbyist for he American Petroleum Institute and was directly responsible for altering scientific reports on global warming, and when exposed resigned and immediately went to work for ExxonMobil. [27]

The Bush Administration systematically used government civil service appointments to further business interests. Under the Bush Administration, the Department of the Interior under Secretary Gale Norton, Deputy Secretary J. Stephen Griles (later sent to prison in 2007 for obstruction of justice), and Acting Secretary Patricia Lynn Scarlett, became a government arm of the petroleum industry, squashing regulations, opening federal lands for drilling, failing to enforce fees petroleum companies owed the government for leasing federal land, and ignoring environmental laws. In gratitude, Bush cut back corporate taxes to the lowest level since World War II.

Tea Party members marched to "take back government." Americans took back government from the British, but the South also tried to take back its separatist government in 1860 so the national government would not interfere with its peculiar lifestyle. What the Tea Party and similar movements did not do, until that is, the "Occupy Wall Street" movement that began in October 2011 in New York and spread across several cities, is protest against the financial and corporate sectors that really sucked money out of middle class circulation and held it, spent it, or stashed it in foreign accounts. Demonstrations are supposed to be inconvenient, to draw attention to a national problem. They are usually cultural, inspired typically by the young, and not counter-cultural. According to an October 2011 *Time* poll, 54% approved of the movement, and 86% agreed that Wall Street and lobbyists have too much influence in Washington.

When younger Americans protested in Wall Street its members were accused, by Congressman Eric Cantor of Virginia among others, of being a "mob," of inaugurating "class warfare," of "pitting Americans against Americans." It's hard enough to keep from laughing at this disturbing and bizarre perspective, if, indeed, it does not illustrate a fundamental hypocrisy. Ironically, a literal "class warfare" is what the South originated in 1860.

But the inequality is not enough. Americans had to listen to the worst of political hypocrisy and plenty of hyperbole from Republicans ingratiating themselves with the right wing of the party. Newt Gingrich collected $300,000 in 2006 and over $1.6 million in fees since 1999 from Freddie Mac, one of the government's the mortgage finance companies, for lobbying members of Congress. He then had the audacity to tear down it as a part of government during the 2011 presidential primary debates. Benefitting lavishly from government contracts and then lambasting government itself is a cheap but deceitful political game. Mitt Romney felt it necessary in his campaign to scrap the *Patient Protection and Affordable Care Act* of 2009, derisively known as "Obamacare," that was virtually identical to the health care bill he got passed as Governor of Massachusetts.

According to a *Time* poll from October 2011, 81% viewed the country moving in the wrong direction, but favored the protestors against financial institutions by 54%, and 73% favored raising taxes on the most wealthy. Those polled were split between those wanting the government to spend more to get the economy moving and those favoring cutting spending. And 65% said the best way to reduce the federal deficit was a combination of an increase in taxes and spending cuts. Only 27% looked favorably on Tea Party solutions.

The following figures are rounded and approximate from 2012 but indicative of stark conditions of our economic dilemma that unregulated and unaccountable financial institutions, globalization and American addictions have combined to create.

25+ million are unemployed but willing and able to work
51 million can't get health insurance
47 million need government help, like food stamps
15 million owe more on their mortgage than their house is worth

Now imagine a middle-aged wage-earner, the head of his family who tries to create a happy existence for himself and his family but who finds himself in debtor's prison. The daughter Amy, employed as a seamstress, is unappreciated by other family members for her selfless work. A friend name Arthur is determined to help but is baffled by the government bureaucrats that can never seem to get anything done right. If this seems like a contemporary picture of hard times, of declining wages and busted mortgages, it is the literary creation of Charles Dickens in *Little Dorrit* (1855-57), a bleak study of a cold society in which struggling people try to make sense of working life. For many Americans it has become a Dickensian world.

Selective facts underscore the growing inequality that threatens a balanced economy and increases social tension. For example, the 400 wealthiest Americans have a combined net worth that is greater than the bottom 150 million Americans. The top one percent have more money that 90% of all other Americans. The average income in the financial sector in 2010 was $361,330. Many chief executives took home more in salary than their companies paid in federal income taxes. Today's bank robbers are the banks. The gaming of the financial system that benefited only the gamers and not contributors has severely damaged and tainted the whole economy. The financial sector enjoyed profits in good years and, unlike consumers, accepted federal bailout money in the lean years. Additionally, the Pew Research Center in 2012 found that two-thirds of Americans believe there are "strong conflicts" between the rich and poor, a nearly 20% increase since 2009. [28]

This vast inequality in wealth is unsustainable for both the economy and relative social harmony. In the decade from 2000 to 2010 the number of suburban poor in the 95 largest metropolitan areas grew by 53%, and the number of poor in the cities grew by 23%. [29] How the nation deals with the loss of revenue from consumer spending and taxed goods, the bankruptcies, and the human toll on frayed relationships, will determine its economic emergence, or not, from a slowly deteriorating lifestyle. The profound economic turn of events has imploded the myth that discipline and hard work would gain access to the American dream of acceptable living standards. We are no longer the affluent society John Kenneth Galbraith once defined.

Protestors had undefined purposes but were propelled by their collective angst and outrage against financial institutions and fading prospects for a quality job and relatively comfortable lifestyle. Such leftist protests reveal the widening of income inequality and the extreme concentrations of wealth. The working class and the expanding poor, vulnerable to propaganda manipulation, have become a magnet for discontent and the focus of the expression of grievances. They are the polar political opposites of the Tea Party but their fear of the loss of financial security is just as precarious. America may never again regain its former lifestyle of living from easy credit. [30]

Americans are just as responsible for the dilemma as the institutions they decry. We overate, overspent, over-borrowed, over-entertained ourselves, consumed what we couldn't afford, went into debt, and gambled away the future. America's physical flabbiness is a sign of its soft, decline-in-reading and decline-in-reading proficiency, intellectual underbelly.

Finally, like other Know Nothing negative movements, the Tea Party and similar arch-conservative movements will eventually fade into obscurity, but not the anti-government theme, and not radical conservatives locked into a dispirited dogma. But because of its long negative legacy in American politics, and Americans' love of buzzwords and slogans that seemingly encapsulate complicated principles and processes in democratic life, groups like it will not disappear entirely from national discourse.

Nor will the conservative agenda of looking inward into the domestic economy as if it were in an isolated country resolving its unique underlying financial issues. Cutting the size of the national government, for example—a truly southern legacy reinvigorated by President Reagan and still held as a primary conservative ideal—is the least responsive of all actions for addressing America's global engagement. It is reasonable to conclude that the lingering southern strategy of limited government is counterproductive to America's active participation in the world's new inter-related economy in which technology transfers, and shifts in labor and capital markets have altered the traditional business model.

Chapter Three
The Libertarian Agenda

Nowadays the mass believes it has the right to impose and lend force to notions deriving from its own platitudes.
(Jose Ortega y Gasset, *The Revolt of the Masses*)

Libertarianism became a political movement in the home of David Nolan on August 15, 1971. He and four associates heard President Nixon announce wage and price controls. For Nolan this was unconstitutional in times of peace. He and his friends met later in Colorado Springs and formed the Libertarian Party partly in response they felt, to presidential usurpation of powers and opposition to the war in Vietnam. The first Libertarian agenda included an initiative for a constitutional amendment to void the income tax.

Nolan had read novels of Ayn Rand (1905-1982), *Atlas Shrugged* and *The Fountainhead*, for political inspiration. This has been a course followed since by like-minded public servants, like former Federal Reserve Chief Alan Greenspan, her protégé, Texas Congressman Ron Paul and his son, Kentucky Senator Rand Paul, and Wisconsin Congressman Paul Ryan (who insisted all his staffers read *Atlas Shrugged*). They all formed their guiding political ideology based on Rand's fiction. Nolan sought to unite Republicans and Democrats behind an unfettered form of capitalism and in maximizing civil liberties, beliefs that today resonate throughout the radical right. Nolan died in Tucson on November 21, 2010, aged 66. His political ideas, formed largely from Rand's novels, influence those who seek limited government intervention in business, and antipathy toward government.

Why have such economically and politically important people taken their ideology from novels and not from serious philosophers? For that answer, we must turn to Ayn Rand herself.

I swear—by my life and my love of it—that I will never live for the sake of another man, nor ask another man to live for mine.
(Ayn Rand, *Atlas Shrugged*, p. 1,069.)

Atlas Shrugged, first published in 1957, is Ayn Rand's epic *magnum opus*, a novel as long as Leo Tolstoy's *War and Peace* (1,168 pages), and equally as rich in narrative texture, story-telling, philosophy, and in some places, approaching inspirational poetry. Rand has visually enticing descriptions of scenes, a remarkable series of gripping dialogues, and clinically nuanced character development of several major figures, a novel that took her over a decade to complete. Rand was politically independent, an amateur philosopher but a fierce individualist.

Atlas Shrugged is the fictional bible of libertarians and radical conservatives who demonize an impersonal and conspiratorial government that taxes citizens mercilessly, and can find no fault with corporations, the enterprises of the nation's creative minds. Like those who believe that Mary Magdalen and Jesus were married and had children in Dan Brown's *Da Vinci Code*, disciples of Rand believe that government is the enemy. But which government: the USSR or America?

Rand was born in Leningrad and grew up under Lenin and Stalin's Soviet communism. This socialist version of government, and not just her experiences of freedom in the U.S., colored her philosophical view of the state that was the glorification of American business and the repugnance of the dull, conspiratorial, faceless bureaucrats of Soviet government. Her followers have assumed her fictional account of a demon American government is the real truth and not her actual, formative childhood and teenager experiences lived in a brutalized and repressive Soviet regime.

The heroic figure in *Atlas Shrugged* is John Galt who symbolizes Rand's own immortalization of an independent modern maverick. Galt is portrayed as a persecuted, misunderstood Socrates-like man of wisdom, or Jesus-like guru persona—even though Rand's message is anti-Christian—or like a mythical Atlas who holds up the world. Her philosophy of a safe environment—again reflective of her lack of freedoms in Soviet Russia as a young adult before she immigrated to America—is like a utopia, the place in *Atlas Shrugged* she calls Atlantis, or like a symbol of those who emerge from enslavement in Plato's cave in *The Republic*. Her utopia is a peaceful country where all her fictional heroic figures retreat to, a place without a government or social rules where intelligent residents can act without coercion.

Another main philosophical principle Rand embodies is as ancient as that of Protagoras (490–420 BCE): that man is the measure of all things. Rand is opposed to any form of altruism, of helping others, and is grounded in self-interest, a philosophy derived from, among others, Jean Jacques Rousseau (1712–1778) and Jeremy Bentham (17481832). Hence, Rand's followers do not want government equalizing incomes or funding welfare programs that help the less fortunate in society.

Rand's self-styled philosophy of Objectivism is composed of a utopia where corrupt and conspiratorial governments are non-existent, and where rational and creative people like herself and her capitalist kingpins can enjoy the company of other intellectuals, just like Plato's philosopher kings. Today's far right anti-government disciples, like the libertarians and the Tea Party followers, have adopted her special perspective on life and the state from Plato (429–347 BCE). But unlike Plato who proposed that wise philosophers actually rule the state, Rand's philosophy is that they should escape the world altogether into a Thomas More *Utopia* (1516), from a Greek word meaning "no place." More's *Utopia* is a socialist welfare state where everyone is engaged in agriculture or a trade, exactly as Atlantis in Rand's *Atlas Shrugged*.

Rand's point is that when government stifles creativity that the people of intellect retreat and let the world collapse so they can rebuild it. The underlying premise is that only the top business people are creative enough to keep the machinery of the economy moving and everyone else, including public servants, are moronic. The metaphor is also Platonic—that the world returns to the cave where they were enslaved after the wise ones have shown them the sunshine outside, a Platonic metaphor for a transcendental world yet to be experienced, a view that appealed strongly to a Christian afterlife. But overall, Rand's fictional world is a powerful indictment of an out-of-control government. Rand's radical right followers are projecting a fictional world onto a democratic government, compounded with a misunderstood role of its constitutional foundations.[1]

Libertarianism is the contemporary political expression of a form of classical liberalism, as old as the ancient Greeks and Romans, a belief that individuals should be free to pursue their own self-interests. Related philosophies like the epicurean or utilitarian espoused by Jeremy Bentham (1748-1832) proposed that happiness and self-interest were the greatest personal goals. In America, and principally under William James, utilitarianism popularized by John Stuart Mill became pragmatism, the epitome of an American philosophy that seemed to embody the spirit of 19th and 20th century accomplishments. The rise of right wing extremism—the province of the South—crowded out this can-do philosophy with an emphasis again on the individual and not what the commonweal could achieve as a collective force for the well-being of all society.

Individualism seems totally inappropriate to parents who nurture helpless children to adulthood. Some measure of genetic altruism, and not just to personal satisfaction, applies to supporting the social order, as it does to parenting one's own young. Libertarian freedom and corporate self-interest can be a powerful motivating source in personal life. But seeking self-interest doesn't prepare an individual for the actions of an impersonal universe where accidents, disease, or the colliding interests of the powerful and wealthy subvert one's comfort and complacency, as the self-interests of financial institutions have done to the economy. Freedom and self-interest do not exist independently of values. Jettisoning all motivations and valuations other than the extremely narrow ones of freedom and self-interest is hard to justify.

Yet Alexis De Tocqueville in his classic *Democracy in America* (in Book Two, Chapter Eight) noted how fashionable and universally accepted was the concept of self-interest even in 1838 among Americans. They often deceived themselves, he said, into believing that all self-interest was honest. In fact, self-interest does not often promote justice nor spontaneously lead to the social improvement of society. Americans, and particularly Republicans, extol self-interest as a comforting, corporate philosophy, but rarely discuss or see its darker, predatory side, especially in businessmen who could care less about the social good and seek only profit for private gain without any sense or regard for the common good. Self-interest without justice is unenlightened vanity and selfishness.

For reasons that influence a conservative religious bias, few Republicans recommend a Darwinian view of progress or self-interest, a more scientifically rigorous, persuasive and justifiable condition than abstract philosophical principles. Even among animals there is altruism for the good of the herd or pack. The ability to even have an interest in survival, or self-interest, is attributable to natural selection and evolutionary progress.

This chapter is an abbreviated example of how American politics, but especially the ultra-Republican agenda, has been controlled by a group of economic hucksters and financiers who have gamed the political system in favor of policies that lack academic and scientific evidence and rigor.

Libertarians are the ultimate individualists, believing that people have the right to control their own body, speech, actions and property. They usually seek to reduce the size of governments, to eliminate personal income tax, and to privatize roads, airports, public parks and education. Their numbers doubled from 2005 to 2010. This means that they, like one of their main exponents, Kentucky Senator Rand Paul—named after Ayn Rand (?) and the physician son of libertarian Texan congressman, Ron Paul—are opposed to portions of *The Civil Rights Act of 1964*, *The Voting Rights Act of 1965*, or similar laws that prevent discrimination, or offer government services paid for by taxpayers.

In May 2010 Rand Paul commented to the Louisville *Courier-Journal* that he thought the *Civil Rights Act* trampled on property rights. It was an argument that would have found sympathy among slave owners in the South in 1860. Libertarians and all their ideological cousins are like bathers in a Turkish bathhouse surrounded by misty fogs of their own making, and believing that that fog is the ultimate reality. For the paranoid among them, the fog is the enemy.

Oddly, the transformation of other politicians can also be traced to the impact of a novel. Representative Michele Bachmann of Minnesota was a Democrat as a college senior until she read Gore Vidal's acidic historical novel *Burr* about Aaron Burr, Vice President under Jefferson, killer of Alexander Hamilton in a duel. He was tried but not convicted of treason during Jefferson's presidency. This one novel's treatment of the founding fathers so irritated Bachmann that she became not only a Republican but a leader of the Tea Party movement and presidential candidate. Her perspective of the founders of the republic is uncompromisingly naïve even though she is a tax lawyer with a J.D. degree from Oral Roberts University. She has said, for example, that they tried to eradicate slavery, which most certainly they did not. It is odd to find that our politicians are unable to separate the world of novels from reality, and build a political philosophy on fiction.

Let's get the facts straight. The signers of the *U.S. Constitution* who owned slave plantations or large farms with slaves included: Richard Bassett, John Blair, William Blount, Pierce Butler, Daniel Carroll, Daniel of St. Thomas Jenifer, Charles Pinckney, Charles Cotesworth Pinckney, John Rutledge, William Dobbs Spaight, George Washington, John Dickinson, Hugh Livingston and James Madison. In other words 35% of the signers (14 of 39) were slave owners. Jefferson, surely the most mythologized of the founders also owned slaves, was Minister in France when the Constitution was written in 1787. [2] Subsequent presidents who owned slaves included: James Monroe, Andrew Jackson, John Tyler, James Polk, and Zachary Taylor. The first president who tried to eliminate slavery was Lincoln.

The ultra-conservative political agenda is not so far removed from the libertarian. Remember when the new Republican victory election resulted in a wave of new members of Congress who promised to reform Washington, who were suspicious of the handsome new president because he wasn't "American" enough with his ivy-league learning, and that the country needed to return to old-fashioned values? They felt the country and Washington with its elite corps of legislators, and the left-wing liberal media was out of step with ordinary Americans. There was talk of dismembering the proposed health care plan, of cutting taxes and lowering the deficit. Sound familiar? That was Newt Gingrich, Republican congressman from Georgia, after the Republican victory in 1994. If, like me, you have a touch of déjà vu, than you have experienced another round of conservative engineers who use similar slogans and catchy phrases without definitive policy initiatives to make campaign promises only slightly adjustable to the times, but with the same dogmatic certainty and fervor the South used to thwart the federal government in bygone decades.

Barry Goldwater, Ultra-Conservative

> The role of government has been expanded to a point where government influence and government decisions exert an overwhelming control over our daily lives. (Goldwater, 1979, p. 15)

Who is it you think of when you hear about a candidate for the U.S. Senate opening his campaign praising federal social programs? On the evening of September 18, 1952 in Prescott, Arizona, Barry Goldwater (1909-1998) "opened with praise for some of the social programs of the New Deal. I mentioned the Securities and Exchange Commission, the FDIC [Federal Deposit Insurance Commission] Society Security, unemployment insurance, old age assistance, aid to dependent children and the blind, and the FHA [Federal Housing Administration]." [3] Barry Goldwater, the ultra-conservative presidential candidate and college dropout, was not always opposed to federal social programs. Candidate Goldwater, a retail department manager and World War II pilot, sounded like a confirmed Democrat at the beginning of his political career.

Goldwater was the descendant of Jewish merchant immigrants who found their way to Los Angeles before settling in Prescott, Arizona. Goldwater absorbed the western frontier spirit and mentality as if he were an open range cowboy fighting against the cattle barons who controlled land and sometimes whole towns. He was a merchandiser but an intimate part of the territorial West. It is that indomitable and fierce independence that made him a rare voice in American politics that owned no allegiance to corporate interests.

But later in his politics he championed opposition to communism, labor bossism, foreign aid, inflationary federal spending, and was in favor of states rights and liberty, issues at the core of Republican and libertarian platforms. His essential code was laid out in *The Conscience of a Conservative* first published in 1960.

> I have little interest in streamlining government or in making it more efficient, for I mean to reduce its size. I do not undertake to promote welfare, for I propose to extend freedom. My aim is not to pass laws but to repeal them. It is

not to inaugurate new programs, but to cancel old ones that do violence to the
Constitution . . . (Goldwater, 1990, p. 17)

This undiluted ideology would cancel all New Deal programs he was so
proud of just a few years earlier. Since Goldwater's stance emphasized
"freedom," it seemed unclear what he thought about Blacks in the South who
had truly limited freedoms. In his personal life, Goldwater was unprejudiced. As
a member of the Phoenix City Council he voted to desegregate the restaurants,
pushed for desegregation of the Arizona Air National Guard, the Senate
cafeteria in 1953, and made donations to the NAACP. [4]

But his public pronouncements seem to offer an alternative explanation. For
example, he said he was in favor of civil rights but was firmly opposed to the
Brown v Board of Education ruling in 1954 that desegregated schools because
he didn't believe that the federal government should be permitted to rule on
anything about education. Apparently it did not occur to him that the Supreme
Court decision had less to do with education and everything to do with
outlawing segregation and states' denial of civil rights. He also said in
Conscience of a Conservative that Supreme Court decisions were "not
necessarily" supreme, which begs the question of what he thought was legally
supreme under the Constitution.

Goldwater held to a stricter laissez-faire doctrine. He believed that all social
welfare programs weakened individual liberties and self-reliance. He wanted to
terminate farm subsidies, social security, federal aid to education, the graduated
income tax, public power programs, and public housing—the very programs he
had praised in his first senatorial campaign. Goldwater's enemy became the
government's whole welfare state, coincidentally the posture of the South for
more than a century.

During the 1964 campaign Goldwater played the law and order card, raising
questions about women not safe on the streets, that there was too much crime
and lawlessness, and that if only a few leaders at the head of government could
be removed these unpleasant realities would disappear. For a conservative that
wanted to keep government out of peoples' lives, to appeal to a sense of moral
superiority using issues that should be addressed locally, is inconsistent. But
painting the opposition in an unfavorable light is not meant to appeal to logic but
to emotion. He was opposed to excessive foreign aid, excessive welfare, to high
taxes, and to foreign policy that was based largely on appeasement and
accommodation.

Goldwater held a private meeting with Johnson and both agreed that on the
nation's most divisive issues, the Vietnam War and civil rights, they would not
sully the campaign with further national divisiveness. [5]

Goldwater's nomination for president in 1964 was a highlight moment for
ultra-conservatism and Republican extremism. As presidential candidate he had
certainly changed his mind and tone about government. That presidential
election year was also a watershed in the pioneering of the modern conservative
movement. Lyndon Johnson was elected with a 22.6% victory margin, the 5th
largest in U.S. history, carrying 44 states. Goldwater's loss was attributable to

sympathy for Johnson, elevated to the presidency by a national tragedy only six weeks after President John Kennedy's assassination the previous November.

Yesterday's ultra-conservatives, inheriting the shield of Goldwater, are today's Tea Party activists with a vengeance who demonstrate a polemical strength disproportionate to their actual numbers, gathering momentum from conservative media outlets. Their intellectual appeal is negligible but powerful to the naysayers who joyride through anger and agitation at government. They look more to Reagan's principles than Goldwater's, though neither is that far apart politically, as both used recycled values from the South's negative response to the North. Goldwater's son-of-the-western-soil zeal, and part Jewish, part Protestant self-reliant work ethic, was the right mixture to produce a traditional veneration for individualistic values appealing to a conservative base.

When conventional wisdom dictates that investment funds should be distributed in a variety of portfolios, politicians seem to reply on only one economic theorist. The two most prominent among conservatives have been Hayek and Friedman.

Friedrich Hayek (1899-1992) & Milton Friedman (1912-2006): Freedom & Political Economy

> There is no culture where there are no norms and standards to which our fellow citizens can have recourse. There is no culture where there are no principles of civil legality to which to appeal . . . There is no culture where economic relations are not subject to protective rules of conduct.
> (Jose Ortega y Gasset, *The Revolt of the Masses*, 1985, pp. 60-61).

Let's emphasize "protective rules of conduct," as Ortega y Gasset notes in the quote above, for economic relations. What a strange idea, when in ultra conservative America the principal idea of capitalism is unrestrained rules of conduct for the business community and free markets. The absence of economic policing norms that protect the public, and the loosening of only those norms that seek the profit motive, according to Ortega, is barbarism. How did such an idea as the lack of government participation in monitoring the economy, come to dominate the Libertarian platform?

Friedrich Hayek (1899-1992) was a world-renowned economist who had academic appointments at the University of Freiburg and Salzburg, the London School of Economics, UCLA, and the University of Chicago. He was an advocate for free-market capitalism. He won the Nobel Prize in Economics that he shared with the Swedish sociologist Gunner Myrdal in 1974. President Bush awarded him the presidential Medal of Freedom in 1991.

Hayek looks back to a previous century, the *belle epoche,* to find his golden age. To attain it again he believes it is necessary to dismantle the welfare state that had few state social supports in the 19th century. Each person, not governments, should be given the opportunity to decide how to allocate existing resources. Hayek believes that government modification of *laissez faire* commercial activities, the marketplace, will lead inevitably to political serfdom or a totalitarian state.

The Road to Selfdom, his most celebrated work published in 1944, turned Congressman Ron Paul's life around, and many of his associates in the Libertarian camp. Hayek argued that state control of the economy leads to tyranny, and that any government expansion tends to socialism. Hayek's definition of socialism is a little more extreme than that bruited about by conservatives today. Hayek's socialism was the result of the abolition of private enterprise and ownership of the means of production and the creation of a planned economy, or exactly the form of socialism in Germany under Hitler, and in Russia and the USSR from 1917 to 1989 and in China under Mao. [6]

Hayek wrote his *magnum opus* during wartime in England, and as Chair of the Economics Department at the London School of Economics, but while at Cambridge to escape the *blitzkrieg* bombing of London by German aircraft. Thus, this work has to be understood against the backdrop of his experiences of the disaster of Austria at the end of World War I, and the Nazi aggrandizement of Europe in World War II, not normal times of quiescent financial activity.

Hayek was writing against the background of a bankrupted and hyperinflationary Europe destroyed by World War I in which he was a disillusioned soldier. It was a time when credit was almost non-existent, every country was carrying enormous war debts and reparations, and housing and food were scarce. World War I ruined he gold standard that Ron Paul wants to revive. Politically, Hitler and the Nazi party would soon control the German economy, Fascist Italy would embolden Benito Mussolini, and a Lenin-led, Bolshevist, and Marxist Russia would torment the free world of capitalism with its brand of totalitarian socialism. Hayek's professional life was circumscribed by the context of real tyrannical governments, collapsed economies and the destitution and starvation in his city, Vienna, at the end of World War I, and not a democracy American libertarians claim is tyrannical. (Vienna would fall to the Russians at the end of World War II, a city that had cheered Hitler like a conquering hero when he entered the city on March 14, 1938 after the *Anschluss*, Germany's unification with Austria). Like all professional writers, Hayek's economics were shaped in an economically devastated Europe and a looming depression that might further devalue money.

Socialism can be the proletarian brand that Karl Marx advocated and that became the standard for a political totalitarianism in Russia, China, North Korea and Cuba. The organization of unions and the collective actions of mostly manual workers in the 20th century revealed the differentiation of what Marx assumed was a unified proletariat. Marxism died as a useful economic theory based on class differences when the USSR imploded in 1989.

But socialism it is not, as is sometimes used loosely today, a true description of the American economy by those who oppose social welfare programs. Hayek is inapplicable to the American economy. All successful forms of capitalism in the developed world are mixed economies in which both public institutions and private enterprises function in relative harmony, just like the Federal Aviation Administration that manages the nation's airspace and corporate airlines that use it.

During times of war governments institute wage and price controls, legislate higher taxes and in general exercise a tighter rein on the economy. Hayek and others feared that after war governments might continue to influence the economy unfavorably with too many controls. Yet some government planning is compatible with economic freedom. The Invisible Hand of the economy, Adam Smith's metaphor, needs some direction with the visible hand of government. How else can there be real democracy if a people, and elected representatives in government, cannot have a legitimate hand in regulating the economy that sustains them? The only question is how much or what kind of intervention should government take in an economy to redress inequalities. The GI bill (*The Servicemen's Readjustment Act of 1944*), for example, is universally acknowledged as a prime example of a government educational program for veterans that simultaneously updated skills and provided employment as a student in a weakened economy.

Hayek was academically trained as an economist and a philosopher, and his collection of essays, *The Constitution of Liberty*, is expressive of his views. [7] Radical Republicans and Libertarians applaud Hayek's endorsement of liberty in the abstract. He speaks about governments as if they were all equal, never distinguishing between a monarchical government in Thailand, Saudi Arabia, Spain, Denmark or Britain, or a socialist government in Cuba or China, or a representative democracy like America or Sweden. Hayek is isolated in his own ivory tower.

He believed, erroneously I think, that the less fortunate in society, as he notes in *The Constitution of Liberty*, would be cared for by the general expansion of private wealth. [8] If we were to admit even the tiniest prospect of the truth of this idea we would have to assume that the distribution of welfare would be uneven, distributed wherever the private provider thought it most advantageous to its business, and probably with parks, theaters, museums close to its workers. Hayek did not believe in the redistribution of income for the purpose of creating more inequalities that resulted in socialism. For the government to provide for unemployment, poor health and retirement pensions is paternalistic, he says, and deprives individuals of the liberty to make their own life choices. One counter argument is that for the government to allow individuals to become financially ruinous, as in catastrophic health problems or massive job layoffs, without a minimum safety net is to undercut the economy and the tax base, and thereby depreciate provisions for other laudable public service programs like national defense or natural disasters not directed specifically at individuals.

There will always be debates over the proper balance between the leverage of individual liberties and the powers of government to regulate social behavior and services. He did not believe in centralized government economic planning. Hayek argues for the dangers of government's increasing control over the economy and individual lives, a theme comparable to George Orwell's literary version in *Animal Farm*, first published in 1945, of absolute state control. Like Hayek's life experiences during World War I and the Great Depression, Orwell was extremely critical of Josef Stalin's version of communism that deprived individuals of all liberties. The Russian and German tyrannies influenced both fiction and non-fiction in the early 20th century.

Nobel prize economist Milton Friedman was one of the most illustrious of such figures to show the relationship between politics and the economy in his landmark study, *Capitalism and Freedom* (1962), a study that only gained increased credibility after Republicans came to power under Reagan.

> Fundamentally, there are only two ways of coordinating the economic activities of millions. One is central direction involving the use of coercion—the technique of the army and of the modern totalitarian state. The other is voluntary cooperation of individuals—the technique of the market place. [9]

What Friedman omits in this quote above is the third way for coordinating economic activities in a democracy and that is with government. Friedman had been a follower of Keynes and spent time in wartime Washington as a government employee compiling data on consumers. Later in his professional life he rejected his previous Keynesian ideals.

Laws based by Congress and judicial decisions by courts also regulate the differences between an individual's freedom and rights and those of a society. To say that the *only* logical possibilities for economy activity are between a totalitarian state and one's individual freedom is to pretend one does not live in a democracy. Friedman establishes a totalitarian straw man he can easily demolish. Thus, like literal interpreters of the Bible, literal Friedman readers can assume, as Tea Party members do, that any intrusion on personal economic freedom is tyranny. Like the South in 1860, they compare President Obama to the "tyrant" Abraham Lincoln for encroaching on their liberty to use slaves as laborers, and after the war to keep the national government from challenging discriminatory laws to maintain White supremacy.

Friedman's examples of manufactured commodities, like his pencil analogy during TV interviews, is simple and understandable—that free markets gather raw materials, workers put them together with other goods, advertise their availability, transport them to suppliers and sellers. But he fails to mention is that the workers had to be trained and educated in public schools, that safety rules for workers had to be followed to protect health and lives, and that public roads were made through public tax allocations. For trade to flourish there had to be police protection of the movement and storage of goods, courts and judges to resolve commercial disputes, hospitals, municipal water and waste administration—in other words, public functions administered by governments.

Although I am a social scientist and not a trained economist, I say again based on my studies and travels that the best economies throughout the world are mixed, a combination of government and businesses together advancing everyone's improved quality of life. Admittedly, this is less true in much of sub-Saharan Africa and parts of Asia. Government and business work best when they function like necessary organs within the same body, the body politic.

Those who buy into a free market exclusively without any government interference are living in an ideological parallel universe, like the flying human figures in Marc Chagall's paintings. Nevertheless, this does not answer how and when the government should intervene in markets, and whether or not officials should rely strictly on theories to apply government action. And it certainly remains to be seen whether the developed economies in Europe, like those of Keynes and Hayek in post-World War I Europe, translate into convenient American parallels. As much as a depressed economy impacts government, and can change elected officials, it isn't clear that government inaction in times of economic stress is acceptable.

So who needs a government at all if markets are free, like individuals, to do whatever they want without consequences to society? The problem is that economic decisions are usually made for political reasons. In effect, economies are delicate self-balancing machines that nobody really fully understands, not economists, and certainly not politicians. Economic policy errors, like pilot errors in airplane crashes, lead to tragic consequences.

How Free are Markets?

One of the most fundamental and important ideas of economics—that business and government have complementary roles as part of a "mixed economy"—has been increasingly ignored, to my amazement and consternation. [10]

So consider the repetitive political conservative appeal to "the free market system," heralded as if it were an unassailable constitutional principle, and often cited as a defense of capitalism and unrestricted business operations. Are free markets simply unmanaged capital markets without corrective principles except that of competition, or economic systems without major flaws? Or are markets free to seek help from both business and governmental partners to keep the economy stabilized so it does not capsize the financial structure, depress wages, erode the currency and the people's confidence? What is it about free markets that make their implied powers so magical and unassailable? The so-called free markets—defense industries, pharmaceuticals, energy, financial services, insurance companies, among others—are not really free but they often have a corporate stranglehold on parts of the economy, though conservatives believe they all should be free of government regulation.

Can self-interest be the only guiding principle in economics but not in one's total social life? Parents cannot pursue self-interest exclusively if they truly seek to be devoted and nurturing to children. So why is it that self-interest should be the only motivation in the acquisition of wealth, and not any altruism, philanthropy and compassion as competing virtues? Are human values to be discarded at the business door? Dogmatic insistence on just one guiding principle is not recommended in philosophy, theology or economics. Thus, market capitalism cannot be unilaterally allowed to run a monetary agenda without the judicious restraints of government to tether excesses.

Business markets under President Herbert Hoover in 1929 and Bush in 2006 were certainly free of government interference. And it is important to remember that Smith's understanding of government was not a democracy but a monarchy. Are there no lessons to be learned from the excesses of 1929 and 2007 that mouthing a slogan of "free market" should make us wary? Indeed there is concern, as even that stalwart of free enterprise Adam Smith would be aghast at the lack of regulation. [11] Smith put almost as much emphasis on the need for external political institutions, such as a government has, to channel and control the potential for abuses by financial institutions devoted to capital accumulation as he does favoring freedom in business. [12] Additionally, Smith favored a progressive tax whereby the rich pay a higher proportion of their income than the poor. [13]

Although the majority of politicians would not equate it to the abuses in American history, such a political invocation uttered in the 1860s would have without equivocation included the defense of slavery, at the time very much a description of the "free market," which was essentially the slave labor economy of the South. Or, to compare the term to more contemporary events, does "free market" refer to the scandalous gangster capitalism that banks played on the American housing market with such creative and unregulated financial devices as collateralized debt obligations, or credit default swaps that nearly bankrupted the economy and disemboweled the savings of millions of Americans? Collateralized Debt Obligations (the infamous CDOs) were essentially insurance policies bungled together as bonds, and were one of the more creative and risky extensions of credit, and in collusion with rating agencies that had no idea what these financial instruments were. The catch was there was no collateral because they weren't really assets, so when the notes came due there was no financial backing and the house of cards collapsed.

The global meltdown of financial voodoo practiced by Wall Street, where financial hucksters were freely able to make risky investments and gamblers and create artificial financial notes like meritless derivatives that crumbled under examination because they lacked collateral, can never again be allowed to operate without enforced government oversight. The International Monetary Fund put the total U.S. financial losses at over 41 trillion dollars. The American public is trying to swim out from under the reckless financial devastation.

I was in Kazakhstan in 1991 shortly after that country's release from the old USSR, the Soviet empire. As a fledgling stock market was about to open Kazakh government officials were asking me what to invest in. Without hesitation, I said to invest in companies that produced goods like chairs, soap, jars of jam, anything that was tangible. The financial industry created worthless pieces of paper they sold as assets and their lackey rating agencies approved.

Worse, the Bush Administration, under Treasury Secretary Henry Paulson, a former Goldman Sachs executive, convinced a confused Congress in September 2008 to pass the *Troubled Asset Relief Program* (TARP) for $700 billion of taxpayer money that Paulsen then passed out to the largest banks to cover their losses. This money was taxpayer gifts not loans. The public got stuck for the check for the stupidity and losses of the banking industry.

Banks were established and incorporated as private enterprises but were protected from certain liabilities much like medieval clergy. Such celebrity banks were thought "too big to fail," meaning they were exempt from default or civil prosecution because of their revered status, the contemporary replicas of medieval ecclesiastical exemptions answering only to a Pope.

Furthermore, the U.S. Supreme Court has over the last hundred years ruled on the federal regulation of businesses to demonstrate that constitutionally the national government has a right to regulate business activity under the commerce clause. Obviously, the "free market system" is not totally free of government regulation. Here is a short summary of some U.S. Supreme Court cases involving the regulation of businesses.

United States v. E. C. Knight Co. (1895)
Northern Securities Co. v. United States (1904)
Swift & Co. v. United States (1905)
Standard Oil Co. v. United States.
Schechter Poultry Co. v. United States (1935)
National Labor Relations Board v. Jones and Laughlin Steel (1937)

In addition, Congress passed the *Securities Exchange Act of 1934* creating the Securities and Exchange Commission that regulated the stock market from fraud on the public. *The Fair Labor Standards Act of 1938* established wage and hour regulations for all businesses involved in interstate commerce.

The Commerce Clause of the Constitution has been the focal source of much national legislation, and the antipathy of strict constitutionalists and far-right Republicans. The clause has been used to pass the *Clean Water Act*, the *Clean Air Act*, the *Endangered Species Act*, the *Fair Labor Standards Act*, and most acutely, the *Civil Rights Act* of 1964 outlawing segregation in the public domain. This expansion of national government for the welfare of all has infuriated conservatives who perennially seek a diminution of what they perceive as interference in personal liberties and state prerogatives. [14]

The South has never forgotten that northern politicians after 1865 attempted to politicize newly enfranchised voters in the South, mostly Blacks, into the Republican Party. Southerners believed this to be a double insult: to place Blacks equally with Whites in the voting franchise, and to empower political figures in states to enlist new voters in an opposing political party.

> A person should be free to do as he likes in his own concerns; but he ought not to be free to do as he likes in acting for another, under the pretext that the affairs of the other are his own affairs. [15]

For example, Article IV, Section 3 contained a fugitive slave provision: "No person held in service or labor in one State under the laws thereof, escaping into another, shall, in consequence of any law or regulation therein, be discharged from such service or labor, but shall be delivered up on claim of the party to who such labor or service may be due." This section was repealed by the 13th Amendment that freed all slaves. But it is still a part of the original document. Do strict constructionists want those constitutional sections preserved, even though later amendments and court decisions have invalidated them?

Returning to the purity of the original document is like attempting to return to the original form of first century Christianity. The original Constitution allowed slavery, and at the time even the slave trade, and did not include any amendments, so there were no personal rights or liberties. Such a view ignores all U.S. Supreme Court decisions for the past 200+ years that have defined American democracy and personal freedoms. Constitutional purists—and many Republican presidential candidates—want America to be stuck in the 18th century where women and slaves still existed without rights, and only men of property could vote.

From 1787 to 1791 prior to the first amendments, what became known as the Bill of Rights, there were no civil rights or liberties—no freedom of speech, assembly, press, or rescue from religious interference or petitioning the government for redress of grievances. If this the Constitution they seek to reconstruct? Will gentlemen have to return to wearing tricorner hats, laces and breeches as a fashion statement? Will there still be a large number of American Loyalists who want to preserve English royalty?

When the U.S. Supreme Court decides on matters where two constitutional freedoms, such as state-imposed compulsory schooling and freedom of religion collide, the decisions become a part of constitutional interpretation and law.[16] The Supreme Court and federal courts are defined in Article III, and hence court decisions are an extension of the Constitution.

> In all the other cases before mentioned, the Supreme Court shall have appellate jurisdiction, both as to law and fact . . . (Article III, 2)

John Marshall was Chief Justice when two brothers named Cohen sold District of Columbia lottery tickets in Virginia. Lottery tickets were legal in the District but illegal in Virginia. Virginia authorities arrested them and fined them $100 dollars. But then Virginia claimed that it was the final arbiter in matters between the state and the federal government. The U.S Supreme Court actually upheld the convictions. But the court went further on the jurisdiction of reviewing state court cases. It unanimously declared that the U.S. Supreme Court had appellate jurisdiction over any case tried by a state court, without the states' permission, a decision that clearly limited the legality of state powers.

Strict originalists or constructionists of the Constitution to my knowledge have never cited any Supreme Court decisions as evidence of current roles the national government possesses as conferred by the supreme judiciary. It is just another example of the intellectual poverty of factions who boast of patriotism while exposing ignorance of democratic governance.

The attempt to counter-balance the omnipotent and volatile will of the majority with the longstanding political divisions results in congressional and state house legislative stalemates, endless political discussions about procedures rather than substance.

Governance in a republic provides for each citizen to have a suffrage voice in voting representatives into office, and in America for assembling peaceably to protest, to write or speak freely, or to file a grievance against government. But the American character also prides itself on diminishing the high quality of expertise and intellectual capacity in leadership positions. For a politician it is more commendable to appeal to local prejudices and passions to win the hearts and minds of the sometimes heartless and mindless, the better to represent their interests. It the era of American slavery, a politician had to favor slavery or be unable to represent the district or state's interests. In the South slavery existed unsteadily in the social environment with Christian religion and morality for more than three centuries.

The Revolution of Congressman Ron Paul

My message is one of freedom and individual rights. (Ron Paul)

Congressman Ron Paul of Texas, a perennial presidential candidate, has been one of the most longstanding advocates for a reduction in the role of the national government, especially in foreign policy. He emphasizes the role of the individual and that most ambiguous and yet emotional word, "freedom." In his words, he wants to "legalize freedom," perhaps unaware that freedoms for individuals are already enshrined in the U.S. Constitution. Yet Paul never discusses whether he favors the revolution that brought an end to slavery in America, a real revolution in civil and human rights and not an independence from Britain, in which the Union fought a bloody war to free people born in the United States who were not citizens, and to punish states for enslaving people. Do these libertarians love the Constitution because it kept slavery as an institution without violating "property rights?" Which section of Paul's Constitution guaranteed liberty and freedom for Blacks and women in this country from 1787 to 1965?

There is another side to that freedom coin. Too many take advantage of what they consider freedom and turn it into license to perform any act that upsets social or civic order. Democratic governments are social engines of law and of the maintenance of order, and therefore people are not absolutely free to do as they please but must also conform to legislated and adjudicated social rules of behavior.

For devoted Marxists there is no individual freedom either as the inevitability of the laws of history predict there will be a proletarian revolution against the bourgeoisie that result in a socialist upheaval. But since few in today's political landscape on the right or left claim to be disciples of Marxian economics, I omit a discussion of Marx's declining influence over intellectuals, politicians and economists.

Libertarians never make the connection that federal courts, and constitutional extensions of the national government, actually protect the denied freedoms of individuals—ethnic minorities, women, and gays. But liberty and freedom are not calls for indiscriminate license to do whatever an individual wants. Is it liberty to be able to breathe all carbon emissions as possible, to drink polluted waters (or swim in them), to dump all health care crises at emergency rooms, to pay whatever credit card companies want to charge customers as "fees." On the other hand, individual liberties are not extended in order to impose upon the liberties of others, or the freedom of the state to impose social controls on all citizens. The maintenance of civic and public order is at least as precious in a democracy as are protestations of individual liberties.

Ron Paul attended Gettysburg College in Pennsylvania and Duke Medical School. But his intellectual persuasion comes from his readings of Austrian economists like F.A. Hayek. Just to be clear, the reason Paul cites why the national government should not agree to conduct any social services for its citizens, or sponsor any program for the "general welfare," is because an Austrian economist was frightened by the Nazi government that tyrannically controlled every aspect of German life and killed people who disagreed, and who left to immigrate to the U.S. where he felt safer. Does this mean that the context of the Nazi regime in Europe in the 1930s should be transposed to America in the 3rd millennium? Would Paul hold the same views about the German government's social programs today?

Paul was a presidential candidate in 2008 and 2012. From 2011 he was Chair of the House subcommittee on domestic monetary policy that oversees the Federal Reserve. His book, *End the Fed*, expresses his views, including that he believes the fed is "a fulltime counterfeiting operation to sustain monopolistic financial cartels." [17] All mixed economies have a central bank. But because Paul doesn't believe in a mixed economy he doesn't think America needs one. In this he follows his guru Hayek who claimed that central banks could never manage the money supply by controlling the business cycle.

Politicians rarely have to debate either/or issues and show that there are very often two or more sides to a topical issue. They just have to state their opinion, sometimes based on a theorist but not necessarily, and argue forcefully for it. So Paul seeks to end the Federal Reserve, to return to the gold standard, to slash a third of the federal budget, and to end all foreign aid, opinions that are outside mainstream political thought. He also opposed the *Civil Rights Act* of 1964, which says much about how he really feels about human liberty.

As an aside, could it be that libertarians and other extreme conservatives view social services the same way southerners viewed the Freedman's Bureau created on March 3, 1865? The Bureau was a federal welfare agency, a legal aid society, a reviewer of land and management contracts, and an educational institution. It established nearly 4,000 schools and over a hundred hospitals, handed out rations and provided transportation. [18] As it turns out, the Bureau benefitted poor Whites as much as Blacks. But the creation of this social service agency rankled the South because it helped Blacks by educating them, an activity forbidden by southerners who feared insurrections from those who could read and transmit messages.

Paul also cites many of the 18th and 19th century politicians and a few other little-known writers to bolster his claim that government is too intrusive in peoples' lives.[19] All libertarian fundamentalists like him return to the time of the American Revolution as if nothing has happened in constitutional law, legislation and social change since then. None of them ever discusses the divisions that incapacitated the country, like slavery, and how that was resolved. In citing the 10th Amendment Paul and others like him never address how states violated the rights of slaves for hundreds of years and how the national government connived in that agreement as a function of protecting property. All this is a good example of how one idea translates into an ideology that keeps pesky historical facts out of the discussion because they undermine the argument.

Paul's political code and manifesto is this: "everyone has a right to his or her life and property, and no one has the right to deprive anyone of these things." [20] We universally agree, as would Ayn Rand, but with this caveat—for three hundred years the states, not the national government, deprived slaves of freedom of their lives and treated them as property. Yet somehow Paul and similar proponents of the libertarian message see the national government as operating with its own set of moral rules, but not the states. Our national history has been a history of collusion among half the states to protect their way of life with the property of enslaved human beings. Why is this issue never raised by those who want a revolution from the national government?

Paul's example of big government, or un-necessary government, is the National Endowment of the Arts (NEA), a bureaucracy he finds easy to mock. Moreover, he believes that the Department of Education "is an insult to the American people, who are more than capable of running their own school without being looted to support a national educational bureaucracy." [21] His "Restore America" goal was to trim $1 trillion from the national deficit by eliminating the departments of: Energy, Housing and Urban Development, Commerce, Interior and Education and abolishing the Transportation Security Administration that manages airport security. He did not explain how he would get Congress to do any of this. We can all pick and choose which federal bureaucracies we want or don't want, but the fact that legislation from the Congress created them and the laws that govern them does not make them unconstitutional or un-necessary. Nor does it mean that presidents can simply disband them.

The obsession with the faults of the national government does not extend to the faults of the free enterprise system, which appears to be sinless and guiltless. How a group can be so victimized by the supposedly wickedness of government—"our system is shot through with government intervention, regulation, mandates and other distortions"—and so attached with blind faith to the heavily bankrolled corporations that brought about economic ruin to the country cannot be explained rationally. [22] The 20 largest financial firms fired 160,000 workers, but five of the highest-ranking officials that received the most in federal assistance took home $3.2 billion from 2006 through 2008.

> My purpose, said Orren Boyle, is the preservation of a free economy. It's generally conceded that free economy is now on trial. Unless it proves its social value and assumes its social responsibilities, the people won't stand for it. [23]

Where is the corresponding outrage from Paul and other libertarians about the free market enterprise fraud and deceit among corporations and their representatives like the U.S. Chamber of Commerce? The Chamber is on record approving of outsourcing. After all, it is financially advantageous to business to locate overseas where labor is cheaper and where profits can be hidden. But during the 2010 congressional campaign, the Chamber, with money coming from foreign sources, palpably campaigned against Democratic candidates for losing jobs in their states. Hypocrisy and deceit are a part of national politics. But the conservative holding of contradictory ideas—pro-life but favoring executions, supporting troops but loathing gays in the military, cutting taxes but also balancing the budget—is notably conflicted.

Should the government have better regulated offshore oil companies in deep water drilling so as to prevent the disastrous BP oil spill such as occurred in 2010 that ruined businesses like fishing and tourism and created a catastrophic environmental blight?

On April 5, 2010 a massive explosion in a coalmine in West Virginia operated by Massey Energy killing 29 miners. It was the worst mine disaster in nearly a half century. A 972-page Labor Department study in late 2011 concluded that Massey's "unlawful policies and practices" were the cause of the tragedy. Paul and his ilk would prefer to remove all such regulatory agencies, like the Mine Safety and Health Administration, and let the free market do as it pleases. There should be an equal distribution of blame and indignation over private as well as public incompetence and malfeasance. Libertarians are stuck on animosity only toward presumed federal public iniquity.

According to Paul, joining the World Trade Organization (WTO) amounts to an "outrageous affront to our national sovereignty." [24] And yet, according to the Constitution Article I, Section 8, #3, Congress has the specific, not just the implied, power "to regulate commerce with foreign nations." How are treaties with foreign nations, about trade, commerce or any other diplomatic means, contrary to the Constitution or in any way and "affront to sovereignty"? In this instance Paul's bias overtakes his constitutional understanding and clouds his judgment. If, as he goes on to state, that "Our Founders never intended for America to become entangled in global trade schemes," how is it they came to give the power to regulate trade with foreign nations to Congress?

Paul opposes the whole apparatus of the national government supporting special interest groups. He calls it immoral and a means of exploiting people. He denounces the financial crisis as the result of easy credit by the Federal Reserve and not banks and the financial institutions that relaxed the rules for home ownership by letting people purchase homes for negligible collateral. His solution is to offer people freedom, an ambiguous word that does not define a program, a philosophy, an ideology or a theory. His denouncements of government interference never extends to the rightfulness of federal courts that do protect civil liberties of all citizens and pronounce some acts of Congress unconstitutional.

He presumptuously states that he knows how the Founding Fathers thought, a dangerous precedent for slave-holding politicians in the 18th century. He writes: "Our Constitution was written to restrain government, not the people." [25] He errs. The Constitution is nothing except the creation of a national government. The restraints he notes are on its powers between the three branches so that none would dominate.

Paul's opinions about limited government are appealing if one has already demonized government as a kind of enemy of civil liberties. But the corrections within the system—Congress impeaching a president, Congress correcting legislation through amendments or letting legislation lapse, courts declaring legislation unconstitutional, and lastly, the electoral process itself by which we change our representatives—are already in place and are working.

Libertarian views on government are an important element in our national discourse because certain ideas about how government functions, or does not function as it should, is necessary to check excesses. Government, like life itself, is a work in progress that always needs adjustments as it moves forward. The solution to this dilemma is that private capital and business markets need to be partners with government in promoting what is best for all citizens, and that neither needs to be demonized as the crazy aunt in the attic, or the only wicked spirit in the room.

A majority of voters in Kentucky and elsewhere want the national government out of their lives, and want the private sector to be left alone to create jobs, and provide their health care. It's amazing when people love the Constitution but hate government when it exercises the powers of the Constitution. They believe that the private sector can never harm anyone in an era when insurance companies, petroleum conglomerates, pharmaceutical enterprises and banks and financial institutions have depleted the pocketbooks of the middle class.

As I noted above, Rand Paul was likely named after Ayn Rand, the author of *Atlas Shrugged* (1957), a novel about how the government stifles innovation and creativity and asserts control over industry. The point is that in such a world the individual is not free to create. The novel advocates for the expression of human freedom, reason and strong individualism. Hence, the liberty theme of the libertarian movement receives its name and ideology from a novel, and the son of a congressman who becomes a senator has the last name of an influential novelist. Living in a world of imaginative fiction is not a strong foundation for understanding the complexities of how government fulfills its function in a global economy.

Paul's extreme view of people's access to government services he sees as a form of slavery. That's right, Rand Paul believes that your right to government-sponsored health care services means you are enslaved. Could a more direct and conscious linkage to our most catastrophic period in American history be more demented than to compare slavery with government provision of services like health care? This twisted logic comes from a senator who happens to be a physician whose specialist income exceeds $340,000 annually, a direct result of government provided health care services.

Lastly, Paul's unique Libertarian strategy appeals to disaffected White extremists that his political team in newsletters in the 1980s and 1990s has subtly courted in the past. Paul himself disavows them though he does not deny their support. How a perennial presidential candidate cannot know of his staff's racial writings is disingenuous. That so many found his discredited views acceptable speaks much about America's tendency to gravitate to the politically ridiculous.

Revolution Comparisons

They mounted up to the heavens and went down to the depths; in their peril their courage melted away. (*Psalm* 107:25-27.)

Tea Party activists and ultra-conservatives want to bring about a revolution. Are they prepared for the consequences when they call for revolutions? Are such political revolutionaries returning to the American Revolution, or are they speaking as if they were Black freedom fighters seeking release from southern slavery by joining the Union army to fight the Confederacy?

The League of the South, a group begun only in 1994, began defending the South and its way of life as its mission. In a short time he advocated racist tendencies and secession. Now its rhetoric is militant as it seeks the collapse of the federal government and the rise of the Confederate South. What began as a social club has morphed into a survivalist, paramilitary organization. [26]

There was tumultuous exhilaration on February 11, 2011 when Hosni Mubarak resigned the presidency after 30 years of overseeing perpetual martial law after the assassination of Anwar Sadat he witnessed in 1981. The peaceful demonstrations of the revolution in Egypt began after a revolt in Tunisia in January 2011. The Egyptian army sidestepped the Constitution about presidential succession, assumed power, dissolved Parliament and began transitioning to democratic rule. The Tunisian, Egyptian, Libyan and Syrian revolts, the so-called Arab Spring, originated with the populace, not from a political party platform that believed presidential policy decisions amounted to tyranny.

And so tyranny naturally arises out of democracy, and the most aggravated form of tyranny and slavery out of the most extreme form of liberty.
(Plato, *The Republic*, Book VIII)

Similarly, the American Revolution was a reaction to the abuse of power by England's colonial government and the lack of American representation in the British Parliament. There is clearly a mental residue about the abuse of power still in democratic government based on our colonial history. Nursed in the American mindset during the revolution was disdain for royalty and a privileged aristocracy, though this was more evident in the North than in the South.

The Tea Party movement hearkens back to that era to solidify that revolutionary connection against Britain. Understandably, it does not look back on the revolution of the South against the North to protect slavery. The comparison of colonial government to today's constitutional government is thin, though the labels, like "Tea Party," and slogans, like "revolution," are appealing to the general public. Violent revolutions, like the American Revolution or those in the Middle East, occur because of human intolerance of the abuse of rights by means of dictatorial powers. Revolutions should not be called for lightly simply because of decisions by a president or Congress that some disagree with when only reform may be necessary. After all, it is the majority that holds the concurrence of power in a democracy, not members of a minority who feel aggrieved.

Let's use the comparison of the French Revolution to see what havoc can be created when the forces of civil concord are released after authority is violently dismissed. The ideas and intellectual ferment that was brewing to create the French Revolution were the same as precipitated the American Revolution. John and John Quincy Adams, Ben Franklin, Thomas Jefferson, and John Jay, co-writer of *The Federalist Papers* and first Chief Justice of the Supreme Court, among others all spent many years in Europe and were fully acquainted with European ideas and revolutionary ideals. By the same token, misplaced southern ideals of superiority are still exhibited in political theater.

The French Revolution made a mockery of civilized reformation, as today ultra-Republicans make a mockery of governance. The French *Declaration of The Rights of Man*, published in August 26, 1789 by the National Assembly, set out the new government's principles. It is easy to think that these sentiments were copied from the *Declaration of Independence*. However, the ideas were standard for the time and had been promulgated through periodicals and books throughout the Enlightenment. Jefferson was in Paris when these ideas were circulating and absorbed them as common expressions he would use in his writings. The prevailing concepts were enunciated by Rousseau, Montesquieu, Locke and Hume, all figures whose ideas were used in documents formative of the American Revolution. The French had class differences and strong church influences. Americans enslaved races they could not agree in their hearts to call people. [27]

Ironically, it was Jean Jacques Rousseau, writing in *The Social Contract* in 1792, years before the French Revolution that anyone refusing to abide by the social contract between individuals would have to be compelled to obey by the general populace. "This means," writes Rousseau, "that he will be forced to be free; for this is the condition which, by giving each citizen to his country, secures him against all personal dependence . . . this alone legitimizes all civil undertakings . . . " To be free for Rousseau means that we have to engage in a social contract which gives us "civil liberty." "Obedience to the law," writes Rousseau, "which we prescribe to ourselves is liberty." [28] This is quite the opposite from Libertarians to only define "liberty" as a personal freedom. Rousseau's idea of liberty and freedom were inspiring to those who created the French Revolution against a king and aristocracy, not against the government, or the embodiment of a more refined social contract.

Other notions in the French's *Declaration of the Rights of Man* in 1789 after the revolution, however, were so arbitrary and obtuse as to be unsustainable. For example, take No. 4: "Liberty consists in the freedom to do everything which injures no one else; hence the exercise of the natural rights of each man has no limits except those which assure to the other members of the society the enjoyment of the same rights. These limits can only be determined by law." [29] This is a declaration for untrammeled personal license, without social bonds, and can obviously lead to anarchy. Is this the liberty libertarians seek? They appear to be enlightened figures, but do not understand theorists from the Enlightenment because they never quote them.

The excessive taste of liberty, unfettered from monarchy, actually led to anarchy in France, as everyone felt unbound by any restraints. Can we forget that it was the French aristocracy that yelled the loudest when Parliamentary demagogues cried for *liberte*, and begged the people to denounce the tyranny of Louis XVI? Are ultra-conservatives calling for a revolution, similarly digging their own graves as did the French nobility by such extremism?

Prior to the revolution in France the peasants paid the dreaded *taille*, the land tax that benefitted the royal state, the aristocracy and the church. Because of a combination of social and economic factors, the peasants and the middle class of merchants soon became an armed force that took vengeance on the aristocracy and threatened the destruction of property. The essential cause of the French Revolution, as indeed most revolutions like Russia in 1917, was the economic disparity between the very wealthy and all others. The poverty of the lower classes and the disempowerment of the Middle Class together is a powerful cauldron for the overthrow of governments. And according to data from the Brookings Institution, America is on a long-term slide toward increasing numbers and rates of poverty.

After the Terror and the guillotines in France, the revolts and political and economic anarchy resulted in November 1799 in the military dictatorship of Napoleon. Revolution does not always lead to democracy but often to dictatorship as it did in Germany in 1933. Neither the *Rights of Man* nor the Constitution said anything about slavery, except that the trade should be abolished.

In the southern states prior to the Civil War, laborers as slaves did not have to be taxed as they worked without wages or freedom. The slave-holding plantation owners, nevertheless, like their French seigniorial counterparts, feared slave revolts. But they detested having to pay taxes that went chiefly to their northern neighbor states and did not return as benefits. In France the peasants revolted against feudal privileges. In the South, states and plantation owners revolted against the northern government for the usurpation of the feudal and aristocratic privileges. It is a drama still unfolding.

American democracy, in a continuing political experiment, has from time to time elected actors, wrestlers, salesmen, tailors, ex-military and wealthy patricians as executives. We presumed that with any legitimate and qualified citizen that virtue and wisdom would accompany that person into office, assumptions that we have often discovered were erroneous because the virtues were absent. The election of anyone who catches our fancy to rule us has been a source of supposed strength in the body politic. But this is quite different from proposing that the structure itself be reformed or overturned, or that a so-called "revolution" should replace elections.

As to the management of government, I know from practical experience that it is a most awesome trust and responsibility, one that requires a high degree of reflection, maturity, depth of knowledge and experience. It is not for the un-initiated. We should uphold for those entering politics the same standards we expect of those in medicine, law or the professions. The American Revolution had such educated men as leaders (one can say elitists) because they debated policy issues until they received a consensus. The French Revolution did not emerge with proven leaders or with a workable, serious plan for governance. The blood-letting that followed in France after its revolution is an example of why inexperienced, rabble-rousing, tumultuous cabals like the Jacobins or Tea Party activists, rarely succeed in governance what they might achieve in overthrowing monarchical governments, or those they like to characterize as tyrannical.

The contemporary American anti-government movement, I believe, will pass soon, and not without a short-term struggle, as did the anti-Catholic feeling at the turn of the 20th century, or the anti-Semitism of the 1920s and 1930s. This movement is not a convergence of outstanding grievances, like the Peasant Revolt in England in 1381, but a reaction to economic hardships, an outpouring of dormant racism, and a rekindling of old animosities toward government itself, a revival of Reagan's belief that government was the problem and not the solution. Government has not become the enemy. It is a misguided movement that has mislaid its grievances at the doorstep of government—but really vehement reactions against the Obama Administration—rather than at that of the financial sector.

In all revolutions—commoners against the monarchy in England in 1649, and working classes against the King and aristocracy in France in 1789—class distinctions and their grievances have been typical bones of political contention. This particular political movement is not primarily revolutionary, in that it seeks a militant revolution because bread prices are too high. It is a political response to the presidential election of an African American, an event that would have been violent as the South was after the passage of *Brown v Board of Education* in 1954. The alliance of even the religious right with any of the social groups has a powerful political influence.

Today's revolutionary members are similarly infected with preachers, or those who like to think of themselves as morally righteous, and the disaffected, angry and petulant. They are mouthpieces subservient to corporate and conservative business interests, ignorant of American history, many of whom know little beyond the sound of deposits in their cash registers, and who want to operate without any governmental interference or regulation.

Those who cry liberty the loudest may be the least entrusted with its preservation. Apart from negative pronunciations, what are their ultimate aims besides propagators of the political gospel of dissent? Certainly a government without the means of changing itself does not hold the reins of its own preservation. The right to be free from government interference, like any other right, is not absolute. Congress has a right to forge solutions to national problems by legislating for all the people.

This vociferous group, the Tea Party among them, has cast a long shadow over American politics. It energized a far right conservative agenda and aired the animosity among a passionate few. The vocal expressions of discontent, however, arose during an election cycle but otherwise remained dormant in an embittered part of the population, among those permanently opposed to any government initiatives, even ones to protect an endangered and depressed economy. For them the national government—not themselves, not banks, corporations, foreign devils and alien invaders—is the primary culprit. From whence did this singular, designated enemy emerge? My thesis is that it arose from conservative southern politicians in pre- and post-civil war America who wanted to keep the national government from interfering with slavery. Anti-government sentiments and expressions have not substantively changed in the centuries since.

The fact that the movement will undoubtedly cease when a Republican Administration returns is a sign that it is a deliberate political movement stroked by conservative media and not a popular uprising, as was true during the student revolts against the Vietnam War in 1968. Pervasive American racism has its origins in the centuries-old history of slavery in the South. Except for Gerald Ford, and with concessions to Southern California for Nixon and Reagan, all presidents in the last half-century have been from the South—Lyndon Johnson, Jimmie Carter, George H. W, Bush, Bill Clinton, George W. Bush. Only Obama, since John Kennedy, has been from the North. The South's suspicion of northerners, from the abolition of slavery to school desegregation and the promotion of civil rights, is historically deep and abiding.

Conservatives defend the idea of a free society and cast a wary and skeptic eye on government encroachment of what they perceive as a socialist welfare state. Why they target just America in condemnations and not nearly all other developed nations, and especially European countries is unclear. They see government as the enemy of individual and corporate freedoms, and a free market as the best guarantee of the existence of liberty. Their unflinching ideological dogmatism is historically myopic and refuses to acknowledge the role of government in the improvement of people's lives. America cannot be truly united until it can overcome its divided political and social past.

A libertarian scholar and author of Reaganomics, William Niskanen, (1933-2011) was a former Chairman Emeritus of the Cato Institute, Acting Chair of Reagan's Council of Economic Advisors and Defense Department official. His book, *Bureaucracy and Public Economics* (1994) is highly regarded in ultra-conservative circles. Like his ideological associates, he believes that government taxes primarily benefit "people in a lower-income component region." [30] He believes the national government should restrict the funding of public services to the lowest level of government—to states and localities. He neglects to see that half of the national government's expenditures accrue to the military, not lower income individuals, thereby benefitting the country as a whole.

The idea of personal liberty among libertarians is misguided because it is only one-half of an ethical philosophy. The other half, as enunciated by all major philosophies, even Rousseau, is the social obligation or social contract. [31] Libertarians want to be left alone to pursue their own license. But in a complex society that is not possible unless libertarians want to become hermits, or cloistered monks or nuns.

The strongest defense for continuing personal liberty is a government strong enough to protect the interests of the people, and a people strong enough to control its government through enlightened understandings.

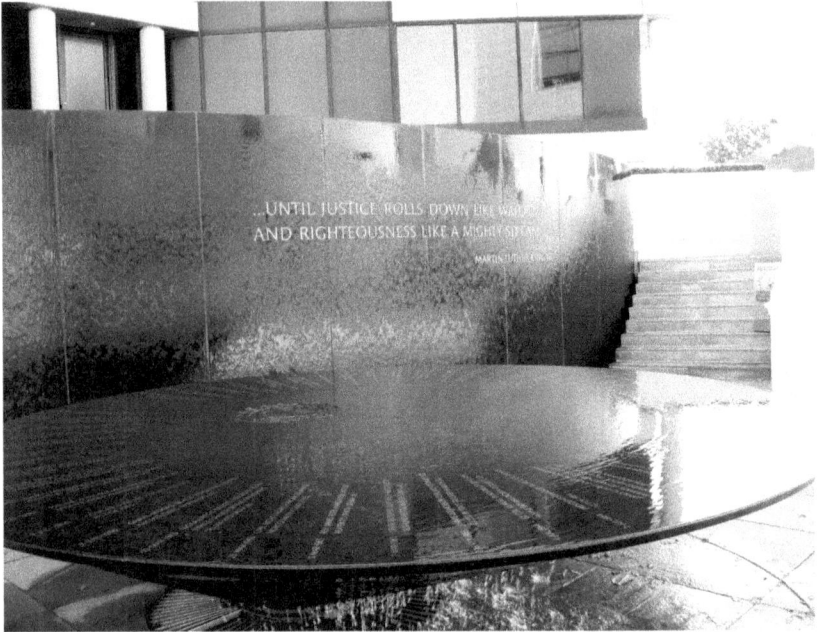

Chapter Four
Love the Constitution, Hate Government

The struggle between liberty and authority is the most conspicuous feature in the positions of history . . . (John Stuart Mill, *On Liberty*) [1]

America was divided North and South from the 18th century by slavery and into the 20th century by racial segregation in southern states. It remains essentially divided today between the two major political parties whose opposing views essentially mirror the North/South divide. It is split, not so much about how to deal with domestic concerns and foreign affairs, but ironically over the role and functioning of the national government. The same political chasm existed during the times of slavery and it is not far-fetched to assume that it is a part of the same lingering political condition, a situation that has now spread throughout the population and is not localized to the South, though it finds its strongest heartbeat there.

Let's begin with the simple facts. In the South Blacks, both before they were citizens and after the 14th Amendment in 1865 when they became citizens, were legally and systematically excluded from public life. They were denied the vote and then had state law restrictions put on their voting until 1965. They were allowed only limited access to courts and could not serve on juries. Whites legally exploited them in any way they could. White supremacy was maintained through violence, condoned by the law, police and public officials, or ignored when done extra-legally. [2] This is just the public record.

A brief historical review of this lingering division in American political discourse will highlight how pervasive this racial legacy is.

The First Continental Congress met in Philadelphia on September 5, 1774 as a result of the closing of Boston port by the British responding to the Tea Party revolt. But the *Declaration of Independence* in 1776 changed the attempt at reconciliation with Britain, and the states agreed on a new form of government. The Continental Congress passed *The Articles of Confederation* on November 15, 1777 in America's second year of independence, and ratified it on March 1, 1781, the year the Revolutionary War concluded. Canada was offered to join the union but politely declined.

A legal agreement among the states could not resolve disagreements among them nor permit them to come to the rescue and defense of other states should the separate states be attacked by other foreign powers. So they came together after the Revolutionary War to form a new national government, and not just a partnership among squabbling former colonies that thought of themselves as sovereign and independent. But they had to compromise because of something that really did divide them more than anything else: slavery.

Before the Constitution, there were five southern states that existed on slave labor and indentured servants: Maryland, Virginia, North and South Carolina and Georgia. Nothing changed after the Constitution that protected land and human property. After the Constitution it was property above all that national government protected, as all signers were either heavily invested property owners with slaves, or lawyers or businessmen.

For conservatives who romanticize the wisdom of the Founding Fathers and signers of the illustrious documents in U.S. history, we need to recall that many were slave owners, fourteen of the thirty-nine signers of the Constitution, including Washington and Madison. But they did not want the government they were forming to interfere with the domestic politics of southern slavery. Those who so enthusiastically extol the founders neglect this essential item in understanding what constitutes our current political division, glued like a Siamese twin to our collective psyche.

> We are happy in a form of government which cannot envy the laws of our neighbors, for it has served as a model to others, but is original . . . And this our form, as committed not to the few but to the whole body of the people, is called a democracy. (Pericles' Funeral Oration, c. 431, in Thucydides, *Peloponnesian War*, Book II, 34-46)

The Articles of Confederation

The political history preceding the Constitution is instructive because some of the discussion from the radical right comes from the era of 1776 to 1787 prior to the Constitution. *The Articles of Confederation* was a contractual union like a limited business partnership among the states, "a firm league of friendship with each other." States had an equal voice in the confederated legislature and each state retained its sovereignty as former colonial entities without British governors. Under the *Articles* states kept their rightful powers but relinquished them under the Constitution. [3] The official government was known as *The United States of America*. The Continental Congress was the dominant authority for the business between the states, including international agreements, and an arbiter of disagreements among them. It had the effect of a consultative or advisory board with no real powers. There were as many as five delegates from each state but each state had only one vote, and nine states, the simple majority, had to agree to everything legislated.

The weakness of the *Articles* is that there was no provision for an executive or judiciary and no agreement for common defense. Foreign invasion was a real possibility when England, Spain and France had adjoining territories in North America. The Revolutionary War had weakened the states militarily. The legislative body could not raise finances, taxes or troops for the war with England. As it turned out, war with England did break out again in 1812. National defense was the primary theme running throughout *The Federalist Papers* that Madison, Hamilton and Jay argued for in New York newspapers on behalf of constitutional ratification by all the states and the people. But from 1781 when war with England ended until a decade later in 1791 when the Constitution was ratified, this initial American government legislation was the only national but politically limited lawmaking body.

Anti-government advocates are hearkening back to the *Articles of Confederation* agreement when states were mini-sovereign entities flush with the excitement of independence from Britain, and prior to legal and binding union in a national government the Constitution created. They have uninformed views of the supremacy of the Constitution in creating a national government superior to any state or group of states, a central government and not merely a legal partnership between states. They are also restating the political ideology of the South to protest national government actions that infringed on their presumed state sovereignty, and that summarily led to their secession.

The idea of a sovereign political entity historically grew out of the various treaties that composed the *Treaty of Westphalia* that ended the Thirty Years religious war in Europe and dissipated the concept of a Holy Roman Empire. *The Treaty of Westphalia* was the fruit of diplomacy and created a new political order in Europe based on the diversified idea of sovereign states governed by a royal sovereign, an idea that later extended to the sovereignty of the people, a truly revolutionary concept in political dynamics.

Respect for the national government grew in the succeeding generations as the jealousies and menaces of the states subsided and as national patriotism increased. Nevertheless, parochialism and sectarian sentiments prevailed until improved communications, like more newspapers, and transportation systems like the railroads, brought people closer into national harmony. Social contact mitigated some local perspectives and biases. Overall, slavery still stood in the way of complete national unity.

Article 1, Section 9 of the Constitution specifically noted that the slave trade was to be maintained for another decade, until 1808.

> The Migration and Importation of such Persons as any of the States now existing shall think proper to admit, shall not be prohibited by the Congress prior to the Year one thousand eight hundred and eight, but a Tax or duty may be imposed on such Importation, not exceeding ten dollars for each Person.

It's troubling to think that explicitly in the Constitution are passages protecting slavery and the slave trade, though to the credit of the founders, it made a proviso to have the slave trade cease in 1808, and President Jefferson signed a bill into law to that effect.

Constitutional delegates could have reformed slavery as they debated the merits of representative democracy. They could have called for freedom from slaves too old to work, and could have negotiated the freedom of children, who could have been paid something for their services while working on a farm or plantation. Politicians and delegates could have proposed a plan that would have allowed slave owners to have slaves work off their purchase price just like indentured servants until a debt was repaid. None of this occurred. Slavery was maintained. Its preservation corrupted the national image, led to war, and insured a lasting moral and cultural dilemma that stains us still.

The Constitution used the phrase that codified how representatives were chosen: "three fifths of all other persons," referring to slaves and Indians. If the

Constitution called them "persons," how could they also be identified and claimed as property? Legally, they should have been free at the moment of ratification except that at the time there was no national citizenship, only state citizenship.

When Washington took command of the Continental Army in 1775 and on July 9, 1776 he barred recruitment of Black soldiers, despite Blacks having fought at the battles of Lexington, Concord and Bunker Hill. [4]

Lord Dunmore, British Governor of Virginia at the time, promised freedom to any slaves who joined British forces. He issued his proclamation on November 7, 1775 to that effect. Within a month 300 Blacks men signed up as recruits. Probably no more than 800 eventually succeeded in the British regiment, but his proclamation inspired thousands of runaway slaves to follow behind the British throughout the war. More than 20,000 served the British. In December 1776 Washington reversed himself and over 5,000 Blacks signed up for the American cause. Though the majority sided with the British, male slaves were willing to fight for either side that would guarantee their freedom.

The Continental Congress created by *The Articles of Confederation* described how patriot leaders hoped to recruit slaves as soldiers late during the Revolutionary War, and to propose that military service would lead to their emancipation. Here are relevant passages from March 29, 1779 from the *Journal of the Continental Congress.*

> That a force might be raised in the said State [South Carolina] from **among** the **negroes** which would not only be formidable to the enemy from their numbers and the discipline of which they would very readily admit, but would also lessen the danger from revolts and desertions by detaching the most vigorous and enterprizing [sic] from **among** the **negroes**. (emphasis in text).

> Resolved, That congress will make provision for paying the proprietors of such **negroes** as shall be inlisted [sic] for the service of the United States during the war, a full compensation for the property at a rate not exceeding one thousand dollars for each active able bodied negro man of standard size, not exceeding thirty five years of age, who shall be so inlisted and pass muster.

> That no pay or bounty be allowed to the said **negroes**, but that they be cloathed and subsisted at the expence [sic] of the United States.

> That every negro who shall well and faithfully serve as a soldier to the end of the present war, and shall then return his arms, be emancipated and receive the sum of fifty dollars. [5]

Representatives chosen from the South were representative of only the White voting population, and clearly were not as equally representative as northerners. The fact that slaves were counted in the Constitution as if they were persons and yet not given actual representation, was more than a cruel joke: it was a perversion of law and justice. The Constitution only delayed the slavery problem for another four generations. [6]

Until 1865 the South was not just stuck in a plantation economy, but in a medieval governance system, a primitive system of masters and serfs prevalent in the 13th century, a dynastic aristocracy controlling ownership of the land and the subjugated people who worked it. Yet the government tolerated this arrangement in order to preserve its artificial unity. It was in practice two nations held together by a legal contract. The real America, the real practical effect of the Constitution, only began after the enactment of the 13th and 14th Amendments that eliminated slavery and created all persons equally as citizens with national citizenship. Would the Virginia delegation debating the Constitution, with Washington, Jefferson and Madison having large slave-holders on their plantations, have voted to ratify a Constitution with the 13th and 14th Amendments included?

John Locke's argument from human nature is quite clear as to when it is justified in overthrowing a government. Slaves would have had a right to revolt for their freedom.

> Whensoever therefore the legislative shall transgress this fundamental rule of society; and either by ambition, fear, folly or corruption, endeavor to grasp themselves, or put into the hands of any other, an absolute power over the lives, liberties, and estates of the people; by this breach of trust they forfeit the power the people had put into their hands for quite contrary ends, and it devolves to the people who have a right to resume their original liberty . . . and provide for their own safety and security . . . [7]

Jefferson and Madison had certainly read this section in Locke's *Second Treatise on Government* and ignored these passages for constitutional arguments, even though Locke's reasoning was absolutely grounded in the theory of human nature that Jefferson had nobly built into the *Declaration of Independence*. Moreover, if a conqueror's rights over captives, Locke argued, did not extend over families and descendants, how could slavery ever be a permanent status? Locke could not have envisioned that the mentality of White Supremacy, cultivated in a people over centuries, could endure through several generations. Nor could the likes of Washington, Jefferson, and Madison divested themselves of their slaves without automatically bankrupting their estates and the sources of all their revenues and power. Without dispute, the wealth and political power of the principal founding fathers came off the unreimbursed work and sweat of slaves.

After the Constitution's ratification in 1791, the South tolerated the new national government as a nuisance, as European medieval lords had tolerated the Church as a necessary irritant. Lord Baltimore founded Maryland. Eight nobles with a Royal Charter from Charles II founded South Carolina. But the South after 1791 and for the next three generations worked assiduously to keep federal powers and their reach nominal, even while compromised representatives and officials and several presidents participated in federal governance and prepared to fight for its independence if any imperial prerogatives were challenged.

Too many officials by their actions upheld slavery rather than their oaths of office to uphold the Constitution. As examples let me cite Jefferson Davis, who served in both houses of Congress, with distinction in the Mexican-American War, and as President Franklin Pierce's Secretary of War. He became President of the Confederacy. George W. Randolph, a grandson of Thomas Jefferson, was an official in the Confederacy's War Department. James A. Seddon had been a congressman from Virginia and became Secretary of War during the Confederacy.

How can so many officials, sworn to uphold the Constitution at one time, later become officials in a rebellious government and support an alternative constitution? One credible conclusion is that until 1860 their allegiances were always with southern states and never with the national government. Even after the Civil War when slavery was abolished and secessionist states brought back reluctantly into the Union, southern attitudes still ran high against national government. It is that same kind of emotional stance that today drives ultra-conservative anti-government sentiments.

Prior to 1860 the South was essentially a medieval feudal society writ large, with a cosmetic overlay of representative democracy, but only for its aristocratic American lords who, just like their medieval counterparts in Europe, inherited land and its working slaves. The southern rebellion and its later defeat in secession in 1865 only partially ended the national dilemma of political and social rupture.

> The judicial power of the United States . . . shall extend to all cases, in law and equity, arising under this Constitution, the laws of the United States, and treaties made, or which shall be made, under their authority . . . to controversies to which the United States shall be a party;—to controversies between two or more States; between a State and citizens in another State;—between citizens of different States;—between citizens of the same State . . . and between a State, or the citizens thereof, and foreign States, citizens or subjects. [8]

Rick Barber, a Republican candidate for Alabama's second congressional district, campaigned in 2010 for impeaching the president and fomenting an armed rebellion against the U.S. government. He got 28% of the vote, which shows how annoyed, uninformed or persistently in revolt against the national government many voters are in contemporary Alabama.

> The great division of interests in the United States . . . lay between the northern and the southern.
>
> (James Madison, June 1787 during the Constitutional Convention)

The Constitution is generally acknowledged to be the most important document in American history, jurisprudence and politics. The document is typically waved aloft at a political rally as if it were sacred scripture. Yet some political candidates, acting as if they were constitutional experts, are as ignorant of its contents and judicial interpretations as the body politic, or at least posture as if they were. The relevance of the document among the general public is not matched by a basic understanding of what it means or the powers it delegates. Many radical Republicans are "originalists" who believe that only the original document, which of course tolerated slavery, contains the true constitutional meaning. [9]

One constitutional clause was a compromise on representation, the so-called "three-fifths of all other persons," who were slaves and some Indians, to be counted as having a voice in congressional voting, though neither slaves, Indians nor women could vote. The 13th Amendment eliminated the Constitution's requirement that allowed slaves to be counted as three-fifths of a person for congressional representation. Without this political compromise to obtain the South's acceptance of the Constitution, John Adams would have been re-elected in 1800 instead of Thomas Jefferson. [10]

The abysmal level of constitutional ignorance has now entered politics and suffused the political discourse. It would take an intense national learning campaign more than one generation for everyone to become re-educated about the Constitution and its judicial precedents so that uninformed politicians could not mislead the public about the basis for our national republic.

Railing against the national government is not just political sport, it is a recurrent appeal to a deep-seated sinister, anti-government attitude that has always resided in the South and is now resident everywhere. Anti-government feelings compete with ignorance about government. Christine O'Donnell, candidate for the U.S. Senate in Delaware, claimed that a U.S. Supreme Court decision was unconstitutional because it violated the Tenth Amendment to the Constitution giving power to the states. To say that states are sovereign is to imply that they have no authority above them, an idea that means that they can act as if they were a mini-nation without recourse even to a superior judiciary.

Former Republican Speaker of the House and presidential candidate Newt Gingrich from Georgia proclaimed on numerous occasions (the latest in a speech to the Values Voter Summit on October 8, 2011) that he believed that elected branches of government should be free to ignore judicial decisions. Because federal judges were not elected, he asserted, they should be subpoenaed to explain their decisions. The judiciary is, and must also be, truly independent of political oversight. This principle is so grounded in American democracy that it could only be acknowledged if it came from a South that had in its past rebuffed Supreme Court decisions *like Brown v Board of Education* in 1954 desegregating schools.

This kind of blatant nonsense may pass for campaign rhetoric but does irreparable harm to public knowledge about a document that requires proficiency in understanding, including past legal precedents, and not just simplistic ideological opinions. When the U.S. Supreme Court rules on a case there is no further appeal, except by constitutional amendment or Supreme Court reversal. Its decision is supreme though not sovereign, a term that implies kingly royalty that a democracy finds anathema.

The Constitution of 1787 is not the Constitution of the third millennium. *Roe v Wade*, among other controversial Supreme Court decisions, is a part of the constitutional landscape though not envisioned by constitutional framers. So it is important to know which Constitution candidates are speaking about, unless of course they do not believe that the U.S. Supreme Court in Article III is a part of the Constitution. Only the U.S. Supreme Court, not the people through amendments by the states, is legally allowed to decide what the Constitution means. It is arrogant to think that anyone in this age can accurately determine what the original framers had in mind for specific applications of the principles they developed. Consider Madison's words in No. 14 of *The Federalist Papers*:

> Is it not the glory of the people of America that, whilst they have paid a decent regard to the opinions of former times and other nations, they have not suffered a blind veneration for antiquity, for custom, or for names, to override the suggestions of their own good sense, the knowledge of their own situation, and the lessons of their own experience? [11]

As so many legal experts say, the Constitution is a living document for which we fought a war among ourselves. After centuries as a civilized nation we have finally established civil and voting rights for everyone and use our legal foundation to modify and improve the quality of our lives and not live permanently in the 18th century. After all, the Constitution is not the Bible, and unlike it has federal courts that have the authority to rule on its meaning.

Who or What is a Sovereign?

> The supremacy of the nation and its laws should be no longer a subject of debate. That discussion, which for half a century threatened the existence of the Union, was closed at last in the high court of war by a decree from which there is no appeal—that the Constitution and the laws made in pursuance thereof are and shall continue to be the supreme law of the land, binding alike upon the States and the people. This decree does not disturb the autonomy of the States nor interfere with any of their necessary rights of local self-government, but it does fix and establish the permanent supremacy of the Union.
> (President James Garfield, Inaugural Address, March 4, 1881)

Does so-called state sovereignty extend beyond the sovereignty of the U.S. Supreme Court in deciding constitutional matters? A positive response would be repugnant to democracy and runs contrary to all legal scholarship. Sovereignty as a designation of state superiority, according to the radical right, is actually a political argument created in the South in 1838 by John Calhoun, propagated in order to reduce the national government's role in impeding slavery, and used today to assert state power against perceived federal interference. What is actually sovereign is the law.

Let's take the case of another form of sovereignty to place the issue in context. The Cherokee nation in 1830 brought a suit to the U.S. Supreme Court arguing to prevent the state of Georgia from encroaching on its territory and violating Cherokee sovereignty. The court ruled that the Cherokee nation was not a foreign nation as described in the Constitution, but that a more appropriate description would be "domestic dependent nation." But the Cherokee lands constituted a state with rights to its lands. In a sense it was a ward of the government, though the Cherokees had several treaties with the U.S. government. [12]

The Cherokees had a constitution, laws and a government with three branches, and had established schools. They became agriculturists, mechanics and herdsmen, and many become Christians. They claimed protection against states seizing their lands since they had treaties with the U.S. government and that states like Georgia that sought their lands were violating existing contracts.

The Georgia legislature passed an act in 1828 to add to its territory the lands inhabited by Cherokees since time immemorial and to make Georgia laws extend to them. In 1829 the state of Georgia passed an additional act to annul all laws and ordinances of the Cherokees. Georgia sought to extinguish the Cherokees and their entitled sovereignty, and seize their land for settlement.

The Supreme Court denied that the Cherokee nation was a foreign state. A year later in *Worchester v Georgia* (1832), Chief Justice John Marshall wrote that the "laws of Georgia can have no force" in Cherokee territory. The court concluded that only the federal government could rule on Indian affairs. Samuel Worchester, a preacher from Vermont, was arrested by Georgia authorities on the trumped-up charge of residing within Cherokee land and operating without a preaching license. The U.S. Supreme Court denied that Georgia could regulate between citizens of its own state and members of the Cherokees. Chief Justice Marshall wrote: "The Cherokee nation, then, is a distinct community occupying its own territory in which the laws of Georgia can have no force. The whole intercourse between the United States and this nation, is, by our constitution and laws, vested in the government of the United States." President Andrew Jackson ignored this ruling and proceeded to submit to Congress the *Indian Removal Act* that sent the Cherokees from their ancestral homeland to Oklahoma. [13]

> Sovereignty . . . is indivisible . . . It is the will either of the body of the people, or only a part of it . . . The conjuring tricks of our political theorists . . . first dismember the body politic by an illusion, then join it together again we know not how. (J. J. Rousseau, *The Social Contract*, 1792)

Some conclusions can be drawn. First, that what is presumed as sovereignty, as Indians did with treaties with the U.S. Government, is precarious. Second, that states that presume they have sovereignty over everything within their territory is also precarious, as it does not extend to Indians with territorial treaties, or to the legitimate role and function of national government. And third, that presidents and officials from the South believe they can with impunity disregard Supreme Court decisions if they don't agree with them. Jackson should have been impeached for violating his oath of office to uphold the laws of the United States. But he had the political backing of southern members of Congress.

The anti-government conservative view has gone viral and spread to numerous state law proposals. One of the more absurd is Arizona's Senate Bill 1393, with the ironic title of *The Freedom to Breathe Act* that allegedly grants the legislature the authority to regulate particulates in the air and greenhouse gases, a crude attempt to invalidate existing federal laws of the Environmental Protection Agency (EPA), established in 1970 during the Nixon Administration. Perhaps members of the legislature believe that air pollutants in Arizona only circulate above the state and do not cross from or into other states. The Arizona Senate wants Arizonans to choke only on Arizona air. This delusional state act is but one attempt to declare congressional laws unconstitutional.

Kenneth T. Cuccinelli II, attorney general of Virginia, wrote to all state attorneys general in December 2010 requesting support for a constitutional amendment allowing states to vote to overturn acts of Congress. The House majority leader, Eric Cantor also from Virginia, thought it was a good idea. It had the support of legislative leaders in 12 states. Utah congressman Rob Bishop (a former student of mine whom I failed in a course on Education and the Constitution as he never completed the requirements) introduced the proposal in the House of Representatives.

The debate about the limits of federal power is symbolic of a wider disaffection among conservatives who believe social programs like health care that Congress legislates are unconstitutional. Many conservatives believe that the national government has grown too big (they never specify which branch), that acts passed by Congress and signed into law by a president are unconstitutional (though they rarely seek remedies through the courts), and intrusions like lending money to automobile companies that they say threatens the free market system.

About 45% of Americans participate in employer-based health programs, and about 26% in government (Medicare, Medicaid, military) programs. About 16%, about 50 million, have no health care coverage. People without health care go to emergency rooms, where they cannot by law be denied treatment, thus raising health care costs for hospitals who pass the cost-overruns on to all customers. The *Affordable Health Care for America Act* (2008) was a study in political contrasts by exposing the ideological differences between those who oppose any government domestic intervention, and those who believe government should find ways to help improve people's lives. The law sought to minimize those uncovered by health care plans, to extend dependents coverage to the age of 26 to be on their parents' medical coverage, and to cover those with pre-existing conditions not be denied coverage.

The core of the legal objection was whether or not Congress has the power to require individuals to obtain medical insurance. Does government take away individual liberty by compelling everyone to purchase medical insurance, or does it enhance it with the knowledge that their health needs will be take care of when necessary and in a way that will not bankrupt them?

Here are a few additional typical twisted Republican definitions used negatively to discredit government actions.

Bailout: A bailout is when you give money for example to a sibling never expecting to see any of it again, but a word Republicans used to help troubled industries or individuals. This is different from what for government was a
Loan Such as federal money lent to a bank or car company paid back with interest.

Takeover: when banks foreclose on a home but used by Republicans to mean any government financial help. This is different from a
Partnership when government intervenes to prevent medical and pharmaceutical conglomerations from stiffing the American taxpayer and adding to Medicare costs.

State sovereignty was for kings, not states that are subservient to national government, including a Supreme Court under the Constitution. This is different from
The sovereignty of the people who can choose whom they want to represent them and to alter the Constitution with Supreme Court decisions and with amendments, as states cannot.

Mandates: something Republican-controlled states believe they can oppose because they are "directive," as opposed to
Laws to be followed by all citizens in a democratic society.

Class Warfare misapplied by Republicans to describe a tax on the wealthiest Americans, more appropriately applied to the French Revolution or Marxist theory than to
Equitable Taxation where everyone pays the fair share according to the law and social justice

Activist Judges judicial decisions opposed by ultra-Republicans because courts
Apply Justice when individuals are discriminated against

Creating campaign language of pessimistic words is a deliberate attempt by an entire political party to confuse the easily deceived public, and feeds into an anti-government rhetoric, divides the citizenry and is not conducive to informative discussion on serious national matters.

Alien and Sedition Acts and State Supremacy Resolves

The Fifth Congress in 1798 passed a series of measures aimed at aliens and the process by which they would become citizens. It also made it a crime to criticize the federal government's actions. Congress feared foreigners coming into the country and fomenting discord. Aliens, the law claimed, would have to wait five years for an application of citizenship to be admitted, and have to have resided in the U.S. fourteen years. Doesn't this sound familiar in today's debates about immigration?

On July 14, 1798 the Fifth Congress passed an act making it a crime to impede the operation of any U.S. law, or to intimidate any officer carrying out such laws, or to "procure any insurrection, riot, unlawful assembly . . . " But the act went further by prohibiting anyone from writing, printing or uttering any derogatory ("false, scandalous, and malicious") statement against the U.S.

government, or to stir up sedition. The sedition part of Congress was clearly unconstitutional and violated freedom of speech and assembly.

As background, Jefferson and Madison were sympathetic toward French revolutionaries, though they could not predict that the French Revolution would result in such bloodshed. Immigrants from France were coming to the U.S. as refugees and aligning themselves with Jefferson's party. Hence the alien laws were an attempt by the Federalist Party, located mostly in New England, to thwart the addition of foreign potential political members coming from abroad and aligning with the southern coalition.

Madison and Jefferson, then Vice President under John Adams, wrote responses known as the Virginia and Kentucky Resolves that placed state sovereignty at the forefront of any action by Congress. These resolves expressly noted that the states had the right to rule on the constitutionality of congressional laws because sovereignty resided in the people and in the individual state legislatures. These resolves became the ideological basis for arguments favoring southern slavery used by Calhoun in 1838 and others. Jefferson and Madison went further to point out that secession from the Union under certain circumstances would be legitimate. The South took their words to heart by the South in the following decades.

Here is what Jefferson wrote for Kentuckians on November 10, 1798.

> Resolved, That the several states composing the United States of America are not united on the principle of unlimited submission to their general government; but that, by compact, under the style and title of a Constitution for the United States, and of amendments thereto, they constituted a general government for special purposes, delegated to that government certain definite powers, reserving, each state to itself, the residuary mass of right to their own self-government; and that whensoever the general government assumes undelegated powers, its acts are unauthoritative, void, and no force; that to this compact each state acceded as a state, and is an integral party; that this government, created by this compact, was not made the exclusive or final judge of the extent of the powers delegated to itself, since that would have made its discretion, and not the Constitution, the measure of its powers; but that, as in all other cases of compact among parties having no common judge, each party has an equal right to judge for itself, as well of infractions as the mode and measure of redress. [14]

The Kentucky Resolves, under Jefferson's pen, continued calling an act of Congress null and void. How and why he could even conceive of such an idea is unknown. But clearly he expressed the view of all southern plantation owners like himself, and all ultra-conservative Republicans today.

> Resolved, That it is true, as a general principle, and is also expressly declared by one of the amendments to the Constitution, that "the powers not delegated to the United States by the Constitution, nor prohibited by it to the states, are reserved to the states respectively, or to the people;" and that, no power over the freedom of religion, freedom of speech, or freedom of the press, being delegated to the United States by the Constitution, nor prohibited by it to the states, all lawful powers respecting the same did of right remain, and were

reserved to the states, or to the people;.... That therefore the act of the Congress of the United States, passed on the 14th of July, 1798, entitled "An Act in Addition to the Act entitled 'An Act for the Punishment of certain Crimes against the United States,' which does abridge the freedom of the press, is not law, but is altogether void, and of no force. [15]

Every since 1798, states' rights advocates like Jefferson (who did not sign the Constitution as he was in France during the summer of 1787) have used the 10th Amendment as their exclusive argument for denying the authority of Congress. Yet apparently Madison and Jefferson, authors and constitutional advocates, were unfamiliar with, or ignored, Article VI (2): "This Constitution, and the laws of the United States which shall be made in pursuance thereof . . . shall be the supreme law of the land, and the Judges in every state shall be bound thereby . . . "

"And the laws of the United States . . . " The phrase could not be clearer, yet it is never refuted in any historical document I have read, or even cited in any argument proposed by those who advocate for the rights of states over that of the actions of the national government. Perhaps they didn't read that far in the document.

In 2011 the Arizona Senate, led by the Senate President, arch-conservative Russell Pierce, introduced Senate Bill 1433 that would negate federal laws the state dislikes. It would nullify, by a simple majority of a 12-member panel of legislators, "a specific federal law of regulation that is outside the scope of the powers delegated to the people to the federal government." This reckless negation nonsense is exactly what occurred in 1838 in South Carolina's legislature. Conservative extremists are repeating the past reactions from the South.

The U.S. Supreme Court decision in *Marbury v Madison* in 1803 resolved the issue. It concluded that the court alone has the authority to decide what laws are constitutional and which not. "It is emphatically the province and duty of the judicial department to say what the law is," Chief Justice John Marshall wrote. States claiming they have rights superseding the powers of the national government never cite this decision that cites judicial supremacy in deciding constitutional matters.

Judicial decisions will remain central to how Americans define themselves under the Constitution. The issues will always be debated—gun rights versus gun control, separation of church and state, freedom of the press and speech, capital punishment, abortion rights, unreasonable search and seizures, the right to bear arms, etc. The majority of federal cases typically involve an overlap of constitutional principles. In fact, the most relevant phrases, like "due process," "freedom of speech," "unreasonable searches and seizures," "cruel and unusual punishment," are themselves ambiguous, subject to interpretation. To insist that judges interpret the Constitution literally, at a time prior to 1791 when Blacks were slaves and women could not vote, is without ethical foundation in the history of constitutional decisions.

Here are a couple of decisions that have defined national government powers. The doctrine of implied powers was defined by the Supreme Court case of *McCulloch v Maryland* in 1818. A cashier of the Baltimore branch of the Bank of the United States refused to pay a tax levied by the state of Maryland on notes the bank issued. Chief Justice John Marshall declared for the majority that Article 1, Section 8 of the Constitution gave Congress the right to carry out its powers to tax, borrow and convey funds for armies. But the real result was that states could not over-ride the supremacy of the federal government in matters within its jurisdiction.

The Interstate Commerce Clause in the Constitution gives the federal government the authority to regulate commerce between the states. Thus, it has jurisdiction over businesses which cannot decide whether or not it wants to admit certain minorities into its stores, as occurred in the South prior to the *Civil Rights Act of 1964*. [16]

Campaigning for Commander-in-Chief

The American public has not generally voted for the clever or the knowledgeable presidential candidate in the past two hundred years, but rather for the average, anti-intellectual, religious candidate or military leader. Politicians rise to power in office by descending and catering to local instincts, and not just to jobs, business and social benefits, but to prejudices. No campaigner would be so independent as to declare that he or she is willing to stand on principle even to the extent of voting against his district's wishes. Would a southern politician in the mid-twentieth century have dared speak out against White supremacy? Recall just a few acknowledged racist politicians like Alabama's George Wallace or Orval Faubus of Arkansas, or Senator Strom Thurmond of South Carolina. [17]

Great talents generally pursue wealth—although occasionally law, journalism or academia—and not politics. Hence politicians must steer simple emotionally appealing slogans and rhetoric to the intellectually average voter lest the audience be lost, and spend vast amounts of money generously given by corporations to achieve such a victory. The 2010 Supreme Court decision, *Citizens United v. Federal Election Commission* (558 U.S. 08-205) determined that under the First Amendment corporate funding of independent political broadcasts in candidate elections cannot be limited. The majority maintained that political speech is indispensable to a democracy, less true because the speech comes from a corporation. Free speech is applicable to a corporation and hence it can spend all the money it wants to voice its opinion. One wag noted that he will agree that corporations are people when Texas executes one.

Polls portray quite accurate the volatility of public opinion so candidates no longer have to guess at where citizens stand or what they desire. "In the long run," noted Thomas Carlyle, "every Government is the exact symbol of its People, with their wisdom and unwisdom." [18]

Every president in my memory, except for Eisenhower, ran on a campaign of anti-Washington feeling, and most won. Running for a government office usually means degrading the conduct or virtue of a predecessor. A campaign for national office must appeal to anti-Washington attitudes, which on the surface appears illogical and incongruous. But such is the nature of American political inconsistency and is consistent with the concept of a divided nation. Americans prefer the average person with some experience to lead or represent them, but disdain the office and government they represent. This is the imperfect harmony of northern and southern interests derived from the early part of the 19th century. Americans love the services government provides, but then detest government's powers. This conflicted relationship in American democracy strengthens anti-intellectualism because people nearly always choose economic stability and not knowledge about how government functions, or how a variety of conflicting special interests survive in a national agenda.

Let me use an example of loving the Constitution and hating government from Tea Party advocate Dick Armey, former majority leader of the U.S. House of Representatives. In his treatise *Give Us Liberty* he extols the Founding Fathers and the Constitution and then has this curious quote: "Government is, by definition, the means by which you are compelled by force to do that which you would not be voluntarily." [19] In fact government is, by definition, what the U.S. Constitution created. So loving the Constitution and hating what the government does when it exercises its constitutional authority is the shallow miscomprehension of radical conservatism, and a description of the political dilemma of the times.

One Republican method of castrating a government agency is to fail to appoint a director empowered by legislation to carry out the laws of the agency. The most notable example is the Consumer Financial Protection Bureau created in 2010 by the *Dodd-Frank Wall Street Reform and Consumer Protection Act* to supervise non-bank financial institutions like payday loans and credit cards not regulated like banks. The Republican House did not confirm a qualified candidate because it disagreed with the creation of the agency in the first place. President Obama bypassed Congress and used a Congress in recess to make the appointment of Richard Cordray, a former Ohio Attorney General as Director. Love the Constitution, but hate legislation that regulates the financial world or that expands government to protect consumers from fraud and abuse.

Lastly, let me also quote one of our nation's truly great thinkers though little-known Presidents, James Garfield, from his inaugural address of 1881. It is the people who agree with constitutional laws or agree to change them with amendments. But it is also the people who must safeguard the constitutional inheritance.

> The voters of the Union, who make and unmake constitutions, and upon whose will hang the destinies of our governments, can transmit their supreme authority to no successors save the coming generation of voters, who are the sole heirs of sovereign power. If that generation comes to its inheritance blinded by ignorance and corrupted by vice, the fall of the Republic will be certain and remediless. [20]

The national government is staggeringly complex because the legislation has created a variety of internal stakeholders influenced by lobbyists with special interests. Government is not only fractured politically, it is dysfunctional

114

in many of its operations, except in dispensing grants, gathering statistical data, protecting us through Homeland Security and in the Department of Defense. At this writing there is little or no long-term economic policy planning, no engagement in an impending global warming crisis—hybrid cars will not suffice—no national plan for the improvement of education, no plan for dealing with the 20% of children living in poverty, no realistic energy program, and no sensible labor market policy. None of these can be left to the whims of the free market or private enterprise. Badgering unions, curtailing voter rights, restricting women's rights, and limiting government's intervention when it is needed are all conservative ideals. But these issues will not solve any of the nation's pressing priorities. The conservative agenda, born and reared in the South, is handicapping America and its destiny.

Chapter Five
The Slave Trade

Slaves, obey your earthly masters with deep respect and fear. Serve them sincerely as you would serve Christ. (*Ephesians 6:5*)

Man is born free; and everywhere he is in chains.
(Jean Jacques Rousseau, *The Social Contract*, 1762)

Michelangelo's unfinished sculptures—An Awakening Slave, a Bearded Slave, a Young Slave, and an Atlas Slave—are symbolic of people trying to escape. Each figure is portrayed as struggling to wiggle free from confinement. It was Michelangelo's idea to liberate figures, not just to craft them from marble. These unfinished masterpieces reveal how they seem to want to explode from their solid encasement. So it is with people enslaved.

Traffic in human beings has been an ancient commercial venture, and the antiquity of its existence and biblical references (*Leviticus, Exodus*, Paul's letters to the *Ephesians* and *Timothy*) were scriptural excuses for its preservation by those who rationalized its trade, even though the Hebrews had been held captive in Babylon and reputedly Egypt, enslavements that were a cause of much biblical resentment. Non-biblical writers like Hesiod, Homer, Aeschylus, Cicero, Virgil, Tacitus and Sallust all universally denounced slavery, so pro-slavery proponents never quote them. The depravity of the trading occupation and its financing by so-called religious adherents, like Ferdinand of Spain, is perfidious enough, but that the slave trade continued for hundreds of years is even more alarming. It went on for so long because it was immensely profitable.

A fully integrated commercial enterprise, supported by most European governments, endorsed by the Church, financed by speculators, extended credit by insurance companies, with ship builders and captains, suppliers of goods, purveyors of slaves in Africa, sellers in ports, and owners in the New World, were all implicated in the practice. Wherever money was to be made from the slave trade, even through to suppliers to slavers, profit triumphed over consciences. The governments of Portugal, Spain, France, and England issued licenses for slave trading and taxed the companies established for operating the business. But like illegal drug business today, even after the slave trade was banned, many profited hugely from its business. [1]

Nobody voluntarily became a slave for life though many, to escape hard times and destitution, or possible imprisonment by authorities, rented out their labor for a few years as indentured servants to gain ship passage to the Americas, Australia and elsewhere.

The Confederacy was one of the first countries in the world (South Africa another) to boldly proclaim, as Jefferson Davis did at the beginning of his Administration, that slavery's existence was based on commercial enterprise founded on Black inferiority. Davis had been a veteran of the Mexican War, a Secretary of War, and Senator from Mississippi. His views above all championed slavery, and he was a Mississippi slave owner. White supremacy and black bondage were the cornerstones of the South. Returning to this period is a way of searching where our deeper, and more divisive, national identity really lay.

Not that the national government was unsullied in enslavement policies as it rounded up American natives throughout the second half of the 19th century, herded them onto reservations whose land held little value at the time, and in effect enslaved a native population overwhelmed by a superior force that had no qualms about enforcing militarism. American Indians, those who survived death in battles or massacres, became wards in their own lands.

Because so many generations are removed from current political trends, it's easy to take the moral high ground and to be indignant about slavery that was engrafted onto the southern psyche. Many slave owners had slaves bequeathed to them as heirs of estates. Freeing them would have bankrupted them and their extended families that relied for revenues almost exclusively on the sale of cash crops. No one seemed to have a sensible answer for what the freedom of slaves entailed if they were to be released in a plantation economy that would assuredly collapse without them. In the end, agricultural revenues overcame all moral persuasions, that is until secession brought war.

As early as 1462 Pope Pius II wrote to an Italian bishop for taking new converts into slavery. He did not condemn slavery, only the enslaving of Christian converts. The enlightened leaders of the Renaissance, even its titular religious head, valued more a captured slave's soul than body. Catholics and Protestants were miles apart of theological matters but united in their acceptance of slavery. Protestants would have no popery, would never be a slave to a Pope, but would have no qualms about having Africans sold as slaves. Catholics involved in the trade simply abandoned scruples, if they had ever had any, and paid homage to their purses and bank accounts.

Yet in French, Catholic Louisiana, plantation owners had to have their slaves baptized into Catholicism. The advantages to the slaves were that they did not have to work on Sundays or religious holidays and owners treated them as fellow religious followers. The principal disadvantage was that they did not have a voice in their religious persuasion or in their freedom.

For nearly 400 years it is reasonably estimated that more than 54,000 voyages transported approximately 11 million slaves throughout North America and Europe of which about a half million came to British North America disembarking at Salem, Newport, New York, Providence, Charleston and Savannah through Caribbean ports.[2] The first slaves arrived in Jamestown, Virginia in 1619. The acts known as "Fundamentals," or "Body of Liberties," legalized the slave trade in Massachusetts as early as 1641. The founders of Georgia originally prohibited slavery but within fourteen years re-introduced it. The West India Company brought eleven Brazilian slaves to New Amsterdam in 1626. By the time of the first census in the U.S. in 1790 there were 757,000 Blacks living in America constituting 19% of the total population. About 9% of Blacks were free. Half of all slaves then lived in Virginia and Maryland.

The Declaration of Independence—a political and not a legal document—boldly declared freedom from British rule and servitude, but never intended to extend that freedom to its slave population. Independence was governmental, freedom of colonial governments from a British imperial government. It was not intended to be the expression of a new government or an extension of personal entitlements. The Continental Congress on Friday, October 14, 1774, prior to the *Declaration of Independence*, declared: "That the inhabitants of the English colonies in North America by the immutable laws of nature, the principles of the English Constitution [there was not then, nor has there ever been an English Constitution], and the several charters or compacts, have the following rights— Resolved 1. That they are entitled to life, liberty and property . . ." Slaves were then and ever after "property," which no one could repudiate. [3]

> Civil government so far as it is instituted for the security of property is in reality instituted for the defense of the rich against the poor, or of those who have some property, against those who have none at all.
> (Adam Smith, *The Wealth of Nations*, 1976-77, p. 715.)

Normally, only a government can secure property rights. A condition under which people were constitutionally protected under the aegis of property becomes morally and ethically unsustainable. Anti-slavery sentiment occurred primarily in the North and never in the South leading to hatred and distrust against the national government. The Civil War did end slavery but not the animosity against government nor the entrenched belief about White supremacy.

Later, in March 1784, Jefferson and others introduced a resolution in the Continental Congress that would have prohibited slavery in new states that today would include Alabama, Mississippi, Kentucky, Tennessee and all of the Northwest Territories. "That after the year 1800 of the Christian era there shall be neither slavery nor involuntary servitude in any of the said States, other than in punishment of crimes . . ." [4] The proposal did not pass. But it is interesting to speculate that had Jefferson been president when the Missouri Compromise bill admitting a new slave state into the Union was introduced in 1820, whether or not he would have vetoed it. [5]

Patriots and conservatives alike extol the founding fathers and their bravery in establishing a democratic republic, but have selected memory loss when we recall that these same founders and the country as a whole willingly permitted slavery in the union. The remnants of that national disgrace have not totally been eradicated. Racism and discrimination are not just endemic in America. But ours is more pronounced and profound because of its governmental toleration, contrived under the useful subterfuge of a functioning democracy, and that states should be allowed to do what they want within their borders.

Madison in #54 of *The Federalist Papers* made clear what everyone already knew in 1787. "Slaves are considered as property, not as persons. They ought therefore to be comprehended in estimates of taxation which are founded on property, and to be excluded from representation which is regulated by a census of persons." The "three-fifths of one person" phrase in the Constitution used for counting representation to Congress was a compromise to slave states as no two states represented the aggregate number of inhabitants or suffrage in the same way. This constitutional stumbling toward democracy would be one of the first concessions to slavery. It would not be the last.

> I believe in shaping the ends of government to protect property as well as human welfare. Normally, and in the long run, the ends are the same; but whenever the alternative must be faced, I am for men and not for property, as you were in the Civil War. (T.R. Roosevelt, 1910)

By 1787 delegates to the constitutional convention reached a compromise about the slave trade. Southern states agreed with the compromise not to interfere with the importation of slaves until after twenty years, though each slave would be taxed. It was an opposing value to Enlightenment principles proposed by the founders, and as enunciated in the *Declaration of Independence*, but felt to be a necessary political compromise. Here is that constitutional paragraph. "The migration or importation of such persons as any of the States now existing shall think proper to admit, shall not be prohibited by the Congress prior to the year one thousand eight hundred and eight; but a tax or duty may be imposed on such importation, not exceeding ten dollars for each person." [6] Within a generation, it was believed, there would be enough fecundity among slaves, and sufficient buying and selling of slaves within the U.S., to replenish any slaves lost through death or escape and hence no need of additional importation.

President Jefferson signed into law the bill eliminating the American slave trade on March 3, 1807, as the Constitution instructed. But until the trial and execution of the American slave trader Nathaniel Gordon during the middle of the Civil War in 1862, no one in the intervening half century had ever been prosecuted for illegal slave trafficking. The failure to prosecute the law against illegal slave trading is an illustration of the complicity of government in the slavery business. Additionally, according to Article IV, Section 2 of the *U.S. Constitution*, slaves fleeing to another state did not avoid their slavery: "No Person held to Service or Labor in one State, under the laws thereof, escaping into another, shall, in Consequence of any Law or Regulation therein, be discharged from such Service or Labor, but shall be delivered up on Claim of Party to whom such Service or Labor may be due."

Because slavery was explicit in the Constitution it was thereafter used as southern justification of a federal responsibility to protect it as an institution. Constitutional delegates understood that even if the trade were to be suspended slavery would still be permitted, because otherwise the Constitution would not have received the support of existing southern states. From 1787 onward the North and South would be sucked into a titanic struggle to maintain additional compromises that sustained slavery even as rising voices in other nations and in the North with the Abolitionist movement argued against it. England's Parliament had banned its slave trade in 1807.

But had Madison or Jefferson or their ancestors not had slaves and the money from the plantation economy that made them wealthy, they would not have had the opportunities to become educated or to get themselves elected to positions of public trust. Had they been born Black in Virginia, no laws would have made it possible for them to succeed. Like royalty, the accidents of their birth provided them with the concomitant aristocratic lifestyle and advantages. Hence it is not surprising that they defended slavery because they were defending their privileges and property. The limited voting franchise helped too, as only White, male property owners could vote. In the 1800 presidential election the United States had a population of 5.3 million. There were only 67,000 who voted in the presidential election, or only one percent of the population. The landed aristocracy or moneyed interests voted only for one of their own.

There are rare examples of freed slaves who, when they became merchants or tradesmen, owned slaves themselves. William Johnson (1809-1851) was born the son of a mulatto slave woman in Natchez, Mississippi. He was freed when he was eleven by his owner, William Johnson, presumably his father, after his mother, Amy, had also been freed. He was apprenticed as a barber, and soon owned several barbershops and a bathhouse in Natchez. As his wealth increased he purchased his own slaves and additional farm property. He owned a three-story brick townhouse in Natchez on State Street just two blocks from the Mississippi River. [7] His business was on the ground floor and his wife, mother-in-law and ten children lived upstairs. The kitchen, dining room and slave dorms were in a separate two-story building. When a boundary dispute arose with a neighbor, Johnson filed a suit. Before the case came to trial the neighbor fatally shot Johnson in the back. He identified his killer before he died but because a black man, slave or free, could not testify in court against a White man, his killer was freed.

Samuel Johnson, of England's first dictionary fame, unleashed his considerable wit on America's slave problem in *Taxation No Tyranny: An Answer to the Resolutions and Address of the American Congress*. "If slavery be thus fatally contagious, how is it that we hear the loudest yelps for liberty among the drivers of Negroes?" [8] Moreover, he argued: "It has been proposed that the slaves should be set free, an act which surely the lovers of liberty cannot but commend. If they are furnished fire arms for defense, and utensils for husbandry, and settled in some simple form of government within the country, they may be more grateful and honest than their masters." [9]

Other forms of compromise included executive appointments. For example, Lewis Cass (1782–1866) had been a general in the U.S army, notable for extinguishing Indian land titles in the Michigan territory, and Governor of Michigan Territory in 1813 until 1831, during which time he amassed a personal fortune. He was Secretary of War under President Jackson from 1831-36, and at the end of his term was appointed Ambassador to France where he argued in a pamphlet against the suppression of the slave trade through searches of American slave ships. He was a Senator from Michigan from 1845-48 and again from 1849-57. He called for popular sovereignty, or the right of the people in the territories to decide whether or not they wanted to be a slave or free state. President Buchanan appointed him Secretary of State in 1858 and it was in this position that he appointed Charles J. Helm, a pro-slavery politician, consul general in Havana, Cuba. Helm granted American slave ships papers allowing them to ply their illegal trade. [10] This deliberate flaunting of American law by an American Secretary of State and his subordinates demonstrated how pervasively southern slave sympathies had penetrated the executive branch.

As late at 1857 New York City was engaged in various ways in the slave trade. Slave vessels were outfitted alongside those cleared for legitimate trades, and financiers funded capital for partnerships into slave trades. [11] New York's garment industry provided most of the cheap clothes for southern slaves. In early January 1861 Mayor Fernando Wood recommended to his cotton council business associates that New York City secede with South Carolina and become a commonwealth composed of Manhattan, and Long and Staten islands so that business with the South would not be interrupted. [12] As soon as southern states seceded and the Confederacy was formed in 1861, the South repaid its northern business partners by repudiating all northern debts.

Would free market capitalists today defend the institution of slavery without government interference, and all those merchants who supported it? Today, that argument must extend to free market advocates and, for example, credit card companies and their sponsoring banks that charged whatever fees and interest rates they chose without government regulation on behalf of the consumer and without financial institutions informing clients of their rights to protest.

At this point it might help to put a face to the slave trading business. The biggest slave trader of them all was not just a corporate sponsor of slavery but the President of the Continental Congress, one of America's first and most prominent politicians.

Henry Laurens (1724-1792)

> Men generally need great and constant efforts in order to create lasting evils; but there is one evil that enters the world furtively: at first one hardly perceives it in the midst of ordinary abuses of power; it begins with an individual whose name history does not preserve; it is deposited as a cursed seed on some point in the soil; then it nourishes itself, spreads without effort, and grows naturally with the society that has let it in: this evil is slavery.
>
> (Alexis De Tocqueville, *Democracy in America*, 2000, p. 326.)

Henry Laurens was a successful Charleston, South Carolina businessman who owned the largest slave trading company in North America in the late 18th century. In the 1750s alone he auctioned over 8,000 slaves. Born of French Huguenot immigrants, he owned rice and indigo plantations on over 20,000 acres, married into a family of rice planters, and fathered twelve children, seven of whom died in infancy.

He fought against the Cherokees in his youth in the South Carolina militia with the rank of Lt. Colonel and won easy election into colonial government. He was a delegate to the second Continental Congress and succeeded John Hancock as President of that assembly. He was sent as Minister to Holland and helped secure Dutch support for the war. On the return voyage, the British captured his ship. Among the retrieved diplomatic papers the British recovered were the American/Dutch alliance contracts. He was charged with treason and imprisoned in the Tower of London, the only American to achieve that distinction. He was held for 15 months and released on December 31, 1781 in exchange for Gen. Charles Cornwallis, the British general Washington defeated at Yorktown.

He was a delegate to Paris with Ben Franklin and others to help secure the peace that resulted in the Treaty of Paris in 1783 and the conclusion of the American Revolutionary War. He was a dedicated patriot, solidly against Britain's trade policy against the colonies and its anti-colonial sentiments, and favored one union between the colonies. He signed the *Articles of Confederation* but not the *Declaration of Independence* or the Constitution.

He lost most of his fortune in the war but apparently saw no contradiction between his slave holding and his other business activities. Slave trading and the buying and selling of slaves drew unscrupulous risk-takers because the profit margins were so high. His pious religious enunciations and writings during his tenure in the Continental Congress give no indication of his policies of enslaving others for personal gain.

The majority of Lauren's writings are business letters largely about slaves, and the capital needed for cargo, clothing, price estimates, the health and mortality rates of the slaves, etc. In a letter to Samuel and William Vernon on January 22, 1757, for example, he wrote: "Our people latterly made as great a difference between prime slaves and such as are Ordinary as any place whatever and will continue to do so as long as our market shall be as well supplied as it was last year." [13] He reported that in 1757 able men slaves sold for 260-270 pounds sterling, a prodigious price by any reckoning.

Laurens' son Jack would return to the colonies from his studies in London and Geneva, enlist to fight in the Revolutionary War and become a part of Washington's staff. He offered Washington over 3,000 of the family's slaves as soldiers to fight for the patriot cause, an offer initially declined. When Jack Laurens' proposal to sell slaves as soldiers was set before the South Carolina legislature, the planters who governed were not about to let their property be thus liberated, even in the defense of Charleston from the British.[14] Nevertheless, Jack's moral resolve toward liberating the slaves was as admirable—more so than any of the other founding fathers—as was his courage, if sometimes reckless and risky behavior, in battles during the Revolutionary War.

A famous legal slave case occurred in England in 1772, while Henry Laurens was in London, known as *Sommersett v Stewart*. James Sommersett had been kidnapped in Africa and taken to Virginia and sold to Charles Stewart. While Stewart was on business in London prior to the *Declaration of Independence*, Stewart brought Sommersett with him to serve in the residence. He escaped, but was quickly recaptured. He was placed on board the vessel *Amy and Mary* captained by John Knowles and bound for Jamaica. Famous lawyers heard about the incident and filed a claim of *habeas corpus* on Sommersett's behalf, a petition the court granted. Sommersett thus came to a court in London in 1772.

Several significant legal issues emerged from this case. First, whether compensation is due a slave owner for property loss. Second, whether ships at sea are granted extra-territoriality in open waters. Third, whether African states are entitled to slavery. And fourth, whether slaves may be granted freedom on public ships or on land. Mr. Hargraves, Sommersett's defense counsel, argued that in England the "claim of villenage," or a form of servitude, was no longer in effect. The defense argued that *lex loci* should prevail, or the law of the land where the event occurred. Slavery was permitted in the American colonies but not in England. Hargraves said: "Our law prohibits the commencement of domestic slavery in England, because it disapproves of slavery, and considers its operation dangerous and destructive to the whole community."[15] Lord Mansfield, the presiding judge, discharged Sommersett on June 22, 1772, and he disappeared into history, but with his freedom.

Forbes v Cockrane in 1822 involving the British was a similar legal case. On the night of February 23, 1815, 38 slaves escaped from the cotton plantation of Mr. Forbes, a British merchant in Florida. Florida was then under Spanish control. But South Carolina, the closest state, permitted slavery. The escapees fled onto the *Terror Bomb*, a British vessel under the command of Vice Admiral Sir A. Cockrane. When the case came to trial in a British court, the judge found for the defendants, and the slaves were freed. The court found that once aboard an English ship British law prevailed, and England did not permit slavery. The laws of sovereign nations took priority when questions of liberty and freedom were at issue.

If the colonies had not declared independence, or had not won the revolutionary war and England had prevailed, would English law have disbanded slavery in America as it did in England? That would have prevented the American compromises about slavery for over a century, forestalled the Civil War and its calamitous consequences, and the disastrous period of Reconstruction and a further century of discrimination.

In 1773 a published poem by an anonymous author appeared entitled *The Dying Negro*. It was a long narrative poem about "a Black" who had run away from his English master, got christened in order to marry a fellow servant, a white woman. He was captured and while on board a ship in the Thames shot himself. A part of the poem reads: "And better in th'untimely grave to rot, The world and all its cruelties forgot, Then dragged once more beyond the Western main, To groan beneath some dastard planter's chain." [16] The prose narratives and legal cases aside, it is evocative to see a poetic response, especially by an anonymous poet, to a tragic episode, like that of Eleanor Rigby, but in the slave trade and ownership business.

To return to the chronicle, the British had been sufficiently persuaded against slavery through public opinion, and the condemnation of illustrious officials and groups like the Quakers, that the British Parliament passed *The Abolition of the Slave Trade* bill into law on 25th March 1807. Three weeks earlier, on March 3, 1807, President Jefferson signed a congressional bill "to prohibit the importation of slaves into any port or place within the jurisdiction of the United States." The *U.S. Constitution* had specified this date in Article I, Section 9. The South through natural procreation had enough slaves for the plantation work, and thought that too many slaves could lead to insurrections, a fear more worrisome than guilt about slavery's morality.

Jefferson and Madison, both plantation slave owners, sought to limit the powers of the national government to what was expressed in the Constitution. Madison said in his State of the Union in 1810: "American citizens are instrumental in carrying on traffic in enslaved Africans, equally in violation of the laws of humanity and in defiance of those of their own country. The same just and benevolent motives which produced interdiction in force against this criminal conduct will doubtless be felt by Congress in devising further means of suppressing the evil." This was a political statement and did not reflect Madison's typical plantation owner's views of slavery. He never freed his slaves. [17]

Hanging Captain Gordon, Slave Trader

The Piracy Act of 1820 declared that any American citizen engaging in the African slave trade was to be considered a pirate, and if found guilty should suffer the death penalty. It was originally a temporary law. But in 1823 it was made permanent. Enforcement proved to be the biggest problem in making the statute workable, as the trade was extremely profitable, and many juries sympathetic to the lucrative business, even if members were only indirectly engaged in the logistics of its interests. Yet there were huge risks—ship confiscation, release of enslaved prisoners, rewards for tipsters, fines, jail time for captains—that made the monetary advantages dangerous too. Yet because the New York business community was so commercially linked with southern interests, few sympathetic juries would convict slave traders, and evidence presented in court was often circumstantial making convictions tenuous. [18]

Nathaniel Gordon (1834–1862) of Portland, Maine had successfully made several trips as a slave ship captain. But he and his ship the *Erie*, flying the American flag with over 900 slaves packed so tight they could not lie down, were captured about 50 miles from the Congo River in West Africa in 1860.

On a previous slave trip before his capture, Gordon, was hired to serve as captain but had stolen a brig known as the *Camargo*, sailing out of San Francisco with a load of hides bound for New York City. While at sea, Gordon won over the crew, possibly with the promise of riches, to become a slaver ship. They threw the hides overboard and once in port in Rio de Janeiro outfitted the ship for a slave ship to Africa. Eluding capture, Gordon landed his slave cargo back in Brazil, burned his ship and escaped clothed as a woman. The sale of slaves far exceeded the cost of the ship, or payoffs to the crew, and eliminated incriminating evidence. [19]

Gordon was convicted in New York City on November 9, 1861, and hanged on February 21, 1862 in the middle of the Civil War. He was the first in 42 attempts to be successfully prosecuted, was tried and found guilty, and had the automatic death penalty applied under the *Piracy Act*. [20] His death sobered the merchants of New York—at the time the largest center of finances and outfitting of slave ships in the world—who had profited from building and requisitioning the ships that later became slavers in Cuba, and from the casual business supplying slave owners throughout the South with clothes for slaves and wares for their owners. His death implicitly censured the reprehensive preachers of the city for not speaking out about the heinous practices.

Gordon's death was a turning point in American history. Gordon was legally executed for doing at sea what had been done for more a century on land legally in states and with the complicity by the national government—the kidnapping and buying and selling of humans as property.

Not the "Blessings of Liberty"

Slavery, wrapt in its own congenial, midnight darkness, can, and does, develop all its malign and shocking characteristics; where it can be indecent without shame, cruel without shuddering, and murderous with apprehension or fear of exposure. (Frederick Douglass, 1855, p. 62)

How does one distinguish between American revolutionaries who believed it was their right to kill British occupiers and men like Denmark Vesey, a free Black, who led the largest slave revolt in American history against people he believed supported enslaving his fellow Africans? Answers usually depend on the ethnicity of the responder. The first revolt was against colonialism, the second against racial enslavement. The American revolt against the British has been glorified by the radical right as the kind needed today against a supposedly tyrannical government. The second revolt is never mentioned. But some Blacks literally sacrificed "our lives, our fortunes and our sacred honor" if caught, just like plantation owners in 1776 pledged in *The Declaration of Independence*.

However, both revolts according to existing laws were illegal. Yet both can be accepted as legitimate revolution against the abuse of human rights. The American Revolution barely succeeded, and only with the help of the French, a foreign power. Slave revolts all failed and slaves were freed only when another foreign power, the USA, subdued in war the Confederacy that held them in bondage.

Denmark Vesey, a Black who bought his freedom from money from a winning lottery ticket, earned the confidence of Whites in Charleston, South Carolina as a congenial resident making his living as a carpenter. What they didn't know, nor suspect, was that he systematically planned and nearly executed the largest slave revolt in 1822 in North America. Loose tongues and Black loyalties to White owners exposed the plot. Vesey and several of his co-conspirators were hanged after a brief trial before judges. Blacks did not have access to jury trials. [21]

What is extraordinary is that Vesey had recruited hundreds of cooperating slaves from Charleston and the adjoining countryside. The plan was to set fires in different sections of the city simultaneously, to kill all Whites, and then to escape to Haiti. Whites feared slave revolts more than plagues or hurricanes because their success would ruin the economy.

Several studies, almost universally conducted by southerners, have been sympathetic toward the South's position prior to and after the Civil War. [22]

Slave owners believed that they lived in a well-ordered society in which classes of individuals fulfilled their providential goals in life, and that menial and laborious tasks were to be performed by slaves. Defending slavery as if the trade had not been repudiated a century and a half earlier in England, and crushed militarily in the U.S. two generations previously, is a ridiculous rationalization from an exhausted culture. None of these arguments is rich in anthropological theory or practice and is only self-justification grounded in a mindset of racial supremacy.

> In the solitude of my spirit I see clouds of dust raised on the highways of the South; I see the bleeding footsteps; I hear the doleful wail of unfettered humanity on the way to the slave-markets where the victims are to be sold like horses, sheep and swine, knocked off to the highest bidder.
>
> (Frederick Douglas in Foner, 2003, p. 32.)

The pro-confederate assumptions about the benefits of slavery, however couched to appeal to southern sympathies, were derived from an odious premise: that owning human beings is laudable for the capital and labor they provide. We never discover in any apologists for southern slavery how noble it was for families to be split up and sold separately, nor how they should be humanely treated. Nor do slavery apologists ever discuss whether or not it would be equitable to have White slaves too, people captured, say, from other countries not in Africa, to plant seeds and harvest crops?

"The region is still carrying the heritage of slavery," wrote the Swedish social scientist Gunnar Myrdal in his monumental study, *An American Dilemma.*[23] Conservative Republicans today are generally opposed to the influence of labor unions because their political ancestors in the South had no need of unions because they purchased laborers as chattel outright. The South raged against the so-called imperialism of the North. Yet nobody asked slaves whether or not they had imperial masters, no matter how benign.

Two quotes from President James Buchanan, who tried to prevent a civil war and was acceptable to the South because of his moderating views of it, will illustrate the mentality of officials in 1860. "The truth is that the people of the South are daily more and more confirmed in the opinion that the security of the domestic fireside requires a separation from the Northern States . . . the worst feature . . . is that they are rapidly losing their respect and attachment for the Constitution and the Union."[24] "The great object of my Administration will be to arrest, if possible, the agitation of the slavery question at the North & to destroy sectional parties."[25]

During this pre-Civil War era federal courts took a moderating stance on other relevant issues that broke along sectional lines. Several cases had arisen that invoked the commerce clause of the Constitution giving Congress powers to regulate inter-state commerce. These cases, *Groves v. Slaughter, Prigg v. Pennsylvania, Rowan v. Runnels*, among others, involved the slave trade within states, not just the trade between Africa and the U.S. The court generally avoided sectional disputes that were sure to arise in the aftermath of portentous decisions by ruling on technical matters, as in the notorious *Dred Scott* decision.

They tended to avoid the central question of which jurisdiction, the federal government or States, should regulate slave trade in the U.S. or jurisdictional disputes involving the *Fugitive Slave Act*, freedom for slaves in one state but not in another, etc. [26] These judicial concerns would soon be decided on the battlefield and not the court room.

It is not my purpose to review the Civil War's battles or its catastrophic destruction, only its lasting political consequences, and some anecdotes, events and figures of how it still influences contemporary American political life.

The March Toward Civil War

The *Kansas-Nebraska Act of 1854*, federal control in the territories, the debates about admitting Texas, the *Dred Scott* Supreme Court decision in 1857, the Lincoln-Douglas debates in 1858, all stroked the most contentious issue in America at the time, and highlighted sectional differences. In the fading weeks of his administration in 1860, just before South Carolina seceded, President Buchanan tried to placate the South by amending the Constitution to recognize states to hold slaves under state law, to protest that right in the territories, and to enforce the *Fugitive Slave Law* more effectively. [27] That wasn't enough for the South. Lincoln had already been elected and his views were clear: that Blacks may not be equal but that slavery would not stand. As Congress debated compromises in December 1860 Lincoln made clear he was totally opposed to any compromise on slavery in the territories. State conventions were held throughout the South to decide how to respond. But South Carolina seceded quickly on December 20th, 1860. All southern states soon followed within weeks. Politicians still threaten secession today, as if they remember nothing from the disaster of the war, let alone the illegality of the exercise.

Seeking independence was one thing, but in seceding southern states also reneged on their share of the federal debt, and immediately began pilfering federal property—buildings, forts and even postal offices, as if ownership suddenly reverted to the states. Not even southern sympathizers have offered rationales for this wholesale larceny of federal property. Inept and obstinate politicians, commercial interests, a mob psychology of vengeance against "northern aggression," all contributed to the widening of sectional antagonisms and war fever.

In 1869 the Supreme Court ruled that secession was unconstitutional by using the argument from the Constitution of forming "a more perfect union." [28] In one sense, the country could have been spared the deaths of over 620,000. Had Lincoln simply allowed secession and never challenged it, the South, without resources and manufacturing capabilities and a lack of diverse economies much like a baronial feudal system, and with a restless and growing slave population that might have created its own secession, would have eventually deteriorated economically within a couple of generations.

Had secession been left to stand in 1860 we would not today have extreme political polarization with conservative politicians still insisting on, for example, "states rights," as if that issue had not been settled constitutionally, militarily and judicially. Lincoln succinctly brushed that flawed argument aside in his *Message to Congress* in a special session on July 4, 1861. Southern states in seceding assumed their supposed sovereignty was equal to that of the federal government after the Constitution, as it had been under the *Articles of Confederation*. In 1860 the North was unprepared to let slavery stand any longer, and the South was equally unprepared to make any racial adjustments.

Moreover, a greater issue was at stake: which view of American civilization would prevail? Half of a nation that tolerates slavery, and another half which hates it and wants to extinguish it, presents contrary perspectives to itself and the world. Maintaining coexistence under these conditions was not a viable option. Under the South's reasoning that states can secede if they want, then if all states were to secede how could there be a national government at all? In his inaugural address Lincoln said: "that no State, upon its own mere notion, can lawfully get out of the Union—that resolves and ordinances to that effect are legally void; and that acts of violence, within any State or States, against the authority of the United States, are insurrectionary or revolutionary . . ." The Supreme Court agreed in *Texas v. White* in 1869.

The bravado and optimism for independence to protect slavery codes and culture have been vividly portrayed in fiction, in Harriet Beecher Stowe's *Uncle Tom's Cabin* (1852) and in Margaret Mitchell's *Gone with the Wind* more dramatically than any sociological text. Although we cannot overlook Joel Chandler Harris (1845-1908), whose stories of *Uncle Remus* I read as a child, a burlesque of literary art, with a dialect borrowed from Harriet Beecher Stowe, and a humiliation of what literature could have been if there had been enough southern artists or satirists.

Other fiction writers have since explored the South's peculiar racial tensions and social class differences, each offering a unique insight into a regional problem: Mark Twain, William Faulkner, Robert Penn Warren, William Styron, Katherine Anne Porter, Thomas Wolfe, Tennessee Williams, Eudora Welty, Harper Lee, Carson McCullers, and Margaret Mitchell, among others. Modern literature about the South paints an agonizing portrait of a South that can't forget its past, even as many Americans are ignorant of the country's history.

> Why reasonable people go stark raving mad when anything involving a Negro comes up is something I don't pretend to understand.
> (Harper Lee, *To Kill a Mockingbird*)

The secessionist states ratified a Confederate Constitution on March 11, 1861 modeled on the *U.S. Constitution* in principle and language. The sovereignty of southern states, and presumably all states, was recognized, as they had been under the *Articles of Confederation*. The document created a new centralized government, which, presumably also was sovereign concurrent with the secession states. This major logical and political inconsistency was not resolved because in the haste the question was not raised of how there could be competing sovereignties. Neither was the question of whether or not a secessionist sovereign state could decide on its own initiative to secede from the Confederacy. The *Confederate Constitution* was ratified by delegates but, unlike the *U.S. Constitution*, was never proposed to the people. [29] In this political mentality the seceding states not only came before the federal government but spoke for southern voters who had no voice in its own constitutional establishment. Comparatively, the *Articles of Confederation* were ratified by the states, but not the Constitution which was ratified "by the people of the United States," as noted in the Preamble.

The insolent aristocracy that was the Confederacy attempted to erect a modern, slave-holding republic, a daunting challenge in itself, and simultaneously remain solidly Christian. These two idealisms were crushed at Appomattox when the misguided, treasonous political experiment collapsed. The Confederate Union and its slaveholding society tried to sustain conservative principles discarded by the western world.

The same principles are upheld today in the radicalized conservative movement—that it is good policy to react against representative government, to curtail programs that enlarge personal and civil rights (like to gays and women who seek abortions), and that re-distributes tax monies to the society's less fortunate. This is not an argument for liberals (in some quarters considered worse than communists) and against conservatives, since all Americans need to be vigilant about government programs and policies. Rather, it is to show how the far right of the conservative movement has borrowed the principles of southern supremacy and anti-government sentiment and cloaked it largely in Christian piety and nationalistic fervor.

Secession did happen; reunion did not. The military and governmental infrastructure of the Confederacy, its livelihood and property was decimated as were the traumatic psyches of those who lost loved ones, as almost all in the population did. But reunion, in the sense that the conquered peoples were joined again in a felicitous bond, did not occur. It was as if antagonistic divorced couples were forced to live with each other again. Contemporary political struggles between extreme conservatives and liberals are a linear descendant of that social and cultural division of which the Civil War was merely a disastrous interlude. The initial unity that glued Americans together in the 1770s was enmity toward Britain. At the conclusion of the American Revolution in 1781, the inherent economic and social divisions between the North and South emerged and widened over the centuries. Economic changes did not occur in the South until the beginnings of industrialization in the 1930s when cotton was displaced as the main commodity and workers began to move into cities, including the North.

Although legal restrictions have been secured ending civil inequalities, there remained social, class and economic inequalities some of which result because of subtle forms of discrimination. Had they not been compelled to do so as a condition of admittance back into the Union, southern states would not have voluntarily accepted the 14th Amendment banning discrimination against Blacks.

> Man over men
> He (God) made not lord, such title to himself
> Reserving, human left from human free.
> (John Milton, *Paradise Lost*, 1667, vii, 64.)

By late 1864 when the South's military cause became desperate, the unthinkable was debated and encouraged—the recruitment and emancipation of slaves to serve as soldiers. The cause of the war was the preservation of slavery. But confederate leaders were futilely searching for ways to sustain its preservation by allowing slaves to fight as "persons," as Jefferson Davis noted, and not as property or commodities, thereby converting pieces of property to lives, corrupting all previous southern arguments, and, by default, appearing to free slaves. [30] Yet recruiting, training and provisioning 200,000 slaves, as was suggested, would imperil the South's food supply, in the latter years of the war already in perilous condition. It was an absurd and desperate assumption for Southerners to think that slaves would fight to maintain their slavery and that of their families left on plantations.

After Admiral David Farragut ran a blockade past the Confederate forts of Jackson and St. Philip in the lower Mississippi delta and began to sail toward New Orleans, hundreds of slaves abandoned plantations in the summer of 1862 and ran to Union lines. By early November 1861 the sugar plantations were nearly empty of slaves. In a sense, Lincoln was compelled to issue the *Emancipation Proclamation* in January 1863. By then all of southern Louisiana was under federal control, and Blacks were not only already free, but free to enlist in the Union army, which they did in the thousands. Twenty-four Black soldiers would be awarded the Congressional Medal of Honor for service in the Civil War. [31]

The South pronounced acidly on the imperialism of the federal government for attempting to eradicate slavery, and yet ironically appeared to endorse Lincoln's tenets in the *Emancipation Proclamation*. The *Confiscation Act* of 1862 declared that slaves reaching Union lines were captives of war and could be set free. Thousands escaped just to join Union forces, or to meet them when Union forces were in the vicinity. They were often received reluctantly since hostility toward Blacks was ubiquitous in the North too. By 1865 there were upwards of a quarter million escaped Blacks in the Union, many appearing in army uniform.

The loss of the western Confederacy and other military defeats in Tennessee, specifically at Vicksburg in April 1865, and the loss of slaves as farm laborers, and a limited supply of soldiers, compelled Confederate officials and military leaders to consider that loss of the war meant the eradication of slavery, their social and economic way of life, and their property. Humiliation of a haughty people would be the least of the results.

And yet Jefferson Davis, Robert E. Lee and other Confederacy officials seriously entertained the arming and emancipation of slaves. The debate brought to the fore that if the South was planning to destroy slavery on its own why it had gone to war at all. In the end, patriarchal plantation representatives in the Confederate legislature killed any law that might empower slaves in the army as soldiers or teamsters. But clearly the fateful debate exposed southern hypocrisy, that graveyard of naïve optimism, in believing their nostrums and fantasy platitudes about slaves willing to risk their lives to save the plantation way of life.

Dr. John Henry Stringfellow (1819-1905), a Virginia native and pro-slavery activist, proposed one solution. He obtained a medical degree in Pennsylvania, went to Kansas to help cholera victims but stayed to secure that territory as a slave state. As Kansas Speaker of the House he persuaded the territorial legislature to pass laws making it illegal to question slavery's legality and barred anti-slavery individuals from holding public office. Returning to Virginia, he proposed to Jefferson Davis that the South free all the slaves because they would have nowhere to go and could be hired as laborers. That slaves would want to return to their masters, and not ride, run or walk to the North toward real freedom, is another southern delusion. The ridiculous idea gained some credibility among confederates, but before it could be seriously debated or exercised the war was lost in April 1865. The belief that southerners thought they had reliable knowledge about their slaves is just one of the pathetic stereotypes emerging from the southern mind.

The myth that Blacks fought alongside confederate soldiers in the Civil War is still perpetuated in Fourth Grade Virginia textbooks. *Our Virginia, Past and Present* notes that two battalions of Black soldiers fought under Stonewall Jackson, who died from friendly fire in Chancellorsville in May 1863. This is pure fabrication, as every notable historian of the period knows. The Confederacy would never have allowed Blacks to have guns, nor would Confederate soldiers have been persuaded to fight alongside slaves or freed slaves.

The end of the Civil War did not bring an end to servitude and subordination of Blacks. Southern strategists rose to assert states rights, that old conundrum used by John Calhoun to resist the Union's right to national legislative authority. Federal troops helped install blacks in elected office during Reconstruction in 1865-70. But an intimidating terror campaign by white supremacists forced blacks out of office. Under President Grant and Hayes, the federalists retreated and the southern states passed discriminatory laws against Blacks. The *Plessy v Ferguson* decision by the U.S. Supreme Court in 1896 solidified the laws of states to segregate. The South's culture of feeling superior to blacks lingered on into the 21st century.

The Confederate flag still flies in some quarters, signaling that its discredited ideals are still embedded in the South and throughout the U.S. where it has migrated over the generations, and has become a persistent undercurrent in American politics. [32]

The history of the 20th century shows an equal animosity toward civil rights. The violence and antagonism toward the *Brown v Board of Education* decision in 1954 making segregated schools unconstitutional, was one indication of how difficult it would be to reverse centuries of prejudice. (See Chapter Thirteen)

Gov. Orval Faubus of Arkansas refused to integrate Little Rock High School, so President Eisenhower federalized the state militia and escorted nine black students into school. It took more than ten years of court decisions for school integration to occur uniformly. President Clinton gave the nine former

Little Rock students Congressional Gold Medals in 1999. Governor George Wallace barred the door of the University of Alabama so a potential Black student could not enter, and he had to be confronted directly by the Attorney General of the U.S., Nicholas Katzenbach. Governors defying the U.S. Constitution were not unusual in the South, and sent the message that southern pride in its segregation policies was more important than adherence to the law.

After the 1954 Brown decision the underlying racist ideology broke loose from its doctrinal slumber and drew support from all social classes. There are still subtle and some not so subtle examples of it in political messages and campaign speeches. For example, this never disavowed statement appeared in a June 1992 Ron Paul newsletter about the Los Angeles riots: "Order was only restored in L.A. when it came time for the blacks to pick up their welfare checks three days after rioting began." [33]

On December 31, 2011, Rick Santorum campaigning in Iowa said in a speech: "I don't want to make black people's lives better by giving them somebody else's money. I want to give them the opportunity to go out and earn the money." Finally, Newton Leroy Gingrich on January 5, 2012 in New Hampshire he intoned: "I'm prepared, if the NAACP invites me, to go to their convention and talk about why the African-American community should demand paychecks and not be satisfied with food stamps." Ronald Reagan was fond of quoting his fable about the "welfare queen." All of these asides are meant to invoke the ire of the bigoted.

By 1964 Mississippi still excluded Blacks from voting, and in other southern states there were still poll taxes (see the 24th Amendment) and literacy tests, as well as threats of violence for Blacks who attempted to vote. Southerners even argued that segregation was better for the "Negro" than slavery. [34] Racial prejudice then and now is a perversion of the declared American quest for equalitarianism.

The passage of the *Civil Rights Act* in 1964 and the *Voting Rights Act* in 1965, and the subsequent bombing of black churches and murders of civil rights workers revealed how little social and political equal rights for all had been achieved in the hundred years since the end of military hostilities. Southern states had vigorously opposed any legislation that would imperil black separation and subjugation.

America had undergone a war with itself, and legislatively and judicially tried to solve its long-standing moral dilemma about race relations. But though the laws have changed, the contemporary radical right, rooted in Christian evangelicalism, still supports a basically White establishment by emphasizing White power values. Hence, it protects large businesses and corporations, largely White, and legislatively tries to restrict government programs that traditionally go to the poor, disproportionately African Americans and minorities. The political strategy is for less taxation, so the government cannot fund social service programs, but tax breaks for the wealthy under the false argument that the money of the rich is invested to fund new jobs.

These advocates are like robotic puppets, making identical platitudinous speeches, as if banal repetition was a way of offering new insights. The far right almost directly mirrors anti-bellum politics, though since the 19th century the political party names have been reversed. But uncompromising policies are a distinct disadvantage to equalizing economic and social inequalities, the same kind of caste policy that pro-slavery advocates stood for.

According to the Swedish sociologist Gunnar Myrdal who came to the U.S. specifically to study race relations the problem is still with us:

> Thus the opportunistic disrespect for law, order and public morals has a complicated causation and a deep-rooted history in the South. The tradition is today still part of the way of life and as such is often patriotically cherished as distinctly Southern. It is certainly one of the most sinister historical heritages of the region. It spells danger for a democratic society that involves serious maladjustments. [35]

The disestablishment of organized religion by Protestant colonialists who converted because of messages from the Spirit and not the pulpit has been transformed in contemporary America into a disestablishment of the prerogatives of the national government. The spirit of dissent is strong in a democracy, as it should be. But in modern America it seems to encroach on the foundations on which that democracy rests. It definitely hearkens back to an earlier era in which slavery was acceptable and antipathy toward the national government endemic.

Chapter Six
Monroe and Missouri:
The Admission of New Slave States

For three hundred years an uneasy compromise existed between free states and slave states. A review of that history is essential for understanding the current political division in America as the split then is similar to today's rift. It's convenient to describe how select sitting presidents dealt with the contentions between North and South so that we can understand the origins of the present political dilemma and appreciate the similarities of America's perpetual struggle to find a presumed national unity from a tradition of sectional opposition.

Let's explore two presidents during the early 19th century: James Monroe and John Quincy Adams. James Monroe was America's fifth president during the days of the Missouri Compromise, a political issue that further divided North and South over the admission into the Union of a state that would have Congress choose it to be slave or free, an issue that had political ramifications in congressional representation. John Quincy Adams, America's sixth president, had an abiding hatred of America's centuries-old conflict with itself over slavery.

James Monroe (1758–1831) and Missouri

James Monroe, the fifth president, was the fourth president to be a slave-owner. When his father died he inherited his family's 500-acre tobacco plantation and its personal property, including Ralph, a Negro boy. He operated a plantation at Highland (now known as Ash Lawn), his 3,500-acre estate in Albemarle County near Charlottesville in sight of Jefferson's Monticello, with between 30-40 slaves. During his presidency Monroe endorsed African colonization as the most effective way to end slavery. And because of this Monrovia was named as the capital of Liberia, the country where freed slaves could immigrate. But most Blacks were not freed slaves.

I distinctly note this about our early slave-owning presidents, a fact often hidden in the laudatory treatment of our first heads of state, because I seek to emphasize that they all had a tendency to protect the plantation economy and its peculiar lifestyle built around slave labor. It was a condition not disguised at the time because it was a part of the political compromise. Consequently, in protecting property rights these southerners did not defend civil rights, for example, as an extension of privileges for everyone.

Monroe at age 17 entered the Continental Army where he fought with distinction. He attended the College of William and Mary, as had Jefferson, where the two courses of study were either theology or the law. He lived near Charlottesville but practiced law in Fredericksburg, and was elected a delegate in the first Continental Congress. He was one of the Virginia delegates at the Annapolis convention that sought to revise the *Articles of Confederation*. In quick succession he became Governor of Virginia, Ambassador, Secretary of State and Secretary of War under Madison, and then President. Where Madison was profound, quick and temperate, Monroe was dull but passionate, ponderous in speeches but plain and unpretentious in behavior. Madison was philosophical and well read. Monroe was practical and not at all bookish.

Monroe was faced with some of the nation's most intractable problems, the most divisive of which was the Missouri Compromise bitterly debated in Congress for two years, an issue as divisive as a contemporary health care or debt ceiling debate. This one issue of a nation's admission of a new state compelled the country to face its singular division over slavery.

Monroe was elected President in 1816, and re-elected to a second term in 1820. He chose two of America's greatest intellects: John Quincy Adams as his Secretary of State and John Calhoun as Secretary of War. The electorate initially hesitated to elect another Virginian to the presidency, as until then John Adams was the only non-Virginian president. But Monroe's solid military, diplomatic and administrative credentials, and his political strength in Congress proved too compelling to resist.

Based on his military experiences in war and his role as temporary Secretary of War when the British burned Washington and exposed the nation's weak defenses, Monroe anchored his initiatives in military preparedness, a feat that marks his presidency. He began his presidency in 1817 with a 16-week long tour of northern military facilities throughout the country. After this exhausting trip, he immediately planned a similar trip in the South through the Carolinas, Tennessee and home via Kentucky, a journey that lasted from late March to August 1819. Wherever he went he was feted with receptions and dinners as if he were campaigning and not already president. But showing himself personally to the people was a political precedent, enthusiastically maintained by his successors.

By 1819 the country was financially distressed. Commodities were severely depressed as were manufacturing, imports, exports and bank credits. Unemployment was at an all-time high and property devalued. This sounds too contemporary. But Monroe took no special steps to call a special session of Congress or to get the national government to intervene in the national crisis. This form of inaction revealed his Jeffersonian and southern version of limited government. Perhaps he presciently knew in advance the impending economic calamity, which is why he decided to flee Washington and roam the country, though his travels would have educated him about the worsening economic condition throughout the South and West.

The economic problems would seem like playground activities when compared to the storm caused by the admission of a slave state. Some of the questions of the day were: Should citizens have the right to be able to choose whether or not to have slavery in their new state? Did Congress have the right to prohibit slavery in the territories? The disturbing social and political topic was the most debated throughout the country. Yet oddly, while it was uppermost on everyone's mind, Monroe did not mention it in his annual message to Congress in 1819, as if slavery were merely a distracting political topic and not the country's most enduring and painful dilemma.

The Missouri Compromise

The Continental Congress in the *Northwest Ordinance of 1787* had prudently provided that there be no slavery or involuntary servitude in new states that would be carved out of the Northwest territories, consisting then of northern Midwest territories like Ohio. This was easy for southern states to concede because this section of the country did not offer the proper conditions to grow cotton, sugar cane or tobacco. By 1818 Missouri, then a part of the Louisiana territory, had enough people to qualify for admission into the Union. Slavery was already legal in the settled parts of Louisiana territory and would therefore be considered legal without further legislation in any territorial extension.

The Congress of the Constitution, however, should have considered abolishing slavery altogether in all territories rather than focusing on admission into the Union of a slave territory. By failing to keep the whole of Louisiana as a territory until slavery itself could be abolished, the U.S. forfeited the opportunity to deal with slavery everywhere. [1] Not diminishing the role of slavery when new lands were opened to admission happened first under Jefferson when he purchased the Louisiana territory. Southern states argued that the Constitution had no power to prohibit slavery in any state. Northern states argued that neither Congress nor state legislatures had the right to establish slavery where it did not exist.

The fact that southern representatives in Congress sought to equalize political representation rather than tackle the core issue of slavery itself says volumes about political maneuvering to accommodate the most pervasive human rights problem in the 19th century. The South argued successfully that since slavery was embedded in the Constitution, Congress could not rescind it. The South also knew that if it could not maintain an equal number in Congress through new slave states it could not legislatively control the North's resistance to slavery.

An amendment to the Missouri proposal in Congress in 1818, introduced by Representative James Tallmadge of New York, stipulated that the state could not import new slaves and would eventually have to free slaves born in Missouri after the age of 25 and after admission into the Union. The amendment passed the House but not in the Senate. Ensuing debates became bitter. Alabama had been admitted to the Union in 1819 as a slave state equalizing the number of slave and free states. The whole country knew the high stakes. In April 1818 representative Arthur Livermore of New Hampshire introduced a constitutional amendment bill to prohibit slavery in any state thereafter admitted to the Union. The House refused to consider the proposal.

Southerners argued that Congress had to admit Missouri as a slave state and not place conditions on the admission of a new state. Yet because Missouri might be considered a slave state, Congress could have refused its admission.

But because most of the settlers to Missouri had come there from the South, everyone expected that it would enter as a slave state.

When Missouri's state constitution came before Congress it included a phrase that excluded entry into Missouri of any free Negroes or mulattos, an obvious unconstitutional action, because in some states free Negroes were citizens. The U.S. Constitution notes: "citizens in each State shall be entitled to all the privileges and immunities of citizens in several States." Admirable men conceded that there was no moral justification for slavery but could not see any way around solving the South's labor problem, or of compensating for the existing investment in humans, or of overcoming the racial bias.

States took sides in their instructions to congressional representatives. New York, Pennsylvania and Delaware, a slave-holding state, told their representatives to vote against the admission of any territory unless slavery was excluded. Kentucky told its representatives to admit Missouri and let the people of Missouri choose whether or not to be a slave state.

In a private letter on January 10, 1820 to George Hay, James Monroe's son-in-law and a Virginia delegate, Monroe wrote his private views. [2] He had decided that states had to be admitted as residents chose and as equals in other states without restrictions. Clearly, he could not openly oppose southern states or any compromise that would damage his reputation in his home state. He thought the admission of Maine into the Union should be granted separately and quickly. This political concession would put the South on the high ground making it easy to admit Missouri as a slave state.

The amendment to the Missouri bill on February 17, 1820 provided for the admission of Missouri as a slave state but excluded slavery from the remainder of the Louisiana territory north of 36 degrees 30 minutes, an enormous political concession southern legislatures apparently did not realize at the time. [3]

This was a significant restriction on future admission of states and a damaging and shortsighted oversight by Southern legislators because it insured that all future states north of 36 degrees would not be admitted as slave states. This line today is within minutes of a degree of the northern designation of North Carolina, Tennessee, Arkansas, Oklahoma, New Mexico and Arizona, a demarcation line that extends mostly across the United States. As more non-slave states were admitted in the years following, southern slave states had unequal congressional votes. John Tyler, as a congressman from Virginia and slaveholder and later the tenth President, knew the importance of this amendment, which is why he voted against the Missouri Compromise bill.

On March 3, 1820 Congress admitted Maine, which prohibited slavery, into the Union, and authorized Missouri to enact a constitution and form a state government without any restriction on slavery. Missouri adopted a state constitution on July 19, 1820, and the House admitted Missouri as a state on February 26, 1821. All knew it was a fitting national political compromise, but only a postponement and not a resolution of slavery.

Lost in this debate was the full context of slavery. Had legislators focused on admitting a state for freed slaves, or offered slave states compensation for freeing slaves, further progress addressing the nature of the slavery problem might have averted the Civil War. Instead, Congress formulated the issue as equanimity of the political balance between states and not as a compromise for reducing slavery itself.

Monroe, with the help of his Secretary of State John Quincy Adams, and advice from ex-presidents Madison and Jefferson, confirmed during his second term in 1823 that the western hemisphere was no longer open to European colonization, and that any such interference would constitute a threat to U.S. security. He thus strengthened the influence of the presidency in foreign affairs, a tradition well established in contemporary executives. [4]

But Monroe's real lasting legacy was his southern inheritance and his belief that states were more sovereign than the federal government in internal and domestic affairs. For example, he sought a constitutional amendment on the extent of federal powers for internal improvements, an issue Congress did not address. Today we would be stunned if we thought the national government could not build and partially fund interstate highways. But Monroe vetoed a bill for a national road from Cumberland, Maryland to Wheeling, Virginia (now West Virginia) and the establishment of turnpikes and tollgates. He did not believe Congress had the right of jurisdiction over state land.

When he left office he had personal financial difficulties and had property in Albemarle and Loudoun counties that he put up for sale. At the time he owned between 60-70 slaves whose families he did not want to separate for sale. He did not live long in retirement. Like John Adams and Thomas Jefferson, he died on July 4th, the last president to have fought in the Revolutionary War to die on that memorable day in American history.

John Quincy Adams (1767–1848)

J. Q. Adams, the second child and oldest son of John and Abigail Adams, who would become the sixth president of the Unites States, spend seven years in Europe with his father, John Adams, then Ambassador to France. John Quincy became fluent in French and passable in Dutch, Russian and German, a language he did not master until be came Ambassador to Prussia. As a teenager he attended classes for several sessions at Leiden University. His father goaded him into studiousness, and Abigail, his protective, stern and vigilant mother, into virtue.

All his life he only wanted to be a scholarly and literary man and not a public servant or lawyer. However, in recognition of his scholarly writings he was elected President of the American Academy of Arts and Letters in 1820. He accepted an endowed chair at Harvard, and served for several years on the faculty. Harvard subsequently published two volumes of his lectures. He was a passable poet of both solemn and amatory verses. A long narrative poem, *Dermot MacMorrough or the Conquest of Ireland*, was published as a separate volume when he was 66 years old. He was renowned for his skillful diplomacy, with postings to Holland, Russia and England, and his acute political and administrative talents, despite a rather testy Yankee temperament.

He graduated from Harvard College and entered the study of law under private tutelage but did not complete the required three years of study before entering law practice in Boston. Within a year he was writing anonymous editorials that were circulated widely in the colonies and Europe. Because his father was Vice-President under George Washington, and because as a young man in his 20s he was known by all key figures in the early days of American federal government, he was appointed Minister to Holland when he was only 27.

He was 45 years old when the particularly difficult year of 1812 found him as Ambassador to Russia. That year Napoleon invaded Russia with a half million troops and America's war with Britain appeared inevitable. His singular achievement in Russia was to secure Emperor Alexander's help in mediating the war between England and America. And for this, President Madison appointed him Ambassador to Great Britain in 1813.

He was barely elected President in 1825 by the House of Representatives, not winning a majority of electoral votes cast between Henry Clay and Andrew Jackson. Jackson received 99 electoral votes, Adams 84, and William H. Crawford 41. When the election of the president went to the House, Henry Clay, who had been eliminated from contention because he received only 37 electoral votes, gave his influence to Adams and this secured Adams plurality. One of Adams' first acts was to appoint Clay his Secretary of State. [5]

What galled Adams the most was that he had been feted and earned the respect in Europe of diplomats and men of science and letters, but in America he had earned only the disrespect and abuse of unschooled and undistinguished partisans. He grew despondent. But melancholy, with its corresponding moodiness, was his habitual lifetime condition. After his defeat for a second term in 1828 by Andrew Jackson, the year his eldest son died, he retired to Quincy but was unexpectedly elected to the House of Representatives where he served with satisfaction to the consternation of his political enemies the rest of his life.

He may have seemed out of his element during the presidency because he was so vilified. Yet he had a vision that seems eminently sensible today, a politics of domestic initiatives that have actually been fulfilled over time. Yet then he was bucking a tendency to downplay the government and to lessen its influence, a political idea popular today. Party politics deepened the antagonism toward him and left the country in dysfunctional turmoil. Adams would be pleased to know that most of his proposals were eventually accepted. And today we can understand how calamitous party divisions are to congressional accomplishment and national unity.

On December 21, 1835 a message came from President Jackson to Congress about an Englishman named "Simonson" who had bequeathed funds to America for the establishment of an institution of learning. Adams recognized the importance of this immediately, as Congress did not. He requested a committee be created to investigate its merits and he was appointed Chair. Adams learned that James Smithson, the illegitimate son of the Duke of Northumberland, had left his entire estate of more than half a million dollars in gold to the United States to increase knowledge among its citizens, the very suggestion Adams had made to Congress in his first annual message as President. Congress tried to divert the funds to trivial projects, but Adams prevailed against these petty contrivances. As a result, the Smithsonian Institution today is the foremost example of a British noble's generous gift to further knowledge of the citizens of a nation its own representatives could not see fit to fund in their own country.

He began his tenure in Congress by confronting the issue of southern human slavery, that permanent and painful presence in the national consciousness. He believed that the Constitution was a compact that guaranteed slavery within certain limits and henc he had no sympathy for Abolitionists. [6]

Adams was a worthy legislative combatant but had to endure his fellow southern colleagues in Congress as they justified slavery as if it were morally essential to southern culture. Some of these representatives, of course, were his political enemies while he was in executive office, so it was with double enthusiasm that he undertook a crusade to expose and defeat them.

Two congressional matters clashed with each other during Adams' tenure in the House. One involved a so-called "gag" order in which southern states and their sympathizers construed a resolution: "Resolved, That Congress possesses no constitutional authority to interfere in any way with the institution of slavery in any of the States of this confederacy." This resolution was adopted by a vote of 182 Yeas to 8 voting Nay, including Adams who believed the resolution was unconstitutional.

But notice that the reference in the resolution is to America as a "confederacy" rather than a "union." *The Articles of Confederation* was the authority that brought together the states. But the *U.S. Constitution* in the Preamble clearly proclaims the need for "a more perfect Union." Southern sentiments were once again bypassing the U.S. Constitution so they could stand tall for the confederacy that gave them "sovereign" status.

The other issue was petitions. Adams believed that a "gag" rule preventing petitions being introduced into Congress was against free speech and the right to petition the government, both constitutional protections. He used petitions like those recommending the cessation of slavery in the District of Columbia to challenge the constitutionality of Congress' gag rule.

He was caustic, biting, always baiting his southern opponents, exasperating and persistent in his beliefs. He consistently took every advantage to savage the idea of slavery and its supporters. At the end of the fierce debates of 1842 he emerged with victories over his person and ideas. His keen, logical mind and his wide knowledge of the law, debating procedures, House rules, and foreign affairs from long experience abroad gave him an tactical edge, though his combativeness gave his enemies continuing strength to challenge and harass though not outmaneuver him.

His participation in one event in particular secured his reputation. It was late August 1839, and a ship without a flag and with a torn sail was discovered off the north Atlantic coast of the U.S. There were 30 Black and two White men aboard. On June 28th, this vessel, the *Amistad*, had set sail from Havana, Cuba for the Cuban coastal town of Puerto Principe bearing 49 slaves including four children, 40,000 in Spanish gold doubloons, and assorted cargo that included silks, glasses, books, pictures and food items. The slaves, several of whom died during the trip, freed themselves from their chains during the fourth night at sea, mutinied, killed the captain and the cook, and ordered one of the captured Whites to sail back to Africa where they were first taken into slavery. Cunningly, the navigator steered erratically toward the east during the day, and northerly at night hoping to reach the southern US coastline. The *Amistad* was spotted by a U.S. Coast Guard brig, the *Washington*, which hauled it into the harbor at New London, Connecticut together with its leader, a man known as Cinque. [7]

What initially appeared to be simply a matter of returning the vessel to its rightful owners soon became one of the most celebrated cases in American jurisprudence involving two sitting presidents (Martin Van Buren and William Henry Harrison), a former president and member of Congress (John Quincy Adams), a Secretary of State (John Forsyth), two Spanish Ambassadors, and the U.S. Supreme Court.

Several intriguing legal questions emerged from what was at first just a question of salvage rights to a vessel. Since Spain had outlawed the slave trade in a 1795 treaty with England, were the Blacks on board legally slaves or had they been kidnapped? Though they were found on board a Spanish vessel, were they even Spanish subjects? Illegal immigrants? Since the U.S. Congress had outlawed the slave trade (but not slavery), as had Connecticut, even slaves on a vessel were technically illegal in American waters. The Blacks were not slaves even by Spanish law, or by American law that prohibited the slave trade. Adams argued for the defendants. The U.S. Supreme Court agreed with Adams that they were free Africans and hence should be returned to Africa and not sent back to Cuba, then a Spanish territory. It was one of his most eloquent and stirring pleas and earned him high esteem.

Wealthy abolitionists in northern states helped with financial costs and paid for the Blacks to return to what is today Sierra Leone where they lived out their days. Several members of the American Board of Missions followed and established a Christian missionary colony in Sierra Leone.

In the session beginning in January 1842 Adams introduced into the House a petition from Havermill, Massachusetts that urged Congress to dissolve the Union because so much federal money was spent supporting southern slave institutions. Kentucky responded by offering a resolution that accused Adams of "the crime of high treason." Adams claimed the right as any citizen to defend himself against the charge of treason and the House became a judicial proceeding. Adams used the tactic into an offensive against slavery. Over a period of two weeks he made personal accusations against individuals he despised in Congress, many he considered the most depraved men in America. The resolution of treason against him was defeated 106 to 93.

He vehemently opposed the admission of Texas into the Union, convinced it would be another slave state. He voted against going to war with Mexico.

On February 23, 1848 he collapsed on the floor of the House from a stroke and died two days later in the Speaker's Room in the Capitol.

Among presidents who succeeded him he had hatred for Jackson, distaste for Martin Van Buren, friendliness for William Henry Harrison—who didn't live long enough as president for the cordiality to be reciprocated—contempt for Tyler and distrust for Polk.

John Quincy would not survive to see the country thirteen years later slide inevitably into Civil War, a predictable outcome of the constitutional compromise in 1787. The country's division was the outcome of the necessity to forge a Union against foreign interventions that became the U.S. Constitution, and of the inability of the South to extricate itself from its abominable practice of human slavery. The Civil War and the 13th and 14th Amendments ended the martial conflict and involuntary servitude but not the lingering anti-federalism resentment that yet prevails in American society.

We might think that contemporary political animosities are just the result of polarized convictions existing in society. I believe rather that they are the historical residue of our long-standing actual national sectionalism, that they became resurgent again during the civil rights era in the mid-1960s and are still in evidence today cloaked in a variety of political subterfuges, slogans and anti-government movements.

Confederate Flag on a House in Montgomery, Alabama

Chapter Seven
Jackson and Nullification:
The First Test of Secession

Liberty and Union, now and forever, one and inseparable.
(Daniel Webster, January 27, 1830 on the floor of the U.S. Senate)

Andrew Jackson (1767–1845)

Without union our independence and liberty would never have been achieved; without union they never can be maintained . . . The loss of liberty, of all good government, of peace, plenty, and happiness, must inevitably follow a dissolution of the Union. (Andrew Jackson, *Second Inaugural Address*, 1833)

Andrew Jackson was a man whose political life began with a scandal. News got out that he had married another man's wife before she was divorced. The scandal so exasperated his wife that she died shortly after he was elected president and prior to him assuming office.

But a domestic scandal was only the beginning of the tempestuousness of his personal life and career. He executed mutineers on the field of battle in Florida. He invaded Florida—many thought without proper authority—killed British subjects, killed Charles Dickinson in a duel in which he was also wounded and carried the bullet in his chest the rest of his life, and had a gunfight with the Benton brothers from Missouri. Any one of these escapades could have been the ended his political ambitions. But it was his decisive victory over the British at the Battle of New Orleans in 1815 that cemented his popularity. It was the single event that catapulted him into the presidency. [1]

Prior to Jackson there were opposing views of national government. On the one hand, the Hamiltonian view was of a centralized government bringing order to the disunity of states. Jefferson stood for limited government as a way of providing unity among states and for White property owners. Jackson believed in the centrality of the people with the president as the only true elected representative of the whole country. He is the first president to create an imperial role for the office, a legacy many successors found favorable.

Jackson's 1824 and 1828 campaigns against John Quincy Adams are symbolic of the political distinctions extant in American political life. Adams was a writer; Jackson a fighter. Adams was a man who could be an equal among European elites; Jackson a poorly educated frontier man who could regale men around a campfire about his combat exploits. Adams aspired to write epic poetry. Jackson was a man who could lead a ragtag army to overcome Indians or the British. In the end, it was Jackson who won the presidency for the common man against the New England professor, son of a president, and a man representative of the literate northern elites. The egalitarian, rough-hewn action candidate won over the urbane, cosmopolitan, professorial and political intellectual that ushered in a popular democratic spirit in the electorate that often spurns mental accomplishments and has a disdain for the learned in society. The vulgar slave-owning backwoodsman, Jackson, bested the genteel sophisticate, Adams, who was solidly opposed to slavery. This political drama that would be played out countless times in future presidential campaigns. Politicians thereafter quickly learned to pander to popular anti-science tastes like creationism and pooh-poohing global warming evidence. America craves leadership but often elects dullards.

The suspicion about experts began with Jackson, the common man's man. The only popularly recognized scientists were in space exploration, neurosurgeons, and agricultural experts at land grant colleges. Everything else, from biology to climatology, was ridiculed, especially if it disagreed with fundamentalist religious views. Yet the founders of the republic, who were experts, literate and scientific for their time, are extolled with encomiums that would embarrass them in real life.

Andrew Jackson's two terms as president (1829–1837) marked a distinct period in American history when regional divisions in the country surfaced and collided. The same divisions have arisen today. The South remained decidedly aristocratic, tied to feudal plantation practices, a more or less single economy, and slave labor. East coast states were also socially static and were built on wealth rooted in mercantilism and prestige. The West, symbolized by the populist Jackson, was bubbling with commercialism, individualism, freedom from governmental restraints, and an adventurous and democratic spirit conquering the untamed land.

Jackson's victory over the British in the Battle of New Orleans in 1815, and his earlier conquests over the Creek and Seminole Indians, made him in the eyes of ordinary Americas the greatest military hero since Washington. America was carried away with his victories even though Jackson himself was a thoroughly odious character unworthy it seemed of leading a republic. His election to the presidency twice says as much about American voters in the 19th century as it does about Jackson the man. The triumph of democracy is that every vote is equal to any other, and the collective mix can help elect any firebrand malcontent like Jackson.

> General Jackson, whom the Americans have twice chosen to place at their head, is a man of violent character and middling capacity; nothing in all the course of his career had ever proved that he had the requisite qualities to govern a free people; so the majority of the enlightened classes of the Union had always been opposed to him.
>
> (Alexis De Tocqueville, *Democracy in America*, 2000, p. 265).

Jackson was born in South Carolina near its northern border, and had two brothers, Hugh and Robert who both died in the Revolutionary War. As a young man, British forces captured him. As president he had ordered military forces to Charleston and privately threatened to hang John Calhoun his Vice President. His family moved to Tennessee where he was elected to the House of Representatives in 1796, and in 1797 to the U.S. Senate but resigned the following year to assume duties as a Superior Court Judge in Tennessee. In 1802 he was elected a Major General in the Tennessee militia, and in 1814 commissioned with the same national rank by President Madison. He fought multiple duels, some aborted, and carried all his life at least two bullets from wounds in duels. Although wounded himself, he killed Charles Dickinson in a duel. That year Aaron Burr visited Jackson for the third time and Jackson gave notice to the militia to be on alert to counteract Burr's expedition to secede. Jackson testified in Burr's trial for treason in Richmond in 1807.

Jackson was commissioned Governor of Florida in 1821, resigned his commission as Major General, accepted Florida from the Spanish, and then resigned the governorship. He was elected to the U.S. Senate again in 1823 and nominated for President in the convention of 1824, resigned his senate seat in 1825, was elected President in 1828 and appointed John Calhoun his Vice-President. He was re-elected in 1832, defeating Henry Clay, the year he sent a response proclamation to the Congress about South Carolina's nullification, which South Carolina sensibly rescinded in 1833.

In his annual message to Congress in 1835 Jackson, himself a slave-owner, recommended prohibiting the circulation of abolitionist literature through southern mails, a clear violation of constitutional free speech. His support of slavery and his orders to remove Native Americans (*Indian Removal Act of 1830*) from their ancestral lands, contrary to a U.S. Supreme Court decision, make him a contemptible symbol of presidential politics. In fairness to his support of the policy, one major issue was whether Indians would agree to abide by the laws of the state they inhabited, and many did not agree. His strong advocacy for the Union, especially during the nullification controversy, even though he was at heart a southerner, is one of his finer accomplishments.

When the U.S. bank charter was up for renewal the controversy flared anew between federalists and states rights advocates, or between the North and South.

The U.S. Bank and States Rights

The United States Bank Act of 1816 was a symbol of national unity after the end of the War of 1812 with England. As Secretary of the Treasury during Washington's presidency, Alexander Hamilton proposed a national bank in 1791. Secretary of State Thomas Jefferson, a states rights man before the term became popular, opposed the idea because it was not a power explicit in the Constitution. Hamilton's argument was that it was implied under the "necessary and proper" clause in Article I. Washington backed the idea and the Bank of England chartered it. Two-thirds of deposits were owned by British interests until 1811 just as the U.S. was preparing to go to war with England.

After the war of 1812 America had a strong tendency to charter its own national financial affairs and put aside its sectarian sentiments. The importance of this chartering of a second U.S. bank is that the House Committee that proposed it, and the votes that created it, were essentially southern representatives led by John Calhoun and endorsed by Madison. The U.S. Supreme Court ruled in *McCulloch v Maryland* (1819) that when the state tried to tax the federal bank because it believed that a U.S. bank was unconstitutional.

The U.S. Supreme Court ruled that the Constitution had "implied powers." Jefferson was furious at Chief Justice John Marshall, his distant cousin, for this ruling.

These same southern representatives refused to renew the charter of the first U.S. bank in 1811, but that was prior to the war with England. States thought that a federal bank would be in competition with state banks. The difference was that a federal bank could raise funds to fund national military operations in time of war, as states could not. Moreover, the government bank refused to accept the deposits from states that did not redeem their bills in specie (approved coin and not paper) on demand. Because the bank used its congressionally authorized power to force state banks to use specie payment, the bank became unpopular and its centralized monopoly became fuel for states rights proponents.

In 1818 Ohio and Maryland laid a tax on branches of the bank in their states. The U.S. Supreme Court in *McCulloch v Maryland* ruled in 1819 that the act of Congress creating the bank was constitutional and that states laws attempting to tax it were unconstitutional. This was the first major defeat of the states rights grievances.

Jackson returned to the idea of letting banks operate only in the states by proposing a federal bank as a branch of the Treasury Department and could not issue notes, make loans or purchase property. It was a clever proposal around the McCulloch decision, as this bank did not need a charter since there would be no shareholders, debtors, or holding of any property. The bank would only manage government funds. This presidential proposal would leave all regular banking within states. Jackson vetoed Congress' act to re-charter the bank and used the popular idea of the bank as a government monopoly as a political platform for re-election in 1834.

Jackson withdrew all the federal deposits from the national bank and placed them in state banks, which almost immediately began extending loans to speculators that in turn caused the financial panic of 1837. Jackson's aim was the same of Jefferson: to take the government out of state-controlled monopolies and let states control domestic affairs.

Doesn't this historical financial act have a contemporary ring tone? During years of government de-regulation of financial institutions, beginning with the Reagan Administration and the Savings and Loan scandal in 1989, politicians have allowed banks and other financial entities to operate with almost unlimited freedom speculating with the public's money as did state banks under Jackson. [2] Beginning at the turn of the millennium, banks, searching for more profits, created hundreds of billions of dollars in high-risk, poor quality mortgages that ultimately plummeted in value, causing huge losses to investors and endangering the whole financial system. [3]

The fundamental fear driving all political and social thinking in South Carolina during Jackson's Administration and thereafter was the threat of a slave revolt. Everything was motivated to maintain slaves and by extension the labor force of the plantation economy. When black sailors under international treaties were allowed to leave their ships docked in Charlestown harbor to visit other blacks in 1822, it was believed that they had conspired in a plot to help slaves revolt. This terrified South Carolinians that then began jailing all sailors who came ashore. The Supreme Court ruled the action unconstitutional. South Carolina ignored the court order. A slave revolt, real or perceived, was paramount to all laws and government actions.

After the elections of 2010 many state legislatures began passing laws that restricted federal laws, such as in immigration, and asserted the predominance of state law over federal law. This one governance issue of which authority should prevail has been perpetuated into the 21st century. State law never prevails over federal law and its continuing presumptive use by states and state legislatures is legally unjustifiable but does pander to popular prejudices. It is an integral part of the anti-government movement and its political advocates pander to the public's ignorance of the long-term legal standing to gain electoral advantage.

When a congressional tariff law in 1832 raised the taxes for the whole country to benefit the manufacturing sector located mostly in the northern states, South Carolina again considered secession. The protection of the lifestyle provided by slavery was more imperative than union with the federal government. The nullification issue would dominate the Jackson presidency as the closest the Union came to dismemberment before the Civil War. For Jackson the unity of the republic was more important than the insolence of the South. Although a slave owner himself—owning about 150 slaves—he had no qualms about slavery. But he did see secession as a threat to democratic unity and the Constitution, and brought all his energies and authority to bear to defeat the secession threat that began in 1830.

Jackson's *Nullification Proclamation* on Monday, December 10, 1832 is a landmark study in his presidency and an enduring American legacy of executive authority. It occurred because of South Carolina's imminent threat of secession instigated by Vice President John Calhoun and 32 years prior to the inevitable civil war.

John Calhoun (1782-1850): States Rights and Nullification

Northerners were nationalists, antislavery and pro-tariff. Southerners were anti-tariff, proslavery, and very much for states rights—rallying cries for an anti-government fixation. Bank disputes and tariff issues were politically resolvable. Slavery was a rock that could not be moved.

Ever since the 1840s protests from the radical conservative right and some militia groups clustered primarily around three issues:

1) Limited federal government and assertion of the rights of states
2) No submission to any federal legislation that seeks to limit gun control
   or other limitations on liberties, such as asserting religion into
   public affairs
3) When all else fails, be prepared to start a revolution and to rebel

The theme of this book is that history repeats itself, and these social forces that prevail today among some radical conservative members are the same that precipitated the nullification of South Carolina beginning in 1828. The linchpin of the southern strategy then and now is the obstruction of majority government rule. The claims of states rights, suppression of minority voting, control of congressional committee chairs, and the filibuster are the tools of resistance.

John Calhoun (1782-1850) emerged politically active in the 1820s at a time when Alexis de Tocqueville was planning to journey to America and write his two-volume *Democracy in America*, the best book on America and democracy ever penned. In so many ways, Calhoun's political lifetime is still evident in America today, when the pursuit of wealth was paramount, and local governments, states and the national government were competing for how to govern a restless, highly individualistic citizenry whose industrialists incessantly lobbied representatives for laws favorable to their interests.

John Calhoun was alternately a member of the House of Representatives, Secretary of War under President Monroe, and Vice President of the United States under John Quincy Adams, and later under Andrew Jackson with whom he founded the Democratic Party. Jackson once mused that he was sorry he never had Calhoun hanged. And this comes from a man who killed in duels and had others hanged on his military orders. Calhoun resigned as Jackson's Secretary of State in 1832 because of the nullification affair. Calhoun was then elected Senator, served as Secretary of State under President Tyler, and re-elected Senator.

Here's the setting of South Carolina's nullification of an Act of Congress. Tariffs were a form of tax on exported goods. But federal tariffs revealed the growing distinction between the economies of the North and South as much as the differences between federal and state powers. At the beginning of the 19th century Thomas Jefferson was convinced that it was necessary that America invest in manufacturing and industries and that federal capital be used to increase productivity in commercial enterprises. Once established or organized, commercial groups petitioned the government for protection from duties, and for no taxes on raw materials or finished products. Democracy accelerated this move to entrepreneurship, limited imports for the same goods by creating new industries that in turn created new social movements and a vibrant mercantile class in northern states. New social classes emerged in the North among factory workers, merchants, business owners, each creating new levels of economic prosperity.

Southern states were still anchored in agriculture, chiefly tobacco, rice, indigo, sugar cane and cotton. Social class divisions were static in the South, where, with few exceptions, there were only plantation owners, a semi-aristocratic collection of agriculturalists who thought alike for the most part, and whose day laborers were exclusively slaves, non-citizens, non-voters whose opinions were never solicited. Whites without property were tradesmen, shop owners or day laborers.

Alexander Hamilton saw that manufacturing industries could not survive without government encouragement and subsidies. This meant that tariffs on imported goods were necessary for a manufacturing economy. The problem was that tariffs hurt the economy of the South more because they relied more on imported goods. A higher tariff lessened the pocketbooks of the South as added transportation costs of goods from the North cost the consumer more. Adjusting the tariff rate so as to protect the manufacturer had to be balanced by not antagonizing clients elsewhere. Tariffs on cotton coming from the South to woolen plants in Boston and New York were especially problematic. Calhoun had argued in Congress in 1816 that a strong economy was essential for national defense, especially if America had to fight the British again, though economic wars are as difficult to win as military ones.

Northern manufacturers wanted tax relief for businesses. Southerners, with their semi-feudal economy and slave labor, and without convertible currency, wanted no tariffs that would primarily benefit northerners. The country was divided, not just by slavery but by a rising manufacturing sector in the north, and by comparison with an institutionalized and non-innovative crop plantation economy in the South. Southerners could not seek refuge in the expansive West without abandoning their slaves. Tariffs, the great economic issue of the age, it was believed, would further impoverish the South. But the real question was the South's attempt at emancipation from national government control and the fear of slave revolts. The tariff issue was a pretext for flaunting government interference. Slavery was always the real issue. But taxation became the principal means of opposing the North. [4]

If the southern states could not outvote the tariff advocates in Congress they would deny the right of Congress to legislate at all on the issue. That has been the argument of states rights' proponents since the days of the *Alien and Sedition Acts* of 1798 that were later deemed unconstitutional, and still is the nullification argument today. States rights' advocates had no sound legal or meritorious political arguments so they relied on strong emotional tendencies within states and an omnipresent popular resentment against national legislative power. The concept of state sovereignty has migrated all over the country.

Calhoun was one of the most respected members of the House of Representatives. But the tariff issue caused him to look again to the Constitution for answers. Arguing from the relevance of national defense and security, a common argument in contemporary political theater, he proposed that a national transportation system of canals and roads was in the best commercial and industrial interests. His reasoning is that it was justified by the commerce clause and the general welfare provision. Having successfully argued for the passage of such a bill, he learned to his surprise that President Madison planned to veto it. Madison, of all politicians understood well the merits of the U.S. Constitution, argued that it was not exclusively enumerated in Article 1, Section 8. Today, this key liberal interpretation, so widely accepted today, was rejected by Madison, the father of the Constitution, in his veto on March 3, 1816, his last day in office, yet ardently advocated by Calhoun, a South Carolinian.

The central question then was how to reconcile vastly different and competing social and economic interests sections of the country without tearing the fabric of the whole union. Calhoun's extensive readings in political economy allowed him conclude that the sovereignty of the states would be a formidable refuge from federal domination and a political protector of southern interests. John Quincy Adams had claimed, in a Fourth of July speech in Quincy in 1831 (the same day that James Monroe died, as had both his father and Jefferson on the same day, July 4, 1826), that nullification of an Act of Congress or the notion of the sovereignty of the states was a hallucination and that it would led to war between the states. [5] The South Carolina nullification occurred on November 24, 1832.

> We, therefore, the people of the State of South Carolina, in Convention assembled, do declare and ordain . . . that the several acts and parts of the acts of the Congress of the United States . . . are unauthorized by the Constitution of the United States and violate the true meaning and intent thereof, and are null, void, and no law, nor binding upon this State . . . [6]

The resolution was signed by 136 delegates. The supreme irony is that while these delegates and the White citizens they represented extolled democracy and the foundational principles of active participation in governance, less than half of South Carolina's people were able to be counted as anything except chattel, and unable to vote even in matters of their own destiny. By 1842 the President, then John Tyler, the President of the Senate, the Speaker of the House, the Chief Justice of the Supreme Court and four of its nine judges were all slave-owners. For slave-owners, democracy meant the mockery of representation by White property owners exclusively.

Oddly, at the end of the resolution was noted that it was signed in the 57th year of the *Declaration of Independence*, a declaration approved by the Continental Congress. It made no mention of the *U.S. Constitution*, even though the former document has its basis in a colonial government that no longer existed, and the latter was ratified by a majority of the states and was then, and remains now, the legal authority binding the states to a national government.

A similar South Carolina Ordinance on March 15, 1833 noted "the fifty-seventh year of the Sovereignty and Independence of the of the United States of America." The *Declaration of Independence* would have been meaningless had America lost the war with England.

Colonies preceded the formation of state governments that did not exist until independence from Britain. But once they bound themselves together under the *Articles of Confederation* they all declared themselves to be a nation and not a loose group of sovereign states. Moreover, the Constitution made clear it was "the supreme law" of the land. Hence no statute supported even unanimously in a state or commonwealth could prevent the execution of laws passed by Congress. Any resistance implied rebellion, as it certainly would in 1860.

Until the 1790s states had their own laws, constitutions, state citizens, currency and unique systems of governing, and usually their own predominant Christian denominations. The South was different from the North because the region had a greater bond with the land and the slave labor that planted and harvested its crops. Because the land and its imported labor constituted nearly the whole economy, the South was unable to develop the manufacturing innovations emerging in northern locales because of the Industrial Revolution.

Its resentment of the North was over constitutional governance and the difference in economies, of which taxation in the form of tariffs that benefitted northern industries appeared as the most odious.

Equally beguiling was why South Carolina did not petition the U.S. Supreme Court, the judicial arbiter under the U.S. Constitution, for a legal interpretation of the tariff law. On the face of it, it would appear that the state and its delegates were waiting for an excuse to disqualify themselves from the Union. To rid themselves of abolitionists and criticism about slavery was the only recourse as dissolution appeared inevitable. A few keen minds in the 1830s predicted war. It would take another generation for the predictable conflict to become real.

In his reply to South Carolina on December 10, 1832, President Andrew Jackson proclaimed, as was his sworn duty, among other considerations, how inane and legally stupid South Carolina's ordinance was:

> This Ordinance is founded, not on the indefensible right of resisting acts which are plainly unconstitutional, and too oppressive to be endured, but on the strange position that any one State may not only declare an act of Congress void, but prohibit its execution . . . that the true construction of that instrument permits a State to retain its place in the Union and yet be bound by no other of its laws than those it may choose to consider as constitutional. [7]

A series of state resolutions quickly followed offering solidarity to Jackson's response to South Carolina, pointing out the unconstitutionality of its proclamation. Southern states like Alabama believed the congressional act to be "unjust, oppressive, and against the spirit and true meaning of the Constitution," but also declared that nullification was not a sound remedy and would lead to revolution and "anarchy and civil discord," which, in fact, it did 28 years later. [8] There was talk and resolves in southern state responses of a southern convention to resolve the issue, and what were perceived to be missteps of authority by Congress.

South Carolina ordered a day of "solemn fasting, humiliation and prayer" for January 31st, 1833. There is no record of how many actually participated in these exercises. But continuing in convention, delegates resolved on March 15, 1833 that "should odious discriminations be instituted for the purpose of continuing in force the protective principle, South Carolina will feel herself free to resist such a violation of what she conceives to be the good faith of the Act of 2nd March, 1833, by the imposition of her sovereignty, or in any other mode she may deem proper." [9]

Calhoun asserted in his book-length, two-part *A Disquisition and a Discourse on the Constitution and Government of the United States*, a laborious work advocating for states rights, that he was merely reiterating constitutional principles and not projecting his own point of view. [10] His argument in South Carolina was so persuasive that Nathaniel Gist named his seventh son States Rights Gist. [11]

Calhoun's argument, like many in contemporary states rights movements, is strictly constructivist that is, examining just the document of the Constitution.

He does not address any laws of Congress or U.S. Supreme Court decisions, most notably *Marbury v. Madison* (1803) on judicial review, *United States v. Peters* (1809) on federal supremacy, and *McCulloch v. Maryland* (1819) on implied powers, all judicial rulings Calhoun would have known. Calhoun's doctrine, first published in 1831, gave impetus to South Carolina's declaration that Congress was usurping constitutional powers.

Calhoun denied there is a national government, only a federal government of all states.[12] Delegates from states in Philadelphia 1787 did create the Constitution not to be a legal partnership between themselves—that is what the *Articles of Confederation* were—but to be a new national government that assumed powers they neither individually nor collectively possessed. Calhoun's deceptive argument survives today as if it were constitutionally sound.

"By the imposition of her sovereignty" is a phrase that today has reverberations but for which no constitutional basis exists. Prior to 1791 the first colonies were ruled by Britain and supervised by British governors. Under the Constitution they were provincial authorities under the national government, and even those powers were distributed through three branches of government. The South Carolina Ordinance of March 18, 1833 repeated the nullification but then declared that not only was the Act of Congress "unauthorized" but was "subversive" of the Constitution, and therefore it was "null and void within the limits of this State." Advocates for states rights never quote Article VI, Number 2 of the Constitution.

> This Constitution, and the laws of the United States which shall be made in pursuance thereof . . . shall be the supreme law of the land, and the Judges in every State shall be bound thereby, anything in the Constitution or laws of any State to the contrary notwithstanding.

South Carolina thought it proper not only to declare a federal law nullified but to demand that every citizen of the state take an oath of allegiance to the state, and then insolently to prohibit anyone from taking an oath of allegiance to the United States, or by implication, any other state in which they could have had a dual residence, and to provide suitable state penalties for so doing. State sovereignty apparently has prerogatives that include vitiating the laws of a nation and, like kings or popes, demanding that citizens acknowledge its illegalities by pledging allegiance to it alone. America history knows no more blatant episode of legal arrogance and despotism, and in the end, treason.

South Carolina and its sympathizers throughout the South preached a cant of devotion to the union while from within separate state asylums challenging the constitutional bond that held them together by threats of cutting and running.

Daniel Webster, Henry Clay and John Calhoun, the triumvirate of 19th century rhetorical and political oratory, harangued the Senate in the early weeks of 1833 trying to influence a compromise to the tariff imposition and South Carolina's nullification. President Andrew Jackson was determined to preserve the Union and had ordered army and naval personnel into place, to use military force if necessary to restore a rebellious state to the Union. The *Force Bill* of 1833 on the imposition of revenues or duties collected on imports, with a compromise proposed by Henry Clay, passed the Senate on March 2, 1833, approved by a vote of 32 to 1. The lone dissenting vote was cast by then Senator, later President John Tyler of Virginia. [13]

South Carolina encouraged the state legislature to adopt legal measures to prevent federal enforcement and to penalize those who acted against the state law preventing it. But it went further still: "That the allegiance of the citizens of this State, while they continue as such, is due to the said State: and that obedience only, and not allegiance is due by them to any other power or authority . . ." This state allegiance was to be subscribed to by the provision of various "oaths or affirmations, binding them to the observance of such allegiance, and abjuring all other allegiance . . ." [14]

After Lincoln's election in December 1860, a special convention met in South Carolina and resolved unanimously to secede. Within weeks, Mississippi, Florida, George, Alabama, Louisiana and Texas followed. In February 1861 in Montgomery, Alabama a confederate Congress adopted a provisional constitution and elected Jefferson Davis, former congressman, senator and Secretary of War under Franklin Pierce, its new president.

> Our new government (the confederacy), its foundations are laid . . . upon the great truth that the negro is not equal to the white man, that slavery—subordination to the superior race—is his natural and normal condition. This our government is the first in the history of the world based upon this great physical, philosophical and moral truth. [15]

By 1864 over 200,000 of these so-called inferiors were fighting for the North, over 80% of them recruited from slave states. More importantly, the document clearly stated what later writers who glorified the South were unable to do: that White supremacy was the foundation of secession.

Contemporary parallels abound. By 2010 South Carolina gubernatorial candidates were equally finding fault of the national government for all state problems. The Attorney General, Henry McMaster in 2010 sued to stop the government from bringing health reform into the state. He attributed the failures in the school system to teachers too busy filling out federal forms they can't teach. According to South Carolina the national government even today is the culprit and source of state problems.

There are multiple examples of states claiming some power over the U.S. Supreme Court and Congress. In 2011 Arizona sued the government to void state participation in *The Voting Rights Act* (1965) because the state is required to get approval for changing election rules and maps. Arizona claimed the law was unconstitutional. Apparently state officials forgot or never knew that *The Voting Rights Act* is simply an extension of the 15th Amendment to the Constitution that grants everyone the right to vote. But once again, conservative southern states act as they did in the South in 1838 to challenge the constitutionality of Congress passing legislation on hard-won but now constitutionally established citizen rights. [16]

Abolitionists

> Congress shall make no law . . . abridging the freedom of speech, or of the press. (U.S. Constitution, Amendment I)

Between 1830 and 1860 northern abolitionists actively campaigned against slavery, promoting the ideas of universal liberty and the principles of human rights embedded in the *Declaration of Independence*. Just as zealously, southerners denied freedom of speech and the press to northern abolitionists who sought to plead their case in the South.

One controversy began in 1835 when abolitionists took advantage of government's distribution of mail through the postal service to send literature against slavery throughout the South. Southerners thought they had a legal right, again to protect slavery, by preventing the distribution of incendiary literature in their communities. On the night of July 29, 1835 a mob broke into the post office in Charleston South Carolina, located a sack of abolitionist literature and burned its contents. On that night southerners incinerated freedom of the press and freedom of speech.

A series of communications passed from the acquiescence of the South Carolina postmaster in agreement with the local community, to the New York postmaster, where the literature originated, asking that no such literature be sent to South Carolina. The Postmaster General entered the discussion immediately and replied that the government had no power to curtail the mail or censor the contents. Had he stopped at this point he was perfectly legal. But in his message he went further and declared that postmasters owned an obligation to the communities where they lived too. This was clearly another compromise to slavery proponents, appearing to relinquish the government's power to permit freedom of the press. An abuse of the mails had clashed with freedom of the press, and again because of the ruse of inciting slaves to insurrection.

President Jackson in his 1835 message to Congress denounced the abolitionists because they were agitating a war. He recommended Congress pass a law prohibiting such literature through the mail inciting slaves to revolt, obviously recommending something that was unconstitutional.

Calhoun argued that only the states could make such laws, not Congress. He recommended that such literature be retained in the post offices, the offensive material burned, and that local authorities not prosecute postal officials. Henry Clay objected that this proposal assumed that the laws of the states prevailed over that of Congress. The Senate rejected Calhoun's proposal.

The result was that the Abolitionists formed a political party. The South was placed on notice that the North was determined to attack slavery, not just wearily acknowledge its existence. There was also a new sense of social defense against the status of slavery. Local communities, and not just slave-owners, grew more jealous of their peculiar class differences and initiated more vigilant police safeguards against runaway slaves and non-official military exercises. The South realized that only the addition of new slave states would keep its congressional balance safe. Southern eyes turned toward Texas that, by 1836, had won its independence from Mexico in the Battle of San Jacinto under Sam Houston and declared itself an independent republic.

The proposed admission of Texas into the Union caused the same kind of apoplexy the Missouri Compromise did, as we shall see in the following chapter.

Andrew Jackson Statue in Jackson, Mississippi

Chapter Eight
Presidents Tyler and Polk

John Tyler (1790–1862): President and Traitor

> Treason against the United States shall consist in levying war against them, or
> in adhering to their enemies, giving them aid and comfort. (Article III, 3,1)

John Tyler was the Tenth President of the United States, a Virginia slave owner and planter, fervid advocate of states rights, and in his final days a member of the Confederate House of Representatives. He had been a President who betrayed his oath of office to join a secessionist state and pledge allegiance to another government. Like so many in the South, he did not view the Confederacy as an enemy of constitutional government. Yet southern states and their sympathizers had been so socially and culturally removed from northern free states for so many decades forming a secessionist government did not appear to be treasonous. Tyler's two primary governance goals in life were the absolute advocacy of states rights and the limitation of the national government, especially over the creation of a national bank.

From Tyler's era onward, taxes and tariffs, together with the so-called rights of states, were one of the primary issues separating the North from the South. Taxes were complicated who could issue bank notes and lines of credit. The Constitution gave the national government control over the regulation of currency, and forbade states from issuing bills of credit. States rights' advocates like Tyler did not want the national government to infringe in any way on state power. On the other hand, as states increased bank notes without the collateral to redeem them, the federal government was losing control over the national currency, and this in turn meant that people in different sections of the country were taxed unevenly because the value of currency was uneven. [1]

Unregulated banking ventures, a feature of radical Republican initiatives and those who believed that federal government was too intrusive, led to the failure of banks, credit and public funds like pensions in 2006.

Tyler was a member of the Whig Party, a political party formed in 1834 in reaction to authoritarian President, Andrew Jackson, whose members had labeled him with tyrannical actions. Its most notable members, after Harrison and Tyler who were elected President and Vice-President in 1840, were Henry Clay and Daniel Webster who became instrumental in creating compromises between North and South over slavery issues. By 1852 the party split its affiliation because of slavery into northerners, who became Republicans, and southerners, who enlisted as Democrats. The party names have since been reversed, primarily after the civil rights legislation in the mid-1960s.

Those who heard Tyler speak, like a reporter who commented on one of his speeches while Tyler was running for Vice President with William Henry Harrison in 1840, said that he was "a graceful, easy speaker . . . but that there was nothing forcible or striking in his speech; no bright thoughts, no well-turned expressions; nothing that left an impression on the mind from its strength and beauty . . ." [2] This sounds as if it could have been any political speech in any age. Those who knew him agreed he was cordial but not charismatic.

As a five-term member of the Virginia House of Delegates Tyler believed that because the U.S. senators had not voted according to the Virginia House wishes that they should no longer be considered senators because of their defiance of the state, and accordingly offered resolutions to that effect in the Virginia House. The Virginia House of Delegates in 1810 had instructed its two senators to vote against a re-charter of the Bank of the United States believing it to be unconstitutional. Contrary to these instructions, the Virginia senators voted in favor. It is hard to conceive how this effected Tyler's belief in the voting franchise, or in the concept of representative democracy. Tyler later voted to suspend a reading of an address proposed by one of the senators in the Virginia House, a vote sensibly voted down by a majority of delegates. But Tyler's irritant vote meant that he was not even willing to grant due process in a state chamber to a hearing for an elected U.S. senator.

Tyler was elected to the U.S House of Representatives in 1816, narrowly beating out his opponent, the former Speaker of the House of Delegates. He was only 26 years old.

Tyler did not run for re-election in Congress in 1821, undoubtedly in order to earn money for his growing family. He did, however, allow himself to be elected to the Virginia House of Delegates in 1823, and in 1825 to the governorship. At the time Virginia's constitution dated from 1776 when the commonwealth was still wary of British governors and so had several restrictions on the executive. The Virginia Governor, elected for only a one-year term, was an honored position without much power. His one principal act was presiding over the ceremonies following the death of Thomas Jefferson—also at one time Virginia Governor—on July 4, 1826, the same day both Jefferson and John Adams died. Tyler was elected to the U.S. Senate in 1827 defeating John Randolph the existing Senator. [3]

As senator he was consistently opposed to any internal national domestic improvements, including the extension of roads or canals. So nearly two hundred years ago southern presidents and politicians were opposed to the national government engaged in promoting infrastructure developments or improvements, just as they were in the third millennium in disfavoring the government's proposals to reform health care. Tyler also objected to appropriating funds for survivors of the Revolutionary War. But in a speech directed against what he perceived were the dangers of nationalism he said: "I have no such word [national] in my political vocabulary. A nation of twenty-four nations is an idea which I cannot realize. A confederacy may embrace many nations; but by what process twenty-four can be converted into one, I am still to learn." [4] Southerners constantly used the "confederacy" and not "union," the word used in the *U.S. Constitution*.

Literally, he was correct: the word "nation" does not occur in the *U.S. Constitution*, though the phrase in the preamble, "to form a more perfect union," suggests a national identity, as does the idea that *The Articles of Confederation*, a document within memory of many of his political colleagues who had lived under it, sought to make that partnership agreement between the states a "union that shall be perpetual."

Advocates of states rights believe that the U.S. Constitution is merely an extension of *The Articles of Confederation* and not the defining and transformative document creating a government superior to the states. Indeed, the sovereignty of the states did exist from colonial times, from 1776 until 1791, but not afterward. As colonies, sovereignty still existed in the sovereign, the king, and not in the colonial governments. Tyler's speech delivered in the Senate on February 6, 1833 attests to his misconstrued belief.

> Do all things necessary to give renewed life and vitality to the confederation of these states, but do not change the articles of our copartnership [sic}. Let us have no monarchical or national Government . . . The attempt is now made to do that very thing that was scouted out of the convention—to convert this Government into a consolidated national Government—from a league among states, which its terms imports, into the Government of a single nation . . . The Government is but a superstructure erected upon the old confederacy . . . The Government was created by the States, is amenable by the States, is preserved by the States, and may be destroyed by the States . . . [5]

Clearly, Tyler saw the Constitution as an improvement on *The Articles of Confederation*, a legal partnership constructed by the States but not in any way limiting their sovereignty or imposing a new one on it. This was not just a lack of trust in government that occurs in the body politic from time to time but a totally different perspective from what the Constitution authorized.

In his Vice-Presidential speech, reported in the Washington DC national newspaper *National Intelligencer* on March 5, 1841, Tyler reaffirmed his adherence to the doctrine of states rights. Harrison's long speech and the importunities of his new office (he was then 68 yeas old) obviously took its toll. Harrison contracted pneumonia shortly after his March inauguration and died on April 4, 1841. Meanwhile Tyler, then 51, had left Washington for his home in Williamsburg thinking he would spend the next four years in quiet contemplation. Since no president until then had died in office it wasn't clear from the Constitution whether the Vice President would assume the office of the presidency or just the "duties and responsibilities." Was he the Acting President, as John Quincy Adams claimed, until the election of a new one, or the new *de facto* President? A House resolution solidified Tyler's interpretation that he was the actual President. He was then 51, the youngest to become President until John F. Kennedy.

Tyler wanted to annex Texas in 1841. A plebiscite of Texans gave a majority in favor of annexation in 1836 but was rebuffed by the Administration of Martin Van Buren because it would have to be admitted as a slave state and, many feared, that would instigate a war with Mexico. As a slave owner himself, Tyler did not see this as a problem, but his brilliant Secretary of State from New Hampshire, Daniel Webster, did. Mexico had said it would declare war if the U.S. annexed Texas. [6]

In the midst of this dilemma, Tyler's first wife, Letitia Christian, died on September 10, 1842 leaving him with seven children. Within five months while President, then aged 52, he courted the socialite from New York Julia Gardiner, then 22, younger than some of his children. Julia initially refused his proposal, but they would marry two years later and she would bear him five more children, the last of them, Pearl, living to 1947. Two of the oldest girls never did reconcile with their new stepmother.

What To Do With Texas?

No one in Texas really knew its boundaries. Several rivers competed for its definition. The Red River—today's boundary between Oklahoma and Texas—seemed reasonable. John Quincy Adams thought that the Sabine River, also flowing to the southeast, was the border. Others thought the Brazos River, just south of the Sabine, or the Colorado River that flows into the Gulf between Galveston and Corpus Christi, or even the Nueches River that flows into the Gulf at Corpus Christi were suitable candidates. As it was, Polk always thought the border was the Rio Grande, and his view prevailed.

The Jefferson Administration assumed that the Red River watershed, now the border between Texas and Oklahoma that drained into the Mississippi River, was a part of the natural boundaries of the Louisiana Purchase. Early settlers in this region further assumed that the land south was also a part of America. A treaty negotiated by then Secretary of State, John Quincy Adams, and the Spanish Minister to the U.S. in 1819 affirmed that the lands south of the Red River were Spanish. Spain controlled the territory until Mexico obtained its independence in 1821. In fact, the territory had never been surveyed or certified, and this presented no problem to anyone in this sparsely populated land.

The ultimate national border of the Rio Grande was not then a candidate for the frontier border with Mexico. That border only became established after the end of military actions in 1848. Andrew Jackson believed that Texas, however defined, was already a part of the Louisiana Purchase. Mexico claimed otherwise.

The settlement history is worth recalling. Moses Austin, born in Connecticut and living in Missouri, journeyed to Mexico where he presented himself as the leader of a group of Catholics who had been discriminated against in America and sought a tract of land for settlement. Mexicans gave him a large tract of land on the Colorado River, but he died before he could settle there. His son, Stephen F. Austin, with 300 families settled as a colony along the Brazos River in 1821, the same year Mexico became independent of Spain. Soon Stephen Austin sought the formation of a separate state, initially with the permission of the Mexican government, and when that failed as a revolutionary commander. A new constitution in Mexico failed to define the rights of citizens, including those in Texas. By this time many settlers were also importing slaves. Several armed skirmishes—Goliad, Concepcion, the Grass Fight, and Bexar—began in earnest in 1835.

Mexico after 1821 was eager to expand trade with the U.S. by allowing settlers in the southwest, and commercial traffic expanded through Santa Fe and beyond. But soon Mexico realized that he had erred in allowing so many settlers who were not Mexicans to live in their territory and not be citizens. These settlers were American frontier people who lived on Mexican land but did not consider themselves Mexican citizens or aligned in any way with Mexico. The massacre of the defenders of the Alamo in San Antonio in 1836 exposed the dilemma. But the rallying of more troops under Sam Houston, former Governor of Tennessee at the battle of a San Jacinto, and the capture of Santa Anna, the Mexican commander, sealed the independence of the Texans but not the political alignment with the United States.

Near present day Houston, where the San Jacinto River flows into Buffalo Bayou next to Galveston Bay, is the site of the Battle of San Jacinto. There on April 21, 1836, after the Texan defeat at the Battle of the Alamo, Texas revolutionary forces defeated the superior forces of the Mexican army. In a battle that lasted about 18 minutes, 750 Texas irregulars under Texan General Sam Houston attacked the Mexicans during afternoon siesta, as they failed to post sentries, and killed 630, losing only nine killed and 30 wounded. The Mexican General Santa Ana was captured the next day. This victory effectively ended the war between Texans and Mexicans, but not between the Mexican and U.S. military. Texas earned its independence from Mexico that spring day in 1836. A convention created the Republic of Texas in 1836. Its entry as a state into the Union, however, was to be another story.

Add to this uncertain mix the character of Sam Houston, a friend of Jackson, who had been Governor of Tennessee from 1827-29 but who left Tennessee after his young wife of only three months left him in tears under the cloud of unfaithfulness. Houston abruptly resigned the governorship and went incognito into Texas territory where his military and administrative career found fulfillment. President Jackson wanted neutrality for Texas because he wanted good relations with Mexico, and feared that Texas might be partitioned in yet smaller slave-holding states. The dual threats of war and disunity were enough to cause sleepless nights among chief executives and members of Congress. President Jackson did not annex Texas but did send a representative in 1837 to recognize the Republic of Texas.

By 1842 Mirabeau Buonaparte Lamar, who had succeeded Sam Houston as the President of the Republic of Texas, was amenable to annexation, and twice in that year offered to join the Union but was rebuffed. Tyler was in favor of adding another slave state but knew the Senate would refuse. Texas took a different political tack by courting England to aid in recognizing its independence. Once Daniel Webster retired, Tyler moved more aggressively to propose annexation. In an odd twist, it was felt that if England, which encouraged the abolition of slavery everywhere, had an agreement with Texas, its influence would end slavery in Texas, and that fugitive slaves would easily immigrate to Texas beginning an exodus of southern slaves.

Martin Van Buren, Jackson's successor, was not keen on recognizing Texas either. Texas requested admission into the Union, but Van Buren used the excuse that admitting Texas would violate a treaty with Mexico. The annexation of Texas was a central campaign issue in the presidential election year of 1844.

Tyler was in favor of annexation. Jackson in retirement in Tennessee had changed his mind about Texas, favoring its annexation. He was partial to Tyler, who in turn respected him greatly, and was also Polk's mentor, almost like a godfather to him. Polk won the presidential election in 1844 by a razor thing margin indicating even then how evenly the population was divided. [7] Southern states was solidly in favor of the annexation of Texas which helped propel Polk into the presidency, and, as many had predicted, into war with Mexico.

Commercial interests helped convince the North of the admission of Texas because trade would be increased. The South would feel more secure in its border and smuggling would be curtailed and it could rely on additional congressional votes for the extension and retention of slavery. If Texas was not admitted, Tyler believed and so noted to Congress, that it would look elsewhere for commercial and diplomatic alliances. Tyler's enemies saw him lining up another sectarian slave state in the Union. The Senate rejected the treaty. Tyler submitted a new resolution to the House for support. Texas was admitted in 1845 shortly after President Polk's inauguration.

Tyler was in retirement at his farm about 35 miles from Richmond but was prescient enough to see the portentous drift between the North and South. As soon as Lincoln's election was confirmed, all cotton states seceded. President Buchanan had urged restraint in his final message to Congress on December 3, 1860, but it was too late. In January 1861 the Virginia legislature passed join resolutions calling for a Peace Convention, and Tyler was named one of the commissioners.

As a member of the convention to resolve the problem of secession, Tyler met Lincoln on February 23, 1861 when Lincoln finally arrived in Washington, DC, the only time the Ex-President and President-Elect ever met. The contrasts could not have been more striking. Tyler was from a proud southern patrician family, schooled at the second oldest college in America (William and Mary), and a dignified and refined gentleman slave owner. Lincoln was from rural poverty, self-educated, a simple, natural, skeptical personality. Their meeting is symbolic of the transfer of patrician to plebian presidents so illustrative of a true democracy.

None of the seceded states sent delegates to the convention. Tyler argued that no arms be used to settle the dispute between the government and the States, though personally he was not sanguine about the outcome. Congress did not accept any of the commission's recommendations. Tyler returned to Virginia naively believing that if the southern states stood together armed conflict could be avoided. In the meantime, Virginia held its own convention. Tyler spoke at it and noted that if there was no hope for a settlement that Virginia should secede. It was surprising that the Union had held together half slave and half free as long as it had.

When the first southern states did secede, Lincoln called for 75,000 military volunteers and asked Virginia to send her quota. In response, on April 17, 1861 Virginia passed an ordinance of secession. In June Tyler was elected to the

Provisional Congress of the Confederacy, but he died the following January 19, 1862. The Confederacy honors him. But even as an ex-president the general opinion is that he was a traitor for violating his oath to uphold the Constitution.

Tyler had been both a respected and maligned man of his times, noted as much for his fecundity—fathering a total of 15 children—than for his political acumen, prized oratory, or the advancement of American progress. But what he lacked in political esteem he excelled in practical sense. He was a devoted family man and stood rock solid on his political principles for the Commonwealth, if not for the constitutional powers of national government.

Tyler knew, as did everyone in the South, that the plantation economy, built almost entirely around cotton and tobacco, could not sustain a protracted war with the manufacturing North and expanding western population. The South had virtually no economy without slavery. With slavery it had no chance at reconciliation with the North or the rest of civilized nations. Slavery was not just one among many factors for the Civil War. It was the central and decisive factor.

The rhetorical language and tired, inaccurate arguments used by southerners during the era of slavery in the U.S. are voiced today by anti-government and radical movements that seek to bring about a "revolution." They seek to end what they perceive is a form of tyranny that existed when the British ruled the colonies. But misinformation about constitutional principles, ignorance of American history, misguided sense of purpose, and over-reliance on worn-out slogans from the days of slavery to propel their cause has exposed the deep social rupture in American society that has been there since the beginning of colonial settlements.

Slavery is extinct. States' rights and the mindset that sustained slavery for so long in America are not.

James Polk (1795–1849)

James Polk was the eleventh president of the U.S. and the seventh slave-owning president. I make this comment about our past presidents because although personal business is normally one's own affair, in the case of owning slaves there is an inherent self-interest in protecting the institution of slavery and in others who own slaves. Though it was common practice in the South to own slaves and to defend slavery, it is a morally bankrupt business practice anywhere and at any time, and could not help but influence the policy initiatives of a slave owning president toward preservation of the custom.

Polk was born in North Carolina in 1795 and was an honors graduate of the University of North Carolina, an institution at the time with only one professor and a couple of tutors. He and his family moved to Tennessee where he served in the state legislature and was elected soon thereafter as a representative to Congress. He served as Speaker of the House from 1835-1839 and resigned to become Governor of Tennessee, a position he later lost twice in future elections.

He served a total of fourteen years in Congress, four as Speaker of he House. He was a vice presidential candidate in 1840 with presidential hopeful

Martin Van Buren while he was Governor of Tennessee. Van Buren and Polk were defeated in 1840 when General William Henry Harrison was elected with Tyler as his running mate, both from patrician families in Tidewater Virginia. But within a month of his inauguration, as noted above, Harrison died of pneumonia and John Tyler was president, the first to assume the duties on the death of a president while in office.

Polk's middle Tennessee neighbor and mentor throughout his political life was Andrew Jackson, whose political coattails he clung to, and who in turn furthered Polk's career ambitions. [8] Jackson lived in The Hermitage on the Cumberland River just outside Nashville, and Polk in middle Tennessee in Columbia on the Duck River about 50 miles south, though in retirement he moved to Nashville.

As Polk waited for Britain to make a proposal on letting the U.S. admit Oregon as a territory, he still had to deal with Mexico. Meanwhile, the House of Representatives had voted to establish a territorial government for Oregon but had added an amendment copying language from the *Northwest Ordinance of 1787* passed by the Continental Congress decreeing that: "neither slavery nor involuntary servitude shall exist in said territory."

David Wilmot of Pennsylvania decided that it would be a useful amendment to include with the funding request for admitting new territories obtained from a Mexican settlement. And so on August 8, 1846 Wilmot introduced an amendment to an appropriation bill that slavery be prohibited in any acquired territory. The amendment passed the House. Significantly, the vote spread was not between parties but between geographies. Northerners supported the amendment, while southerners, like Alexander Stephens, Robert Toombs and Howell Cobb, universally rejected it. Once again, slavery had entered into the admission of territories, not just within states, and totally consumed national attention. A filibuster did not allow the Senate to vote on the House measure that year.

A similar appropriations bill was introduced in 1847 for the negotiation of territory acquired from Mexico, and a similar amendment was passed in the House but the amendment was excluded from the Senate bill and thus failed. The election of 1848 highlighted the slavery issue and further divided North and South as the country expanded.

Polk had risked war with Britain by claiming all of the Oregon Territory. At the conclusion of the Mexican-American War in 1848, Mexico ceded New Mexico and California for $15 million and damages. But though Polk is remembered for extensively enlarging the boundaries of the country, he is less known for a southern interpretation laws that favored the states so they could retain slaves. His views on federal-state relations were clearly outlined in his Inaugural Address in 1845. "Each State is a complete sovereignty within the sphere of its reserved powers. The Government of the Union, acting within the sphere of its delegated authority, is also a complete sovereignty." How there could be competing sovereignties, as if there were two kings exercising absolute authority simultaneously, is not addressed and is logically and legally inconceivable. Moreover he had a misinformed opinion about the role and function of national government, as outlined in the Constitution. He said in his Inaugural Address on March 4, 1845:

> To the Government of the United States has been intrusted [sic] the exclusive management of our foreign affairs. Beyond that it wields a few general enumerated powers. It does not force reform on the States. It leaves individuals, over whom it casts its protecting influence, entirely free to improve their own condition by the legitimate exercise of all their mental and physical powers. It is a common protector . . . of every man who lives upon our soil, whether of native or foreign birth...

Two points are relevant from this quote. The first is that Polk, like so many strict constructivists, overlooks the role and function of the U.S. Supreme Court that exercises absolute legal authority over citizens, states, the President and Congress. So his statement about competing powers is not just between states and Congress, but between all other federal powers. But it's obvious that when he refers to "unfortunate collisions" that have "disturbed the harmony of our system and even threatened the perpetuity of our glorious Union," he is referring to sectarian quarrels over slavery.

But it is that final sentence, that the federal government's role is to protect "every man who lives upon our soil, whether of native or foreign birth," that is puzzling. Polk, as a slave owner, clearly did not have in mind slaves when he penned these words. Perhaps he didn't consider them "men." A similar statement in his address merits a dumbfounded expression: "Minorities have a right to appeal to the Constitution as a shield against such oppression." Or this: "All distinctions of birth or of rank have been abolished. All citizens, whether native or adopted, are placed upon terms of precise equality. All are entitled to equal rights and equal protection."

Slaves were not minorities to Polk, nor were they to most southern politicians, and did not count as citizens or worthy of equality under the law. But the irony is so thick that a President of the U.S. could even utter such a sentence at a time when slavery was the most controversial topic in the nation, one that emerged whenever a state petitioned to enter the Union.

As a southerner he would understandably espouse the traditional argumentative line of the South, first articulated most eloquently by John Calhoun, of states' rights and prerogatives and the limitations of national government not to interfere in state affairs, which meant hands off slavery.

Polk did expand enormously the territory of the U.S. through diplomacy, war and war reparations to Mexico. But he also is known as one who narrowly misconstrued the *U.S. Constitution* and the operation of the national government to favor the southern strategy of keeping the national government from infringing on slavery, the only domestic subject that truly separated the South from the North.

Jackson, Calhoun, Tyler and Polk, all slave owners, championed the cause of annexing Texas into the Union, and did not seek to interfere with its slavery, even if it meant war with Mexico, a decision many considered the doom of America. The curse everyone feared might come, a war to eradicate slavery, did not come for another fifteen years, and then not because of the admission of new states but because of the antipathy of southern states against a northern president, Lincoln, who would not tolerate even the admission of a new territory with slaves.

President Tyler actually made the decision to annex Texas into the Union as a state in the final hours of his presidency, but with the concurrence of Polk, the President-Elect. In his inaugural address, Polk defended the cause of slavery saying, "It is as source of deep regret that in some sections of our country misguided persons have occasionally indulged in schemes and agitations whose object is the destruction of domestic institutions existing in other sections—institutions which existed at the adoption of the Constitution and were recognized and protected by it." The plea to keep slavery as it had existed at the time of the *U.S. Constitution* was soon to be tested.

War with Mexico (1846–1848)

The Mexican-American War may be largely unknown and conveniently forgotten if known as a key event in American history. It is not so for the Mexicans, for whom the war was the beginning of suspicion and mistreatment at the hands of Americans. Mexico had barely gotten used to its independence from Spain in 1821 when it faced possible war with the U.S. over territorial encroachment and failure to resolve slavery that Spain and Mexico banned in 1810. The admission of slave states like Missouri and Texas was a political football in the early 19th century that would benefit the South in its control of the legislative agenda protecting slavery.

The war began because a group of American settlers in Texas, whose numbers exceeded that of Mexicans living in the territory in the mid-1830s, wanted to secede from Mexico. When American settlers outnumbered the Mexicans, Americans believed that the land belonged to them. Led by Sam Houston, a former Governor of Tennessee, they declared independence in 1836. Mexicans attacked Zachary Taylor's American army that had been sent to protect American settlers in 1846. Technically, Taylor's forces had invaded Mexico beyond the treaty boundaries near the Rio Grande River.

A treaty was signed during the Polk Administration April 12, 1844 that the Senate accepted and incorporated Texas into the Union. Tyler had sent army and naval forces to the area to protect Texas pending treaty negotiations. Polk kept that same military policy.

It is clear from diplomatic and personal correspondences of the day that Texas was admitted into the Union in order to keep it as a slave state. Mexico had legally abolished slavery and had never recognized the Republic of Texas. [9] Even John Quincy Adams argued that annexing Texas would result in a war with Mexico for the purposes of extending slavery into a territory that had been free. He also argued that Congress had no power to annex a free country into the Union.

Polk ordered General Stephen Kearny, Commander of the Armies of the West, out of Ft. Leavenworth to proceed immediately to Santa Fe and thence to

California to secure these southwest territories for the U.S. in advance of war with Mexico, and to hold them until peace had been concluded. Polk also ordered Kearny to enlist Mormon emigrants recently driven out of Missouri and make them a part of his command. Hence 543 Mormons were recruited from Council Bluffs, Iowa. Polk wanted them in the army rather than as an opposing army. The Mormon battalion is the only army unit recruited specifically because of religion. True, Mormons once wanted their own country of Deseret in the late 19th century with a stretch of territory from Utah to San Diego so Mormon missionaries would have an outlet to the sea. The Union had to squash that secessionist movement too.

Once mustered out of the army in 1847, most Mormons returned to Salt Lake City where Brigham Young had settled with his pioneers. In 1849 Brigham Young asked for territorial status carved out of former Mexican land that was to include what is today Utah, Nevada, New Mexico, Arizona and southern California. When New Mexico and California petitioned for entry as states, Young changed his mind and requested entry as a state because Mormons believed that non-Mormons would be appointed to positions of authority thereby diluting a Mormon theocracy. [10]

Brigadier General Zachary Taylor, a slave owner with farms in Kentucky and sugar plantations in Louisiana, later to become president, was under orders from Polk's War Department to hold the border at the Rio Grande River. When a Mexican patrol came upon an American scouting party and fired on them with ensuing casualties, Taylor had to engage and the war was on. Freshman congressman Abraham Lincoln from Illinois wanted facts. He wanted to know from Polk in 1847 if the spot where American blood was shed was on American soil. Lincoln was on firm legal grounds because only Congress can declare war, and Polk had not asked for permission from Congress when he invaded Mexico.

In one of those paradoxical twists of history, former comrades-in-arms and junior officers in the Mexican War, Lt. Ulysses Grant and George Meade, would later face Joseph Johnston, Lt. James Longstreet, Capt. P.G.T Beauregard, Capt. Robert E. Lee and Lt. Jefferson Davis as enemies in the Civil War. Jefferson Davis, an officer in the Mississippi Rifles, later Senator from Mississippi became President of the Confederacy. All the other former cadets at West Point were promoted to generals.

America invaded Mexico under the pretext of protecting American settlers in the territory of Texas though it was legally Mexican. Polk was criticized for starting a war that did not have congressional approval. The war lasted from 1846-48 with an American victory. *The Treaty of Guadalupe Hildalgo*, signed in a settlement just outside Mexico City, ceded much of the west to America including the states of Texas, New Mexico, Arizona, Utah, Nevada and California. The treaty was supposed to protect the rights of Mexicans now living in the U.S., but in practice speculators and new settlers stole much of the land.

As Jackson rejoiced in Texas being admitted, he penned a final letter to Polk. During that interval, Sam Houston was hurrying from Texas to see

Jackson at his Hermitage home outside Nashville. He arrived three hours after Jackson died. Polk had lost his friend and mentor.

General Zachary Taylor's victory over the Mexicans in Mexico City concluded the hostilities and the *Treaty of Guadalupe Hidalgo* ceded Texas and the lands of New Mexico and California to the United States aided with a requisition of $15 million dollars.

In the summer of 1848 Polk turned his attention to Oregon. The question of slavery in the territories arose again like a recurring nightmare. Polk, ever the conciliator, noted in his message to Congress on July 27, 1848 that he wanted America to maintain a proportional balance so that southern slave states would not lose equal representation. On July 27, 1848, the Senate passed the Clayton Compromise, a solution to the issue of slavery in the territories, essentially letting the courts decide the issue. In a Speech in Congress, also on July 27, 1848, Abraham Lincoln said: "Although volume upon volume is written to prove slavery a very good thing, we never hear of a man who wishes to take good of it by being slave himself."

The slavery issue arose again in 1848 at the end of the Mexican-American War when the Senate debated the inclusion of Oregon, California and New Mexico as territories in the Union. Provisional laws had already been passed in Oregon that prohibited slavery and Congress admitted Oregon as a non-slave state. But Congress deferred slavery in California and New Mexico until those territories had governments that would decide on the issue. Southerners like John Calhoun urged Polk to veto the Oregon admission on the grounds that any antislavery provisions were beyond the powers of Congress. California was admitted as a free state in 1850, but the territories of New Mexico and Utah were admitted without mentioning slavery, though it was clear to all that the high desert and mountainous terrain was not conducive to a slaveholding, plantation economy.

In his message to Congress on August 14, 1848, Polk transmitted his thoughts about the admission to Oregon as a territory as the subject of slavery had again emerged.

> But one such question can now be agitated in this country, and this may endanger our glorious Union, the source of our greatness and all our political blessings. This question is slavery. With the slaveholding States this does not embrace merely the rights of property, however valuable, but it ascends far higher, and involves the domestic peace and security of every family. . . I do not doubt that a similar adjustment of the questions which now agitate the public mind would produce the same happy results. If the legislation of Congress on the subject of the other Territories shall not be adopted in a spirit of conciliation and compromise, it is impossible that the country can be satisfied or that the most disastrous consequences shall fail to ensue.

On August 14, 1848 Congress created the Oregon Territory, an area that today includes Oregon, Washington, Idaho and parts of western Montana and Wyoming, leaving aside the question of slavery. [11]

After watching the inauguration of Zachary Taylor—after Washington, Jackson and Harrison, the fourth military general to be elected president, and who was to die 16 months later—Polk made a triumphal tour through the South, and, likely contacting cholera, came home to his unfinished house in Nashville and died June 15, 1847 only 53 years old.

Zachary Taylor won many military battles but won the presidency with southern support even though he had no platform or plan for governance. It is a political scheme still used by contemporary congressional candidates who hope that the force of their personalities without a national agenda, or with a consistent anti-government message, will win electoral favor. Taylor bested Henry Clay in the 1848 presidential election, helped by a concerted southern effort, because they thought they could manage Taylor better than Clay who had a more independent streak. [12]

Polk, on the other hand, was a diligent and effective administrator, almost a micro-manager of government affairs, who had a vision commensurate with America's frontier and expansionist tendencies. His territorial expansion, coupled with his wartime administration and political acumen, were extraordinary among presidents. He was of course a creature of his times, a southerner with all that implies in an age when slavery was tolerated and defended. He is more remembered for his uncanny abilities in a compromised era than for his slave holding actions. He wrote in his will that should he survive his wife it was his intention to free all his slaves. He did not survive her, and she did not die until 1891. Slaves everywhere were freed by the 13th Amendment in 1866.

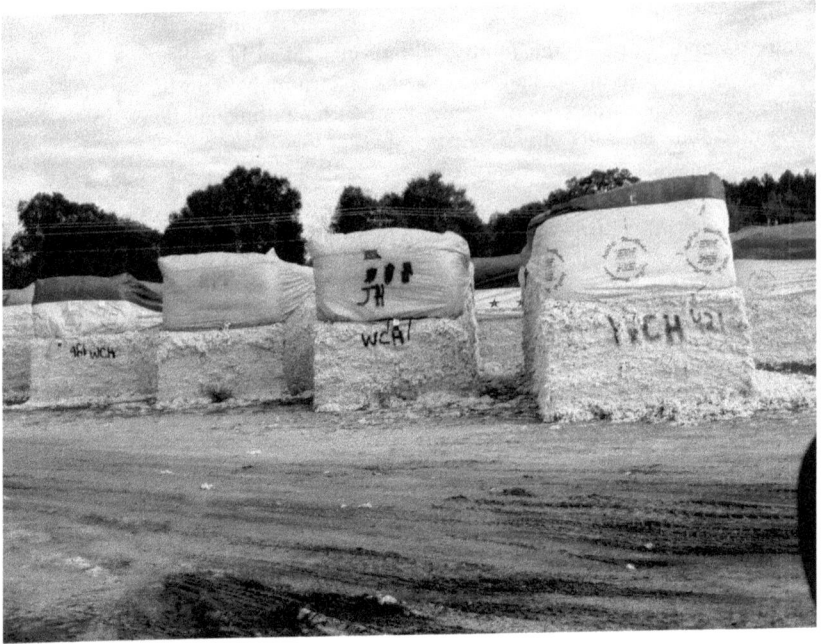

Cotton Bales in Rural Alabama

Chapter Nine
Slavery and Its Advocates

The natural liberty of man is to be free from any superior power on earth . . .
but to have only the law of nature for his rule . . . and not to be subject to the
inconstant, uncertain, unknown, arbitrary will of another man.

This is the perfect condition of slavery, which is nothing else, but the state of
war continued, between a lawful conqueror and a captive.
(John Locke, *Second Treatise on Government*)

Harry Washington escaped as a slave from Mount Vernon in 1776, the year
Jefferson wrote "that all men are created equal," who were said to have
"inalienable rights" to "life, liberty and the pursuit of happiness" in *The
Declaration of Independence*. Harry was the property of George Washington.
Like many other escaped slaves he tried to leave with the British, with whom he
would have been declared free, when they abandoned Boston. With about 1,500
hundred other escapees, he finally settled in Nova Scotia in 1783. But life there
was cold, harsh and unforgiving. Harry then journeyed to Sierra Leone where he
and other families were promised free land, which turned out to be a false
promise. Harry was elected chief of a rebel group just months after his former
owner died at Mount Vernon. [1] Harry was one of the fortunate ones to have
escaped slavery and not been recaptured, and from among one of the esteemed
national founders and the country's first president. America's legacy of slavery
and injustice began long before the Constitution.

John Locke (1632–1704), in the quotes above and throughout his *Second
Treatise on Government*, made clear that slavery constituted a state of war since
it violated the laws of nature and human freedom. The legal issue between the
Constitution and the states trumped the venomous nature of human enslavement
in America for over 250 years under the protected guise of property rights. The
niceties of political compromise were preserved because they were deemed
more important than human captivity.

To relate this history and political theory today, consider that the American
Third Position is the nation's newest political party, a white supremacist group
that advocates the deportation of anyone with any "ascertainable trace of Negro
blood." This of course would have included President Barak Obama, and maybe
that was the point. This thinking is unquestionably a legacy of southern slavery
and the bigotry accompanying it, and I don't believe it is localized to fringe
groups.

The history of slavery and its trade has been documented in a more
scholarly way elsewhere. But a short summary is instructive.

A Dutch ship brought African slaves to the first English settlers at
Jamestown. Virginia enacted a law that said that a child born to a slave mother
was also a slave. The Stono Rebellion in South Carolina in 1739, when over a
hundred slaves went on a rampage trying to reach Spanish territory and freedom,
rattled the slave-owners. The result was a law making it illegal for slaves to

learn to read and write, and legalized excessive punishments by owners. The North profited from the slave trade by, among other business activities, building ships for the slave trade.

There was a pyramidal structure to slave-owners. Many were small farmers who worked the farms themselves with from five to seven slaves. A larger group of middle class slave owners had 15-20 slaves. These were the descendants of wealthier families and they were better educated. The 3,000+ planters with 100 and more slaves were the aristocrats and owned hundreds of acres of land. [2] This last group of slave owners included Presidents George Washington, Thomas Jefferson, James Madison, Andrew Jackson, John Tyler, James Polk, and Zachary Taylor, who himself vehemently opposed secession but whose son served as a general in the Confederate army.

A typical wealthy economic base was Laura Plantation along the Mississippi about 50 miles north of New Orleans. The plantation began as a grant of land given to Guillaume DuParc, a French sailor wounded in the battle at Yorktown helping Washington's troops fight the British. Jefferson gave him a land grant for his services in 1804. His family managed the estate for another two hundred years. The unprecedented growth of the sugar cane industry led the family corporate business to expand into slave breeding. [3] In 1830 the family purchased 30 females to add to the existing slave workforce of 32 females and 60 males. It was more economical in the long run to propagate slaves than to purchase them, but this demeaned them further since they were bred like farm animals for coerced labor. The jobs creation bill in the South during this era was to breed humans.

But in Catholic Louisiana the church had more influence on the treatment of slaves than did civil authorities. The so-called *Code Noir* meant that Catholic slaves could not work on Sundays or religious holidays, and slave marriages could not be arranged by owners but had to be by choice.

By 1860 the Duparc family owned 960 acres of sugar cane and 1,134 acres of cypress forest tended by 183 slaves who lived in 69 cramped cabins. The plantation had 10 horses, 75 mules, 15 milk cows, 25 oxen, 80 sheep, 30 pigs and 30 beef cattle. That year it harvested 460,00 pounds of granulated sugar and 30,000 gallons of molasses. The plantation was self-sustaining, contributing to the national economy, a family corporate structure that ultra-Republicans today value as they do all corporations, while under-valuing government sponsorship of worker benefits and social programs.

The South's method of preventing revolt and organized rebellion among slaves was to deny education and learning and to prevent transmission of ideas. Secretly the government cooperated by not allowing even freed slaves to transmit the mail as such individuals could carry messages from community to community, and maybe even tell slaves that they had natural rights to freedom like Jefferson proclaimed in *The Declaration of Independence*. The maintenance of slavery in the South relied on the denial of human rights and constitutional privileges extended to other citizens.

The slave was robbed of liberty, promised by the founders as a fundamental condition for all. The White laboring man in the South was deprived by the slave system of the just rewards of his labor because he was in a context where a class of slaves worked without wages. America invited fugitives from other lands to its shores and feted them for their courage. But fugitives from its own land were hunted down with dogs, and legally arrested or shot. "The existence of slavery in this country," wrote Frederick Douglass, "brands your republicanism as a sham, your humanity as a base pretense, and your Christianity a lie." [4] Lincoln was a reluctant liberator of slavery and an even more reluctant conciliator in agreeing to racial equality and Douglass was. Their personal relationship tells us much about our current dilemma illustrated in our political fractiousness. The nation still flinches from the truth of our historical racial reality.

The ideological differences between the two regions of the country about the time of the Civil War were based on economic interests and widening social class differences. The South was an aristocracy built on slavery, and on limiting the powers of the federal government that might infringe on its fragile economy and unconscionable social and labor distinctions. The North was mercantile built on manufacturing, and generally wanted an expansion of government favorable to business.

Plantations in the antebellum South were usually far from urban centers producing all foodstuffs, but this resulted in social and intellectual isolation as well. The plantation economy intellectually impoverished, as well as disenfranchised, the Black population by denying them the main pillars of western civilization—the rule of law, forbidding basic literacy and access to knowledge, participation in communal activities, and the right to elect representatives and leaders, all rights the central documents in American history had guaranteed for all others.

The southern plantation patriarch ruled in his domain as a kindly family despot, exercising his hierarchical status like a medieval lord. Ex-slave Frederick Douglass comments on this antiquarian outlook in his autobiography from his own experiences.

> In its isolation, seclusion, and self-reliant independence, Col. Lloyd's plantation resembles what the baronial domains were during the Middle Ages in Europe. Grim, cold, and unapproachable by all genial influences from communities without, there it stands; full three hundred years behind its age, in all that relates to humanity and morals. [5]

The only social contact of the family and laborers was between immediate and extended families. The South was profoundly rural and its rituals and rhythms were based on the seasons and practices associated with agricultural life, cotton planting and picking, corn shucking and hog slaughtering among them. It was this static, rustic and provincial existence that the South sought to preserve intact without manufacturing capabilities that would doom it to economic erosion. The destruction after the Civil War exacerbated the fragile economy to starvation in some southern regions.

Today's extremist groups exhibit this same kind of social and intellectual insularity, with anti-science and anti-government attributes among others. As a group members appear to be blithely unaware of the complications of modern domestic life. Among anti-social and racist groups like the KKK members maintain an ordered hierarchy just like a plantation owner. Biases are formed and maintained by simple slogans and not independent or liberating thought. Moreover, the anti-government and radical conservative movements today have their origins in both regions of the country, but principally in the South. Former secessionist-minded religious groups like the Mormons, who once sought to form their own country in the Utah territory, also harbor strong anti-government sentiments.

George says to Eliza in Harriet Beecher Stowe's *Uncle Tom's Cabin* first published in 1852: "My master! and who made him my master? . . . I'm a man as much as he is. I'm a better man than he is. I know moe [sic] about business than he does; I'm a better manager than he is; I can read better than he can; I can write a better hand . . . and what right has he to make a dray-horse of me?" [6]

Uncle Tom's Cabin galvanized the abolitionist movement in the North, alienated the South and made the region fear slave rebellions. The book convinced Leo Tolstoy that as a novel it was "one of the greatest productions of the human mind." It was the most accurate descriptions of slave life ever conceived and had the most eloquent narrative and dialogue portrayals of slave experiences. In short, it was a literary masterpiece and a social and political indictment of America's greatest crimes against humanity.

Slavery, religion and marriage characterized the antebellum South, and in many ways it still does. These values combine to define today's extremist and militant groups (See Chapter 14). Racism has replaced slavery and exists as a form of snobbish exaltation of a racist's social standing, as if he were the heir of a long-gone southern plantation mentality. The South always had a mixture of regional xenophobia, racist feelings of superiority and a practice of social Darwinism, all hidden under the cloak of righteous Christianity. Apologists from the South who defended its ways always seemed to write under a haze of romantic tobacco smoke about the placid South and its happy denizens.

It may be that the link between our slavery past and anti-government feelings today appears tenuous and thin. But I believe that we cannot so easily rid ourselves or our history, tradition or culture and that the seeds of our racist past are buried deep within us still.

Fugitive Slave Law (1850)

> *SEC. 6. And be it further enacted, That when a person held to service or labor in any State or Territory of the United States, has heretofore or shall hereafter escape into another State or Territory of the United States, the person or persons to whom such service labor may be due . . . may pursue and reclaim such fugitive person . . . or by seizing and arresting such fugitive . . .*

On August 29, 2011 a federal judge blocked enforcement of Alabama's proposed immigration law (SB 2011-535). The Alabama law would have made it a crime to be an undocumented immigrant in Alabama. It criminalized renters of residences, nullified contracts of anyone who is undocumented or who makes a contract with them, and required the police to check the papers of anyone suspected of being undocumented. Businesses that knowingly employ undocumented workers would have lost licenses. School officials would have had to check students' immigration status. Anyone harboring an undocumented worker could have been charged with a criminal act. Similar laws had passed in Arizona, Utah, Georgia and Indiana.

The Justice Department and ACLU sued arguing that the law was an unconstitutional intrusion on the government's authority to craft immigration laws. Church leaders of three denominations—Episcopal, Catholic and Methodist, but oddly not Baptist—also denounced the law and filed suit saying that the law vitiated religious acts of compassion and charity. Is it coincidental that such state immigration laws so eerily resemble Fugitive Slave Laws?

Not only was Alabama's law patently unconstitutional, because it over-reaches state powers to intrude on a federal prerogative, but its ill-conceived strictures exposed its crude attempt to exclude non-Whites. In one of the more comical consequences, an executive of the Mercedes car company, visiting Alabama where a manufacturing plant was located, was arrested for looking foreign and not having resident papers.

Congress passed a *Fugitive Slave Act* in 1793 to prevent slave rebellions, a perverted sense of chattel property, thus criminalizing the act of helping a slave to escape. Congress passed an updated *Fugitive Slave Law,* signed into law by president Millard Fillmore that created new commissioners who had the judicial power to compel citizens to assist in pursuing runaway slaves, who could be fined for refusing to cooperate. There was no statute of limitations and no court trials for recaptured slaves who were without judicial relief, unrecognized as citizens. This law, a compromise to the South for admitting California as a free state in 1850, infuriated abolitionists and helped create a system of over 3,000 safe houses, known as the Underground Railroad, for fugitives avoiding capture. Defiance of this law accelerated in the North and the South grew increasingly restless. The updated law was part of an artful compromise that was crafted over several months by a few of the cleverest minds and oratorical speakers in congressional history—John Calhoun of South Carolina, Daniel Webster of Massachusetts, and Henry Clay of Kentucky—that kept the South from seceding for another decade.

The Great Compromise of 1850 intimately engaged the North in the perpetuation of southern slavery. Constitutional framers had initially avoided slavery in order to cobble together a unified governmental compact, the *U.S. Constitution.* Succeeding generations also tried to avoid facing the issue until Americans became alarmed that slavery states were actually dictating terms in a democracy, like whether or not new states could be slave states. This compromise once again postponed the country facing the issue head on.

The chief congressional leader in the effort to save the Union while permitting slavery to continue to exist was Henry Clay (1777-1852), a lawyer and Kentucky slave owner. He was under thirty years of age when he was elected in 1806 to the U.S Senate to fill a vacant Senate seat. In 1810 he was elected to the U.S. House of Representatives in his own right and chosen Speaker of the House on the first ballot. [7] It was a contentious time when northern legislators sought to restrict the spread of slavery into new territories, and southern legislators just as eagerly sought to expand it to maintain congressional equality.

The Compromise of 1850 was an extension of the first Missouri Compromise to be admitted it as a slave state during the Monroe Administration in 1821. The 1850 Compromise comprised a series of five legislative bills that prevented sectional strife, at least for another decade. California was admitted as a free state. New Mexico and Utah were admitted and allowed to choose slavery but did not. The former independent Republic of Texas would yield its claims to the New Mexico territory and receive $10 million to pay a debt to Mexico. Finally, slavery was abolished in the District of Columbia.

Though he owned as many as 60 slaves on his Lexington plantation, Henry Clay always said he was ideologically opposed to slavery. He argued in writing for the gradual emancipation of slaves, and helped establish the American Colonization Society, a group that sought to find homes for freed slaves in Africa, and established Monrovia (named after President James Monroe) in Liberia for that purpose. Members included Bushrod Washington, James Monroe, Andrew Jackson, and Francis Scott Key.

Nevertheless, when he was in Washington living on Dupont Circle, Clay had domestic slaves Aaron and Charlotte Dupuy and their two children as house servants. Charlotte's lawyer filed a lawsuit for her freedom based on a promise of freedom from her former owner. She lost her case but refused to return to Kentucky, so Clay had her arrested and then transported to New Orleans. Clay freed her husband Charles in 1844, and Charlotte and her daughter in 1849. After losing several bids for the presidency, Clay retired to his estate in Lexington, Kentucky only to be re-elected in 1849, and returned to Congress to influence the 1850 compromise. [8]

The South's promotion of slavery for the newly acquired lands of New Mexico and California created intense agitation among ultra-abolitionists in the North and slavery advocates in the South, widening the division in the nation. Nine southern states held a convention in Nashville in June 1850 resolving that the Union needed to be preserved, and Congress did not have the right to prohibit slavery in the territories. Jefferson Davis, then a Senator from Mississippi, claimed that Congress could not prohibit slavery in the territories. If that were true Congress had no authority to introduce it into territories either.

There was strong talk of dissolution of the Union. Southern states were anxious that congressional equality would be diminished and that they would thus be unable to maintain a defense of slavery. On February 7, 1850 the following resolution was introduced on the Senate floor: "Mr. Hale presented the petition of John J. Woodward, and others, praying that a plan may be devised for the immediate peaceful dissolution of the Union." [9] Both Methodist and Baptist churches had split over slavery and the fragile political union was beginning to fracture as the religious union had.

A supreme court in Wisconsin declared the *Fugitive Slave Law* unconstitutional. States like Connecticut attempted to give captured slaves trials so they could be freed. Some members of Congress tried to uphold funds for the law's administration. Northerners had more or less universally ignored or actively disobeyed this law. By the time Buchanan became president in 1856 slavery had completely divided the country socially and politically. During the Civil War Congress passed an act on July 17, 1862 that made any slave in territory occupied by federal troops free. Lincoln's *Emancipation Proclamation* did similarly on January 1, 1863.

Thus prior to the Civil War the seeds of national disunity were sown. The perpetual acts in Congress were extensions of the stalemates in the 1840s and 1850s when Congress debated procedural issues that were in essence profound ideological differences between slavery opponents and advocates. Contemporary anti-government political expressions of limited government are a direct linear descendant of these divisions and appear especially noticeable during congressional election and presidential campaign cycles.

Popular Sovereignty and the Nebraska Bill

Mine eyes have seen the glory of the coming of the Lord,
He is trampling out the vintage where the grapes of wrath are stored,
He has loosed the fateful lightning of His terrible swift sword,
His truth is marching on. (*Battle Hymn of the Republic*, Julia Ward Howe)

As the railroads expanded benefitting travel and commerce, business interests clashed with slavery and non-slavery interests. Stephen A. Douglas, who won the Lincoln/Douglas debates in his senatorial re-election campaign in Illinois in 1858, had presidential ambitions and desperately courted southern votes. He was instrumental with concluding arguments in the Compromise of 1850, following Henry Clay's exhausting two-day speeches (he was then 73), who, to recover, went north for a few months to take the summer waters off Rhode Island.

A few years later, Douglas introduced a bill in the Senate in 1854 that new states like Kansas, under the slogan "popular sovereignty," would allow states to choose whether they would be free or slaves states, a bill that enraged anti-slavery forces in the North. He won the South's favor when the bill invalidated the Missouri Compromise. The full effect of this legislation was to satisfy his presidential ambitions but deepen the chasm between North and South.

With the help of President Franklin Pierce, after the House passed the bill, Douglas saw the *Kansas-Nebraska bill* adopted in the Senate in 1854.

It being the true intent and meaning of this act not to legislate slavery into any Territory or State, nor to exclude it therefrom, but to leave the people thereof perfectly free to form an regulate their domestic institutions in their own way, subject only to the Constitution of the United States . . . [10]

This bill invalidated the provisions of the Missouri Compromise bill that would have prohibited slavery from both the Kansas and Nebraska territories, but allowed new states to choose whether they wanted to be free or slave states.

Congressman Lincoln spoke out vigorously against this legislation and he joined a lengthening list of anti-slavery advocates. Ironically the legislation, while not acknowledging any rights for slaves as "persons" under the Constitution, took pains not to impair the rights of the Indians living in the territory. The Democratic convention in 1856 gave unanimous endorsement to the *Nebraska Act* and elected James Buchanan of Pennsylvania for President. The Republican Party platform that same year voted no extension of slavery and for admission of Kansas as a free state.

Kansas in 1855 was to become the literal battleground for slavery prior to the Civil War. Both sides sent ruffians, drifters, villains and fanatics into Kansas as part-time settlers to vote for or against the defense of slavery. John Brown led the anti-slavery group known as the Free State Party. Barn burnings, riots, and murders characterized the encounters of these hostile bands of intruders. In time there were two territorial legislatures in Kansas both of suspicious legality.

The legendary firebrand John Brown was a descendant of Puritans and Revolutionary War soldiers who honed his fighting skills from 1856 onwards. After fighting proslavery settlers in Kansas with incendiary fervor and weapons, Brown formed a new eighteen-person guerilla band in that fateful year of 1859, a watershed year. John Dewey was born in Vermont. Charles Darwin published *The Origin of the Species*. And John Brown raided Harper's Ferry and attacked the armory to seize weapons and free slaves. It was a bold but doomed plan from the beginning but one of America's largest failed conspiracies.

He held the armory for about a day and a half before the townspeople and surrounding residents killed most of his militia, wounded Brown and captured him. [11] The commanding officer of the federal troops was Robert E. Lee with help from his deputy J.E.B. Stuart, both later Confederate generals. Lee and federal troops discovered thousands of guns and weapons at the safe house Brown had established a few miles distant from Harper's Ferry indicating how extensive they believed their uprising would be.

According to reports, Brown said during an interview to reporters: "You had better—all you people at the South—prepare yourselves for a settlement of that question that must come up . . . You may dispose of me very easily; I am nearly disposed of now; but this question is still to be settled—this Negro question I mean—the end of that is not yet." [12] Brown was not the biblical prophet he imagined but his vision was somewhat prophetic about America's central social division.

When all northern newspapers universally condemned Brown, the civil disobedience guru Henry David Thoreau gave a speech, "A Plea for Captain John Brown," on October 30, 1859 in Concord, Massachusetts praising Brown for his integrity, heroism and firm principles. [13]

Brown had an idealistic Puritan mentality, seeing himself as a biblical Gideon filled with religious fanaticism for the evils of slavery and its abolition. Though he had fought pitched and running battles in Kansas he had too few recruits and little sense of military strategy, as his capture of Harper's Ferry showed. His raid brought terror to the South that such an uprising came from White evangelicals, and elation to northern abolitionists at the boldness of the scheme literally to rescue all southern slaves. Brown's willingness to use violence to end slavery accelerated the march toward war.

Ten of Brown's raiders were killed at Harper's Ferry, including Watson Brown one of his sons, six others including Brown were captured, four escaped and two of those died in the Civil War. Brown was tried in Charleston (then still a part of Virginia but now in West Virginia) and hanged on December 2, 1859. One witness was John Wilkes Booth. One of Brown's last acts was to hand a guard, who had asked for an autograph, this scribbled statement instead: "I, John Brown, am now quite certain that the crimes of this guilty land will never be purged away but with Blood. [14]

The bloodshed would not come close to equaling the human devastation of the Civil War but its military audacity emboldened the North to the ills of human bondage and stiffened the South in resistance to institutionalized human property rights.

> Our foes are in our midst and all about us. There is hardly a house but is divided against itself, for our foe is the all but universal woodenness of both head and heart, the want of vitality in man, which is the effect of our vice; and hence are begotten fear, superstition, bigotry, persecution, and slavery of all kinds. We are mere figure-heads upon a bulk, with livers in the place of hearts.
> (Henry David Thoreau, "A Plea for Captain John Brown.")

The country became even more divided and reconciliation became nearly impossible. In a demonstration of how important the issue was to the South and its congressional representation, pro-slavery settlers entered Kansas in droves from the South in order to vote overwhelmingly for slavery. Kansas as a territory passed a death penalty law for anyone helping a slave to escape, and two years for even possessing abolitionist literature, a clear violation of 1st Amendment rights. Because of violence and the establishment of two opposing state legislatures, and both pro- and anti-slavery settlers moving in to decide the fate of the new state, Congress refused to recognize the constitution of Kansas. It was finally admitted into the Union on January 29, 1861 at the beginning of the Civil War as a free state, as by then anti-slavery settlers, who fought pro-slavery opponents in pitched gunfights, outnumbered pro-slavery voters. Pro-slavery proponents drifted back into the South to fight in the Civil War for the Confederacy. The Missouri Compromise squandered the chance for Congress to end slavery in the U.S., and simultaneously strengthened the power of states to regulate internal affairs.

Presciently, Senator Jefferson Davis, late President of the Confederacy, said in the Senate: "If we are not protected in our property and sovereignty, we are therefore released from our allegiance, and will protect ourselves out of the Union." [15]

Alton, Missouri and the Lincoln/Douglas Debates

A 45-minute drive north from St. Louis is Alton, Missouri, a crossroads in the struggle of runaway slaves to reach safety. The author of the 13th Amendment freeing slaves, Lyman Trumbull, lived here. So did Elijah Parish Lovejoy (1802–1837), class valedictorian of Colby College in Maine, a former schoolteacher, Presbyterian minister and abolitionist publisher who was gunned down on November 7, 1837 while trying to prevent an angry mob from destroying, for a fourth time, his printing press. Lovejoy was driven out of St. Louis because of his abolitionist views published in *The St. Louis Observer* and set up shop in Alton where he published the *Alton Observer*. The partisan mob burned his printing house, shot him five times, shot others protecting him, and threw his printing press in the Mississippi.

That day could be said to be the beginning of the Civil War as, besides the mob murder of a civilian, the defilement of the constitutional freedoms of the press and speech were equally attacked by forces favoring slavery who were willing to kill anyone opposed to their views. The printer with the improbable name of Lovejoy was a martyr to freedom of the press and to the war that would divide and ravage the country.

In Alton's town's plaza stand two life-size statutes, one of Stephen Douglas and the other of Abraham Lincoln. Lincoln and Douglas debated here in 1858 while campaigning for the Illinois senate seat. They debated in two and three-hour sessions at each stop over several months in the campaign of 1858. They did not debate about immigration, western expansion, railroads or any topical issues of the day. They debated about whether or not territories could admit slavery, and new states like Kansas could enter the Union as free or slave states. Douglas favored letting states decide for themselves. Lincoln favored an end to slavery and allowing all new states to enter only slave free.

Douglas, like today's anti-Washington campaigners, won re-election to the Senate. But Lincoln, who had served in Congress, gained national recognition for his oratorical style and message in these debates that served him well in the Republican convention to choose a presidential candidate in the 1860 election. Lincoln said at the time: "We, the majority, would not strive to dissolve the Union; and if any attempt is made it must be by you. We don't want to dissolve it, and if you attempt it, we won't let you." [16] These literally became fighting words.

After Brown's Harper's Ferry disaster, the South was convinced that Abolitionists in the North intended to bring about insurrection among slaves. In this torrid atmosphere the presidential conventions of 1860 began. Lincoln was chosen as less of an extremist on slavery than other candidates like William Seward of New York or Salmon Chase of Ohio, both later to be a part of Lincoln's cabinet.[17]

The Civil War and the addition of the 13th and 14th Amendments to the U.S. Constitution ended the legal questions but not the social and political ruptures. President Richard Nixon beginning in 1968 inaugurated a "southern strategy," a pandering political move to win votes for his presidency that reinvigorated the old battles of disenfranchising or ignoring Blacks and emboldening disaffected southerners.

Dred Scott (c. 1800–1858)

> So I returned and considered all the oppressions that are done under the sun:
> And behold, the tears of those who were oppressed, and they had no comforter;
> and on the side of their oppressors there was power, but they had no comforter.
> (*Ecclesiastes* 4: 1-3)

Roger Brooke Taney (1777-1864) was born into a wealthy Maryland tobacco producing slave-owning family. Educated as a lawyer, he married the sister of Francis Scott Key. He entered politics and became Attorney General of Maryland and helped President Andrew Jackson draft a veto of the second bank charter in 1832, for which Jackson appointed him Secretary of the Treasury in order to withdraw funds from the federal bank. In retaliation, the Senate refused to confirm his appointment. Because of his favoritism of states rights, Taney was appointed Chief Justice replacing John Marshall.

Dred Scott was born a slave in Virginia in 1795 but traveled extensively throughout the western U.S. because his military owners moved around the country. The U.S Supreme Court under Taney that adjudicated his notorious case in 1856 concluded that he was not a citizen and therefore not entitled to freedom, a decision that delighted the South and horrified the North.

Dred Scott had gone west from Virginia with his owner, Peter Blow, traveling to Alabama and finally to St. Louis where Peter Blow died. Scott was sold to Dr. John Emerson, an army surgeon, who moved to Illinois, a free state. Emerson then moved with Scott to Wisconsin, a free territory at the time. Because he had resided in Illinois, a free state, Scott had an opportunity to file a claim for freedom but did not, perhaps because he was unaware of his entitlements there.

The army transferred Emerson to St. Louis and then Louisiana where Scott journeyed with his wife whom he had married in Wisconsin. Emerson died in 1843 and his ownership of Scott transferred to Emerson's widow who loaned him out to another army captain. It was then that Scott filed a claim for his freedom in St. Louis, where Emerson's widow lived. His argument was that because he had lived in a free state and territory he had a right to be free. A circuit court in St. Louis ruled that Scott and his family were free, but the Missouri Supreme Court reversed the lower court's decision. Scott's lawyers appealed to the U.S. Supreme Court. [18]

Previous court decisions had given the states the power to determine the citizenship status of their inhabitants. But at the time prior to the 14th Amendment there was no national citizenship. Seven members of the U.S. Supreme Court, whose Chief Justice was Roger B. Taney, had been appointed to the court by pro-slavery presidents, and five members of the court came from slave-holding families.

The court ruled that Scott was not a citizen and thus had no right to sue. This decision seemed to imply that under a slave-owner's property protections, any owner could take slaves into any state or territory, regardless of that state's laws, and that Congress had no right to decide their status. This decision also declared that restrictions imposed by Congress on the territories, such as those during the Missouri Compromise, were unconstitutional.

Although Taney was complicated in his personal life toward slavery—he freed his own slaves and offered them pensions—and denounced slavery in speeches, throughout his life he leaned toward southern sympathies. The conclusion of historians is that his logic in the *Dred Scott* decision was flawed. His decision exacerbated the national dilemma over slavery and citizenship.

The fallout from the *Dred Scott* case continued to open the gaping wound of slavery on the American consciousness. Although the legal case can be made that since slaves were not American citizens, nor citizens in any state, they had no legal claims. But rather than confronting the problem of slavery at its core, this decisions merely delayed any resolution. For decades the U.S. Supreme Court skirted around tackling slavery forcefully until the *Brown v Board of Education* decision in 1954 that finally excluded segregation in public schools.

From 1846 to 1860 men of enlarged vision knew that war was inevitable. Winfield Scott knew as early as 1850 that war was in the air, and both Lincoln and Seward declared that the country could no longer exist half free and half slave. And yet in the North nothing was done militarily for its preparation. Southern politicians openly declared that their purpose was to secede and become dissolved from the Union. Most northern politicians dismissed these soundings as high-sounding bluster. Southerners were ready to secede when General John Fremont was anticipated to win the presidential election in 1856. Instead, everyone was surprised when Buchanan became president. Because of his appeasing tendencies, the South backed off its immediate plans to dissolve. But the bitterness had been building for decades and would eventually burst.

The warning signs were everywhere for anyone to interpret, yet it was not until southern guns fired on Fort Sumter that the North hastily began to assemble a fighting force to force the South to rejoin the Union. No one predicted the ferocity, devastation or length of the civil cataclysm. At the end, the country was left with slack-jawed astonishment at the havoc the war had wrought. But to individuals of some vision and understanding of the currents of the time, all the predictable signs were there decades earlier. Men of distinction tried to prevent its inevitability but the cultural lines were too deep, the economies too distinct, the animosities too ingrained. Radical far right conservatives today are the descendants of this social and political polarization born and nurtured in the South and now scattered across the American spectrum.

Only in the South was menial labor classified as "nigger work," and where poor whites were called trash. White migrants coming from Europe moved to the North, not the South, to avoid the taint of slavery. Only in the South was education so impoverished that it was frequently non-existent, and absolutely forbidden for slaves. Only in the South did baronial and patriarchal slaveholders, as did their medieval aristocratic counterparts centuries earlier, prohibit to Blacks free speech, freedom of assembly, freedom of discussion and the press, but constitutional rights granted to them. [19]

The economy is national, the patriotism is national, but the cultural division is sectional. Arguments once used by the South to perpetuate anti-government sentiments have migrated throughout the nation and infused national politics. This is corrosive and not merely attributable to differences of political opinion common in democracies. Nothing quite like it, for example, exists in European democracies, though the former Yugoslavia and today's Belgium are exceptions. The surprise is not that the cultural distinction continues to hang around but that it has not dissipated over time. The social and political disunity, generally between North and South, is pervasive in American politics and results in quarrels over governance hindering the furtherance of national unity and domestic harmony.

That most insightful observer of the American character, Alexis De Tocquevlle, as early as the 1830s perceived the dilemma slavery posed to the future of the nation. He thought that the fight would be a race war in the South, a fear echoed by most white southerners.

> The more or less distant, but inevitable, danger of a struggle between the blacks and whites who populate the South of the union constantly presents itself as a painful dream to the imagination of the Americans. Inhabitants of the North discuss these perils every day, although they have nothing to fear from them directly. They seek vainly to find a means of averting the misfortunes they foresee. In the southern states people keep silent; they do not speak of the future to foreigners; they avoid explaining it to their friends; each so to speak hides it from himself. The silence of the South is something more frightening than the noisy fears of the North. [20]

As it happened, the struggle De Tocqueville predicted came true, but it would be between the two sections of the country. It would be a war over the tyranny of the Whites over its kidnapped and imported slave labor, as we shall see in the following chapters. The struggle to accept Blacks as equals has not found resolution in the culture or the politics, not even in the election of the country's first Black president.

The Mississippi State House

Chapter Ten
Secession, Dissolution and Civil War

Scarlett, our southern way of living is as antiquated as the feudal system of the
Middle Ages. The wonder is that it's lasted as long as it has.
(Rhett Butler in Margaret Mitchell's *Gone With the Wind*, p. 238.)

The traveler Frederick Law Olmsted toured the southern seacoast states in 1853 and even then, years prior to the Civil War with his keen observer's eye, saw trouble brewing. "The commercial success of the free states is the offspring of their voluntary labor system. The inability of the Virginians to engage in commerce is the result of their system of involuntary servitude. The condition of the laborers predetermines the condition of all the people." [1] He was more prescient about what this entailed. "Unless the West is more intelligent than it has thus far shown itself to be, the State (Virginia) will yet, for an indefinite time, be wholly ruled by the slave-holders, and everything else will continue, as heretofore, to be sacrificed to what they suppose to be their interests." [2] He predicted "revolution and a reorganization of society" nearly a decade prior to the war. "Whether this process shall be spasmodic and bloody, or gradual and peaceful will depend on the manner in which it is resisted." [3]

America had grown with two distinctly different social and political systems. The North was a young democratic nation. The South was despotic and feudal. The South cultivated a militant, dictatorial subjugation over its slave population and an undemocratic subjugation over its non-slave-owning Whites. The political opposites, and certainly not the vast social distinctions inhabiting the same continent and pretending to be one country, could not abide.

Moreover, the South, unlike the rest of the developing world, did not seek a manufacturing or industrialized economic base but rather a land expansion that would reap continued agricultural profits from a slaveholding society. That is why the incorporation of new slave states like Missouri and Kansas so dominated the political discussion beginning in the early 1800s. The collision of these two opposing views of America was inevitable. The ideological collision is a contemporary residual of diametrically opposite political stances.

As the nation readied for war we might look back at a population unprepared for its looming catastrophe. The census in 1860 reported the U.S. population was a little over 23 million. [4] Southern states had about 11 million, seven million Whites and about four million slaves. About 40% of White farmers owned no land at all. These men and their families cultivated rented land or hired out as tenant farmers or sharecroppers. They were as impoverished and un-educated as the slaves, unless they were among those who migrated west to find land and job opportunities. Those that remained in the South would form the core of the Confederate army.

The Table below is a summary of slave-holding state populations both free and slave from the 1860 census. Slaves constituted about a third of the total population in southern states. Nearly four million people were completely disenfranchised, with no rights, privileges or immunities and no citizenship. The greatest concentrations of slaves were along the Mississippi River and along the coastal regions of South Carolina. But though the numbers are significant, what is equally relevant, and not easily quantifiable, is the mentality of the White slave-owners toward their slaves, a disposition of individual superiority and animosity toward the national government for attempting to disrupt this labor-intensive economic system. All these people would soon suffer from the nation's delay and persistent ignoring of its race problem.

1860 CENSUS

States	Free Population	Slave Population	% of slaves
South Carolina	301,271	402,541	57.2
Mississippi	354,700	436,696	55.1
Louisiana	376,280	333,070	47.0
Alabama	529,161	435,132	45.1
Florida	78,686	61,753	43.9
Georgia	595,007	462,232	43.7
North Carolina	661,586	331,081	33.4
Virginia	1,105,192	490,887	30.7
Texas	421,750	180,682	30.0
Arkansas	324,323	111,104	25.5
Tennessee	834,063	275,784	24.8
Kentucky	930,223	225,490	19.5
Maryland	599,846	87,188	12.7
Missouri	1,067,352	114,965	9.7
Totals	8,289,953	3,950,343	32.2

Secession, as a way of opting out to form a new republic, occurs for a variety of reasons. Tecumseh (1768-1813), warrior chief of the Shawnees and a brilliant military tactician, formed a large tribal confederacy, and allied his forces with the British, to oppose territorial encroachment by the United States in what was then the Northwest Territories of Ohio, Indiana and Michigan. He did not want to secede as to defend lands he believed belonged to American Indian tribes and not new settlers. Indian defense of ancestral lands would be fought for the next hundred years as frontier people migrated westward. As Indian tribes in the West were defeated, reservations were established by which certain lands acquired a kind of semi-sovereign status as foreign nations within U.S. territory.

In modern times, some American Indian groups proposed forming a Republic of Lakotah, a combination of land that stretches across Montana, Wyoming, Nebraska and the Dakotas. A minority political party, the Alaska

Independence Party, believes that the state, physically separated from the lower 48 states, should split off and privatize its public lands. Some Hawaiian Islanders want a return of their monarchical kingdom. Texas has long harbored secessionist proposals since it was admitted as a state from the independent republic it formed after it declared its independence from Mexico in 1845. It gets sillier. Some residents in Pima County in southern Arizona decided they had had enough of state government. State Senator Paula Aboud proposed an amendment that would allow Pima County to secede from the state. Ironically, the amendment was attached to a Republican bill allowing the legislature to decide which federal laws it would or would not support.

The first secession was when all states declared they were independent of England in 1776. The Revolutionary War followed. Thus, secession from a colonial power was not only a bold political move for states and the fragile union, but a political legacy that when some form of perceived tyranny occurs it is appropriate for a state or group of states to disengage. So when all southern states withdrew from the Union in 1861 and formed a new confederacy with a new Constitution, the war to cement its self-declared independence to protect slavery finally erupted. Southern secessionist states became a separate country that was never recognized by any foreign country. Although the Confederacy no longer exists legally, it does culturally. A part of that cultural baggage is that revolts from the government are sanctioned by a long tradition that began with independence and, for some, outright secession.

It's unclear whether or not radical conservatives are ignorant of American Civil War history, or if they are still a part of it, harboring the same adversarial ingredients. Disillusionment with government and its policies is a typical human ailment, and proponents of change begin revolutions for what are often incomprehensible reasons and then engage in warfare with reprehensible means.

> No State shall enter into any Treaty, Alliance or Confederation . . . keep troops . . . enter into any agreement or Compact with another State, or with a foreign power, or engage in War . . .   (*U.S. Constitution,* Article I, Section 10)

Secession began on December 20, 1860 when 169 men gathered in the ballroom of St. Andrew's Hall in Charleston and issued a 158-word statement, an *Ordinance of Secession* that declared South Carolina a separate country, ironically just days after the unification of Italy and he abolition of serfdom in Russia. [5] Southern states soon followed in January of 1861 before Lincoln's inauguration that was then held in March. In ten of the southern states Lincoln did not receive one single popular vote. [6] What is significant to note in this act is not only was the issue about the protection of slavery, as the ordinances so clearly declared, but that this traumatic political and treasonous act was never ratified by the people of South Carolina. Where was southern democracy by the voting public when it was most needed?

It's unclear what might have happened had these delegates only declared independence and not openly seized federal property and fired on federal troops. Northerners did not recognize nor acknowledge the seriousness of the rape of federal property, not just documents declaring dissolution. In Louisiana, men were openly enlisted in an army, officers appointed and war initiated. [7]

Forts at the mouth of the Mississippi were seized and the U.S. flags removed. New Orleans militia captured the arsenal at Baton Rouge and the garrison sent off and arms distributed. No one in the North was sounding an indignant alarm at these seizures of federal property, as they certainly did with John Brown's seizure of property at Harper's Ferry, as both were acts of war. During the voting by Mississippians on whether or not to favor secessions, many suspected of Union sympathies were hanged, an ingenious and perverse method of obtaining the politically correct vote. [8]

> Slavery is the great and foul stain upon the North American Union . . . If the Union must be dissolved, slavery is precisely the question upon which it ought to break. [9]

Insightful men like John Calhoun understood that the slave question could eventually produce dissolution of the Union, and that the South would have to form an alliance with Britain, its principal trading partner for cotton. As much as Britain needed cotton for its manufacturing mills, it realized that the South was a rural, folk society that needed a manufacturing society for its goods. Without the North, the South had no major industrial capacity. More prescient men also knew that if the South were to become a military community that would mean the eventual emancipation of the slaves.

The South could not abandon slavery without admitting the collapse of their economy built mostly around tobacco, cotton and sugar cane. That in turn would mean a massive readjustment in the hired labor of cultivation, or in manufacturing which would put the southern states in direct and unequal competition with northern states.

Slavery in southern states universally referred to Blacks. Plantation owners would have had their reputations ruined if they employed a white domestic servant. Because slaves were always and everywhere Blacks, they were property, and unworthy of legal privileges or immunities. The idea of servitude did not extend to all activities, only to manual labor. This commingling of ideas of manual labor as equal to servitude, and White dominion over other humans as freedom from manual labor, was a perversion that corrupted southern culture. Worse, Christianity was invoked as a defense of the practice, while southerners cringed in horror at the possibility of extending human rights to Blacks. But this peculiar form of Christianity was cosmetic, a veneer of self-righteousness covering a twisted sense of morality but defended as if it were God's plan.

Before Lincoln took office in March 1861, seceding states in January 1861 seized post offices, customhouses, the mint in New Orleans, revenue cutters and other ships and small forts. But Fort Sumter was another matter, and 28 federal troops were stationed there whose provisions were about to expire. If federal troops withdrew to prevent war the government would appear weak in the teeth of rebellion. Would the evacuation of Fort Sumter hold Virginia in the Union that had not yet seceded? On the other hand, Lincoln thought, would any concession hold the Union together?

Lincoln fought to hold the Union together but he was not in favor of equality of rights for White and Blacks. In this respect, he was a White supremacist too, and was "in favor of having the superior position assigned to the white race," as he noted in one of the debates with Douglas in 1858.

But in 1861, after gentlemanly exchanges between from P.G.T. Beauregard, Brigadier General of the Confederacy and Major Anderson about the surrendering the fort, a ten-inch mortar was fired at Fort Sumter at 4:30 AM on April 12, 1861. Thus began the Civil War. The fort was in no sense a threat to Charleston. South Carolina meant to initiate the rebellion militarily and emphasize their dissolution from the Union. The firing continued from both sides, though, unbelievably, no one was killed. Jefferson's Davis's order and Beauregard's guns now defined the conflict that would ravage the nation and leave a deep and lasting scar.

General P.G.T. Beauregard reached the strategic railroad center of Manassas Junction in Virginia the night of June 2, 1861. Federal troops had already occupied Alexandria, just down the Potomac River from Washington DC, so the Confederacy knew that the next federal incursion into Virginia would be to seize the vital railroads nearby. Beauregard's address to his soldiers that night encouraged gallantry. But then he noted that their forefathers had defended liberty against a foreign tyrant. [10] This is the same rhetoric used today by radical Republicans in political campaigns. But equating the tyranny of King George to constitutional powers of the president and Congress is clearly misguided but politically popular for an uninformed or biased populace.

There was a further, unforeseen secession when counties of northwest Virginia beyond the Appalachian Mountains that did not possess large plantations and therefore slaves and that held Union sentiments, decided to secede from Virginia and declared themselves separate from Virginia. President Lincoln formally admitted West Virginia into the Union in 1863. [11]

> And the king of the south being provoked shall go forth, and shall fight against the king of the north, and shall prepare an exceedingly great multitude . . . and he shall cast down many thousands, but he shall not prevail.
> (*Book of Daniel*, 11:11-12).

It was not only the bloodiest conflict and the most important event in American history, but it was necessary to end slavery. It did not end the culture of White supremacy. The Civil War, fought by over three million combatants from 1861-65 was inevitable. It resolved what congressional legislation, the lack of even gradual emancipation, ineffective legal compromises, adjudication by the courts, and ethical resolve could not. Nearly all the battles were fought on southern soil. About 620,000 were killed, about 360,000 northerners and 260,000 southerners. On the march to Gettysburg, Confederates kidnapped freed Blacks, perhaps to keep them from fighting for the Union army, and shipped them back into slavery in the South, a double crime and a reinvigoration of the slave trade. [12]

In one of those incongruities fate bestows on the unwitting, the South had to raise lots of money to prosecute the war. The Confederate Congress passed legislation for draconian taxes and bonds that crippled the southern economy, inflicting more so-called tyrannical measures than the North was accused of. Confederate money soon became worthless, as commodities grew scarce when owners didn't extract exorbitant prices.

When war began in 1861 both sides believed that God was on their side. Christians were divided. Religious zeal about whose side God was on did not stave off the hunger that ravaged the cities as much as it did soldiers and horses. The South had rushed like a religious awakening into secession and war without the thoughtful planning that would sustain a protracted war—like many recent wars—and paid the price for reckless enthusiasm for its doomed system of enslavement. Those in the South saw slavery as a blessing for the Blacks. Those in the North believed that God favored the Union as a covenant of the American people with God. Northern Christians could not abide slavery any more than they could tolerate adultery, drinking and gambling. If a person could be reborn in a personal conversion, they thought, why not a country without slavery. The inconsistencies between accepting Christianity and slavery as equally good were odious to northern Abolitionists. Church bells and slave auction bells chiming in concert were a disharmonious sound, anathema to northern ears. How could Christian southerners, they reasoned, uphold the laws of the sanctity of marriage and allow slave owners to separate marriage partners, much less to brutalize slaves.

Julia Ward Howe wrote *The Battle Hymn of the Republic* in 1861 after she heard soldiers singing *John Brown's Body*. Her theme was that God was taking vengeance on the country with "the fateful lightning of His terrible swift sword" for allowing slavery to exist so long.

> *He is coming like the glory of the morning on a wave,*
> *He is wisdom to the mighty, He is honor to the brave,*
> *So the world shall be his footstool, and the sound of wrong His slave,*
> *Our God is marching on.*

Both sides invoked God as the champion of their cause, yet God could not take sides because only one side could achieve a victory. Lincoln was conflicted by this dilemma and agonized over it until he concluded that the Union had to take precedence. In his Second Inaugural speech he said that God had punished the nation because of slavery. Previous presidential addresses had only mentioned God perfunctorily. But Lincoln's invocation of God, justice and righteousness repeatedly was a new angle in presidential messages to Congress.

Six weeks later after this address he was shot and killed. Preachers in the North immediately made him into a martyr for God and country, a person who, like a sacrificial lamb, had to atone for the sins of all. With Lincoln's death the nation itself was supposed to be reborn in a religious sense. The slaves would be free, but reunion would be an illusion.

Figuring out the mind of a slave was not complicated. The easy part was that they all wanted to be free to choose their own kind of labor, trade, or journey in life. That's why they came out of their cabins and hovels whenever the Union army marched near and rode mules and walked with soldiers, following the North Star at night to reach any place except their plantation abodes.

Slavery ended in the South but not human and civil rights violations for another hundred years. Residual feelings harbored by American descendants play a significant role in defining political and social divisions in American today. If you can imagine a Confederate soldier screaming his rebel yell and charging into the ranks of the Army of the Potomac, then a similar exhibition of guts, intensity and zeal defines the current radical Republican political braggadocio.

I am reminded of apartheid South Africa, that I first visited as a government guest in 1988. South Africa gained independence in 1934 from Britain, and Whites, who constituted only 17% of the total population, administered the country and denied Blacks the vote and participation in social institutions. By the late 1980s there were urban bombings and violence in ghetto, black townships like Soweto. The government had also established so-called independent "homelands" for certain tribal groups. Segregation was institutionalized. President P. W. Botha, an ardent segregationist, was pursuing a modest policy of constitutional reforms urged on by international pressure.

The first multi-racial elections were held in South Africa in 1994 under the courageous leadership of President F. W. de Klerk who engineered the end of apartheid and released Nelson Mandela from prison after 27 years. Mandela won the next election. But the more important conclusion was that because of bold leadership civil war was averted in a majority, white segregationist government, a lesson never learned in the American South. De Klerk and Mandela both received the Nobel Peace Prize in 1993. When I returned to South Africa in 1998 to a Black majority rule, there was increased migration from other southern African nations and sporadic crime. But the violence and devastation of a civil war had been not occurred in South Africa as it did in America.

Contraband: A Slave Euphemism

Take Highway 64 East from Richmond, Virginia and follow it past Williamsburg and Yorktown. Before you take the Hampton Roads Bridge tunnel bridge that crosses the Chesapeake Bay into Norfolk, exit at S. Mallory Street, take a right at East Mellen Street that turns into Ingalls Road, and head into Fort Monroe. It is situated on the spit of land that forms the southernmost tip of the peninsula between the James and York River estuaries. Fort Monroe, named after the fifth president, a military outpost since the founding of Jamestown in 1620, was surrounded by the Confederacy but remained in Union hands throughout the Civil War. It was built beginning in 1819 using slave labor. Jefferson Davis, former President of the Confederacy, was garrisoned here as a war prisoner in 1865.

What happened there on the night of May 23, 1861, a little more than a month after the start of the Civil War, modified the nation's relations with runaway slaves. [13] May 23rd, 1861 was the same day citizens of Virginia ratified the ordinance of secession to join the Confederacy, so these escaped slaves chose a meaningful date in Virginia and U.S. history.

Frank Baker, Shepard Mallory and James Townsend were Virginia field hand slaves in 1861 working under their owner, a newly appointed Virginia militia Colonel named Charles Mallory. They were ordered to build artillery emplacements among the sand dunes along the James River. They learned that they might be shipped south soon to build fortifications in North Carolina. They agreed to flee and try their luck with Union forces, not knowing if they would be treated as prisoners of war, felons, or traitors since they had been working for the Confederacy. They rowed a boat across the estuary and a guard escorted them into Fort Monroe where they spent the night.

The following morning they met with the fort commander, Major General Benjamin F. Butler (1818–1893), a lawyer from Lowell, Massachusetts whose father and brother served in the military. Butler had only been a soldier for a month, had little military training or preparations though solid political connections, and was assigned as commander only the previous day. The three fugitive slaves presented Butler with a conundrum. *The Fugitive Slave Act* was still in effect that required anyone finding a slave to return him or her to the proper owner as legal property. Lincoln had made it clear that he did not want to interfere with slavery as a southern institution, but only to maintain the Union and end secession. [14]

Yet Butler's canny legal mind went to work. He had not invited the slaves into Union territory, nor had he instigated their escape. As he was pondering his unique problem and preparing a message to the Administration, he was interrupted by another messenger—Major John Baytop Cary of the Virginia 115th—who arrived at the Fort under a white flag of truce. He wanted the slaves returned and argued that under the *Fugitive Slave Act* Butler was constitutionally required to return them. Butler argued that he had no constitutional obligation to grant any such commitment to a foreign country, as Virginia had just seceded. Since the Confederacy considered slaves as property, Butler would do the same, just as if, for example, the slaves were captured guns. Since Virginia had seceded it had dissolved its rights under the Union, and henceforth Butler would consider the slaves as contraband of war, since they had been used in the construction of war defenses. If the Confederacy treated them as property, so would the Union.

Butler used a novel legal argument, a clever description of status that in effect freed slaves from bondage. Contraband of war was a defining euphemism that everyone in the North found acceptable, and that southerners could not legally or logically refute. Within days hundreds of slaves entered Fort Monroe and were put to work on military defenses, freeing soldiers from working on necessary services and trades. More importantly, slaves as contraband property became the description of those who escaped into Union territory for the remainder of the war. The irony was that they were not considered persons, had no constitutional rights, and were not legally emancipated. But once accepted into the Union army they were treated as war workers and not slave laborers beholden to master owners. And for the next four years they fled into the Union by the hundreds of thousands.

Lincoln's Anti-Slavery Messages

In his message to Congress on July 4, 1861 Lincoln wrote his argument for the war. In succeeding messages he outlined his plan for how slavery was the root cause of the war and how he planned to exculpate it from the republic.

> And this issue embraces more than the fate of these United States. It presents to the whole family of man the question whether a constitutional republic or democracy—a government of the people by the same people—can or cannot maintain its territorial integrity against its own domestic foes . . . So viewing the issue, no choice was left but to call out the war power of the government; and so to resist force employed for its destruction, by force for its preservation.[15]

A war would have to determine slavery where constitutional and political compromises and half measures had not. The majesty of democratic governance had been insulted by the installation of slavery, but its constitutional preservation, and would not have to be dissolved through warfare. Lincoln's *Emancipation Proclamation* of January 1, 1863 made all slaves in rebellious states free. It was the signal document that proclaimed the Union as it was meant to be from its inception, and not with a constitutional compromise that condoned slavery. It had a profound effect overseas. [16]

The Emancipation Proclamation threw down the ultimate gauntlet. General Robert E. Lee was fighting for a negotiated settlement so the South could return to its previous political and economic policies of servitude. Lincoln avoided any discussion of a negotiated settlement and undermined the whole southern economy of slave labor by freeing them. The South then knew that there was to be no backing down and the army would have to win military victories or succumb to a profound changed lifestyle. Thus, the carnage from the war was just beginning. In his Message to Congress on December 6, 1864, Lincoln was more unaccommodating.

> For myself, I have no doubt of the power and duty of the Executive, under the law of nations, to exclude enemies of the human race from an asylum in the United States. If Congress should think that proceedings in such cases lack the authority of law, or ought to be further regulated by it, I recommend that provision be made for effectually preventing foreign slave traders from acquiring domicile and facilities for their criminal occupation in our country.

Further in the message he encouraged Congress to re-introduce legislation proposing a constitutional amendment freeing the slaves.

> At the last session of Congress a proposed amendment of the Constitution abolishing slavery throughout the United States passed the Senate, but failed for lack of the requisite two-thirds vote in the House of Representatives.

> Although the present is the same Congress and nearly the same members, and without questioning the wisdom or patriotism of those who stood in opposition, I venture to recommend the reconsideration and passage of the measure at the present session.

Here is more of that poignant message to Congress that reveals much about the mind of Lincoln and the enormity of what was at stake.

> On careful consideration of all the evidence accessible it seems to me that no attempt at negotiation with the insurgent leader could result in any good. He would accept nothing short of severance of the Union, precisely what we will not and cannot give. His declarations to this effect are explicit and oft repeated. He does not attempt to deceive us. He affords us no excuse to deceive ourselves. He cannot voluntarily reaccept the Union; we cannot voluntarily yield it. Between him and us the issue is distinct, simple, and inflexible. It is an issue which can only be tried by war and decided by victory. If we yield, we are beaten; if the Southern people fail him, he is beaten. Either way it would be the victory and defeat following war. What is true, however, of him who heads the insurgent cause is not necessarily true of those who follow. Although he cannot reaccept the Union, they can …
> In presenting the abandonment of armed resistance to the national authority on the part of the insurgents as the only indispensable condition to ending the war on the part of the Government, I retract nothing heretofore said as to slavery. I repeat the declaration made a year a ago, that "while I remain in my present position I shall not attempt to retract or modify the emancipation proclamation, nor shall I return to slavery any person who is free by the terms of that proclamation or by any of the acts of Congress." If the people should, by whatever mode or means, make it an Executive duty to re-enslave such persons, another, and not I, must be their instrument to perform it. In stating a single condition of peace I mean simply to say that the war will cease on the part of the Government whenever it shall have ceased on the part of those who began it.

Lincoln wanted to end the war, to reanimate the States, and get state governments operating again and return to the Union. [17] He made this clear in a conversation he had with officials on the morning of April 14, 1865, the day he was assassinated. The details of battles, names of the principal actors in the military drama, the incompetence of leaders, the terrain, the confusion, smoke, and sundry atrocities can all be found in the standard histories of the Civil War. Lincoln had a whole series of incompetent, timid generals, beginning with McClellan and Meade, who were too busy with tables of organization and lines of authority to actually conduct a war that would defeat an enemy army and follow it to elimination. Unlike Robert E. Lee, the exasperating northern generals, and except for Grant, the northern generals and the War Department relied on weighing risks instead of seizing opportunities.

Lee was deified in 1870 after his death, extolled as a kind of Christian saint in the South and his legend grew. Even presidents like Theodore and Franklin D. Roosevelt hailed him as an American hero in order to win southern votes.

Apparently, being responsible for the deaths of hundreds of thousands to preserve a slave owning society is enough to earn such sanctification.

The contemporary Republican strategy that parallels the disenfranchisement of Blacks prior to, during, and after the Civil War is the denial of basic democratic rights of which slavery was only the most persistently visible. Today, besides the folly of wanting to actually see President Obama's birth certificate—an issue that had never before emerged in presidential politics— Republicans controlling certain state houses with governors and predominantly cohort legislatures seek to erode Democratic Party voting patterns by passing legislation that restricts voter access. The majority of Democratic voters in most states are the less fortunate in society—the young, the elderly, and minorities.

The perversity of this transparent strategy is that not only does it corrupt the political process by abusing the power of the state to restrict another political party's ability to mobilize voters but debases the idea of democratic process of self-expression in choosing representatives in our republic. Sadly, it is the same strategy southerners used to keep Blacks from voting prior to the *Voting Rights Act* of 1965.

Why should it have taken Americans more than two hundred years to enact legislation that gives everyone an equal right to vote? And why are Republicans attempting to place barriers and restrictions on that right? The answer, as I have claimed, is in our history where an identifiable group was denied fundamental rights. We still have a culture that believes some of those people should not vote because they will not normally vote Republican. How very un-American; but how very culturally southern.

We need to raise the unity bar higher as Teddy Roosevelt suggested in a speech in 1910: "We can admire the heroic valor, the sincerity, the self devotion shown alike by the men who wore the blue and the men who wore the gray; and our sadness that such men should have had to fight one another is tempered by the glad knowledge that ever hereafter their descendants shall be found fighting side by side, struggling in peace as well as in war for the uplift of their common country, all alike resolute to raise to the highest pitch of honor and usefulness the nation to which they all belong." [18] A century later that goal of true national unity has slipped back into sectarianism.

The Museum of the Confederacy in Richmond Virginia glorifies and reinterprets the Civil War calling it the "Lost Cause," as if somehow the cause of slavery should have endured. [19] How can the loyalty to a "lost cause," to a regional identity, be reconciled with a disavowal of the institution of slave labor? We can find virtue in the heroism of soldiers and the endurance and stamina of a people, but not as a justification for kidnapping and forced indentured servitude. There may be righteousness in some rebellions. But there is no rectitude in keeping humans in bondage. Few today seek a return to slavery. But too many cling to White supremacy as if it were a noble American virtue, and to the attitudes, like anti-government feelings and states' rights, that sustained the South in its struggle to hold on to its peculiar institution.

Chapter Eleven
Treason, Traitors and Their Allies

> But once citizens have been corrupted by some kind of lunacy and have
> become traitors to their country, you may be able to stop them destroying the
> state, but you can never constrain them by force or conciliate them by kindness.
>
> (Cicero, *Against Catiline IV*)

On December 18, 1860, former six-term Mississippi congressman and Secretary
of the Interior in the Buchanan Administration Jacob Thompson left Baltimore
and sailed down the Chesapeake River to North Carolina. Thompson had been
born in North Carolina in 1810, attended the University of North Carolina and
maintained strong ties to his home state. But in 1860 he was a well-known
Mississippi Democrat and lawyer who had been named as a Mississippi
Commissioner to attend a secession convention. He arrived in Raleigh and
immediately met the Governor and urged the delegates to secede. [1] Thompson
did not resign his Administration post, so while ostensibly professing allegiance
to the Union he was plotting to secede and thus violating his oath of office.

Prior to the Civil War southern politicians, journalists and strategists
painted the upcoming struggle as an attempt to decimate slavery. [2] After the war
this strategy was abandoned as revisionists sought to paint the civil conflict as a
struggle over differing concepts of constitutional liberty, reframing the causes of
the war to their political advantage. This idea of constitutional liberty and the
right of states to challenge the national government on domestic issues is still
the prevailing theme in conservative Republican circles, as is the deceptions
about their actual plans compared to campaign pledges.

It is ultimately impossible to discern the motives of those who betray their
country while claiming to serve it. It would be easy to categorize the motives as
self-interest, but that sweeping generalization contains too much ambiguity. In
today's climate, traitors are often uncovered in the military attempting to sell
state secrets to foreign nations. A few Muslims like Faisal Shahzad, the
attempted Times Square bomber in 2010, lied, as he said he did, when they take
the oath of citizenship and then plan terrorist attacks.

In the presidential campaign in 2112 Governor Rick Perry claimed in 2010
that he thought it might be a good idea to secede if the federal government "goes
too far." He thought that if the Chairman of the Federal Reserve decided "to
print more money," that that would be tantamount to treason. He believed that
the federal social security program (FICA) was unconstitutional. So the idea of
seceding, calling federal officials traitorous for doing their constitutional
obligations, or claiming that the laws of Congress operating for more than 75
years are unconstitutional, is not as far-fetched in modern times for serious
presidential candidates like Texas Governor Rick Perry and his allies as it was
for southern politicians in the middle of the 19th century.

For a southern state governor and his allies, the public voicing of secession, the vilification of federal officials, and proclaiming that congressional laws they disagree with are unconstitutional, is an eerie contemporary echo from a disquieting American past. Inciting to secession can certainly be borderline treason. Let's reluctantly give a necessary concession to the hyperbole of campaign rhetoric. Nevertheless, such talk is also a reflection of our painful and divided past still present in our national discourse.

The Civil War provided the most widespread cases of treason and conspiracy to commit treason as any period in American history. Many in that troubled period, like Alexander Stephens, congressman and Vice President of the Confederacy, were conflicted and did not want southern states to secede, but when they did believed they owned allegiance more to their home states than to the Union. Nevertheless, Stevens also painfully felt that slavery was indispensable to the South, and that there was no equality between the races.

Land was at the heart of the original cultural clash. To place all early American land disputes in perspective it is relevant to recall that all European claims on land in North America were spurious and legally challengeable from the beginning. Europeans imposed their concepts of land and its inheritances on a continent inhabited by natives whose own ideas of land did not endorse individual ownership. Consider what might have occurred in the 15th and 16th centuries had American natives sued in European courts (if any could be found that were independent of the King) over European occupation and claims of royal ownership based on their property claims of previous habitation and uses for survival.

The Treaty of Paris concluded the war of independence between America and Britain, but also involved land claims of Spain, France and Holland. [3] It was America's first important document in international diplomacy. As a part of the treaty, Spain gained control of Florida from the British. A signal provision of the treaty was the delineation of the boundaries and land claims of America on the continent.

In 1762 France ceded Louisiana to Spain. But in the *Treaty of Ildefonso* in 1800 Spain ceded Louisiana back to France. Boundaries were not well defined. France then sold Louisiana to the U.S. in 1803 so Napoleon could raise funds for his European wars. Because of undefined borders, the national fear was that thieves, murderers, escaped prisoners and slaves, and not just pirates and buccaneers, would infiltrate American territories.

Louisiana is a rare case in point. Napoleon had sacrificed more than 20,000 Frenchmen in a failed attempt to curtail the slave rebellion on Haiti in 1803, at the time known as Saint-Dominique. Hence, he was keen to renounce all his land claims in North America. New Orleans was a rare ethnic mix of creoles of Caribbean origin, and Cajun, of French origin expelled by the British from Arcadia, Native Americans, French, Spanish and sundry Caribbean. Thomas Jefferson, so often cited by neo-conservatives for his principles about liberty, thus allowed the extension of slavery in new-acquired American land.

Seminole Indians beginning in 1812 had provided safety to escaped slaves. U.S. troops sent to retrieve them met stiff resistance. When settlers from Georgia attacked Seminole villages, Seminoles retaliated by raiding Georgia settlements. Andrew Jackson was dispatched in 1818 to punish and/or liquidate the Seminoles. He captured Pensacola from the Spanish, elevating his prestige and chances for candidacy to the presidency. Eventually all of Florida, including West Florida, which at the time extended from the east coast to the Mississippi, was acquired from Spain in 1821. The conclusion of the Seminole War resulted in American land acquisition through military conquest. More such encounters would follow throughout the West.

Outnumbered and outgunned Indians would soon be conquered. But slaves were property and usually came with land. So when Jefferson acquired Louisiana a provision in the *Treaty of Cession*, a part of the Louisiana Purchase agreement of April 30, 1803, noted in Article III:

> The inhabitants of the ceded territory shall be incorporated in the Union of the United States and admitted as soon as possible according to the principles of the federal Constitution to the enjoyment of all these rights, advantages and immunities of citizens of the United States, and in the mean time they shall be maintained and protected in the free enjoyment of their liberty, property and the Religion which they profess. [4]

The U.S. government acknowledged that it would protect the inhabitants of the property of the new province and its slave-owners. However, by 1819 seven of the original 13 colonies had abolished slavery, and six had retained it. Subsequent states—Vermont, Ohio, Indiana and Illinois—forbade slavery, but Kentucky, Tennessee, Alabama, and Louisiana permitted it. By 1812 Louisiana consisted of a slave-holding commonwealth and a slave-holding territory to its north. The Missouri Compromise complicated the American dilemma over slavery and raised the perpetual issue of governance and authority between states and the national government. Northern hostility to slavery clearly colored northern state arguments as much as it did the angst that encouraged southern states to exaggerate constitutional claims about the powers of Congress.

Traitors are as diverse as Vice President Aaron Burr who became an active insurrectionist, Governor William Blount, signer of the U.S. Constitution and insurrectionist, and Commander of the Army, General James Wilkinson, traitor and spy for a foreign power. I also regard John Tyler, the tenth president of the United States as a traitor since he joined the Confederate Congress, thus violating his oath of office to defend the Constitution, but died before the Confederacy convened.

National and state political candidates and leaders today are perilously close to secessionist ideas if not the radical steps that lead to treason and political disassociation. They voice misconstrued and ignorant ideas about government and America's unique governance system as any political leaders in the developed world, and cater to a biased public with discredited and disavowed beliefs that led to a humiliating and horrific civil war and decades of segregation. Reviewing a short history of some of these traitors is a way to remind us of our troubled past and how easy it is to repeat it.

Aaron Burr (1756–1836):
The Vice President as Insurrectionist

One of the first attempts at secession, and one of the most notable treason trials in U.S. history, occurred during the Jefferson Administration when Aaron Burr was Vice President. Born in New Jersey, Burr was the son of the second president of Princeton, and a grandson of the colonial preacher and author Jonathan Edwards. He graduated at age 16 from the College of New Jersey, later to become Princeton University, a year behind Madison. He served as a colonel in the Continental Army under Washington. Subsequently, he served in the New York Senate, supporting a bill to abolish slavery in the state. He was appointed as New York's Attorney General, besting General Schuyler, Alexander Hamilton's father-in-law. It was an act that Hamilton never forgave and that eventually resulted in their duel when Burr killed his bitter and scurrilous rival in 1804. He was appointed U.S. Senator and was nearly elected President when he tied Jefferson in Electoral College votes. The House of Representatives elected Jefferson President and Burr Vice President. [5]

By all accounts Burr was a devoted husband, an attentive and loving father to his daughter Theodosia, a dedicated public servant, and the country's first notable insurrectionist. His enemies, including Washington, Jefferson and Hamilton, dogged him with surrogates in the press to repudiate his reputation and damage his political influence. From all available accounts—and there is little documentary evidence about him—he was conniving and a despicable man, however brilliant.

On July 11, 1804 he shot and killed Alexander Hamilton in a duel in Weehawken, New Jersey across the Hudson River from New York. Hamilton and Burr hated each other as political and personal enemies. Historians differ on the exact motive of this duel. A few weeks later, New Jersey indicted him for murder and a New York grand jury indicted him for killing a New Yorker in a state where dueling was prohibited.

Burr lost the race for Governor of New York and assumed his political life though his personal finances were in ruins. The following month Andrew Merry, Ambassador to the U.S. from Britain wrote in code to his superiors that the Vice President of the United States, Burr, was offering his assistance to Britain "in any manner they would think fit to employ him." At the time Burr wanted to separate the western part of the U.S. from the Union.

For motives unknown, he approached Spanish representatives as Vice President to disengage the American southwest and to get that territory, a part of the Louisiana Purchase after 1803, to secede and place him as its chief. He planned to attack Mexico. He journeyed west with collaborators from Tennessee and Kentucky to raise an army but failed to recruit more conspiratorial followers or additional militia. Burr planned a war with Spain for its North American territories in Florida and Mexico. But mostly he spoke often against the national government and sought an army to satisfy his military and political ambitions.

Burr journeyed down the Ohio until he landed on Harman Blennerhassett's island, then a part of western Virginia, a location he thought perfect for gathering an army to separate the western territories from the Union. Blennerhassett (1764–1831), educated as a lawyer at Trinity College, Dublin, was a naïve and perfect Irish immigrant foil for Burr's charm and his romantic idea of revolution, but he agreed to participate. Blennerhassett had to come to America to escape Irish clerical and civil statutes for marrying his niece. He sold his inherited estate in Ireland for less than value and built a castle on the island in the Ohio River, now restored and popular as a tourist attraction. Burr sought him out in 1805 to help finance his insurrection thinking Blennerhassett had more money than he actually did. [6]

Slaves cheered when they heard Burr's name mentioned in the South during his travels to rally support because they believed they would be freed if his insurrection succeeded. Planters feared him because he represented a clear a threat to the established order. Territorial courts like Alabama and Mississippi at the time had no statutes regarding treason, so when Burr was indicted by grand juries in Kentucky and Mississippi judges had to release him. He had three grand jury indictments, attended each and invited inquiry and won acquittal each time.

Capt. Moses Hook, under orders from Governor Wilkinson, appeared in Mississippi at Burr's third indictment with a squad of non-uniformed officers. Sensing dread, Burr failed to appear in court one day and the judge ordered him a fugitive. Burr was indicted again this time in a federal court, arrested while trying to escape to Florida. He was tried for treason beginning August 3, 1807 in a Richmond court headed by Chief Justice John Marshall. Congressman John Randolph, a cousin of Thomas Jefferson, got the House to pass a resolution against Burr so President Jefferson could respond to Burr's escapades.

Jefferson had prejudiced the public against Burr in a message to Congress denouncing him as a traitor. No unbiased jurors could thus be found and Jefferson assumed a verdict of guilty that only a court may pronounce. The law, of course, as Jefferson the lawyer knew, requires the assumption of innocence until convicted by a court.

> Treason against the United States shall consist only in levying War against them, or in adhering to their Enemies, giving them aid and comfort. No Person shall be convicted of Treason unless on the testimony of two Witnesses to the same event, or on Confession in open court.
> (U.S. Constitution, Article III, Section 3.)

The statute regarding English treason was debated during the trial because no cases of this magnitude had been adjudicated previously. According to the combined treason statutes dating from the 25th year of the reign of Edward III in 1351, a person was guilty of high treason (petty treason was a different crime) if they planned the death of the King, violated his "companion" (apparently this applied to wives and mistresses), or the King's daughters or wives of his eldest sons, or levied war against the realm, "giving them aid and comfort." Treason in any country is dangerous because it turns into revolution if successful.

I note this historical episode because so many of the radical conservatives during election campaigns have publicly voiced that revolution is necessary, and it isn't clear if they have more armed revolutions in mind, as Aaron Burr did, and are not just using metaphor to make a point.

During the trial Burr demanded to see the original presidential documents against him, and the court issued a subpoena to President Jefferson. The court has jurisdiction to summon any person in defense of another, especially one on trial for life. But could the court request the president's presence and leave the country without a functioning chief executive? Jefferson declined to appear but in a compromise did release the relevant documents. The judicial power of the courts, even over presidents and claims of executive privilege had been established. This legal principle would be invoked again against President Nixon during the Watergate scandal when the courts demanded documents and tape recordings. Nixon refused and impeachment hearings were initiated. Government prosecutors during the Burr trial argued that Burr's physical presence was not necessary for treason, a legal standing in British common law. But the U.S. Constitution was more specific and Marshall ruled that "levying war" means the actual conduct of violence and not merely traitorous talk. [7]

Judge Marshall found that it was unclear that a war had been levied, that no weapons had been used in the alleged conduct of treason, no military was presented to offer war, and that the accused, Burr, was not actually with the so-called conspirators, or supported by two witnesses as the Constitution requires, when treason was alleged to have occurred.

A jury acquitted Burr. "We of the jury," declared foreman Edward Carrington, "say that Aaron Burr is not proved to be guilty under this indictment by any evidence submitted to us. We therefore find him not guilty." A verdict of "not proven" leaves open the question of treason for potential challenge since the jury reached its conclusion based on presented evidence. Additional evidence might prove the defendant's guilt, though he could not be tried again for the same offence, as that is double jeopardy. Historians generally agree that Burr was a traitor, but that two witnesses were needed for a guilty verdict. At his trial the prosecution produced only one.

This trial demonstrated that assembling to talk about revolution is not enough to be convicted of treason. The court set the precedent that the law is the master of freedoms against possible tyranny and abuse by government. Burr's bold and outrageous bid to get a portion of the U.S. to secede is a landmark in radical American history. The court ruling on his behalf is also a legal context for judging contemporary radicals and insurrectionists. [8]

> Only we want a little personal strength;
> And pause us till these rebels, now afoot,
> Come underneath the yoke of government.
> (Shakespeare, *Henry IV, Part II*, IV, 4)

William Blount (1749–1800)

Blount was born in North Carolina and was paymaster in the Continental Army and a delegate to the Continental Congress, and to the constitutional convention in Philadelphia in 1787. He was a signer of the U.S. Constitution. President Washington appointed him Governor of the southwest territories, at the time the land south of the Ohio River. He was Superintendent of Indian Affairs from 1790–96. When Tennessee, a territory he helped develop, was admitted as a state in 1796, he was elected its first Senator.

Blount was a strong endorser of a central government. He envisioned the West as a land of great opportunity. However, he injudiciously conspired to incite the Creek and Cherokee Indians to rebel against the Spanish in the lower Mississippi valley. Based on his extensive administrative experience with the Indians and his knowledge of the territory, he realized the importance of a well prepared and regulated militia. Accordingly, he organized the territorial militia and with this army he must have seen its possibilities in use against other foreign interests in the West, like France, Britain and Spain. But he hoped his conspiracy would accelerate his land speculations.

Blount had speculated heavily in land in the area, and in North Carolina, hoping to realize extensive profits from prospective settlers in western lands. He soon was recognized as one of the largest landowners in the U.S. But he also conspired with the British against the Spanish, hoping to seize Spanish lands so settlers would move into his lands without Spanish interference. A letter to one of his conspirators found its way into the hands of President John Adams who sent it to Congress. Blount escaped to the West with federal marshals after him. He was expelled from the Senate, and the House impeached him for violating the *Neutrality Act*. The Senate dropped the charges because he was no longer a senator. He was subsequently elected to the Tennessee state senate and chosen its president, acts that revealed Tennessee's confidence in his abilities but also its attitude toward serious federal charges of even for one of its adopted son of the soil. He died a couple of years later of a fever, age 50, nearly penniless. [9]

Though a soldier in the Continental Army, a delegate to the Continental Congress and the constitutional convention, and a signer of the U.S. Constitution, he involved himself in scandalous and possibly treasonous activities injurious to the nation. The actions of southern and western states in nefarious and conspiratorial actions of their citizens unfavorable to national interests shows how such states often disregarded whatever crimes the federal government attributed to them. Today, Blount would be arrested by federal agents and could be indicted and tried in a federal court for "aiding and abetting" the enemy, or acting as if he were a designated agent of the U.S. in dealing with foreign powers.

Blount's service to the nation is overshadowed by his treachery for personal gain. Today, congressional representatives shelter contributions under the aegis of campaign contributions so they cannot be accused to its personal use. [10]

James Wilkinson (1757–1825)

Two of America's earliest generals and Commanders-in-Chief could not have more different in character. George Washington became the first president, while the other, James Wilkinson, was a traitor and a spy in the pay of the Spanish.

Wilkinson was born in Maryland the younger son of the minor gentry. Because he was not the eldest he would not inherit the estate. He grew up in the same kind of slave-holding, plantation world that Washington knew. He was commissioned a captain in the Continental Army in 1775 and two years later, not yet 20 years of age, appointed lieutenant colonel and assigned to Horatio Gates's chief of staff. He fought in a bloodless duel with Gates then left the army in anger.

He married Ann Biddle and into a distinguished Philadelphia family. His extravagant tastes always left him short of assets. In 1779 he accepted the post of clothier general of the army. He resigned within two years when deficiencies emerged in his accounts, and he moved to Kentucky to seek his fortune. Kentucky had citizens bitter at the national government for not dealing with the Spanish who had closed the Mississippi River to trade. Wilkinson helped his new neighbors push for independence from the U.S. He journeyed to New Orleans to convince the Spanish to let him entice Kentucky into Spanish possessions. In a secret document in 1787 he swore allegiance to Spain for money and became known as Agent 13. From then on his double life began. Within a few years settlers in Texas would also swear allegiance to Mexico in return for good land.

In 1791 Wilkinson rejoined the army and was offered the rank of brigadier general and second in command while he was still in the paid employ as a spy for Spain. If discovered he would face court-martial and quite possibly the death penalty. By 1797 he was made commander-in-chief of the U.S. army, the highest rank military officer ever in American history that was a spy for a foreign power. Jefferson had heard rumors of Wilkinson's perversions but continued to trust him. Then in 1804 Jefferson appointed him Governor of the Louisiana Territory, a vast area that included all the land west of the Mississippi and north of New Orleans. Wilkinson, who had originally conspired with Aaron Burr in 1805-06 to wrest the western territories from the rest of the nation, eventually betrayed Burr, endearing him to Jefferson who hated Burr. Later, Madison relieved Wilkinson of his command, and Wilkinson was court-martialed but acquitted for lack of evidence. Wilkinson returned to army service as supreme commander in the War of 1812 along the Canadian border. Subsequent inquires also found him innocent.

He was vain, extravagant, devious, flamboyant, selfish, corrupt, unscrupulous, and a traitor, an officer who reached the pinnacle of army service and rank while remaining in the hire of enemies. He even deceived Aaron Burr into thinking he was a co-conspirator willing to separate American territory from federal control while he was in bed with Spain. Then he betrayed Burr.

Americans denigrate Benedict Arnold, but Wilkinson is the more odious army general who defected but was never found guilty for his crimes.

Jefferson Davis (1808–1889)

The military tradition and entrance into the army in the early part of the 19th century was much stronger among southerners than northerners, which is why so many military institutes, like Virginia Military Institute, still flourish in southern states. The existence of slavery made the fear of slave revolts likely and military expertise was considered indispensable to avoid any such rebellions. Jefferson Davis, Joseph E. Johnston and Robert E. Lee, who graduated second in his class, attended West Point, and several others who became military officers during for the Confederacy.

While at West Point, Jefferson Davis, "with the flat cheeks and cold eyes of an ascetic, his thin round lips set firmly," as Margaret Mitchell described him in *Gone With the Wind*," was twice court-martialed for behavior not condoned by the army. The sentences were suspended. He acquired multiple demerits, and graduated 23 out of a class of 32. While serving as a second lieutenant in the frontiers in Michigan and Wisconsin among Indians, he was court-martialed again in 1835 for insubordination, but was acquitted and shortly thereafter resigned from the army.

In 1835 he married Sarah Taylor, daughter of then colonel, later General and President, Zachary Taylor. The newlyweds moved to Louisiana to visit one of Davis's sisters. Both contacted malaria and Sarah died three months later. Davis became a recluse for several years after moving to a Mississippi plantation on 800 acres staffed with 10 slaves his older brother Joseph, a lawyer and one of the largest plantation owners in the South with over 3,000 acres, had advanced him.

His cotton plantation was successful enough that he increased his slaves from 10 to 40 by 1840. By 1845 according to Warren County records he had 61 slaves and 113 by 1860. Slavery was indeed profitable regardless of how kindly and paternalistic biographies of plantation owners like Davis are portrayed. [1] The tragedy of the South is that no one ever spoke publically against the debased morality of slavery, and no one made any concerted effort to reform the state laws or abolish slavery, even in a gradual way, despite the North's persistent condemnation.

After a few notable speeches in the region, particularly in Vicksburg, in 1844 Davis was elected to Congress. In his freshman year he campaigned for the entry of Oregon and Texas. As hostilities increased between Mexico, Texas settlers and the U.S. army under Zachary Taylor, his former father-in-law, Davis resigned his congressional seat in 1846 to fight in the Mexican-American war and was commissioned a colonel in the Mississippi militia. He brought his horse, Tartar, and male servants with him into battle. He distinguished himself in the Battle of Monterrey where he was wounded in the foot. President Polk offered him a brigadier generalship but he refused saying that only states could offer such promotions, an odd idea from one who attended West Point to acquire an officer rank in the U.S. army. Mississippi's Governor Albert G. Brown appointed Davis in 1847 to fill the vacant seat in the U.S. Senate of recently deceased Jesse Speight.

Besides the vast territories in the Southwest acquired by the military victory over Mexico, and the purchase of additional lands through the Gadsden Purchase, the Union was still imperiled by the addition of more slave lands. The Mexican campaigns also proved to be training grounds for several southern junior army officers at the time including Lee, Bragg, Stonewall Jackson, Johnson, Beauregard and Longstreet.

When Congress began discussions to admit California directly into the Union as a state, bypassing territorial status, southerners were horrified, as this would upset the congressional representative equilibrium. Like Missouri and Kansas, the legislative issue of admitting new states as free or as slave holding would pop up as the overriding topic and expose the lengthening problem that divided the country. A bipartisan southern convention held in Nashville in 1850 actually threatened secession if California's measure passed. But southern strategists had no problem with Davis as one of their leaders in the Senate seeking the entry of Cuba into the Union, as this would enlarge the slave-holding states.

Once again a compromise was proposed for California's entry, this time by Henry Clay of Kentucky. California would enter as a free state, but the territories of Utah and New Mexico would leave the question of slavery to themselves, and whether or not to extend a new fugitive slave law. Mississippi's congressional delegation resisted the compromise. Arguing in favor of slavery, as Davis did in Congress, was arguing on behalf of economic preservation for all southern states. No southerner would vote for representatives sent to Washington unless they were sound pro-slavery. [12]

The arguments sustaining slavery were two-fold: that the prerogatives of the states come before that of the federal government, and that the Constitution has to be interpreted strictly as protecting slavery. These are the same two arguments, with the exception of slavery, that impel radical conservatives in today's political debates. The hardening of ideological beliefs, even about a non-brainer as slavery, kept southern men of talent and minimum virtue, and sympathizers like President James Buchanan, from seeing any way out of the moral impoverishment of an economy supported by slave labor.

The election of Lincoln was merely the final episode in a national feud. Southern states had used the argument of states rights, a code phrase for disobeying any law of federal judicial finding they thought infringed on slavery. Once they collectively decided to secede in 1861 they formed another government just like the one they had withdrawn from. Paradoxically, the power of the rebellious states was curtailed in the Confederate Constitution of March 11, 1861, giving the lie that the states were somehow sovereign and exposing the political hypocrisy. Without slavery there would have been no war. [13]

Jefferson Davis was selected President of the Confederacy because he represented a South that was primarily interested in protecting its economic and socially distinct way of life, a European aristocratic and feudal life of masters and slaves perpetuated in modern America. Davis's chief administrative duties were in asserting states rights and strict constitutional liberties. When he was asked as an experienced planter and naysayer legislator to administer a country consisting of seceded states, his inexperience in management acumen became apparent. As he focused on the military campaign he was unprepared to manage the southern economy, its weak transportation system, food supplies—planters wanted to plant more cotton and tobacco and not enough food for troops—logistics, finances and even diplomacy.

His appointments to key government cabinet positions were often hapless. In the end inexperience and mismanagement proved disastrous. Not only did the South not have sufficient resources to manage a war, it did not have enough capable administrators to manage a domestic economy during wartime. After all, the South had always argued that such matters should be left to states. The South had persistently castigated the national government for intruding into the South's interests. Yet when the South formed its own government, the military campaign notwithstanding, it was incapable of managing its own regional affairs. Had slaves not been able to provide enough food the Confederacy would have collapsed sooner from starvation. Nevertheless, to demonstrate its protection of slavery, the Congress of the Confederacy ordered the execution of any White northern officer of Black troops. [14] The one legislative act alone was decreed not for military but racial reasons.

Davis was captured in 1865, imprisoned, and finally released on bail in 1867 and never brought to trial. [15] His recollections, *The Rise and Fall of the Confederate Government* (1881), declared that the confederates did not fight to preserve slavery—this was a lie—but "constitutional liberty". Proud, inflexible, a symbol of an honor-bound people, Davis never accepted any responsibility for the defeat of the South and its peculiar institution. Although eventually pardoned by President Andrew Johnson his citizenship in the United States was never restored.

The following list below of officials does not include military personnel from the South, like Jubal Early, Richard Ewell, Nathan Forrest, Wade Hampton, William Hardee—all Lieutenant Generals for the Confederacy who fought for the secessionist cause. It does include U.S. Members of Congress and Senators who aligned themselves with Confederate secessionists. Because secession is constitutionally illegal and violates a representative's oath to defend the Constitution, the ones cited below are American traitors, and their villainy so noted. Section 3 of the 14th Amendment specifically excluded all civil officials "engaged in insurrection or rebellion" from holding public office again.

The *Confiscation Act* of 1862 authorized the President to pardon anyone involved in the rebellion. On April 9, 1865 Gen. Grant offered generous terms of surrender to the troops of the Army of Northern Virginia that allowed the men to return to their homes and observe the terms of their paroles. Additionally, thousands more sought amnesty and personal pardons from President Johnson and almost universally received them. On Christmas Day 1868, Johnson granted an unconditional pardon to all Civil War participants except high-ranking military and civil officials.

In May 1872 the *Amnesty Act* gave the right to hold office again to almost all Southern leaders (Confederate States of America, CSA) who had been excluded from public office. But a select list of these men of distinction who turned treasonous to the Constitution shows how deeply southern intransigence went.

Judah Benjamin (1811-84) was a U.S. Senator from Louisiana who became CSA Attorney General, Secretary of War and Secretary of State.

Thomas Bragg (1810-72) was a U.S. Senator from North Carolina who became CSA Attorney General.

John Breckinridge (1821-75) was a U.S. Senator from Kentucky and U.S. Vice President under President Buchanan. He was a candidate for President but lost to Lincoln. He became a Major General and Secretary of War for the CSA.

John A. Campbell (1811-89) was an Associate Justice of the U.S. Supreme Court, who strongly opposed secession, but who became an Assistant Secretary of War for the CSA.

Howell Cobb (1815-68) was U.S. Secretary of the Treasury, and a Major General in the CSA.

R. M. Hunter (1802-86) was a U.S. Senator from Virginia and later CSA Secretary of State and a Confederate Senator.

Stephen Mallory (1813-73) was a U.S. Senator from Florida and CSA Secretary of the Navy.

James Mason was a U.S. Senator from Virginia and CSA Commissioner to Great Britain.

John H. Reagan (1818-1905) was a U.S. congressman and Senator who became Postmaster General in the CSA and Acting Secretary of the Treasury. After the war he was imprisoned for several months, but was re-elected to the U.S. Congress for five terms and then to the U.S Senate until 1891.

Edmund Ruffin (1794-1865) is credited with firing the first shot at Fort Sumter. He fought at 1st Bull Run and committed suicide in 1865 after the Union army destroyed his Virginia property.

John Slidell (1793-1871) was a U.S. Senator from Louisiana who was sent as the CSA's Commissioner to France.

William Smith (1796-1887) was a U.S. congressman from Virginia and made a Major General in the CSA, and later became Governor of Virginia.

Robert Toombs (1810-85) was a U.S. Senator from Georgia who was the Secretary of State for the CSA.

As an example of a man of distinction who did not become a traitor, Thomas Hicks (1798-1865) as Governor of Maryland refused to convene the pro-southern legislature thus preventing the state from entering into secession.

The trauma of the war created heroes and heroines, treason and traitors. But the national rupture also left residues of the reason there was a civil war in the first place, the culture of enslavement it engendered in the southern population, and the lingering seeds of racism that exists still in American society.

Thus when Tea Party candidates and members want to bring about a revolution, are they thinking about the kind of southern secession that engaged this nation from 1861-65? Because they use as their revolutionary statement the revolt against the British, they seem to be symbolizing the rebellion against a foreign power. But that is exactly the way the South viewed the North in 1860. America's hostility toward the national government, a government that guarantees its right to oppose it, simmers yet in its politics.

Alexander Stephens (1812-1883)

(Jefferson's) ideas, however, were fundamentally wrong. They rested upon the assumption of the equality of races. This was an error . . . Our new government is founded upon exactly the opposite idea; its foundations are laid, its corner–stone rests, upon the great truth that the negro is not equal to the white man; that slavery — subordination to the superior race — is his natural and normal condition. (Alexander Stephens, March 21, 1861, Savannah, Georgia) [16]

Georgia Congressman Alexander Stephens (1812-1883) became Vice President of the Confederacy, and Governor of Georgia. Stephens, "with dark burning eyes deep socketed in a face that had known nothing but sickness and pain," as Margaret Mitchell described him in *Gone With the Wind*, purchased his first slave in February 1841 for $600, or slightly more than a year's rent at a Washington DC boardinghouse when he was a member of Congress. Initially, he had not been a vociferous defender of slavery in principle, but over time he did become one of its most vocal advocates. He tried to apologize for its existence and explain away its more regrettable aspects.[17] Most southern politicians were a part of the culture and could not easily escape it. They were allied with, or related to, the large plantation owners who had the majority of slaves. They became defensive when attacked by northern abolitionists or slavery opponents and hence the cultural chasm widened. They may have opposed slavery but felt compelled to defend the South's cultural way of life.

In 1850 Stephens, a very intelligent man who was perpetually frail and sickly, weighing sometimes less than a hundred pounds, owned 13 slaves and had 5,000 scattered acres, about the same amount George Washington had on his non-contiguous plantations in and around Mount Vernon. Within a decade Stephens had quintupled his assets and owned 32 slaves on his estate, Liberty

Hall, near Crawfordville, and was one of the largest slaveholders in Warren country, Georgia.

He was elected to the Georgia special convention to vote on secession and wanted the South to remain in the Union. But in his Cornerstone Speech (see quotation above) he was clear that the foundation of the Confederacy was slavery. Later, he was adamant in his criticism of Jefferson Davis' Administration, the suspension of *habeas corpus* and conscription of soldiers. But in this opposition Stephens was thinking like a lawyer and not a commander-in-chief who, like Lincoln, felt the need to suspend some civil liberties to win the war. The South not only suspended civil liberties, it didn't even provide them to most of its residents. States rights meant not giving any rights, not even state citizenship, to slaves.

At the end of the war Stephens was imprisoned for five months near Boston. He returned to Georgia, where he was elected to the Senate but unable to serve because Georgia had not yet been admitted into the Union. For the following two years he wrote histories and tedious defenses of the discredited southern position. He was subsequently elected to the House and served for four terms until his service as Governor in 1882 where he died in office.

Like Stephens, too many southerners were lulled by the composition of their own siren song of state sovereignty, a dead horse legal issue that blinded them to Supreme Court decisions and national imperatives. I mentioned earlier about the sovereignty of the Cherokees for which Stephens' state of Georgia had no respect and sought only to requisition Cherokee land for new settlers. Georgia forcibly confiscated Cherokee sovereign land, bound by treaties with the U.S. for decades. That's what the South thought of sovereignty for others. It thought that state sovereignty was only that southern states used repeatedly as a rationale for their supposed independence from national government. The racism and ethnic cleansing that Georgia practiced on Indian inhabitants was cloaked with the smokescreen of absolute state authority to do what it wanted within its borders regardless of overriding national authority to protect all citizens, especially those with which it had treaties. So-called "states rights" discussions permeate American political discourse today.

In his two-volume history of the conflict between the North and South, Stephens dedicated his *magnum opus* to "all true friends of the Union under the Constitution" that he called a "Federative System." That is why he and all others sympathetic to the southern cause can still designate the Civil War as a war between the states. In fact, it was a civil war between a national government and rebellious and secessionist states. He cast his study under the rubric of a dialogue like Plato and Galileo, but his discussion partners are straw men for his exposition of so-called state sovereignty and states' rights.

Stephens would argue in his history, as would all who saw the Constitution as merely a re-ratification of the old *Articles of Confederation*, to be a limited partnership agreement between the states and not the origin of a new national government with powers superior to that of states.

Like strict constitutionalists today, Stephens never elaborates on the role of the U.S. Supreme Court, that final arbiter of the Constitution and its intent. I assume he does not because there exists a whole corpus of decisions by the high court giving precedence to the supreme authority of Congress over the states. Quoting these decisions, or even acknowledging their existence and legality, invalidates the argument.

Stephens wrote: "The Government of the United States was created by the States." [18] He errs. As we saw in Chapter Four, The *Articles of Confederation* was a compact created by delegates appointed by States in which state law did prevail. The Constitution, on the other hand, was ratified by the states *and by the people*, only after votes from the people in each of the thirteen states. This one misunderstanding has been constantly repeated throughout the decades and permeates our political discourse, as if continued repetition would make it true. The gist of his argument was that the Constitution was nothing more than an *Articles of Confederation* updated, a partnership agreement approved by the states and nothing more ("A Confederated Republic, or Confederacy . . . and not a Consolidated Government"), even though it contained a new chief executive, a judiciary, and a legislature with expanded powers, and specifically stated it was a new national government and not merely a revision of the old Articles. [19]

It is doubtful that this idea about the limited role of the Constitution as the formative document creating national government would ever had arisen had not slavery been the sole and constant irritant. Slavery and state advocates simply ignored Article VI of the Constitution. Can there be debate about what "supreme" means, or that congressional laws override state laws?

> Allegiance is due no Government. It is due the power that can rightly make or change Governments. [20]

The U.S. Supreme Court ruled in 1869, the year after Stephens' book was published, in *Texas v White* that Texas had never really left the Union to join the Confederate States because neither the *Articles of Confederation*, which declared the Union of states as "perpetual," nor the Constitution, "to form a more perfect union," permitted states to secede. The legal issue was permanently settled, that secession was unconstitutional, though not the philosophical quibbling about the role of states. Hence, the palaver about state sovereignty is rhetorical hyperbole, a shibboleth of the days from defending slavery and designed to diminish the role of the national government. But the differences between how the states relate to the national government have been long-lasting points of political contention.

In a rousing speech in Montgomery on March 21, 1861 Stephens said that the new Confederate Constitution laid out the questions relating to slavery and "the proper status of the negro in our form of civilization." This was his true view and that of the South in 1861. But in his writings, there were no such phrases about slavery, because frank discussion about slavery disappeared after the war. [21] The talk then was only about state sovereignty, as if that alone were justification for states upholding the institution of human bondage. Stephens was a hypocrite as well as a traitor. Even then, politicians would begin to cover their true intent under invented code words designed to appeal broadly to a sympathetic public, even if the issue were civil rights, or the domestic capabilities of government, and not just slavery. We can admire the argumentative audacity but still despise the professed principles.

Stephen's constitutional views were the standard southern views of the time and the common views of strict constitutionalists and many ordinary citizens. But the view of most constitutional scholars is that he and his allies were in legal error on this crucial issue. His lengthy volume is repetitious to tedium, but lawyerly and argumentative. It is difficult reading because of its redundancy. The lasting point is that it has become a pervasive if erroneous belief among the populace, and used by politicians in election campaigns to perpetuate a fundamental fallacy in elementary civics.

Stephens had a clouded judgment about many men he associated with. He introduced little legislation in all his congressional years that had any salubrious impact on the country, or even his state, though many excuses can be offered for his incessant physical irritants, disabilities, his melancholy and miserable illnesses that confined him for long periods to bed. He was in essence a provincial man, a state man, a slavery man. America's house was divided in the 1850s, the 1860s, and into the 1960s. It's still a house divided.

Like most southern gentleman during Reconstruction, P.G.T. Beauregard (1818-1893), former Confederate General, a Creole from Louisiana, in a letter on May 24, 1867 believed that Blacks were naturally indolent, ignorant and inferior. He honestly believed that within 75 years the coloreds would disappear together with Indians and the buffalo. [22]

After the Civil War, Beauregard founded the Louisiana Unification Party in 1873, on the basis that "Negro political power was a reality and might as well be accepted." The committee advocated political equality for the Negro, an equal division of state offices between the races, and a plan whereby Negroes would become landowners. It denounced hiring discrimination because of color in laborers or in selection of corporate managers, and called for the abandonment of segregation in public conveyances, public places, railroads, steamboats, and public schools. It was an extraordinary document, yet no one in the South beyond the reach of New Orleans intellectuals would accept Blacks as equals. Blacks too were suspicious of Negroes in Louisiana and disinclined to follow their leadership. [23] Beauregard and his committee members had appealed to the magnanimity and kindness of southerners at the end of the war when those virtues were unavailable.

I revisited the South again in late 2010 and early 2011 to gain information and conduct "man-in-the-bar" interviews for this book. I found nothing to lead me to believe that the prevalent attitudes I have described have in any way abated. I found self-segregated restaurants and bars and racist literature openly available at gun shows, among other signs of social separation. The same attitudes and segregated practices persist as they did after 1865, as we shall see in the next chapter.

...UNTIL JUSTICE ROLLS DOWN LIKE WATERS AND RIGHTEOUSNESS LIKE A MIGHTY STREAM

MARTIN LUTHER KING JR

Chapter Twelve
Putting The Union
Back Together

. . . and that government of the people, by the people, for the people, shall not
perish from the earth. (Abraham Lincoln, *The Gettysburg Address*)

America freed itself from the subjugation only to find itself embroiled in
guerrilla warfare. Economic and political dislocation followed the ultimate
military withdrawal after independence. The war ended with over 4,000 troops
killed.

If this sounds painfully contemporary, applicable to a foreign conflict, it is
actually the situation when America entered the defeated South in 1865. A
similar series of miscalculations and misjudgments occurred when
assassinations of black political aspirants and white idealists and opportunists
forced a political concession under the Hayes administration. The total
withdrawal of northern troops in 1877 ended federal occupation. As soon as the
southern states reconvened their legislatures, they immediately passed laws
known as the "black codes" that discriminated against freed Blacks. Whites
began a guerilla and vigilante war against those Blacks bold enough to seek
elected or appointed offices. Whites would not accept Black rule where it was
allowed to occur with new freedoms, voting franchises, and federal intervention.

When social barriers were shredded in the Civil War, many southerners
turned to class, ethnic and governmental hatred to channel collective
frustrations. Poor Whites who hadn't worked in a plantation economy realized at
the end of the war that they too had no skills, just like freed slaves, and that
there wasn't any work. Soldiering for them was no longer an option, but
vigilantism was. The KKK was the organization that provided southern
militancy against freed slaves and northern intruders. Scalawags—a term for
worthless livestock—described southerners who cooperated with federalists
during reconstruction, and carpetbaggers described northerners who went south
to help Blacks. [1]

The central questions that needed uniform answers seemed obvious: Were
freed slaves supposed to form a new society on their own, or were they
supposed to merge somehow with former slave owners as equals? Were the
former states to be treated as a foreign power, their admittance based as if they
were territories, as had been done with Native Americans? How were the
rebellious states to be punished, or were they? Should freed blacks be left to the
states to provide or should the federal government take care of them? Should
freed slaves have the same rights as other citizens? No budding social scientists
rushed to the South to seek answers as their lives, and certainly their research,
would have been in danger.

Northern idealism about slave freedom, but without plans for freed slave integration, and the hostility in the South to any emancipation of Blacks, made the whole business of executive, military and legislative reconstruction as unrealistic as Republican compromise today. Reconstruction deepened hostility toward the federal government, a resentment that still permeates American society. The South had three hundred years to try and eradicate slavery and failed. The world's oldest bureaucracy, the Vatican, had instituted more changes. It's a sad part of American history, which is why it's necessary to revisit its origins since its presence in contemporary politics is so pervasive.

Turn O Libertad

Turn O Libertad, for the war is over . . .
From the chants of the feudal world, the triumphs of kings,
  Slavery, caste,
Turn to the world, the triumphs reserv'd and to come—give up
  That backward world . . .
  (Walt Whitman, *Turn O Libertad*, 1923, p. II 92)

The Faults of Reconstruction and Hatred of Government

The cause of the great War of the Rebellion against the United States will have
to be attributed to slavery. (U. S. Grant, 1886, p. 542.)

The hatred Reconstruction created, the political and administrative bungling it exposed, and the court decisions that invalidated initial legislative enthusiasm, still lingers in societal animosity toward national government. Although it isn't always possible to trace absolute links between the historical past and the present, especially in politics, where there are sufficient parallels it is possible to conclude that the turbulent history of north/south relations is a part of our national culture and influences social and political dynamics.

This historical division in part still cleaves the approach to modern politics, ambiguously divided into the vague categories of liberal and conservative. The current radical movement in conservative Republican politics is rooted in the politics of the old South, and extends through the period of Reconstruction in the South from 1865-1877 and until the new civil rights era in the 1960s. The South was never flooded with immigrants like the North was, and so experienced neither a labor revival nor innovative entrepreneurship. Racism, which had always existed, rejuvenated when a Black President was elected.

Despite the moderate urbanization in the early part of the 19th century in Charleston, Savannah and New Orleans, the South had for decades been living in an agrarian time warp presided over by an extensive, landed feudal aristocracy who believed there was nothing to change. The South was then, and largely still is, a combination of cotton, cattle, corn, cane and timber. In fact, the lack of manufacturing that had been sweeping the newly industrialized countries in Europe and in the North was only a symbol of a deepening cultural and educational chasm between the South and North. Communication and transportation systems, particularly the railroad, in the North broadened commercial activities while the South stayed agrarian and relatively isolated from economic developments.

Literacy was never an option for Blacks and it was a southern felony to teach them to read or write, though many learned from each other. Even by 1880 the White illiteracy rate was about 25% throughout most of the South, higher in North Carolina, compared to only 9% nationally in the North. Illiteracy was about 70% for Blacks. Even by 1900, only Kentucky of all southern states had a compulsory school attendance law. The average southern adult female had twice as many children as the average adult female in the North. The amount of taxable wealth per child in Massachusetts was six times as high as it was in North Carolina. Additionally, the South had two separate school systems with a dual corps of teachers and facilities. [2]

There was no middle class in the South. The region had prided itself on its so-called superior civilization that was grounded in racial bigotry and not in regional philosophical, artistic, creative, cultural or aesthetic accomplishments. The economy revolved around the plantations, its production and service. After the Civil War, the economy, the infrastructure, and the system of slave labor were totally destroyed. The South was in ruins, as the diarist Mary Chestnut noted: "Columbia is dust and ashes—burned to the ground. Men, women and children left there, houseless, homeless, without one particle of food—picking up the corn left by Sherman's horses in their picket ground and parching (it) to stay their hunger." [3] Southerners had been dislocated and disillusionment was one of the milder psychological symptoms.

One of the turning points in the deepening North/South relations, as noted in Chapter 9, was the *Fugitive Slave Act* (1850) that forced the whole country to participate in slavery. Previously, the North had disregarded the South's slavery hoping it would not impinge on his lifestyle. But the escape of so many slaves to the North compelled a reluctant Congress to make escaping slaves a national problem. For a decade northern marshals were forced to become slave catchers diverting themselves from policing their home districts. This gave impetus to the Abolitionist movement as northerners became disenchanted with the slavery issue that had legally migrated to the North with runaway slaves.

After the war Reconstruction faltered and lunged forward but with political misgivings, lack of thoughtful clarity, and differing managerial tactics. President Johnson, Lincoln's Vice President who assumed the presidency on Lincoln's assassination, granted over 14,000 pardons. Johnson rejected the idea that Blacks had the same rights of person and property as Whites. He vetoed the *Freedman's Bureau Bill*, saying it bloated the size of government, and the 1866 *Civil Rights Bill*, both vetoes that Congress overrode.

President Andrew Johnson began his pardoning policy incautiously while Congress was not in session, a policy that seemed to reward the South instead of reforming it. Northern legislators were alarmed because it appeared as if southern rebels could return to their former status prior to the war, arm themselves for further rebellion, or possibly even secede again. Johnson even pardoned Nathan Bedford Forrest, a Confederate General who had summarily executed all Black Union soldiers after his victory at Fort Pillow. No one agreed with Johnson's indiscriminate pardoning, especially not Union soldiers who believed secessionist leaders were not held accountable.

Many in Congress and the North felt President Johnson from Tennessee was too lenient in pardons thereby seeming to allow citizens to vote themselves back in office so that they could admit states as if they had never seceded. Southern states in 1865 immediately began electing former Confederate leaders to state legislatures who quickly passed vagrancy laws and Black Codes that severely limited Black movement, ownership, and work. Some states defiantly refused to accept the terms of surrender and secession. Apart from the issue of freed slaves, the irony was that the South had voted back into elected office the very individuals who had voted to secede.

With the tacit encouragement of President Andrew Johnson, Mississippi convened a legislature that passed a series of Black Codes that did everything but enslave Blacks again by prohibiting them from renting land or quitting their jobs so they couldn't become independent farmers.

There are contemporary parallels. As southerners did during the days of Reconstruction to keep Blacks from voting, in 2011, Republicans in 32 states were promoting restrictions on voters that would impact the young, like college students, first time voters, those recently released from prison, the poor and minorities, or, in other words, those who tend to vote Democratic. Stripping voters rights, or placing any kind of restrictions on voters, is as malicious as it was in the South in the late 19th century with literacy tests, and as it continues in southern states like Texas and Florida that exposes the political kneecapping of the democratic process.

On the other hand, during Reconstruction the dilemma was that it was impossible to grant civil rights to freed Blacks and not to Whites, whether or not they had been rebellious. The difference was that Whites would never treat Blacks as equals, in voting, citizenship, or respect because it would make a mockery of secession and the war. Yet to grant votes and license to hold public offices to newly freed men without money, homes, education or security was tantamount to folly and an invitation to failure. No one had thought through the painful but necessary transition needed to become incorporated in the culture of mature citizenship for those who had been treated as little more than beasts of burden.

Ever since this period, the two main political parties have cultivated two groups—White conservative southerners, generally courted by Republicans, and African Americans, minorities and women generally by the Democrats. Consequently, American society possesses this racial divide in its voting blocs that represents the social divide between free states and slave states since the earliest dates of the republic. [4] Politicians play the race card, the gun card, the religious card, and any other topic in the population that will give them a voting edge. But racial identity is the more enduring, and both White conservatives and Blacks tend to vote in opposing blocs.

The war "struck down an aristocratic oligarchy . . . but there was no other class ready to assume the responsibility of government." [5] Historians usually noted that: "the storm united the nation and knit it into one great whole as no slower process could have done." [6] Reconstruction, as Nevins and Commanger note, assuredly *did not knit the country together*, and in fact drove them farther apart because of the clumsiness of President Johnson, the incompetence of President Grant, and the vindictiveness of Thaddeus Stevens and other legislators who sought to punish former rebels. No one had any conception of how to rebuild a torn region into a nation. Or had America, split between non-slave states and slave states from the beginning, ever really been a united nation? I claim that it was in name only.

Southerners, many Grant had faced in civil war battles, were ready to use force to reverse the outcome of the war. The weary and often vengeful North gradually backed away from enforcing its own laws and allowed the South to subjugate Blacks again. The passage of the *Amnesty Act of 1872* in effect absolved all but the most hardened of those who espoused treason.

Congress, led by Pennsylvania Representative Thaddeus Stevens, had a different strategy from Johnson, and pushed a punitive program through Congress, insisting that only Congress could pass the necessary laws to aid in reconstruction. Congress nearly impeached Johnson, and his Senate trial failed by only one vote. Under rules allowing the chamber whom to seat or not seat, Congress refused to authenticate members appointed by southern governors until Congress was satisfied the state was qualified for admission. Congress permitted each state to enter only if it subscribed to the 14th Amendment. Most southern states actively opposed it.

Thaddeus Stevens (1792-1868) and Reconstruction

Pugnacious Thaddeus Stevens, a man who thought and acted like a biblical prophet, who was dubbed "the scourge of the South," led the fight in Congress for emancipation of the slaves and the guarantee of full U.S. citizen and civil rights for all. He was ruthless in his implacable hatred of southern hypocrisy and rebellion and always sought to punish the region and its people for adhering to slavery. From 1865 to 1868, the year he died, he was the most powerful politician in America and used his unique oratorical and strategic skills to pass the most momentous legislation since the Constitution itself. If the North thought they had in him a reconstruction savior, he was vilified in the South for ruining their way of life. [7]

He was partisan in politics, generous to the downtrodden and those in need, highly intelligent, unforgiving to enemies, and had an uncommon determination and unselfishness to achieve his objectives for the country. He was unfazed by applause or praise, without overweening ambition, with a tart and satirical wit, and without the vanity that usually accompanies power. He had a single vision in fighting for the rights of the disenfranchised.

The South may have been conquered in 1865 but it was not subdued. While Congress was in recess, President Andrew Johnson in 1865 attempted to ease southerners and states into the Union by limiting Black suffrage and admitting states under their own conditions. South Carolina's legislature refused to ratify the 13th Amendment because it thought the amendment empowered Congress to dictate terms to the people in the state. Mississippi also refused to ratify the 13th Amendment and elected as a governor an ex-Confederate General, Benjamin Humphrey. Georgia elected the deposed Vice-President of the Confederacy, Alexander Stephens, who was at the time in prison awaiting trial for treason. [8]

Johnson's policies pleased the South since it left states free to dictate the terms of their readmission. Johnson's mistake was in conducting Reconstruction on his terms without congressional consultation while Congress was in recess. Thaddeus Stevens was furious, and he was an indignant man under normal conditions. When Congress finally met, he tactically persuaded Congress to use its powers to decide which members from southern states to seat in Congress, as Congress has the power to admit whom it chooses. He obtained congressional permission in December 1865 to form a Joint Committee on Reconstruction of the Senate and House, composed of 15 members. The Committee agreed that no elected member or state from the South would be admitted until the committee had made its recommendations.

The 800-page report contained no startling revelations unknown about the status of Reconstruction: that everyone in the South still hated Blacks, that suffrage was opposed everywhere, usually with violence for which there was no justice, and that defeated members of the Confederacy still insisted on the right of secession and wanted the national government out of the South.

The northern Republican Party did try to impose its politics on southern voting procedures to gain a greater majority in Congress, and there were obviously self-aggrandizing motives in this. [9] However, the Democratic Party in the South had been a secessionist participant and it was complicit in rebellion, and therefore its candidates, Congress thought, should not be readmitted as representatives. The attempt to "republicanize" the South was to prevent the Democrat Party in the South from forming in order to secede again. But previous office holders, though considered insurrectionists, were nevertheless the most qualified, as freed slaves were not, nor usually were northerners sent to help perform managerial duties. After the South regained political control of the respective states it returned to one-party Democratic rule as before.

Andrew Johnson vetoed the 1866 *Civil Rights Bill* that Stevens had crafted, but Congress overrode his veto. The 14th Amendment was Steven's triumph because it extended citizenship to everyone born in the U.S. and in the state where they resided, thus overturning the *Dred Scott* decision based on slaves not having citizenship in any state. Extending the 5th Amendment's prohibition against depriving anyone of "life, liberty or property without due process of law," the 14th Amendment extended this prohibition to states and forced all states to acknowledge equality of all persons under the law. The Supreme Court in time would have a legal opinion about these legislative acts, as we will see.

Stevens left an enormous footprint on America's legislative legacy, a tribute to the end of slavery, equal rights, and the meaning of human rights and citizenship. In his earlier years as a lawyer he helped free fugitive slaves in Pennsylvania courts, assisted in getting colored soldiers into the northern armies, and the long, tenacious battle for emancipation. He helped establish the

Freedman's Bureau, enjoined Congress to pass the first *Civil Rights Bill* in 1866, the 13th and 14th Amendments, and prepared the way for the passage of the 15th Amendment.

Let's reflect a minute on the meaning of citizenship, so critical to reconstruction, to freed slaves, to the immigrant issue today, and to how politicians in South Carolina still view the issue of citizenship by birth.

Sen. Lindsay Graham, Republican of South Carolina, questioned the 14th Amendment, which grants the right to citizenship to anyone born in the United States. In 2010 he said it was "a mistake" to allow American-born children of illegal immigrants to become citizens automatically. He said he would amend the 14th Amendment as a way of discouraging future unauthorized immigration. "We can't just have people swimming across the river having children here — that's chaos," he said on a TV interview. He could have been a politician speaking in 1868.

But political comments on the 14th Amendment were only the beginning. By October 2010 lawmakers in 14 states were announcing efforts to make changes in granting citizenship to infants born in the U.S. to illegal immigrants. *Legislators for Legal Immigration* planned state legislation to issue state birth certificates that would request parental birth certificates. The group wanted to force the issue at this writing before the Supreme Court for a ruling.

As a comparison, the laws signed by Adolf Hitler as Chancellor of Germany took away the citizenship of German Jews. Documents about the denial of citizenship were admitted during the Nuremburg Trials for Nazi war criminals in 1945. Gen. George S. Patton deposited them at the end of the war initially at the Huntington Library in Los Angeles, which has since released them to the National Archives where they now reside.

Citizenship is precious and who decides who becomes a citizen, and who remains one, is a matter of ongoing debate. The 14th Amendment gave Blacks, formerly slaves, state and national citizenship that had been denied them. But citizenship implies voting privileges. For the Blacks in the South until the latter part of the 20th century, that privilege was tenuous. The 15th Amendment reads: "The right of citizens of the United States to vote shall not be denied or abridged by the United States or by any State on account of race, color, or previous condition of servitude." *The Voting Rights Act of 1965* simply extended the same privileges to all in the South during the tumultuous period of civil rights agitation when southern states placed voting restrictions on Blacks.

And if you think this amendment finally restored privileges to those who had been so long denied basic human rights, then recall that Arizona—in its multiple attempts to assert its state's rights and question the sovereignty of Congress and even U.S. Supreme Court decisions—on August 26, 2001 challenged the constitutionality of the *Voting Rights Act*. This brazen palliative to Arizona conservatives revealed the same kind of discredited sympathy for southern politicians in 1866 in resisting by any means possible any federal intrusion on what the states could do to prevent full human rights for all.

Grant, Hayes and the Unraveling of Reconstruction

After the 13th, 14th and 15th amendments, Congress passed a series of *Enforcement Acts* in 1870 and 1871 designed to force requirements for social equality on southern states. Few at the time realized that the passage of legislation was only the beginning of national social rehabilitation. Ebullience for legislative victory soon gave way to realistic acceptance of southern intransigence toward northern influence of any kind, even after the end of military hostilities. The lack of sufficient federal troops, judges and prosecutors in southern states, inadequate funds, intimidation of Blacks serving on juries, overcrowded jails, and the ambiguity of the legislation made many convictions unlikely, and undermined the fragile efforts at restoring order and integrating all citizens.

Lincoln had appointed Ulysses S. Grant General-in-Chief after successive victories in the Mississippi Valley, especially after his victory at Vicksburg on July 4, 1863, the day after Robert E. Lee's defeat at Gettysburg. [11] Grant's military accomplishments were enough for a national reputation, which is why he easily won the presidential election in 1868. At one of the most crucial periods in American history, his successful military strategies, however, did not translate into administrative and political competencies.

Grant's capricious and inept performance and spasmodic efforts at both appeasement and martial law gave southern states the opportunities to vote White legislators back in power. The following is a list of examples of Grant's conflicting behavior and signals of what the objective was in just the year 1874.

On January 12, 1874, in a letter to Texas Governor Davis, Grant refused to send federal troops to Texas to prevent violence. On April 18, 1874, however, he ordered troops to protect telegraph lines in Arkansas. On September 2, 1874, with increased reports of abundant murders everywhere in the South, he issued a proclamation for Louisiana "for disorderly persons to disperse," and issued a similar one for Mississippi on December 21st. On December 9th Grant wrote to Governor Kellogg in New Orleans that: "It is exceedingly unpalatable to use troops in anticipation of danger." If troops were molested, Grant continued, "the question will be determined whether the United States is able to maintain order within its limits or not." [12]

The naivete of these tendentious documents shows how far removed he was from real and impending atrocities. He seemed unable to transfer his special military strategies from the war into sensible political realities during an ill-conceived and executed plan of reconstruction, a process indispensably needed to repair the rift between the country's sectors.

To be fair, it was an abnormal era when the executive and legislative authority of the federal government were literally in unknown territory, not knowing when to use military force as a domestic police action, or a conquering army to control disorder, or when to compel states to install Blacks as voters and elected legislators. Moreover, there was a lack of constitutional direction, as secession and reconstruction had not been on the agenda of constitutional framers. Coercion toward the South could not replace democratic consensus. Yet the irony was that southern democratic consensus would vitiate the whole return to formal unity and undeniably revert to disunity, if not secession again, if allowed to return to its power bases. The civilian White southern population was unanimously opposed to any federal intervention, and used paramilitary apparatus to achieve that objective. The anti-government movement was reinforced in southern minds during and after Reconstruction. It remains as a political movement in the national constituency to this day.

The Rutherford B. Hayes Administration in 1877 finally abandoned reconstruction and let southern states run their internal affairs. Freed blacks were soon reduced to subordinate status with the passage of discriminatory Black Codes in southern states until unchained legally by the civil rights movement in the late 1960s. [13]

Northerners and government officials did not delude themselves in supposing that hatred of the North, contempt for the Negro, and alienation for government disappeared because the war was over, or that these feelings were confined to politicians. Documentation from this era is clear and unremitting about the suffering, starvation, loss of property, goods, and eradication of the economy that left everyone without provisions, embittered, and in despair. The most outrageous instances, according to southern whites, were when Black federal troops reappeared in their districts, were quartered in towns where they were once slaves, and bullied their former owners and other citizens. The tables had been turned.

A report signed by W. A. Poillon, Assistant Superintendent of the Freedman's Bureau, and reported in U.S. Senate documents, No. 2, 1st Session of the 39th Congress, detailed multiple murders committed just in Alabama of gunshots, drowning and lynching of freed men in July 1865. Vigilant groups waited by rivers to catch ferried victims and along roadways to waylay any Blacks and murder them. [14]

The U. S. Supreme Court in the Slaughterhouse cases originating in New Orleans, where scores had been killed in riots, defined the 14th and 15th Amendments as applying only to violations by states and not by individuals. Hence, the *Enforcement Acts* passed specifically to deal with the KKK, which did apply to individuals, also became unconstitutional. The court reaffirmed this position in *United States v. Cruikshank* in 1876 where it held that the provisions in the 14th Amendment of due process and equal protection applied only to states and not to individuals. As a result, Blacks were left to unmerciful states that did nothing to protect them as citizens from marauding bands of vigilantes. The U.S. Supreme Court overturned and ruled unconstitutional, except for the 13th Amendment, all the legislative attempts to bring civil rights to freed slaves.

The Supreme Court's decision in *United States v Cruickshank et al.* (92 U.S. 542, 1876) rebutted the national government's argument to interfere in the state's prosecution of ordinary felons. The ruling came to the court based on a massacre of Blacks in Colfax, Louisiana in 1873. The court ruled in favor of the states in protecting citizens from: "any outrages, atrocities, or conspiracies, whether against the colored race or the white race, which do not flow from this cause, but spring from the ordinary felonious or criminal intent which prompts to such unlawful acts, are not within the jurisdiction of the United States, but within the sole jurisdiction of the states . . .." The problem was that southern states had no intention of prosecuting Whites who violated the civil rights of Blacks. Hostility to Blacks and the re-instatement of White supremacy was the sole motivating force of the South in this era, and it doomed Reconstruction.

As an historical side note, Jesse James and Cole Younger and their gang were former Confederate soldiers and robbed Union banks using the same tactics practiced during the war. For them and their southern sympathizers and White Line terrorist militia groups the war had never really ended.

The Supreme Court's decision in *Williams v. Mississippi* helped states disenfranchise Blacks by voiding state discriminatory jury selection. [15] Williams had been indicted and convicted for murder by an all-White jury and he sued claiming jury discrimination. The court disagreed and this decision paved the way for southern states to exclude Blacks from juries for all practical purposes. This decision was not overturned until the *Civil Rights Act* of 1964 and the *Voting Rights Act* of 1965.

Within a decade after the Civil War, by a combination of intimidation and violence, southern Whites regained political control, in effect nullifying all federal attempts to alter the social, racist mindset. Within a decade the combination of inept and uneducated freed slaves, corrupt northern officials and a few southern radicals, theft by rampaging militias, armed militancy, bungling by the Grant Administration, and voter fraud, allowed the South to regain its lost status and to reinstate its racial prerogatives.

By 1877, absent ostensible slavery, the country was as divided politically and culturally as it had been prior to the war. The anti-government movement today, from Tea Party members and their sympathizers, is a southern historical legacy that has not been eradicated.

Ku Klux Klan

> Our main and fundamental object is the MAINTENANCE OF THE SUPREMACY OF THE WHITE RACE in this republic. (original emphasis) [16]

Violence, rampant fraud and low turnout marred the election results that seriously undermined the fledgling government's legitimacy. Insurgent fighting the legitimate government killed opponents.

That was the case in Kabul, Afghanistan in 2010 as it was throughout the South from 1866-77. Militant and dangerous groups emerged, apart from the occasional violent incidents even in the Senate, as when on May 22, 1856, Preston Brooks of South Carolina caned Senator Charles Sumner of Massachusetts in the Senate, gashing his head open and crippling him for life.

In May 1866, the Ku Klux Klan arose as a kind of band of brothers that turned into a white supremacy movement in Pulaski, Tennessee. [17] It was reorganized in Nashville in the summer of 1867 with Confederate Lieutenant General Nathan B. Forrest (1821-1877), pardoned by President Johnson, a barely literate former slave trader, as Grand Wizard. Forrest had earned more than one million dollars trading slaves by 1860, entered the Confederate army as a private, raised his own battalion with his own money, and during the war was promoted to a Confederate Lieutenant General. By the end of the war he was financially ruined but was elected Grand Wizard of the Klan.

By 1868, according to Forrest's newspaper interview with a reporter from the Cincinnati newspaper *Commercial*, there were 40,000 Klan members in Tennessee and over a half million throughout the South, in effect constituting a counter-revolutionary army, almost like a replacement or vigilante group of self-appointed assassins of the defeated Confederate army. Many ex-confederate soldiers were members. This news alarmed congressional legislators and citizens in the North. The KKK went by a variety of names depending on where it existed: Knights of the White Camelia, Constitutional Union Guards, the Pale Faces, the White Brotherhood, the Council of Safety, etc. Its reign of terror extended until 1877.

In the 1920s it boasted over four million members with klaverns everywhere in the U.S. Since then its membership has fluctuated, but it remains an active group with the twin goals of white supremacy, colored with Christian overtones, hate and violence to achieve its aims. Inspired by the bigotry of D. W. Griffith's inflammatory silent movie *The Birth of a Nation*, the Klan became a kind of American patriotic civic group, and spread its fears and hatred everywhere, more popular in the North than the South. Lynching was its primary means of intimidating Blacks in the South until the 1960s. Its unfashionable and bizarre dress code of facial disguises, long white robes and hoods was meant to give historical cache to its members and to frighten superstitious individuals, and, according to contemporary reports, succeeded. Its puerile rituals, laughable costumes and ideology of bigotry exposed it for the fake Americanism of unity it vainly espoused.

But it persists. The Klan is now the oldest terrorist group in the United States with 221 known Klan groups throughout the U.S. in 2011.[18] As a contemporary comparison, many of today's 1.4 million soldiers are either from the South or come from rural communities that share southern Christian sympathies. These zealots, and groups like Military Ministry, Valor, and The Navigators, are trying to turn the military into a Christian army with anti-Semitic elements. This revivalist subculture of religious intolerance is overt, disturbing and another facet of the rise of the southern mentality so imbued with fundamentalist Christianity.[19]

The Klan's origins were in part to help bring law and order to parts of the South experiencing the lack of police action and disorder, primarily theft, arson and murder. An Englishman by the name of Somers who traveled throughout the South from 1870 to 1871 discovered how little the mandated government was able to prevent social anarchy. Many freed slaves, released from all supervision and obligations, became disorderly, in some cases terrorized white women, and refused to work.[20] The Klan was almost universally accepted because, although many members were racist—essentially the same ideology as the whole South—its presence created the semblance of order in rural communities. Its avowed purpose was to intimidate the freed slaves from voting, from seeking or holding office, and its methods were violent and ultimately successful.

The KKK became the chief organization for rebuilding white supremacy in the South by delegitimizing emancipated Blacks through murder, terror and intimidation. Additionally, and most despised, northern reconstruction leaders— some teachers with good intentions, and others the dregs of society hoping to enrich themselves—coming into the South became marked persons. These were the carpetbaggers. Few who entered stayed long enough to enjoy success. Schools were burned where northern teachers taught black children. The Klan was the organizational vehicle for reasserting what the South had been prior to the war. State governments and the police, many of whose officials were also Klan members, made no attempt to control or derail the Klan whose organized violence and terror intimidation was endemic, and whose murders of elected Blacks went unpunished. Its activities did bring reluctant order to virtual anarchy after a breakdown in social controls.

Alabama passed an Anti-Ku Klux Statute in 1868, as did other reconstructed states, that forbade any disguised person "away from his home by night, or by day, in company with others, or alone, and wearing a mask, or disguised in other costume, shall be guilty of a high crime . . ." [21] I'm unaware of whether or not this statute was over-turned, but it would have made Halloween celebrations dangerous, at least in Alabama, for the penalty was $500 and a minimum of six months jail time.

The passion that fed the southern male to fight for the Confederacy resurfaced after the war and got channeled into the Klan, the same kind of state militia he had previously served, but that was now secret. The cause was the same—to defend the South from northern encroachment, to keep Blacks inferior and to guarantee White political supremacy. [22]

The national government knew the seriousness of opposition to the KKK presented, and on April 20, 1871 Congress passed the *Third Enforcement Act*, known as the Ku Klux Act, aimed legislatively at making its activities, particularly aimed at jurors, or at hindering the enforcement of federal laws, criminal acts. President Grant went so far as to suspend the writ of *habeas corpus* in South Carolina in a conspiracy for permitting the KKK to operate freely as a militia and a rebellion impeding federal laws. [23]

This was an imposition of federal control over states, which southern states were unused to tolerating, and, in the case of freed slaves, unable to stomach without resistance. Ever since, every modern president has had to stoop to appeal to a distrustful public, and to a standard campaign topic of running against Washington, as if the town itself was a big bully and the culture of Big Government was the scariest form of tyranny. This attitude is a direct leftover fear from the days of Reconstruction.

Imagine a Confederate soldier screaming his rebel yell at the top of his lungs and charging into the ranks of the Army of the Potomac in 1864. The guts, intensity, and enthusiasm is the equivalent today of the zeal of radical Republicans who demand lower taxes while stripping domestic programs that benefit the poor and minorities, especially Blacks, mouthing platitudes and epithets meant to convey substantive content but really only braggadocio and racial and anti-government discontent.

With the Klan's help, the South returned to Black servitude without the need for slavery legislation with state passages of so-called Jim Crow laws, anti-African American segregation laws in schooling and public facilities that remained for nearly a hundred years until outlawed by the U.S Supreme Court's *Brown v Board of Education* decision in 1954, and the *Civil Rights Act* in 1964 outlawing discrimination in the use of public facilities.

The Klan reached its apex in 1925 with a 40,000 person march down Pennsylvania Avenue in Washington DC. Its influence rose again when Martin Luther King began his protests against blatant discrimination throughout the South. In the 1960s, yelling "white power" slogans as its message of white supremacy, it continued its tradition of violence and the threats of violence against Blacks and Jews.

From 1947 to 1965 over fifty bombings occurred in Birmingham, at the time the most segregated city in America. On September 15, 1963, in a racially motivated terrorist act, the Klan bombed the 16th Street Baptist Church in Birmingham, Alabama, killing four teenage girls, ages 11-14, who were in the basement at the time preparing for their Sunday lessons. Bob Chambliss, the chief Klan member involved in the bombing, was tried and acquitted, along with two others (one had died in the meantime). The three Klan members were brought to trial again in 1977 with the federal charge of violating the civil rights of the murdered girls and convicted. Chambliss died in prison in 1985.

On June 21, 1964, a Mississippi man, James Chaney, and two New Yorkers, Michael Schwerner and Andrew Goodman, who had been working to register Black voters, were murdered near Philadelphia, Mississippi after they had been arrested on trumped-up charges and then released so the Klan could track their car. A court later discovered that a conspiracy existed between the law enforcement and the Klan. State prosecutors refused to try the case, but the FBI arrested 18 men in connection with the killings, and seven were convicted. The case as reopened in 1999 and Sam Bowers, the head of the White Knights of Mississippi, was convicted for conspiracy to commit murder more than 30 years after the crime.

When Klansmen lynched a Black teenager in Mobile, Alabama, Southern Poverty Law Center lawyers, led by retired Director Morris Dees, argued that the Klan was responsible and should be held financially accountable. In November of 2008, the court ordered the United Klans of America responsible and made them pay $7 million, effectively bankrupting the organization. Their headquarters was sold to pay for the verdict. The Center has been responsible for winning large jury verdicts against hate groups, like the Imperial Klans of America, and Christian Knights of the KKK.

Members of the KKK later firebombed the offices of the Southern Poverty Law Center (SPLC). By October 2010 more than 30 individuals had been convicted of crimes in connection with plots to assassinate Morris Dees, the founder, and staff members.

So with charity to all Whites and violence to all Blacks, the KKK marches on with its simultaneous message of Christian belief and exclusivity for Whites. How it maintains this cross-purpose, inconsistent mentality is one of the most irrational of American traditions. The Patriot movement is the offshoot of the Klan, and its members now dress in battle fatigues and not hooded robes.

> Segregation now, segregation tomorrow, segregation forever.
> (George Wallace, Governor of Alabama)

By the end of the period of Reconstruction, Blacks were excluded from voting. Whites again had more disproportionate representation in Congress. The violence did not end when freed slaves were disenfranchised again, or when federal troops and Carpetbaggers were evicted, or poor Whites subdued. The South had only one quarter of the North's population but four times as many murders in 1890, a generation after the war. An average of six northern states had 24 murders while an average of eight southern states had 102 murders according to census data for 1890, and the instances of murders in the South were likely underreported. [24]

The Compromise of 1877 was an agreement in which a presidential race was thrown into an Electoral Commission in Congress to resolve. Southern Democrats and northern Republicans agreed that Rutherford B. Hayes, a former Union Major, Ohio Governor and congressman, would become President if federal troops were withdrawn from the South. Southern representatives would receive preferential treatment in the Cabinet and funds for industrial production, especially railroads. For all practical purposes, southern states had regained control of their affairs, had reduced Blacks to subservient status again short of slavery, and negotiated to keep the federal government from interfering. In a letter to his Secretary of War, George W. McCrary, on April 3, 1877, Hayes removed troops from South Carolina and a few days later from Louisiana. During the War Hayes as a Member of Congress wanted to let the South remained seceded. [25]

The election of Hayes to the presidency was a secret compromise that was negotiated over at least a year. The southern Democrats gained control of Congress and adjourned without appropriating funds for the army, which meant that federal troops serving in the South would not be paid. In exchange, the South held the North financially hostage, and wanted the removal of troops and guarantees of non-interference. [26] The North wanted a restoration of Black suffrage and adherence to civil rights. The South reneged on their part of the bargain, gave its votes to Hayes who wanted conciliation, but abandoned commitment to universal suffrage for Blacks.

Fast forward to Tuesday, September 21, 2010 when the Senate failed to override a Republican filibuster of a defense authorization bill so the army didn't get paid. Procedural tactics were raised, but they were inconsequential. But the filibuster did prevent the opposing party from claiming any kind of political victory.

The Civil War ended rebellious insurrection and eradicated slavery but did not resolve the social isolation from the North, except in commercial activities, nor diminish racist attitudes. Except for the legal abolition of slavery, southern states by 1877 after the withdrawal of federal troops returned to subordinating Blacks and passed a series of their own discriminatory legislation, and began a public relations campaign of idealizing a discredited past. Was the war really over or were hostilities just at an interlude? By the 1890s, according to C. Vann Woodward, one of the most distinguished scholars of the South, "A cult of racism disguised or submerged cleavages of opinion or conflicts of interest in the name of white solidarity, and the one-party system reduced political intolerance to a machine of repression." [27]

The Civil War ended in a northern victory but the South reinstalled its racist soul. Substantially, after federal troops departed and the North grew distant and weary from the social conflict that followed the war, the South began *de facto* segregationist policies and legislation, in effect returning to secessionist state governments without a united Confederacy, and a lingering hostility toward the North and national government.

Reconstruction failed, and the reasons are complicated, because it isn't clear it could ever have succeeded whatever legislation or judicial adjudication occurred. After all, the South did not politically participate in the proceedings that passed the 13th, 14th, or 15th Amendments, not that they would have agreed, so states never felt obliged to submit to them, until forced to as a condition to reenter the Union. The North thought that legislating social behavior for the South would be enough to ensure compliance, and it wanted quick results. The North was too eager to cry out, "Mission Accomplished" before any objective had been attained.

The South lost everything in the war including its misplaced pride in slavery as the sole solution to agricultural labor. It was unwilling to submit just to "northern" documents that dictated what they thought or how they behaved toward others, so laws were either unanimously ignored or repudiated. When troops arrived to impose some law and order, there was immediate resistance. Southern paramilitary responses killed freed slaves and northern officials sent south to help them enter society, crimes largely condoned. Midnight raiders endured for years without retribution so widespread was the sympathy for their cause.

Subsequent presidents left the South to its own segregation devices, were in sympathy with them, or pandered to its culture to win votes. President Grover Cleveland was in accord with the South on racial policy. [28] Both Theodore Roosevelt and Howard Taft had inducements to southern sentiments, praised confederate traditions, make sympathetic speeches and laudatory overtures to racial divisions.

The Southern bloc again returned to power under Woodrow Wilson in 1912. [29] But from Lincoln to Wilson, and with the exception of Andrew Johnson elevated from the Vice Presidency at Lincoln's death, no southerner had even been nominated to a national party position. From the beginning of the Civil War to the beginning of the 20th century the South had been politically isolated. Franklin D. Roosevelt didn't need southern votes to continue his winning ways since the power of labor unions and bursts of federal spending on World War II and the creation of new jobs catapulted him into repeated electoral victories. J. Strom Thurmond's creation of the Dixecrat party in 1948 attempted to consolidate the old southern vote that had remained loyal to the cause, a focus almost exclusively on race. [30] The old South had not disintegrated or altered its social attitudes. It never really went underground until, under the Obama Administration, it raised its annoyingly bigoted and repugnant head.

Not much has changed. Multiple unsavory instances of painting political opponents as unworthy of representation continue. Lying about the life of opponents in political ads, or by political leaders of what congressional legislation embodies, appear to be the most popular. Unethical and immoral standards are now somewhat common in political discourse, further alienating the public from the high standards one would like to see in electoral politics. But what is at heart undermined is belief in politics and government. This is why we see the emergence of people who seek revolution, sometimes even by armed means, to restore confidence in the federal government, if they even think that is possible.

The U.S. Supreme Court in 2010 *Citizens United v Federal Election Commission* struck down the McCain-Feingold bill, *The Bipartisan Campaign Reform Act of 2002*, that had made it a crime to pay for "electioneering communication." The court ruled that First Amendment guarantees of free speech prevailed in campaign contributions and not the amount of financial contributions. Thus, the campaign reform act was therefore unconstitutional. As a result, corporations, advocacy groups, and wealthy individuals pour millions into secret election funds without public scrutiny. Giving money, the court declared in a 5-4 decision, is the same as expressing yourself without government interference. By equating the giving of money in a political campaign to freedom of speech the court in effect disenfranchised the public from knowledge of how elections in this democracy can be swayed.

The same kind of reconstruction mistakes have been made in this age in foreign policy as the military, sent to a foreign country to root out terrorists, becomes involved in something called "nation-building," even in countries that previously were not really nations but a loose federation of tribes, similar to the loose federation of states that existed in colonial America. Unsuccessful at home at social reconstruction, American policy-makers believe they can fictionally construct a nation as a liberal democracy when before invasion the country, like Iraq or Afghanistan, was an opposing confederation of ethnic and religious rivalries held together by the iron arm of a dictator or a brutal regime.

A democracy is built around the power of the people to channel the laws that govern them, and the people chosen to represent them. At issue in America in the 19th century was, ironically: who were the people to make this decision? Many in the South did not consider Blacks human. The Constitution did not consider them as eligible to vote, and only to be counted for representation, so they were without citizen rights. The 13th Amendment freeing slaves did nothing to resolve the ingrained culture of Black inferiority in the North or South. The scramble for northern political advantage in gaining Black votes from the South, and the South's hostility and resistance to any Black advantages, defined

America's struggle to reunite the country, and its perennial racial dilemma. It still defines us. Nationalism has not completely triumphed because no national settlement was achieved, only a partisan stalemate, no matter how many stand for the National Anthem. Sectionalism in race permeates the culture.

White conservatives fled the Democratic Party in droves after the passage of the civil rights legislation in 1964 and President Johnson's social programs of the Great Society. By the 2010 election White southern moderates fled to the Republican side too. Though the South today is traditionally pro-business, averse to taxes and government regulation, religiously conservative, against abortion and gay rights and any form of gun control, it is heavily reliant on federal programs like financial assistance from natural disasters, farm subsidies and defense contracts. Politicians who complain about wastage of federal taxpayer money always accept federal funds, like farm subsidies, flowing into their states or localities. The ideological standoff in America is drifting toward the extremes, and the loss of moderation is widening the rigid political chasm.

President James Garfield, remembered most for his untimely assassination after only four month in office, a professor and college president Hiram College in Ohio) and Major General in the Civil War, was one of America's most illustrious presidential intellectuals. At his inaugural address on March 4, 1881 he noted:

> The elevation of the negro race from slavery to the full rights of citizenship is the most important political change we have known since the adoption of the Constitution of 1787. NO thoughtful man can fail to appreciate its beneficent effect upon our institutions and people. It has freed us from the perpetual danger of war and dissolution. It has added immensely to the moral and industrial forces of our people. It has liberated the master as well as the slave from a relation which wronged and enfeebled both. It has surrendered to their own guardianship the manhood of more than 5,000,000 people, and has opened to each one of them a career of freedom and usefulness.

Although his lofty aspirations would not be fully realized, his prescience in acknowledging the ideals of the nation was thoughtful and proper. The country is not without discrimination and prejudice because of its fateful legacy, and equal suffrage is a matter still to be resolved.

Rosa Parks Statue in Montgomery, Alabama

Chapter Thirteen
Battles For Civil Rights
And Domestic Entitlements

In a free government the security for civil rights must be the same as that for religious rights. (James Madison, *The Federalist Papers*, #51)

The chief political issue was slavery in the 19th century. In the 20th century it was civil rights. In the 21st century the political battle is obstructionism of governmental initiatives that seek to benefit the greatest good for the greatest number. Compassionate conservatism is a dead campaign slogan and an unfulfilled policy initiative. I'd like to review in this chapter the more than half century of civil rights legislation and its presidential opposition to show this profound cultural division and its impact on a polarized country and the dysfunctional politics that results.

As is true with most presidents with the possible exception of Lincoln, politicians have tip-toed around civil rights and treated the issue with velvet gloves because they knew it alienated voters. They did not want to kick a hornet's nest. Yet for nearly two hundred years equal rights for all has been the primary social and political issue that separates American voters into nearly equal dual constituencies. Taxes, the size of government, federal intrusions into the private sector, an activist judiciary, are all a part of this legacy of the struggle for civil rights.

The presidents I feature here came from all backgrounds and locales, from small town America, from tradesmen, professionals and families of privilege, with varying ideologies, and differing levels of agreement about the equality of all Americans. Prior to the government's serious engagement with civil rights, the nation had to battle the deteriorating economy beginning in 1929, and a decade later engage in a global war on two fronts. The embattled president was Franklin Delano Roosevelt, a son of patrician privilege. His legacy and domestic involvement set the stage for the political animosities and dilemmas of the 20th and 21st centuries.

Franklin Roosevelt: Groping Through the Depression

Roosevelt was a political pragmatist, unafraid to change his mind. In 1922 he spoke out against government regulation of business. In 1929 speech when he was Governor of New York he decried the dangers of a government relationship with industry. In 1933 he did not favor the federal insurance of bank deposits. Congress created the Federal Deposit Insurance Commission (FDIC) anyway. Each of these political stances would today mark him as a conscientious Republican. Yet for all his charm and beguiling personality, he was a practical man willing to experiment with policies, not an ideologue. And he did change his mind as the times warranted. Despite his Republican-leaning ideas, as President he promoted some of the most far-reaching domestic programs in the history of America. He created farm subsidies, bank regulations, relief programs and social security. One of the unemployed men who found work in the government's relief program known as the Works Progress Administration (WPA) in Illinois, acquired because he had campaigned for Roosevelt, was John Edward Reagan, father of Ronald Reagan. [1]

Almost immediately after his inauguration he proposed the *Emergency Banking Act*, the *Civilian Conservation Corps* (CCC), the *Agricultural Adjustment Act* (AAA), the *Tennessee Valley Authority* (TVA) that served seven states with rural electrification. Lastly, he got Congress to pass the *National Industrial Recovery Act* that allowed businesses to become more corporate, not your normal progressive, or Democratic Party agenda.

All of this legislation in 1933-35 put people to work and, as with the CCC, gave them schooling as a part of their work assignments. Beginning in 1933 the CCC provided jobs for three million unemployed youth and aided park and forest development, disaster relief efforts, control of soil erosion, wildlife protection and historical preservation—all programs the country needed to protect and preserve the national heritage. Its results are still visible today in our national parks and, for example, in cabins built by CCC employees along the Appalachian Trail where I've stayed with my family. No such job bill, though one was sorely needed in 2012, would have passed the Republican obstructionist House in Congress.

The most historic piece of legislation passed in 1935 is the *Federal Insurance Contributions Act* (FICA), otherwise known as social security. Funds are deducted from paychecks and used as a financial distribution for persons with disabilities and as a retirement system for the elderly.

Practical economic programs dictated Roosevelt's executive actions based on a re-evaluation of his own political values and his keen political acumen. Hence the New Deal—his umbrella term for all his programs—was not a coordinated set of strategic policies but a set of improvisations not anchored in any grand economic theory. [2] As a child I had to remain absolutely quiet in the warmth of my paternal grandmother's kitchen while the adults listened on the radio—the acknowledged medium of the day often crackling with static—to Roosevelt's fireside chats.

By the time of undeclared naval war in 1939 against Germany, and the declared war in December 1941 with Japan and Germany, the New Deal had exhausted its influence and full-throttled manufacturing production revived the economy and put people to work. We should not automatically conclude from this that war is good for a flagging economy. What we can conclude is that a determined Roosevelt and a revived American economy and manufacturing base helped defeat the forces of tyranny and aggression from Germany and Japan within five years, from 1941-45.

Roosevelt may have recognized the discrimination in the South, but the national economic depression and the war prevented Roosevelt from initiating any sustained initiatives. But he did recognize southern poverty. According to the presidential report, *The Economic Conditions of the South*, when Roosevelt was president during the Great Depression, the "South presents right now the

Nation's No. 1 economic problem." [3] Rather than address civil rights directly, Roosevelt focused on how the South was economically disadvantaged. FDR did not believe that businesses should make all the essential decisions on society, or that government should pursue a policy of disinterest in the economy, or that popular government was dangerous—all policies advocated by the Tea Party movement. [4] Roosevelt thought of solving problems, not about upholding political dogmas.

In 1938 there was a disproportionate number of adult workers to dependents in the South, as many workers were displaced by machines, notably tractors, and White workers were taking over jobs once reserved for Blacks, while the most skilled workers migrated to the North. The level of poverty was great throughout the nation but acute in the South. This could only deepen the ethnic divide through wage manipulation and taxes to support schools. The South was educating one-third of the nation's children with one-sixth of the school revenues. Teacher salaries were four times less. As a result, there was nearly four times the illiteracy in the South as elsewhere. Economic setbacks in jobs, schooling, health and housing are still the context for the South's coming to grips with its civil rights past. [5]

Roosevelt's opponents on the right were typically conservative in response to the New Deal, that flurry of legislation in 1933 that plunged the government headlong into the nation's economic recovery. Contemporary opponents of government intervention react just as strongly today to government's provisions in health care. [6]

The Swedish sociologist Gunnar Myrdal's classic study of southern race relations in *An American Dilemma* in 1944, and Stetson's Kennedy's 1946 *Southern Exposure*, a realistic critique of the undemocratic South, both laid bare the racist and economically underdeveloped underbelly of the nation. After World War II the South still held a firm, White grip on politics and economics. States routinely disenfranchised Blacks and circumvented the 15th Amendment ratified in 1870 by requiring a poll tax or literacy test for Blacks to register to vote. Today, several Republican-controlled states have passed laws reducing early voting and legislated other voting restrictions, like requiring photo ID under the ruse of voter fraud, that tend to disenfranchise minority voters who tend to vote Democratic.

Roosevelt had to defeat the forces of tyranny in Europe and Asia. The challenge today is to defeat the one-sided, extremist attempts to limit individual freedoms like family planning, gay rights, and at efforts that weaken privacy laws, and attempt to impose religious beliefs. The continuing struggle for civil rights is but one example of why we have failed to integrate the nation.

Truman's Surge for Civil Rights

President Harry S. Truman (1884-1972) oversaw the end of World War II after the death of President Roosevelt in April 1945. Among notable achievements, he ordered atomic bombs dropped on Hiroshima and Nagasaki, attended the end-of-the-war conference with Churchill and Stalin at Potsdam, inaugurated the Marshall Plan for the rebuilding of Europe, helped create NATO, advocated for a Jewish homeland and recognized Israel, presided over the beginnings of the Cold War with Russia, and over the Korean War that began in 1950. But it was Truman's advancements in civil rights not his foreign policy actions that were one of his most successful and courageous policy initiatives.

Truman was alarmed when he received a letter from R. R. Wright, a veteran of the Spanish-American War and World War I stating how a Black soldier returning for World War II was beaten within hours of getting off a bus in Charleston, South Carolina by White police officers who gouged out his eyes. Truman wrote to his attorney general, Tom Clark, seeking his advice about establishing a presidential commission to prevent such occurrences. [7]

Truman issued an executive order on December 5, 1946 creating the Civil Rights Commission, known by its popular title *Freedom from Fear*, to investigate ways to prevent all Americans from violence. At the time there were no substantive federal laws for upholding civil rights, only parts of the Reconstruction-era Enforcement Acts. Returning Black veterans were facing domestic violence after their war duty defending the country from external enemies, returning to the South to face racist enemies at home. The aftermath of World War II had not integrated the South's mentality nor mitigated discrimination by states. Even police were not fearful of indictment for crimes against Blacks, even violence against returning veterans. Southern courts even failed to prosecute let alone convict perpetrators of mob murders and lynching against Blacks.

The report of the commission, *To Secure These Rights*, was a treatise that enunciated the country's need to advance civil rights.[8] The first recommendation was an appeal to morality. The second appeal was economic and for non-discrimination, that the country needed an abundant force of capable workers to rebuild a post-war economy. An expanded Office of Civil Rights in the Department of Justice and in the FBI was to vigorously pursue instances of discrimination. The report contained multiple recommendations for Congress and states to protect individual rights from discrimination in schooling, housing and voting rights. [9]

Throughout 1947 Truman made civil rights a national topic, even addressing the NAACP. In the election year of 1948 he made civil rights a campaign issue. Governor of South Carolina Strom Thurmond, later senator, and his delegation walked out of the Democratic Party convention in 1948 when the civil rights resolution passed, and formed his states rights party known as the Dixiecrats, pledging to preserve segregation. [10] Thurmond, an avowed racist, won four electoral states. The Black vote in the North secured Truman's election. The southern Democratic bloc had been resisting Truman's attempt to interfere with incidents in the South against Blacks since 1946 and began a program aimed at nullifying his efforts through distortions and demagoguery. Many within the party in the North wanted to soften Truman's approach to appease southerners to maintain party cohesion. Previous presidents always stressed party devotion to constitutional rights. The difference with Truman is that he actually believed it and meant to apply it throughout government. Truman never traded principles for votes and would not relent even to keep party unity. He easily won a second term in 1948.

After the election victory, Truman called a special session of Congress demanding reforms to halt inflation, to ease the housing shortages, to fund more for education, and to enact civil rights reforms. The Republican Congress did nothing—echoing a contemporary lack of accomplishment—a move that showed Republican unwillingness to acquiesce to a Democratic president even for major domestic problems. On July 26, 1948 Truman issued an executive order to end segregation in the armed services. [11]

The Eisenhower Years, 1952 to 1960

The end of hostilities in Japan and Europe did not end animosities for Blacks in the South, even for combat veterans. No one in the federal government wanted anything to do with civil rights, not the FBI under J. Edgar Hoover, neither the Justice Department nor members of the House Un-American Activities Committee that preferred to harass communists instead of white supremacists. Federal officials treated civil rights violations as a nightmare to be forgotten. Nevertheless, Eisenhower established regulations for integrating the federal civil service. He got Congress to pass a weak Civil Rights act in 1957, and was successful in implementing the integration of the armed services that began under Truman.

For those with long memories, Eisenhower's democratic opponent was Adlai Stevenson who chose avowed segregationist Alabama Senator John Sparkman as his vice-presidential running mate. Even into the 1952 presidential campaign it is felt politically necessary to pander to the south.

Dwight D. Eisenhower (1890-1969), born in Texas but raised in Kansas, was a former Supreme Commander of allied forces in Europe, former president of Columbia University, and the first Supreme Commander of NATO. He had an acute military mind but an otherwise conventional one. He was relatively inarticulate, as I recall from listening to his rambling press conferences, and was handicapped by his Vice President, Richard Nixon whom he sensibly sent on foreign missions to keep him from political mischief in Washington.

He favored civil rights but wanted to avoid a confrontation with the South and its elected officials who resisted any attempt at racial integration. In this he continued a historical tradition of pacifying southern feelings, even though the South's renegade attitude consistently damaged the nation and America in the world's image. Perhaps Eisenhower's most enduring civil rights appointment was California Governor Earl Warren as Chief Justice of the U.S. Supreme Court. He never appointed a southerner to the court.

The Supreme Court's unanimous 1954 decision of *Brown v Board of Education* under Chief Justice Earl Warren judicially ending school segregation was chiefly ignored throughout the South. Less than two months after this decision the first White Citizens' Council was formed in Indianola, Mississippi, and was cheered when announced in the state legislature in Jackson. Soon, other white supremacist groups formed: States' Rights Council, the Society to Maintain Segregation, and the Southern Gentlemen. [12]

Arkansas Governor Orval Faubus promised Eisenhower, in a face-to-face meeting in Newport, Rhode Island, that he would handle the anti-government and anti-northern sentiment brewing in his state. He did not. Eisenhower was furious at Faubus because he didn't want to avert the riots that followed in Arkansas. Faubus believed that the court order should be ignored, as did much of the South. That tradition of dismissing the law by not actually supporting it continues with similar statements from former Republican presidential candidate Newt Gingrich.

Ignoring or finding ways of subverting Supreme Court decisions has become a classic Republican tactic. While the country was struggling to find jobs for America's unemployed, the Republican-dominated 112th House of Representative was debating amendments to a bill to thwart federal funding for abortions, a rehash of a bill that already existed. Republican presidential candidates talk of how they, if they become president, will undo *Roe v Wade*, the 1973 landmark decision that favored a woman's right to choose an abortion.

Orval Faubus (1910-1994) was a career politician, a World War II veteran who survived six consecutive terms as governor of Arkansas. Schools did not desegregate after the 1954 decision, nor did they after the 1955 decision that urged schools to desegregate "with all deliberate speed." Segregationists resisted, and loud and persistent segregationist voices made Faubus a moderate on racial matters. He was nervous about his re-election, as he knew he could not win against a segregationist politician. On September 23, 1957, the attempt to integrate Little Rock Central High School began. Faubus called out the state's national guard to block the admission of nine Black students to Central High School under the pretext of averting violence. A federal judge ordered the militia removed. Local police escorted the students out of the building for their own safety.

Eisenhower was forced to act swiftly like the military commander he was. He dispatched 500 paratroops from the 101st Airborne Division, 500 other troops, and federalized 10,000 troops from the Arkansas National Guard. The South was as horrified as they had been when Sherman's Union troops burned Atlanta. The South felt that northern Reconstruction had returned. And in fact these were the first federal troops sent to maintain order since they left the South in 1877. The troops stayed throughout the school year. Even though the school board had drawn a plan for gradual integration, the Board of Education closed the school in 1958 to avoid further integration and disorder. A national campaign of repugnance forced the schools to open in 1959. Faubus was elected four more times.

Faubus used the rationale of peace and order to refuse to carry out a direct federal judge's order to desist and integrate, and the U.S. Supreme Court order to desegregate three years earlier. American democracy is founded on laws and its elected officials are sworn to uphold the law. Yet somehow in the South from 1838 to 1957 southern politicians felt obligated to follow segregationists rather than established law and Supreme Court decisions. Multiple conservative states, no longer just in the South, have now assumed the same role by pressing state legislatures to bypass or restrict congressional laws and assert the rights of states over federal control. By the mid 1950s the nation was definitively not unified because half the country did not accept the supremacy of the Supreme Court to rule in a democracy.

Faubus did not address the racists who had gathered in front of the school and jeered and cursed the Black students, nor did he publically renounce the use of violence, or suggest to the people that he was compelled to uphold the law. His political ambitions over-ruled his sworn fealty as a public official to uphold the Constitution and the law. Faubus is a reasonably good example of the divide between North and South in the 1950s, a hundred years after the beginning of the Civil War. He is also a prime example of how politicians in the South, regardless of their moderating personal feelings, feel obliged to reinforce bigoted constituents. [13]

Within weeks of this traumatic event in 1957 so-called White citizens' councils originated in Mississippi, supplanting the need for the Klan, and then sprang up in towns throughout the South. The White councils could not prevent the integration of "Ole Miss," the University of Mississippi, during the Kennedy years. The aim was to prevent a re-enlistment of the notorious KKK and to give the impression that southern citizens could control any agitation. In effect, these bigoted councils were replacements of the KKK (though the Klan too was still active and expanded after 1957) to handle segregation issues. Violence was bad for business and many council members were businessman. [14]

Fast forward 60 years. Mississippi Governor Haley Barbour, considering a run for the presidency in 2012, tried to whitewash the citizens' councils in his hometown of Yazoo City by comparing them to an organization like the PTA, "an organization of town leaders." Barbour must have thought that his comparison would pass without critical questioning. Quickly, historians and journalists pointed out that these councils, even then known as "white collar Klan," carried out harassment attacks on Blacks even in Yazoo City. The Governor, another politician attempting to smooth over the known bigotry of the South, had to backtrack publically from his deceptive and misleading remarks.

On the afternoon of December 1, 1955, Rosa Parks, a seamstress, sat in one of the ten first seats on a public bus in Montgomery, Alabama reserved for Whites. Blacks were 75-80% of all bus riders in the city. Racial incidents were a frequent occurrence on buses in Montgomery, and each had raised the ire of the Black community as Blacks were put off the bus or arrested. The bus driver asked Rosa to leave her seat and she refused. She was arrested and jailed. The defiant response to Rosa and segregation occurred on December 5, 1955 when 50,000 Blacks refused to ride the segregated buses in Montgomery, a boycott that lasted 13 months. It took the federal courts to order buses integrated. [15] In the interim, Martin Luther King was elected President of the Montgomery Improvement Association, an organization that promoted non-violence.

There is something endearing about Americans who want to return to the guileless Eisenhower years before desegregation. For them idealism has never gone, disappointed that the 1950s did not stay around forever. Now they are panicked, in a state of political neurosis, because the world has moved on without them and transcended their worst fears about permanent national stability, but without persons of color in the social mix. These White conservatives, agitating against abortion and for God and guns, who can find no wrong in the activities of corporations and business and everything wrong with government, have become the mainstay of the right wing of the Republican Party.

John F. Kennedy: A Revival of Leadership

John Kennedy was another president who understood the political danger in siding one way or the other on civil rights. I recall being impressed with his candor and oratory when I heard him in a presidential campaign speech in 1959. He had secured an extremely close election against Richard Nixon in 1960, less than 200,000 votes separated them, when the chief issue had been Kennedy's Catholicism. His presidency is remembered most traumatically for the Cuban Missile crisis in 1962 when nuclear war with Russia was at the edge. [16]

Kennedy's initial domestic program was aid to elementary and secondary education, to provide access to public housing and job opportunities, and medical insurance for the elderly. But he refused to place a civil rights initiative before Congress when the South was still segregationist in public affairs. He believed that a political alignment of southern Democrats and northern conservative Republicans would defeat his proposed legislation. Politicians wanted to let the South, as they had for decades, keep the racial problem in their local hands so the national government would not have to get involved. That "hands off" approach exploded when America's perennial racial problem burst onto the global stage and the romanticized image of the land of the free was exposed as the idealistic political fraud it had always been.

Kennedy, whose motivation was not more than the maintenance of order and prevention of violence, sent troops to protect Martin Luther King's peaceful marches through the South in May 1961 during "freedom rides" aimed at desegregating transportation. King's motivation was to bring the racial repression to national attention urged on by Robert Kennedy, the Attorney General. Then in 1962 President Kennedy failed to get Mississippi Governor Ross Barnett to provide for the safety of James Meredith to matriculate at the University of Mississippi. Kennedy sent federal troops to escort Meredith into the university.

James Meredith was a 29 year-old Black air force veteran who planned to enroll in the University of Mississippi in 1962. Everyone in the Kennedy Administration knew it would be another confrontation such as challenged Eisenhower at Little Rock. Kennedy tried to be as conciliatory as he could toward Governor Ross Barnett. Barnett refused to intervene in the demonstration or to prevent violence as federal marshals tried to escort Meredith onto campus. Molotov cocktails were thrown, the Klan was heavily in attendance, guns were fired, and white students staged an all-night row. Kennedy increased the force to three thousand armed troops and Meredith entered. Kennedy, like Eisenhower, had naively trusted southern governors to maintain order. Only massive federal troop intervention succeeded. But burning resentment of southerners deepened against the government. Kennedy steeled his resolve, and re-calculated his poor historical reading of the South during Reconstruction.[17]

Suddenly a series of racial incidents exposed more than the arbitrary indignities imposed on Blacks. The crisis in April 1963 resuscitated national attention when Martin Luther King issued his *Birmingham Manifesto,* a call to end public segregation. King's followers began sit-ins in publically segregated facilities. King was arrested and held in solitary confinement in a local jail where he wrote *Letter from a Birmingham Jail*, a classic of protest literature. Hundreds of youth began protest marches and all were arrested. Then on May 2nd the police chief "Bull" Connor sent in fire trucks and trained dogs. Police dogs attacked peaceful protestors and high-pressure water hoses knocked them off their feet.

Television images portrayed bigots shouting obscene and racist slogans at marchers that were broadcast around the world, and brought to life as no other media can the violence-prone southern racism still boiling a hundred years after the Civil War. Kennedy saw civil rights as an image of America in the international arena and framed his speeches as a moral cause. On June 12th Medgar Evers a veteran of the D-Day invasion and political activist was shot at the door of his home in front of his wife and children. Kennedy was confronted by a rising tide of defiant social discontent, and with state legal remedies that were unavailable to stop harassment against Blacks in states and municipalities. Local and state police were in sympathy with White protestors, and were frequently Klan members.

On June 19, 1963 Kennedy addressed the nation, praised the admission of two blacks to the University of Alabama, and said he would ask Congress to enact an expansive civil rights act that included the elimination of public discrimination, the enforcement of the desegregation of schools, and voting rights. But Kennedy would learn the hard way—just as presidents Lincoln, Grant, Hayes, and Eisenhower and Speaker Thaddeus Stevens did—that southerners do not negotiate with the national government, and are stubborn and unrelenting when it comes to preserving presumed prerogatives and that special brand of White superiority. Not much has changed.

Within five months, Kennedy was assassinated in Dallas, Texas on November 20, 1963 and Lyndon Johnson (1908-1973) was sworn in as the next president.

Lyndon B. Johnson: Legislative Consolidation

As Senate Majority Leader in 1957 Johnson had been consistently opposed to civil rights. Though he was somewhat insulated from the southern racial divide living in the Texas hill country, his southern exposure actually left him clueless about the predicament of Blacks living in the South, as he explained in his autobiography. [18] Like America, he grew to understand its racial problems and to deal with them. He voted for the Eisenhower's civil rights bill in 1957 though he tried to weaken its passage. [19] Johnson realized that if he wanted to run for president he would have to abandon his southern, regional bias.

Johnson himself was horrified as was the country by the riots and the police response in Birmingham in the spring of 1963. Within months the government began its slow and painful embrace of the racial problem that had always confronted the nation. Thirteen months after Kennedy had addressed the nation on the government's initiative on civil rights, and asked Congress to approve an expansive civil rights act, President Lyndon B. Johnson signed into law the *Civil Rights Act* on July 2, 1964 that granted equal rights to all persons, making discrimination illegal. Senator Richard Russell (1897-1971) of Georgia, the main opponent, in a senate speech on June 18, 1964, bitterly resisted any measure that would bring about racial equality in southern states and used the filibuster to block votes in Congress. Later he agreed to end the vote on cloture (a vote to end debate which is not a filibuster) and the bill passed 73 to 27.

One of the more disconsolate media events occurred days earlier, on June 21, 1964, when the murder of three young civil rights workers near Philadelphia, Mississippi shocked the nation, an event I noted in an earlier chapter. Michael Schwerner, 24, from Ohio, James Chaney, 21, a Black from Mississippi, and Andrew Goodman, 20, from New York, had cooperated with several civil rights groups in organizing the registration of Black voters. They were arrested by Deputy Sheriff Cecil Price, charged with speeding, jailed overnight, and released at 10:30 PM the following night. The Klan tracked their car, stopped it, and murdered them with police collusion, a fact that horrified the world. Robert Kennedy called in 153 FBI agents who combed the backwoods looking for the bodies. (President Ronald Reagan went to Philadelphia, Mississippi right after his Republican convention to deliver a major speech, a locale choice that says much about his sentiments).

In October 1964, after gathering testimony, the FBI arrested 18 men, but state prosecutors refused to bring the case to trial citing insufficient evidence. In 1967 seven men were convicted on conspiracy charges. On January 7, 2005, 41 years after the event, Edgar Ray Killen, 80, was charged with organizing their murders and assembling the mob that killed them. He was tried, convicted and received 60 years in prison.

Sam Bowers (1924-2006), a World War II Navy veteran, in 1964 was the Imperial Wizard of the White Knights of the KKK, the most militant of the Mississippi Klans, who had instigated scores of murders. He was charged with the firebombing house murder in 1966 of Black voter registrant Vernon Dahmer, a trial that ended in a deadlocked jury. A 1969 jury was also split on conviction. But in August 1998, he was tried again, this time convicted and sentenced to prison where he died in 2006, aged 82, of natural causes.

For southerners, Schwerner and Goodman were carpetbaggers and scalawags, unwelcome in the South. For the North, all citizens should be free to live and work anywhere in the U.S. This was 1964 not 1864. But nothing in the cultural world of southern radicals had changed. The murder of unarmed, well-intentioned young men rocked the nation and the world, and exposed the soiled underbelly of latent southern violence against any northern, or national intrusion and unity.

Senator Russell was the longtime leader of the anti-civil rights movement and a leader of its southern white supremacist opposition, a proponent of southern discriminatory practices that did not lend support to his presidential ambitions in 1952. Russell supported Johnson and saw to it Johnson became majority leader, but generally opposed him on civil rights. [20]

The 1964 law prohibited discrimination in public accommodations, the integration of school and public facilities and made employment discrimination illegal. [21] The passage of laws requiring non-discrimination had almost no immediate effect in the South. Initially, bureaucrats in the U.S. Office of Education and other agencies relied on paper agreements from southerners on compliance with the laws. The term "freedom of choice" arose as an ostensible explanation for keeping lack of desegregation in the South to a minimum. When "freedom of choice" is used today in educational circles for charter schools or school voucher plans, it still has this southern twist and taint to it.

The passage of the *Civil Rights Act* did not end southern violence. In March 1965 state troopers and Sheriff Jim Clark used tear gas, whips and clubs to beat peaceful marchers in Selma, Alabama. On March 9, 1965 Rev, James Reeb, a Unitarian minister from Boston was beaten to death with clubs and leaden pipes in front of the Silver Moon café in Selma. Martin Luther King called for another march in Selma. Governor George Wallace, who had hired KKK members on his staff, refused to provide protection for the demonstrators. President Johnson federalized 1,900 of the Alabama National Guard, and added another 100 U.S. marshals and FBI agents.

On the evening of March 25, Viola Liuzzo, a mother of five, who had grown up in Georgia and rural Tennessee, but lived in Detroit with her Teamsters' union husband, was driving volunteers for the marches. That night she had LeRoy Moton, a Black native of Selma as a passenger. The Klan members saw the Michigan license plates and followed her car from Selma to Montgomery when, at speeds of nearly a 100 miles per hour they pulled alongside her car and emptied their guns, killing her instantly. LeRoy Moton survived. The Justice Department brought suit against three klansmen on December 3, 1965 and the defendants were convicted for violating Liuzzo's civil rights under the new law.

Civil rights and equal rights, in the broadest sense, has been the key social issue dividing the country, of which slavery and involuntary servitude were the most odious features. With the abundance of national legislative history, has civil rights been unanimously accepted in the American culture? The answer depends, with all the information and polling numbers available, on how you perceive the great American social, cultural and political divide. Although there are many complicating economic factors and social class differences, the country is socially divided still about civil rights. These intertwining principles of anti-government feelings and lingering white supremacist sentiments define far too many of us.

Richard M. Nixon: Civil Rights Dissembler

Richard Nixon (1913-1994) began his political career in Congress on the House Un-American Activities Committee with Senator Joseph McCarthy. As president, Nixon, ironically became friendly with the largest bloc of communists in the world. He promised the public truth in the campaign of 1968, and then lied more to the public than any known president. He backdated a deed to avoid a half million-dollar tax. As a pacifist Quaker he ordered an extensive Christmas carpet-bombing bombing over North Vietnam. The late artist David Levine (1926-2009) caricatured Nixon with a bulging, red nose, blackened eyebrows and an evil stare, looking as if he walked out of a version of Dante's *Inferno*.

He opened dialogue with China in 1972, proposed détente with the USSR, initiated environmental legislation and the establishment of the EPA, and proposed the Family Assistance Plan. [22] These foreign and domestic policy accomplishments were overshadowed by his personality disorders, lack of moral imperatives, massive use of deceit for his own advancement, melancholy and paranoid delusions, self-destructive behavior during televised appearances during the Watergate scandal as the whole country cringed at his persistent, public lies. After his resignation and pardon by President Ford, his personal disgrace never led to an apology for the crimes committed disgracing the country. [23]

> All the time I've been in politics there's only two people I hate, and [Nixon's] one. He not only doesn't give a damn about the people, he doesn't know how to tell the truth. I don't think that son of a bitch knows the difference between telling the truth and lying. (Harry Truman, quoted in Genovese, 1990, p. 2.)

President Harry Truman was right about Richard Nixon decades before the Watergate scandal broke in 1973 that led to Nixon's impending impeachment. Senator and 1964 presidential candidate Barry Goldwater called Nixon "basically dishonest." Goldwater wrote: "I have characterized Nixon as a loner, a cold man with great self-confidence and a one-track mind centered on the advancement of Richard Nixon." [24] It was said by Europeans that the American presidency after Nixon resigned had come full circle: with Washington who could not tell a lie, to Nixon who could not tell the truth.

But the Watergate scandal brought Nixon down, vitiated the stature of the presidency, and corrupted the idea of national public service. I could never afterwards locate anyone who admitted voting for him.

I resigned in 1973 from my position as Technical Director in the Office of Deputy Commissioner for Development and returned to academic life, feeling betrayed and humiliated by presidential corruption. Returning to this era and the national traumatic events, and reviewing my own minor federal administrative role, brought back the feelings of pride in government service, national and professional loyalty and yet feeling stained by malfeasance at the presidential level. The Greeks invented *hubris*, the arrogance of power, for men like Nixon.

And yet, in further evidence of my thesis to demonstrate how divided the country was, and I believe still is, Nixon in the 1968 election barely won with 43.4% of the public vote with Hubert Humphrey trailing with slightly less than a percentage point at 42.7%. George Wallace who ran as an American Independent, but really as a segregationist, received 13.5%, a percentage I still believe closely resembles the overtly bigoted portion of the population. Nixon was elected with the same coalition of southern voters who had been opposed to civil rights for Blacks, and in return he would favor them by dampening any attempts to enforce civil rights laws. [25] He repaid the southern voters with neglect and inattention to civil rights and voting rights. Chiefly for his own ambitious political agenda, Nixon courted the South for votes just like former presidents Martin Van Buren and James Buchanan, and never tried to challenge southern racist policies to achieve real American moral and political unity.

Nixon's policies on civil rights were incoherent, but purposeful. On the one hand, he appealed directly to southern segregationists with his "southern strategy" used in the 1968 election campaign and proposed a constitutional amendment to ban busing as a means of achieving racial balances in schools. Under his Administration there was a deliberate attempt to reverse the progress in school desegregation, a cynical appeal to the dark side of the southern spirit and a moral insensitivity to the aspiration of Black Americans.

As president he abused the power of his office to subvert the independence of the IRS, the FBI, the CIA, and the Justice Department whose director, John Mitchell, Nixon's former campaign manager, was the first Attorney General in U.S. history to be convicted of illegal activities. Nixon ordered my colleague Eliot Richardson, U.S. attorney general at the time, to fire the independent counsel, Archibald Cox, an office created to investigate the president. Richardson courageously resigned instead.

Nixon fired then director of the Office of Civil Rights, Leon Panetta in February 1970 on the grounds of excessive zeal in carrying out the laws on desegregation. [26] The various bureaucracies responsible for implementing the laws on school desegregation and non-discrimination had a push/pull battle within the Administration: the agencies tried to implement the laws and federal court orders, and the Nixon team tried to slow or curtail their efforts. John Ehrlichman, Nixon's right-hand assistant, kept squashing any intrusion into southern sensitivities and any Secretary, Assistant Secretary or Director who hastened to apply the law too enthusiastically. The official line was that the laws must be followed but that more time was needed for implementation, a classical political non-starter.

Everyone in Washington wanted to know what the Nixon Administration's policy was on civil rights, desegregation and busing. The answer was there was no policy except to derail, obfuscate, and delay any initiative from the Justice Department or HEW. Yet on October 29, 1969 the U.S. Supreme Court gave the final word in *Alexander et al. v. Holmes County Board of Education*: "Continued operation of racially segregated schools under the standard of "all deliberate speed" is no longer constitutionally permissible. School districts must immediately terminate dual schools systems based on race and operate only unitary school systems." [27]

This dilemma of a sitting president appeasing a southern constituency for the favor of its votes, against the federal bureaucracy compelled to administer the law is exactly why America has been two sectional identities. The South, so deep was its racial history, would resist any attempt to compel Whites to be the equals of Blacks. Desegregating schools and public facilities was only the outward symbol of the profound social distance between the races and the split personality in the nation.

The volatile issue of immigration contains the same seeds of how some Americans fell victim at the expense of others. Thus, while the issue of desegregating schools in the South and elsewhere for Black children, the same kind of issue arose for Latino children in other parts of the country. The issue is not simply one that occurred in the civil rights era or when Nixon was president. How America copes with its non-White citizens, whether indigenous or new immigrants, will always be a political hot potato.

Yet during Nixon's tenure the times were ripe for a more salient policy. The U.S. Supreme Court had ordered a series of decisions about busing to achieve desegregation of schools so Nixon could have seized the opportunity to advance civil rights because he had sworn to uphold the Constitution. Instead, he tried to pacify the South, as did most of his presidential predecessors except Lincoln. [28]

The Watergate complex is alongside the northern edge of the Potomac River in Washington DC. It includes expensive apartments, restaurants, and offices. In 1970 it housed the offices of the Democratic Party that became the target of Watergate burglars on the early morning of June 17, 1972, an operation initiated from the White House, possibly by Nixon himself, though this was never proven. An alert security guard caught the bungled burglary attempt and when the White House connection was discovered the scandal began to unravel. The White House denied that it was responsible but this too proved to be false as Congressional testimony probed witnesses and secret informants gave information to *Washington Post* reporters. [29]

Let me describe briefly a summary of the Watergate scandal because it goes to the heart of the character of Nixon and the people he gathered around him, many of them, like him, criminals in public employment. To Nixon, therefore, the lack of pursuit of civil rights was merely a brazen attempt to capitalize on political expediency. The Watergate scandal unraveled Nixon's character and violation of his constitutional oath. Nixon's neglect to implement the laws on civil rights was only a part of his plan to get re-elected in 1972 at any cost, much of it that turned out to be what became known as "dirty tricks," which were in fact a series of illegal activities that led to his impeachment proceedings. [30]

By the time impeachment hearings began in the House, bureaucrats were literally lugging portable TVs into their offices to watch the dramatic events. Washington was transfixed with itself and a presidential impeachment. The prepared articles of impeachment for Nixon included perjury, burglary, forgery, illegal wiretapping, obstruction of justice, destroying evidence, witness tampering, bribery, and conspiracy by involving federal agencies in illegal activities. Nixon's actions besmirched the presidency. No other president, and few other lawyers as Nixon was, have been accused of so many crimes or abused the high office so universally and injuriously. Vice President Spiro Agnew was convicted of bribery and tax fraud. Gerald Ford, whom Nixon appointed Vice President to replace Spiro Agnew, became president when Nixon resigned on August 8, 1974, and pardoned Nixon.

Attorney General John Mitchell, the nation's top law enforcement officer, was convicted of perjury. His successor, Attorney General Richard Kleindienst, was found guilty of refusing to answer questions to the congressional committee. In addition, seventeen members of the White House staff, nearly all of the chief officers, and re-election committee members were found guilty of obstruction of justice, conspiracy and perjury. [31]

Since independence from England, America has politically compromised and appeased its southern slave colonies and segregationist states in order to preserve a tenuous unity but fractured by more fragile compromises and venomous opposition. In fact, as I have tried to show throughout this study, and regardless of nationalistic rhetoric about "one nation under God" and similar slogans and obligatory patriotic symbols, we have always been two cultural nations under one national legal umbrella.

The political compromise reached a peak in 1860 with the election of Abraham Lincoln who was committed to not preserving a country that was half slave and half free. A hundred years later, the country nearly unraveled again when John Kennedy, who welcomed civil rights reform in his campaign, was barely elected by the narrowest margins and then ignominiously assassinated in the South. His successor Lyndon Johnson signed another civil rights act that transformed the country, but was reluctantly tolerated by southerners because he was from Texas and therefore one of them, and because America does not vote a sitting president out of office during a war. After only four years in office, Johnson decided not to run for re-election in 1968.

In succession, Richard Nixon, a conservative Republican, ran a "southern strategy" to win southern votes. Gerald Ford, though a conservative congressman from Michigan, was given a polite bye from southern hostility because he was selected after Nixon's resignation. Jimmie Carter was acceptable because he was a former Georgia governor. Ronald Reagan, a confirmed anti-government contender, appealed directly to southern votes, and was even endorsed by the Klan. [32] George H. W. Bush was from Texas, and Bill Clinton a former Governor of Arkansas. George W. Bush was also from Texas.

Republicans generally campaign on the issue of fiscal restraint, less taxes, reduced spending, waste in government, and deficit reduction. During Nixon's presidency from 1968 to 1974, federal spending increased 53%, the federal debt increased 37%, and the purchasing power of the dollar decreased 34%. [33]

Barak Obama was elected president in 2008, the first from the North since Kennedy. Almost immediately, the social and political transformation of America turned divisive and abusive. Gun sales skyrocketed. The political debate turned ugly and often ludicrous, reflective of gut-reactions to growing social changes, the exposure of so many radical candidates who were uninformed about American history and constitutional principles, and the fact that an African American man had been elected to the highest office.

The constant theme from a far-right fringe of the conservative Republican Party was a virulent anti-government invective that had not been heard for decades, a commitment to the right to bear arms, and preparation for a revolution that sounded eerily like an armed revolt. Every sort of smear by the radical conservative bloc, through politicians and media voices, attempted to disparage the president, challenging his birth in the United States, blistering his domestic policies, and in Congress obstructing every legislative initiative. It looked like a re-run of the days preceding the Civil War, and more recently the violent reaction in the 1960s to any civil rights imposed on southerners. The vitriolic reaction was the resurrection of a dormant social repugnance against minorities in general and Blacks in particular ingrained in the American consciousness since the first days of slavery.

Ronald Reagan: Loosening Federal Regulation, Busting the Economy

> There is no question about maintaining social programs for people in need.
> (Ronald Reagan, *Time* Interview, January 5, 1981)

Ronald Reagan (1911-2004) spanned the 20th century and appeared to give us the courage and optimism to believe in ourselves. With his sonorous voice trained in radio and a smile from the movies, he was a tall, mid-western icon who embodied the indomitable, small town American spirit with its innocence, naïve optimism, and simplicity about the world and the workings of government and representative democracy. His lack of intellectual distinction, his moral relativism and strident anti-government strategy was his enduring legacy. He spoke with artilleries of platitudinous, soothing and forgettable phrases that bespoke nothing about his intentions.

He was virulently anti-communist but otherwise clueless about foreign affairs and opposed to government domestic policies and interference in business. His appointments to key cabinet positions were filled with avaricious business cronies anxious to deregulate rules, slash domestic budgets and corporate taxes, neuter any anti-trust actions against corporations, and eliminate or stifle public servants that imposed regulations on the private sector. Reagan and his team were out to make government a tool of business, and they succeeded. The aristocratic rich—those who felt really entitled—under Reagan took over the administration of government and gutted the prosperity that had endured for half a century, in effect decapitating the referee between the people and corporate abuses.

Reagan's anti-government policies reversed an economic tradition of a mixed economy, of government working with business under both Republican and Democratic administrations in the 1950s and 1960s, to create one of the greatest advanced lifestyles and a vibrant Middle Class the world had ever seen. All was to be dismantled by this talking mannequin and his ideologically misguided message, preempted, managed and funded by corporate America whose subsequent excesses led to savings and loan, energy, telecommunications, banking, pharmaceutical and financial sector scandals. All could have been prevented with the maintenance of government regulations that he had eviscerated.

Reagan imbibed his mother's evangelical religion, the Disciples of Christ, and attended that religion's Eureka College in Illinois graduating without distinction in 1932. From 1927-33 he was a lifeguard on the Rock River in Illinois and is credited with saving 77 lives. He moved to WOC radio, became a sportscaster in Des Moines, and in 1937 found his way via college acting to Hollywood where he starred in scores of forgettable movies.

During the anti-communist frenzy after World War II he had personal experiences with the violence of communist sympathizers and their protests and strikes. As President of the Screen Actors Guild and because of threats from communists, he began carrying a gun for personal protection. From this time forward, his anti-communist posture never left him and became one of his chief foreign policy objectives as President to the extent of funding a secret war against communists in Nicaragua.

In the 1950s as a TV spokesman for General Electric he traveled and learned how government intruded on businesses, but never appreciated the role of government in protecting the public from shady business practices. From this period he acquired a disdain of government and an anti-government sentiment that became his second most important policy initiative. He used his corporate role as spokesperson to good advantage when he shaped his mellow message to the public that covered his real intent of dismantling government. He duped the public with his convivial style yet played to its prejudices.

He served as California's Governor beginning in 1967, and was elected President in 1980 beating Jimmie Carter by a landslide, taking 44 states. He believed, as a former lifeguard, that he was rescuing the U.S. from cynicism, economic distress, feelings of national doubt, and rankles from the Iranian hostage crisis that reminded Americans of their vulnerability. He then managed to plunge the nation into its highest unemployment since the Depression, at over 10%, and with his strange ideological arithmetic to mismanage the economy abysmally. [34]

Reaganomics was presented to Congress on February 18, 1981 in a message that called for tax cuts, a deregulation of business, and increased spending on the military—all of which continue to be conservative policies. Based on these policies, the stock market collapsed in 1987. He deregulated commerce, crippled labor unions, starved the public sector, called for the privatization of schools, and accelerated the growth of temporary work agencies. [35]

In 1952 under Eisenhower, he corporate tax rate was 32.1%. Under Reagan in 1980 it was 12.5%. By 1983 it was 6.2%. He cut taxes for the wealthiest from 70% to 50%, a trend Republicans continue to demand. Reagan had effectively starved the government of revenues while enormous corporate profits expanded, especially for agribusinesses like Continental Grain, Cargill and Archer Daniels Midland, putting small farmers out of business. Reagan was a credit card president who left the nation in debt, a stage-managed actor who just read the lines fed to him by his political handlers.

Reagan's first national economic plan was a 30% tax cut that targeted the poor most acutely. His budget cuts were in all new public housing assistance, food stamps, legal aid to the poor and rural development projects. Regan believed, erroneously, that federal programs that helped the poor were at the heart of America's economic woes, and so he and his team demonized the poor as freeloaders and "welfare queens". The former General Electric pitchman was better at pitching for corporations than at helping the average Joe and Jane. Reagan's political public relations staff sold America on the belief that the poor were bankrupting the country and not entitled to government largesse. Reagan asked Gorbachev to tear down the Berlin wall and instead what he tore down were relief programs that divested the poor of virtual the wall that kept them from destitution.

> Pay them their wages at the end of each day, because they live in poverty and need the money to survive. If you don't pay them on time, they will complain about you to the Lord, and he will punish you. (*Deuteronomy* 24:14-16.)

Because of his anti-communism he preferred huge increases in defense spending to balancing the budget and never did submit a balanced budget to Congress. By 1982 the country was in a deep recession made more traumatic by high interest rates. Businesses failed and the unemployment rate soared to 1930s levels. He accelerated government domestic deregulation, but ramped up intervention in foreign policy with non-essential and intrusive campaigns in Central America, Lebanon, and Granada.

Reagan, an amateur actor who always just played himself, has been celebrated as the conservative visionary. But as even his three children have noted, he was an assortment of personalities, affable yet remote, without close friends, too complex and contradictory to pigeonhole into any one category. He attended college but remained under-educated because he never tried to achieve academically, and only got sufficiently acceptable grades to remain eligible for football. He was a Midwesterner filled with folk wisdom, more comfortable with commonsense solutions and not book learning: a simplified B grade movie script and not a reasoned argument.

As president he presided over the end of the Cold War and the collapse of the USSR, but was muddled and confused by the Iran/Contra affairs when the context and content of foreign affairs seemed to elude his comprehension. For example, Oliver North and others were sent on a secret mission to Teheran May 25, 1986. With the utmost conviction but obvious ingenuousness, they carried a Bible with a handwritten verse from President Reagan, and a chocolate cake in the shape of a key, as well as three sets of chrome-plated Magnum pistols and some spare parts for a Hawk missile. These gifts were supposed to open the dialogue with Iranian leaders in the middle of a war with Iraq. But apart from the simplicity of the diplomatic opening, lay the utter naivete of the Reagan

Administration in understanding Islam or any other culture. Reagan embodied the country's ignorance of foreign countries but understood the country's short attention span for involvement abroad.

His domestic agenda revealed his true conservatism. Reagan's policy of loosening federal regulation can be encapsulated in the history of how media frenzy where talk radio and TV commentary rule the airwaves was once regulated by the Federal Communications Commission (FCC). Section 315 of the Communications Act of 1937, enacted when radio was young, required stations to offer equal, balanced and fair treatment to all political candidates. The Fairness Doctrine was a regulation developed in 1949 by the FCC that attempted to ensure that all coverage of controversial issues was fair. In the 1940s the FCC even prohibited editorializing. The argument was that the airwaves were public and that stations were trustees of the public and had an obligation to report contrasting points of view. The Supreme Court in the 1969 case *Red Lion Broadcasting Co., Inc. v. FCC* ruled in favor of the FCC rule. [36] When Reagan became president this regulation was dissolved in 1987.

The commercialization of American society began early but gained momentum during the Reagan years. The penetration of corporate advertising has peeked into every corner, public and private, and invades all conscious life, from dropdown airline lap pads, the margins of all web sites, to pitches of soda drinks and junk food to schoolchildren. [37]

One of Reagan's more successful attempts at dismantling government was the politicizing of government personnel, a move that continued through all Republican presidents. By the summer of 1981 nearly 60% of sub-cabinet appointees had no experience in government management, nor did 78% of appointees at independent agencies, or 100% of those at regulatory agencies. Political appointees at cabinet and sub-cabinet offices are traditionally political. But starting with Reagan so-called liberal bureaucrats throughout the government were replaced, transferred, had their operational programs deleted, and the pay scales diminished. It was a direct assault on the civil service whose protections were in place for about a hundred years to curtail the intrusion of politics into government service. By 1990 federal executives were making on average about 40% less than executives with the same skills in the private sector. This meant that by the third millennium few top individuals sought careers in national government public service, which was exactly what Republicans had always sought.

When he was shot in an assassination attempt in 1981 we all needed therapy. When it became apparent after his presidency that he had Alzheimer's disease, we grew more sympathetic. He knew so little, but achieved so much in a domestic war against the government he administered. Ordinary Americans came to appreciate his optimism, compassion and kindliness. That Reagan myth has turned into idolatry by far right Republicans who view his Spartan ideals about limited government inspiring and as a chief mantra for their ideological platform.

Reagan believed in cutting taxes mercilessly and that that this alone would create investments and jobs. He believed that it was necessary to slash social welfare spending to drive down the debt. He believed that deregulating the financial sector benefitted the consumer. He solidly backed corporate mergers and hostile takeovers that benefited boardrooms but led to wild financial speculation, ethical malfeasance, joblessness, corporate scandals like the saving and loan crisis and Enron, and that eventually bankrupted the economy. Using capital to buy companies and not invested in manufacturing to compete in the global economy led to a perversion of sensible investment policies.

All of these beliefs in the absolute values of the marketplace without restraints—now the province of the ultra-conservative political base that insist on adhering to them as absolute public policy principles—have no historical evidence for success, but plenty for their failures. [38]

America under Reagan had an external enemy in Soviet communism and an internal one in government expansion. Today, ultra Republicans turn their wrath only to one enemy—government, the same as did the South from 1830 onward.

George W. Bush: Wars and Domestic Disassembly

Katrina is not a common female name, nor was its aftermath a common disaster. Besides the turbulent violence of its category 5 hurricane unleashed on New Orleans in 2005, the costliest in U.S. history that killed 1,836 people, Katrina exposed the politicizing of the civil service in a hurricane zone and the governmental neglect of America's poor and vulnerable. The reaction to this one disaster is a symbol of the operating ideology of conservative Republicans I have traced throughout this study as a larger part of an anti-government posture. George W. Bush is a prime exemplar. [39]

Compare Japan's response to the displaced people in the wake of the earthquake and tsunami in March 2011 to America's weak, and in some cases, non-response to the people in New Orleans after Katrina. The Japanese quickly found the homeless shelter and provided them with blankets and food. In contrast in 2005, the Federal Emergency Management Agency (FEMA), by all accounts, was totally unprepared for the scope of the catastrophe—though it was announced days in advance—and could not even find adequate supplies for the scattered homeless. A part of this was surely the result of the Bush Administration's appointment of political loyalists, such as Michael D. Brown to head FEMA, and not specialists in disaster relief efforts. Brown resigned within weeks of Katrina. Media photos of thousands huddled in the Louisiana Superdome for days without food or water while FEMA officials tried to locate supplies is only one pathetic example. America was little better prepared than Haiti, the poorest country in the hemisphere, for a natural disaster. And the sad reason for the lack of an adequate response for Katrina was Republican failure of leadership to use the resources of government that it had sought to reduce to impotence.

It is usually taken for granted that the government, especially the richest in the world, provides safety for all its citizens after a large-scale disaster. This traditional belief was shattered during Katrina because of the Republican belief that it is necessary to slash all federal programs, even those that prepare for national disaster contingencies. Levees went un-repaired, city transit systems unfunded, and evacuation plans—one of the programs gutted during Bush—resulted in vehicular gridlock exiting the city. [40]

Katrina revealed that the priority for Bush Administration and Republican leadership was to outsource money to friendly contractors but provide negligible funds for public sector projects even in known disaster areas. This priority had its full revelation during Iraq when billions of taxpayer funds were squandered on contracted private enterprise projects, usually without bids, that had no government audit accountability.

Bush's forcible attempt to privatize Social Security, a program that Americans opposed cutting by a margin of 64%, was a crude maneuver that exposed the ideology of disemboweling social programs. Most Americans wanted Bush's tax cuts that benefitted wealthier Americans to be retained but with lower limits on income. According to the Gallup Poll, a majority of Americans in 2010 favored letting the Bush tax cuts expire for the wealthy. While 37% supported keeping the tax cuts for all Americans, 44% wanted them extended only for those making less than $250,000 and 15% think they should expire for all taxpayers. The Republican-controlled Congress extended them as they were.

Together with a compliant Congress, Bush passed Medicare Part D, a medical drugs program that benefitted the pharmaceutical industry. The bill debating it started at about 3 AM, and passed about 6 AM on November 16, 2005. At the time the House was chaired led by Rep. Doc Hastings. The call to vote was set for 15 minutes but turned into three hours when not enough Republicans voted for the bill. The president was phoned at 5:00 AM and a cell phone passed around for him to lobby reluctant house members. Congress made no appropriation for its payment leading inevitably toward the nation's deficit woes, a Republican strategy for decimating national social programs.

Regardless of who the Republican president is, or those who seek to be, the domestic policy initiatives will be predictable. Typically, Republicans moralize about what they want from others sexually and about religion, but with hypocrisy do not often practice themselves. Former Speaker of the House and presidential candidate Newt Gingrich played to the evangelical crowd by asking forgiveness for his past sins but condemned the acts of others. At the time he was committing adultery he was leading the charge to impeach the President Clinton for his sexual peccadillo in the White House. He blamed the media for asking questions about his former marriages and his long-term affair while married—a point that goes to his character.

But ultimately, it is above all the dissolution of America's social compact with its citizens embodied in Social Security, Medicare and Medicaid programs that Republicans seek. Tax relief, usually not tax reform, will top the agenda, as will any form of deregulation on business and corporate activities, always believed to be sinless and excusable. Low taxes on the rich do not lead to prosperity for all. The rich paid much higher taxes during the Clinton Administration and the economy added 11.5 million jobs.

It has been the standard set of anti-government belief since the early part of the 19th century. Southern slave states had no need for government taxation, or social programs or any attempt to disrupt the independent, business way of life they enjoyed under slave labor. Conservative Republicans are the direct descendants and embodiment of the slave-owning, segregated and secessionist South.

Typical grievances about civil rights often arise from individual discrimination and class action suits. The reasons for discrimination are sometimes broader and usually more insidious. The sources are stereotypes and bias against particular groups: the elderly, women or ethnic groups. A recent study demonstrated how Blacks face discrimination even in bankruptcy proceedings. [41] Even in areas of the country that have a low rate for Chapter 13 bankruptcies, Blacks, under attorney advisement, filed a higher rate than other groups.

The post-Civil War amendments, particularly the 13th and 14th which advanced due process and equal protection of the laws, attempted to correct for civil rights omitted in the U.S. Constitution. African Americans are now persons under the Constitution and women have rights and can vote. The slow and steady advancement of civil rights, and the protection of individuals and groups against discrimination, will always be high on the American agenda. The particular prejudice against African Americans is still acute and will be a perpetual source of social and legal conflict because of our peculiar legacy of centuries of slavery and our horrendous war to eradicate it.

Chapter Fourteen
Conspiracy Theorists, Militias, Hate
And Extremist Groups

Lo! Thy dread Empire CHAOS! is restor'd;
Light dies before thy uncreating word:
Thy hand, great Anarch! Lets the curtain fall;
And Universal Darkness buries all.
(Alexander Pope, *Dunciad*, 1743)

Alexander Pope's last lines from his clever, satirical poem *Dunciad*, first published in 1728 satirizing British foolishness, is symbolic of the anti-government and militant mentality that characterized the American South 150 years ago. It is now fully interwoven into the fabric of American political discourse. Proclaiming Christianity and appealing to the gun culture has become the latest badge of honor and staple of political appeal. These twin themes are still vibrant today as I discovered in man-in-the-bar interviews and encounters during time I spent touring Alabama, Mississippi and Louisiana for this study. Values are hard to change and I discovered that resistance to changing the southern mentality I thought I might find, I did find.

Over several beers in restaurants, saloons and blues clubs in Natchez, Mississippi in one evening encounter, my two drinking buddies, by the kinds of questions they asked me over a few hours, gave me insights into the southern mind. One owned a car dealership and the other was a carpenter. Normally a relatively wealthy businessman and a tradesman do not mix socially unless they are bonded in other ways, like belonging to a similar club or organization. Social or political views, or clan memberships, are what unite them.

The first question was where was I from. Phoenix was an acceptable answer because, like most southern states, it is extremely conservative, whose legislators love guns and loath immigrants. [1] I was also truthful when I responded that my ex-father-in-law was from Winona, Mississippi, and that I had had projects in Greenwood, Mississippi.

Earlier that day I had attended a gun show and they asked me if I had attended, and I said yes. What kind of gun did I own? "A Walther," I replied which evoked a loud exclamation of admiration since, except for a Sig Sauer, a popular gun with white supremacist groups and Navy Seals, an expensive Walther handgun is admired for its German quality. Within a short period I was classified as "good people," obviously a token of acceptance, because I not only owned guns but had used them. I elaborated on how as a youth my family and I had hunted for food, every year killing deer and often an elk, and seasonally shooting pheasants, ducks, and quail, and fishing for trout, salmon and bass in the local rivers and lakes for family dinners.

A second question for me later in the evening was about my religion. I told them the religion I was raised in, but noted that I was not particularly devout or practicing in any denomination.

The third question was when did I think the revolution would start. I replied that I thought it had already started. This short exchange never became detailed, for many obvious reasons. I was metaphorical in my response but I believe that they were thinking literally, and further discussion to a stranger might have exposed which particular group they either admired or consorted with.

I did not solicit these questions or invite them in any way. But because I was questioned about the topics that mattered to them, and did not myself question them, their cultural beliefs were exposed. The conversation topics did not surprise me. But because I tested my supposition with white males in their drinking and clubbing habitats, and was able to converse about guns, Christianity and the coming revolution with authenticity, I was accepted. I was able to speak knowledgeably about these topics though they do not define me.

You can conclude a lot about a locale from what's missing as from what's present. I ate in restaurants and attended Blues clubs in Natchez, Vicksburg and Jackson. Blues originated in African American communities in the Deep South. But in these clubs there were no African Americans. Natchez is a self-segregated community. Whites and Blacks have their own separate eating and social facilities as if nothing had changed in the world for the past hundred years. Confederate sympathizers, like that of John Wilkes Booth, of a lost cause that a war decided, still live in the South.

You can hear the cry now. "I'm mad as hell and I'm not going to take it anymore. So it's time to kill some federal Yankees." This sort of talk did occur in Tocoa, Georgia (population 27,000) in the late fall of 2011, as it certainly did in the late fall of 1860. No one could have imagined that the Waffle House in Tocoa would be the venue of conspiracy by senior terrorists like navy veteran Frederick Thomas, 73, Dan Roberts, 67, Ray Adams, 65, or Samuel Crump, 68. Yet these four were arrested for plotting to blow up federal buildings and kill federal employees and scores of people using the toxic and fatal poison ricin made from castor beans. This is the sort of hair-brained revolution from self-appointed militia men that is supposed to "make the country right again." The group had links to the Georgia Militia, a militant hate group. But they might just as well had donned confederate army caps and waved the confederate flag as they threw ricin from car windows and detonated explosive devices. Anti-government beliefs, and the militancy that often accompanies it, is still alive in the South. Some southerners are still planning guerilla attacks against the national government in a war that has been over for more than a century and a half but which they believe is ongoing.

> I only say that the injustice is ours, the South's. We must expiate and abolish it ourselves, alone and without help . . ."
>
> (William Faulkner, *Intruder in the Dust*, p. 199.)

In the third millennium there has been an explosion of radical militant Patriot groups, a rise of 244% between 2008, when President Obama was first elected, and 2009. Hate groups increased from 602 in 2000 to 932 groups in 2009. Patriot groups increased from 194 in 2000 to 512 in 2009. [2] Population increases, unemployment, the collapse of financial markets and the housing bubble cannot explain this social phenomenon. Race and bigotry toward President Obama plays a large role. By 2010 there were 1002 active hate such groups, 433 of them in the South. Alarmingly, Neo-Nazi, hate, and white supremacist groups are all responding to changing demographics that feature more racial and ethnic minorities and immigrants. The media portrayal of individual and ethnic groups helps recruitment for hate organizations, some of which hope that anti-immigrant feelings will be a step toward a race war. [3]

This is the underbelly of the South, the virulence of hate against any opposition to its militant aims. This is the kind of hate and pernicious violence the sleazy and White supremacist side of this national divide still cultivates under the cover of free speech and gun addiction.

The League of the South, a neo-secessionist, neo-confederate movement with over 10,000 estimated members, led by Michael Hill of Killin, Alabama, is one example of the rise of militant fringe groups. [4] A greater fear is that white supremacist groups will infiltrate the military. A group of soldiers at Fort Benning Georgia were uncovered in 2009 for supplying hate groups with stolen military weapons. [5]

The Southern Poverty Law Center has identified 309 extremist Nativist groups, or those who oppose immigration of any kind and are usually racist about immigrants. In Arizona, where discussion about immigration reached a peak in 2010, there were 21 such organizations, many with branches in several cities. They include: American Freedom Riders, Federal Immigration Reform and Enforcement (FIRE)—though it is not a federal group at all—Maricopa Patriots 1st Division, Minuteman Civil Defense Corps (MCDC), Mohave County Minuteman, Patriots Border Alliance, Patriots Coalition, Riders Against Illegal Aliens, Warden Burns, and Yuma Patriots.

One of the more militant groups is the Neo-Nazi movement that had a combined membership of about 13,000 in 2011. Neo-Nazis are a part of the National Socialist Party, echoing the party of Adolph Hitler in Germany in the 1930s that was anti-Semitic and anti-immigrant and promoted White or Aryan supremacy. In the name of their ideology of hatred, the Nazis murdered over 11 million Germans.

In the U.S., George Lincoln Rockwell spearheaded the Neo-Nazi movement. Rockwell was not religious but decided to use Christianity as a unifying force in his movement. He was assassinated in Arlington, Virginia on August 25th, 1967. The Neo-Nazi movement is active in 33 countries and on six continents, and they have a willingness to commit violence.

The current head of the American Nazi Party is Rocky J. Suhayda. Its members are often known as skinheads and the wearing of Nazi flag and other symbols is often compulsory. They are totally racist, opposing all Blacks, Jews, gays and homosexuals and minority groups. Some outshoots are: the Christian Identity movement, the Aryan Nations—formerly led by Richard Butler and now by August Kreis—and similar American Nazi groups. They are universally pro-American, though their palpable racism is antagonistic to the nation's multiracial and pluralistic leanings, and their slogan is "White Power." [6] The group most in opposition to the American Nazi movement is the Anti-Defamation League.

National government acts on behalf of the plurality of its citizens, not any particular individual needs. Extreme militants claim that government is using their tax money for purposes they do not endorse. In addition to regulating affairs to prevent financial or community disorder, Congress attempts to balance a redistribution of a nation's wealth to social and domestic needs. Extremists view this as despotism and distrust government to use any taxes for social redistribution, especially for the more economically dispossessed in society and ethnic groups they despise. There are multiple examples.

Four members of the Alaska Peacemakers Militia were arrested in March 2011, accused of planning to kill judges and Alaska state troopers and to burn their houses. Lonnie Vernon, 55, and his wife Karen, 64, and two other co-conspirators were indicted for conspiring to kill a judge, family members of the judge, an IRS employee, and preparing to wage guerilla war in the state.

Jerry Ralph Kane, 45, and his son Joseph Kane, 16, shot two Arkansas state police officers on May 21, 2010 near Little Rock after a traffic stop. The father and son duo used AK-47 assault rifles, not your ordinary rabbit hunting guns. The elder Kane had difficulty accepting authority figures, believed in government conspiracy theories, and had previously had issues with law officers in several states, and was once charged with assault in 2004. He drove without a car license and did not use a set belt. Kane was known to belong to a sovereign citizen movement, an extreme anarchist group who believed that government has no legitimate authority. He gave seminars across the country on how to avoid debt by not paying taxes and avoid government interference.

Officers in several states beginning in 2002 were concerned that a potential lethal confrontation might occur. Kane had publically threatened to kill officers. He did, and the angry father, who recruited his 16-year old son as an accomplice, shot two officers before fleeing. They were tracked to a Wal-Mart parking lot where police shot them both to death.

Arizona was the most aggressive state in attempting to pass laws against immigrants. Senate Bill 1070 was the harshest state law requiring police to check stopped vehicles to see if passengers were illegal or not. A federal judge ruled it unconstitutional. There were Arizona bills requiring hospitals to report suspected illegal immigrants to law enforcement officers, and to prod the Supreme Court to rule against automatic citizenship for children of illegal immigrants born in the U.S. (guaranteed by the 14th Amendment). The Arizona Senate rejected these bills under intense pressure from the business community. The reality of lost revenue from tourism and the boycotting and cancelling of conventions, and the international negative reaction to the bad publicity, triumphed initially over conservative ideology.

Trigger Happy?

Militants or psychotic individuals operating alone, not just leaders of groups, sometimes linked with disciples with varying degrees of commitment, can commit the most horrendous terrorist attacks.

Jared Lee Loughner, 22, attempted to assassinate Representative Gabrielle Giffords, 40, and killed federal district judge John Roll, 63, and five other innocent bystanders in Tucson on Saturday, January 10th, 2011. Although a victim of mental instability, his act played out in the context of political candidates referring to "armed revolution" and to Second Amendment privileges as a way to solve political problems. His crazed action renewed debate about gun control and mental health. According to the Gallup Poll, 42% of Americans believed that political rhetoric was a major or minor factor, while another 42% said it was not a factor at all. Still, Loughner chose a political event and targeted a member of Congress to make his murderous statement, and not a workplace environment like his community college. [7]

On the other hand, some scholars disagree that even psychopaths are not politically influenced. According to Professor James W. Clarke:

> Over a long academic career, I have researched and written about 21 American assassins, would-be assassins and domestic terrorists. It is pure nonsense to suggest, as some have, that the political environment has nothing to do with the actions of very disturbed individuals . . . who plan and attack political figures in public venues. [8]

This one event in Tucson can now be included as a part of the American legacy of violent assassinations like Birmingham (church bombings), Memphis (Martin Luther King), Dealey Plaza (President Kennedy), the Ambassador Hotel (Robert F. Kennedy), Oklahoma City (Timothy McVeigh), Columbine High School and the Virginia Tech massacres. Now we have the Tucson Safeway killings as a reminder of the violent side of insanity forever linked with invective politics. More people were killed in Tucson in 2011 than in the 1881 shootout at the OK Corral in Tombstone, Arizona, ironically a town within Giffords' congressional district. In the 1880s visitors to Tombstone had to check guns on arriving into town at the Grand Hotel or the Sheriff's office.

The political discussion abruptly changed to questions about American identity and cohesion and the nature of how democratic discourse can agitate people on the fringe who take metaphorical messages and anti-government feelings literally. Cultivating a toxic climate where political opponents are viewed as enemies shatters complacency about the soundness of our national identity and its increasing paramilitary visions.

Gifford's unsuccessful political opponent in 2010, Jesse Kelly, had a campaign event where voters were invited to shoot a M-16 with him to represent an assault on her campaign. Another unsuccessful Arizona candidate for Congress, Pamela Gorman, ran a campaign video of her firing off several gun rounds several times. Sarah Palin's ("Don't retreat, reload") web page (since deleted) showed a map with gun targets on selected congressional districts, one was on Giffords' Arizona district. Alabama congressional candidate Rick Barber said, "Gather your armies." Sharron Angle, senatorial candidate from Nevada talked about "domestic enemies" in Congress and said: "I hope we're not getting to Second Amendment remedies." All were Republican candidates for Congress. Politicians pander to the gun lobby and gun owners. The rhetoric becomes muted when someone, even someone deranged, takes gun violence literally.

We may never know exactly what the framers of the Constitution meant by "a well regulated militia, being necessary to the security of a free State, the right of the people to keep and bear arms, shall not be infringed." But surely one interpretation is that the protection of the State is the principal reason, not the protection of individual liberties against state infringement. Hence, if a State is slave-holding, as all southern states were, then the militia is White and the guns are to prevent slave rebellions and not to fight off the British. The judicial decisions have traditionally held that the bearing of arms extends to all individuals. I believe it was initially intended to keep state militia armed, certainly not Blacks, in order to uphold slavery and prevent uprisings. Cato's Conspiracy in 1739 in South Carolina and the New York slave rebellion, both Black slave uprisings were both within memory of the writers of the Constitution.

Politicians were tapping into a more spiteful citizen electorate and not merely expressing a principled viewpoint. The Gallup Poll reported in 1990 that 78% of Americans wanted stricter firearm sales. By 2010, the percentage of the population that wanted stricter gun laws was only 44%. Americans had shifted in two decades toward a more liberal attitude toward citizen gun rights and politicians were catering to that belief. In 2010 Arizona's Governor Jan Brewer signed a bill ending the requirement for a permit to carry a concealed weapon. Utah created a law declaring the Browning M1911 semiautomatic pistol the official state gun, joining the beehive and the sugar beet as state symbols.

Hardly anyone conducts research on the impact of firearms because the National Rifle Association (NRA) convinced Congress to nearly eliminate funding from a safety and health division of the Centers for Disease Control. In 1996 Arkansas representative Jay Dickey, now retired but then a member of the House Appropriations Committee, pushed through an amendment that stripped $2.6 million from the budget for firearms research. Dickey said that we have the right to bear arms because of the threat of government taking over the freedoms we have. Such illogic is supposed to pass for reason.

As soon as the Arizona legislature met in 2011, Senate President Russell Pierce sent a memo to lawmakers giving his permission to carry guns into the legislative chambers, noting that a member of the Legislature does not lose his or her Second Amendment rights when coming to work. Although state statutes prohibit guests from bringing weapons into the building, and even gun lobbyists have to surrender their guns, he has the authority to make rules within the building. He also introduced a bill forbidding Arizona colleges from keeping students from carrying guns into classes.

The more distressing conclusion is that politicians on the far right are reflecting a more acrimonious attitude toward government and divisive and inflammatory political expression among the population at large. Gun control and the diminishment of mental health programs are two factors that intersect with the shooting of Congresswoman Giffords. In a previous generation, the figures on the far right included Robert Welch's John Birch Society members, Phyllis Schlafly, Pat Robertson, Barry Goldwater and convicted felon House Majority Whip Tom Delay. Today, it is Donald Trump, Glenn Beck, Russ Limbaugh, Sarah Palin, Michele Bachmann and Rick Perry, and a few who believe in conspiracies by Jews, Freemasons, the Illuminati, or aliens.

Mobs and Militia

It's time to discuss a little of the history and the swaggering nature of this radical movement symbolic of this extremist shift to see how intolerance, hatred and violence arise from time to time to tarnish our politics and test our patience. According to the Gallup Poll we know that about 7 in 10 national adults, including 88% of Republicans, say it's important that Republican leaders in Congress take the Tea Party movement's positions and objectives into account as they address the nation's problems, except that the movement's disciples have no positive program for government involvement, only opposition to any domestic policy or program.

A certain amount of mob rule was tolerated in early America, certainly during the riots in Baltimore in 1812. Mobs were seen as an extension of the political majority and therefore quasi-legitimate. Force was seen as a necessary expedient to achieve political ends that did not lead to revolution or armed revolt but as a convenient form of extra-judicial justice.

As a U.S. revolutionary comparison, Alexander Contee Hanson published tracts in his paper, *The Federal Republican* at No. 10 Charles Street, Baltimore, against America's involvement with the British in the war of 1812 against President Madison. Hanson accused the government of harboring French spies. Mobs had previously burned down his printing ship on a summer night. Hanson had fled the city for Georgetown but returned a few weeks later. Baltimore at the time was sympathetic to southern interests and brooked no dissent against Madison for his decision. Officials thought it best to escort Hanson and his defenders to jail for protection. The following night another crowd assembled outside the jail and were escorted into the jail by a sympathetic jailor. Then the tar and feathering began. The mob unleashed its fury upon the beleaguered captors by drawing them along behind a cart and torturing them. A man named Lingam, a Revolutionary War general and hero, was beaten to death.

Similarly, riots in 1968 after the deaths of Martin Luther King and Robert Kennedy in many major cities including Washington DC were a venting of frustration at the loss of two primary movers of civil rights. I was in Washington DC that summer of 1968 and recall night curfews keeping us in our hotels. Rioters ruled the streets patrolled by soldiers in the back of jeeps with mounted machine guns. No one knew where or when the conflagration would appear next, what destruction it would unleash, or whom it might engulf. The twin conflicts of the push for civil rights, after the enactment of the *Civil Rights Act* in 1964, and the atrocities of the Vietnam War, generated additional riots and demonstrations, a few ending fatally.

But right-wing revolutionary radicalism is taking a more violent turn. Those who contemplate revolt the most are those who have the least to lose. It is not the wealthy most vocal in discontent. Radicals and those who turn to militancy may live in a moderately prosperous society, but do not feel prosperous, and may also believe they have been disenfranchised. Militants may act against legitimate police authority to maintain public order as despots out to take away some of their freedoms. They have a misguided sense of the need for the use of authorized force needed to uphold the law and to thwart criminals.

Timothy McVeigh: Mass Murderer

David Koresh and his radical Christian followers found refuge in a compound in Waco, Texas. His group stocked illegal weapons, and actually manufactured machine guns in the barns. The Alcohol, Tobacco and Firearms (ATF) division of the Treasury Department, sought to confiscate these illegal weapons. A standoff occurred from February 28, 1993 to April 19th when federal officers began a forced entry. Several police were killed, the compound was set afire, and the inhabitants incinerated. The one event, according to his own testimony, enraged Timothy McVeigh (1968-2001), who committed mass murder on April 19, 1995 when he exploded a van laden with 7,000 pounds of explosives in front of the Alfred P. Murrah federal building in Oklahoma City killing 168 and wounding over 700. His anti-government resentment began years earlier.

McVeigh was born in Pendleton, New York, north of Buffalo. His father worked in an auto plant, and he had one older and one younger sister. When his parents divorced his younger sister moved in with the mother and Timothy with his father. As a youth he got attached to his grandfather. He was picked on in high school and hated bullies and later viewed the government as a bully. After a year at a business college he enrolled in the army just in time to take part in Desert Shield the first war with Iraq in 1991. He was assigned to the 1st Infantry and was a Sergeant in the field. His signal achievement was killing two Iraqi soldiers with one shot.

After the Iraq war he tried out for a Special Forces unit at Ft. Bragg but dropped out, ostensibly because of exhaustion. He left the army after four years and began to demonize the government. Suddenly he discovered repression everywhere that he attributed to the government and become more disillusioned and angry. He possibly had undiagnosed Post Traumatic Stress Syndrome and a nervous breakdown.

He began an odyssey by driving around the U.S. attending gun shows and discovering the sub-culture of the militia movement. He camped outside Waco for four days. Later he expressed his rage about the Waco incident to journalist Michelle Rauch who interviewed him in prison. "I felt absolute rage," he said. "What are the rules of engagement? Kids are fair game; women are fair game."

He had already read *The Turner Diaries*, authored by William Pierce (pseudonym for Andrew MacDonald), a Neo-Nazi member of the National Alliance. The work is supposedly a diary of Earl Turner an underground White supremacist who describes the coming revolution against the United States. One scene chillingly describes how a rented truck filled with explosives explodes in front of a federal building.

He contacted former army buddies Terry Nichols and Michael Fortier, fellow survivalists, for help in starting a revolution. He rented a 20-foot Ryder truck and filled it with 7,000 pounds of ammonium nitrate fertilizer and nitromethane racing fuel and packed it with 13 plastic barrels. He stopped at Oklahoma's Geary Lake where it took him four hours to build the bomb that included a five-minute fuse.

While driving along the I-35 corridor to Oklahoma City he said he felt as if he were going into combat. In Oklahoma City while at a stoplight he lit the fuse, parked in front of the Murrah federal building, left the truck and walked to a Mercury Marquis he had left as a getaway vehicle, but had difficulty starting it. At 9:03 AM the bomb exploded tearing off the front half of the several-storied building. As he drove through Perry, Oklahoma, two hours after the blast he was arrested for not having license plates on the Mercury, and for carrying a gun without a permit, and so spent the night in the Noble County jail.

Within three hours investigators found the truck's rear axle with the identifying number. The truck had been rented at Eliott's Body Shop injunction City, Kansas. McVeigh was arrested April 21st, just three days later. His friend, Terry Nichols, was arrested and agreed to cooperate with authorities.

Until the end he was hostile, lacking any sensitivity toward his victims, without pity or remorse. He was executed on Monday morning, June 10, 2001 at the federal penitentiary in Terre Haute, Indiana. Three months later foreign terrorists would kill Americans for different reasons.

Shortly after the Oklahoma City federal building bombing in 1995, a CNN/Opinion Research poll asked Americans if they agreed that the federal government was "so large and powerful that is poses an immediate threat to the rights and freedoms of ordinary citizens." Surprisingly, even after the worst domestic terrorist attack on innocent victims that killed 168 men, women and children in a day care center in the building, 39% of respondents agreed.

In March 2010 the same polling asked the same question and 56% responded positively. Citizen anger became more ominous. Politicians and many media outlets capitalized on this disturbing trend. The Tea Party movement is just one example of the negative movement filled with right-wing ideas of racism, hate groups, armed revolution, and conspiracy theories. From 1995 to 2009, there were 75 plots, conspiracies and racist rampages uncovered, and 28 law enforcement officers murdered by domestic right-wing extremists.

The consequence of this shifting radical thinking has caused politicians to adapt to its language and anti-government feelings in order to get re-elected. Moderate politicians got defeated in 2010. Yet if they adjust their rhetoric to match the prevailing public mood, encouraged by the donations of large corporations and billionaire sponsors, they move farther away from reasonable legislative compromises—the lifeblood of legislative activity—and towards actions that gut previous laws, and cave in to partisan business interests. Since the country itself is divided, Congress becomes stalemated and the public's perception of Congress receives the poorest of reviews, only 9% favorable in 2011.

Religion and Anti-Government Movements

Members of the media and even members of Congress helped accelerate this resurgent and disturbing extremism. On March 29, 2010, a federal grand jury indicted nine residents from Indiana, Ohio and Michigan on charges of seditious conspiracy to kill police officers using weapons of mass destruction, specifically improvised explosive devices. All were members of a Christian patriot group known as Hutaree. Members believed they were on a mission to oppose the Anti-Christ with violence if necessary. From 1995 to 2010, Patriot groups killed 32 police officers.

Here is a scenario of events leading to their indictments.

- Several members of the militia tried to travel on February 6, 2010 to Kentucky for a militia summit. They did not reach their destination because of bad weather. They tried to make IEDs. From August 13, 2009 Hutaree members used email, the Internet, and phones attempting to use explosive bombs and mines against local, state, and federal law enforcement officers and vehicles.

- On August 22nd and again on February 20th, 2009 militia members used firearms to conduct seditious conspiracy and attempted the use of Weapons of Mass Destruction (WMDs).

- The head of this militia planned a "covert reconnaissance exercise" for April 2010 "during which exercise anyone who happened upon the exercise who did not acquiesce their demands could be killed." [9]

This was not a group of overly eager boy scouts learning to fire weapons for hunting, or immature adults seeking to avoid un-named conspirators. This was a paranoid group who thought evil spirits had inhabited law enforcement and so they had to kill them to start the next revolution for Christ. They wanted to protect Michigan from invasion and seek "to defend all those who belong to Christ and save those who aren't." It's hard to know what those who are not Christian are being defended from. Religiously misguided extremists who believe they can extirpate their grievances by killing others are increasing. Mixing religion and guns does not lead to improved social conditions. Home grown terrorists are a rising concern, and the presiding judge was right to keep them locked in jail without bail bonds until trial. How can anyone tell the difference between a dangerous militia member from one who is not?

Angry anti-government individuals stray beyond the confines of civility. Federal agents charged Charles Wilson, 64, of Selah, Washington on April 6, 2010 with threatening to kill Washington Senator Patty Murray because of her vote on the health care reform bill. Police arrested Gregory Lee Giusti, 48, of San Francisco, in April 2010 because he made 48 threatening phone calls to House Speaker Nancy Pelosi and her husband because of her passage of the health care reform bill. Within a couple of months, congressional lawmakers had received 42 threats between January and March 2010, nearly three times the amount received in 2009, according to the U.S. Capitol Police. For domestic terrorists Christianity often appears as a cover and a justification for violence, although some who make threats have serious mental health issues. For Muslim terrorists, religion is unquestionably the primary rationale for violence as it is embedded in the Koran.

On February 8, 2010, Michael Oren, Ambassador to the United States from Israel, was scheduled to speak at the University of California at Irvine. Shortly after he began his remarks, male Islamic students rose one by one after a few minutes of his speech to beginning shouting slogans and martial epithets. Police escorted them out of the auditorium after each incident. Within a few minutes the whole contingent of Muslim students, more than one hundred, walked out in a sign of protest yelling and deliberately disrupting the speech and the audience gathered to hear his remarks. The university President and sponsors were incensed and promised punitive university action on the students as eleven students were arrested after being led from the hall. Muslims students knew they would receive hearty congratulations in their home countries, and be hailed as stalwarts of Islam everywhere in the Muslim world for standing up to Jews. The Muslim Student Union disclaimed responsibility and said that individuals caused disruption of the speech. But the organization did not condemn the behavior of its members.

On April 2, 2010 the non-violent, fringe organization known as *Guardians of the Free Republics*, sent letters to ten state governors, scattered somewhat randomly throughout the country, asking them to leave office or "they would be removed." Their insane plan to restore the republic by dismantling existing state governments can be found on their website.

> And finally, we constructed "The unanimous Declaration of the sovereign People of the united States of America to restore and reinhabit [sic] the free American Republics" to be a shining covenant with the Creator. His charging the People with dominion over all the earth in the Book of Genesis is declared in the very first paragraph as the foundation for the restoration. In so doing, the Declaration is established in history as a genuine covenant with the Creator in honor of the Law. [10]

The scribe or recorder apparently did not complete or never enrolled in Composition 101, as it is difficult to comprehend the full meaning of this message, the introduction of the group's mission. These are not Thomas Jefferson's sentences or Ben Franklin's ideas. The writer or writers seem to be playacting as self-appointed founders of a new form of government. Nor do misguided members seem to have a grasp of how existing governments function, certainly not American democracy. Was their newly proposed government to be "of the people?" If so, without having taken a poll—one way of determining current thinking—how would they know what people want? But there are more crazy passages:

> With restoration of the de jure judicial institutions in Phase 2, we are also enacting the: Bill of Rights of Law to prevent once and for all the 'legal' franchise perversions of law into at-law, territorial, admiralty/military aberrations.

> There will be no such entity as a non-Article III court, even when administering the admiralty law venue for genuine issues of the high seas and international commerce.

> The Bill of Rights of Law has been authored to address the perversions of law through statutes, Rules of Evidence, and Rules of Civil Procedure which have hijacked the law of the Land for the bar associations and converted the common law grand juries into prosecutorial kingdoms and slandered them as "runaway juries" instead of the fourth branch of government historically charged with OVERSEEING GOVERNMENT and PROTECTING AGAINST TYRANNY BY GOVERNMENT OFFICIALS. [11]

What seems clear is that the foundation of the group's purpose is rooted in the Bible, specifically *Genesis* and perhaps other holy books, but not in any philosophical or political science theories of governance, and no rationale for why existing government is inadequate or un-necessary.

Radical fringe groups, whether or not they are militia-minded or tend toward violence, are ill-informed, poorly educated—as evidenced by the sample writings—and emboldened by group fear and a desire to eliminate present national government in all its forms and start over, whatever that means to them. It is easy to dismiss such individuals as marginalized workers and homeowners who felt aggrieved and ignored and who, with an extremely limited understanding of state controls, constitutional principles and government actions, seek to reformulate what they think is an imperfect structure. The most charitable response would be to have them return to an elementary civic class and to start their education over.

A survey by Quinnipiac University found that these people are overwhelmingly White, evangelical Christians, less educated than the normal population, and often in debt or unemployed. This radical group appears alarmingly favorable within the mainstream Republican Party, particularly key leaders in Congress. These groups hold conventions and issue documents outlining their position, some of which conclude that if people believe that their liberties are being infringed then that constitutes an "act of war," and they have the right to rebel, as did southern states in 1860. For some this means with weapons, which makes the prospect decidedly unpatriotic.

These groups are vocal though shouts and vitriolic slogans that have reverberating emotional ring tones but contribute little except passionate emotional expression, and offer nothing positive to the debate on complicated issues. They argue that government should not be running banks, automobile or insurance companies or health care, but want the government to find ways to reduce job loss, and don't want any cuts in their Medicare or Social Security.

Protesting is a part of the fabric of American society, but from time to time its most vocal and radical element assumes prominence. The anti-war movement in the 1960s, Students for a Democratic Society, which at one time had about 100,000 members, eventually abandoned its goals but left behind the smaller Weather Underground, the radical core that escalated violence.

The social divide in Natchez is a representative example of the social divide in many parts of America, particularly in the South, but doesn't completely explain the current political chasm. Political reality also involves overlapping issues, power relationships, loyalty to a party or ideology, and acceptance or opposition to government activities. But I believe there is an additional variable––the genetic or inherited unwillingness to admit into social contact those outside the familial, clan or tribal identity. Unless we can rise above our suspicious fears of those "others," we limit the boundaries of social intercourse. The stranger in many cultures like the Arab is typically welcomed into the tent of the locals. But outside the region, the stranger is just as often feared.

Except among professional classes, college students and the genuinely altruistic there is no universal social integration between African Americans and others. Housing, schooling and restaurants in Natchez and elsewhere are racially distinct, and this fact, more than the legal integration in public facilities like libraries, reveals the true nature of a divided society. The fact that 70% of Mississippi state legislators are African American is a sign of the strength of population demographics and less the level of multiracial acceptance.

The South's culture is Christianity within accepted denominations, and guns are its priority. Elvis Pressley, born in Tupelo, Mississippi, bought 32 handguns for his personal use for Christmas in 1969. [11] According to the 2010 Gallup Poll, for the second year in a row, a record-low 44% of Americans say laws governing the sale of firearms should be made more strict, while 42% say gun laws should be kept as they are now. Only 12% say gun laws should be made less strict.

Patriot Paranoia and Conspiracy Believers

As so-called sovereign citizens, is it necessary for anyone to pay taxes to the IRS, to obey laws, or do anything imposed by the national government?

Is America in the grip of Jewish financiers?

Is government run by representatives who are opposed to personal liberties?

Can federal officers confiscate firearms, declare martial law and place you and me in a concentration camp for personal beliefs?

Believing that selected individuals and government agencies or religious groups are in the business of confiscating your personal items or usurping your freedoms has reached alarming proportions. Self-styled Patriot groups are in the forefront of conspiracy theorists believing that the federal government and its officials, sworn in fact to uphold the Constitution, are deliberately threatening democracy. These groups rapidly expanded, fueled by the rants, ignorance and deceits of media personalities who are often conspiracy theorists. They perceived the election of President Obama as a socialist enemy of American sovereignty.

Conspiracy theories take many forms and those who commit violence, like shooting police officers, Holocaust museum guards, or federal IRS workers, usually believe in one or more radical conspiratorial ideas. They may also be psychotic or paranoid and untested for mental disability. They may feel a lack of power and success and so they can more easily envision an evil, invisible force that threatens them. The danger now is that conspiracy theories seem no longer to be just a fringe movement, but have blended into the mainstream political process. Popular movies and television programs about the influence of the preternatural and science fiction and the sub-textual and presumed prevalent influence of the intelligence agencies feeds this movement. Providing factual evidence will not convince them. A further danger of the expansion of these groups who, through ignorance and belief in conspiracies that stretch reason, is that they oversimplify the political process and enable politicians to cater to paranoia to feed anxieties and fear.

The individuals who compose these groups are not all high school dropouts, though they may behave as if they are. Richard Mack, 57, is the former Sheriff of Graham County, Arizona. Ted Gunderson, 81, is a former FBI agent for nearly thirty years. Chuck Baldwin, 57, is a Baptist minister. Jack McLamb, 65, is a former Phoenix police officer. Stewart Rhodes, 44, is an army veteran and graduate of Yale Law School, a former congressional aide to Texas Congressman Ron Paul and founder of the Oath Keepers.

The rise in entertainment media commentary posing as news, and the role of preachers and politicians responding to the radical movements is demonizing non-White Americans and fomenting dissension, hate and militancy. The collapse of the housing bubble and the unethical practices of the financial sector have added to the social discontent and pushed politics to extremist poles. But whatever the deteriorating context of American economics or politics, the ugly head of bigotry has never been fully purged from American society. Neither has the dark history of America's racial relations. It may be impossible to eradicate hate from people's hearts. But no nation will tolerate any antagonism toward others to erupt into violence, or shredding of its laws, or the protection of the life, liberty and happiness of all its citizens.

An angel looks down at the book of life as one of the life-sized sculptures hovering over the Natchez city cemetery on the Mississippi River bluffs. We may have to summon one or more of them to oversee the living to help us resolve our polarized democracy.

EPILOGUE

At a time when our discourse has become so sharply polarized, at a time when we are far too eager to lay the blame for all that ails the world at the feet of those who think differently than we do, it is important for us to pause for a moment and make sure we are talking with each other in a way that heals, not wounds.   (President Obama, Tucson Memorial Service, January 12, 2011)

Is our national citizenship and patriotism enough to define us? Or are we really defined by our political identification? I believe our collective citizenship does not fully define us and that our social and political beliefs break into distinct patterns that have been the legacy of our troubled history. This dual and distinctive mentality is reflected into our political system because it is embedded in the population.

Beginning in 2009, the year Obama became President, Republicans systematically derailed and negated every proposal he initiated, primarily so as to deny him legislative victories. Ordinary political disagreements aside, I believe it was a cynical strategy to deny a sitting president any domestic policy plan that might get him re-elected in 2012, even when such policies are beneficial to the electorate. When senior politicians who command half of Congress claim that their first priority is to defeat an incumbent president you can begin to shudder for the problem-solving fate of the country when its imperial, historical, southern hubris is reflected in political impotence.

Every argument created by radical Republicans proved to be mythical. The stimulus package of 2009 did help boost not hinder the economy, according to the Congressional Budget Office. The deficit is not the nation's biggest problem. Job growth is. Lower taxes are not the best solution for growing the economy. Government spending is. Clinton raised taxes in 1993 and the economy blossomed. Bush lowered taxes in 2003 and the economy faltered. Small businesses are not worried about government regulations—corporations are— but about loss of consumer demand. The "trade weighted value" of the dollar, according to data from the Federal Reserve, remained steady under the Obama Administration. It lost value under Reagan and Bush I, gained value under Clinton, and lost under Bush II. The rich do not provide jobs because all economies are linked to international investments. There is no trickle down workable economic theory except in ideological minds unconvinced by evidence.

America is filled with college graduates horse-tied with bulging student loans but unable to find jobs to repay those debts. Men have been laid off and can't find jobs that will pay the bills. Women are likewise saddled with unemployment while scratching for milk money and shoes for their children. Retirees are scratching their heads wondering where the promised money for their pensions went. Those who have jobs can't afford health insurance when only a serious illness away spells bankruptcy. The ultra-Republican response to this is to promise to a lobbyist never to raise taxes, and certainly not to pay for foreign wars, and to claim the enormous loss of wealth is all government's fault.

The fact that this obstructionist and deceptive scheme evaded the nation's severe employment problem was startling to Americans conditioned typically to have the two political parties compromise to solve the nation's problems. The political dysfunction was one-sided, viciously partisan, but rooted partly in our divided history. The 112th Congress mirrored previous Congresses composed of a large southern voting bloc that repeatedly sought to bar or frustrate federal legislation from benefitting the North or disfavoring the South. This book has been an extended argument with some interviews, anecdotes, examples and archival evidence to demonstrate the truth of that hypothesis.

This has not always been the case. The vision of many Republican leaders has been decidedly pragmatic in the past, in favor of sensible solutions to political difficulties. Republican president Teddy Roosevelt, for example, in a major speech in Osawatomie Kansas in 1910, advocated for equality of the distribution of wealth, [1] keeping special interests out of politics, [2] passing laws that prohibit corporate funds corrupting political decisions, [3] active participation of government in business and economic affairs, [4] and a graduated tax on big wage-earners, [5] all issues today that ultra-Republicans disavow. During his presidency over a century ago, Republican President Roosevelt knew it would have been folly to prevent the development and expansion of the banking system, and equally folly to not have government control them. Government, he knew, had to protect labor from corporation abuses and to subordinate them to the public welfare. [6]

What has happened in the century since T.R. Roosevelt addressed the nation's problems and offered his reasonable solutions and contemporary Republicans who obstruct all legislation with ideologically driven obstructionism? I believe that antagonism toward the election of an African American president ranks high on the list of probable responses.

Disdain for the government is at an all-time high, paralleling the antipathy prior to the Civil War. The deep-seated animosity to government and the rise of libertarian and limited government thinking has paralyzed social legislation everywhere, except for abortion. According to the Gallup poll conducted in August 2011, only 17% of American had a positive view of the national government, while 63% had a negative view, or at the absolute bottom of the list of all organizations for the first time. A poor economic climate is perceived as at least as pernicious as a plague, and government's inability to redress the nation's finances makes its relationship to citizens bleak.

In contemporary America, negativity toward government is surely misplaced and should be directed toward financial institutions, and perhaps themselves as purchasers, bearing too much debt. But viewed as a condition of centuries of internal division, it is really an extension of a southern mentality that has always existed. I grant a large swath of probable cause of divided government to political maneuvers and gamesmanship, but still believe history is a greater source of our political dysfunction.

Anti-government persuasions, embedded in our political system since he founding of the Republic, has paralyzed Washington just as bold action is required for America to adjust to a global economy. Huge political contributions and limited taxes benefitting entrenched financial interests have strangled government initiatives. All of this political inertia, as Jeffrey Sachs reminds us in *The Price of Civilization*, comes with a loss of civic virtue, respect and compassion. [7]

Moreover, the injection of religious imperatives into politics has always been a tonic for many conservatives. A significant part of the electorate is fed by religious fundamentalism and the denial of scientific evidence. Half of the newly elected representatives to Congress in 2010 denied the compelling science of global warming. According to the Center for American Progress, approximately 39% of incoming representatives signed on to end birthright citizenship under the 14th Amendment. The representatives of the religious right will favor repealing existing laws on prayer, abortion and science-based evidence in such matters as health care, and prevent the enactment of necessary laws to advance the economy, reduce the deficit, and improve lives. This level of religious fundamentalism is unparalleled in western societies, with the possible exceptions of Italy and Spain.

We don't have to search far for examples of the religious imperatives in legislative life. While the American public overwhelmingly wanted government to engage in finding jobs, the 112th House of Representatives was active in proposing abortion bills and restricting women's access to suitable health care. This activity favored the religious right even while the House knew the Senate would consistently reject new abortion amendments.

The South too, throughout history, championed its Christian religious base while upholding the cause of slavery with equal fervor. Thus could a contemporary Congress plan religious laws that have nothing to do with the nation's problems, but everything to do with its furtherance of religious imperatives.

Meanwhile, the widening chasm between the very rich and other Americans has already exposed unequal tax laws. In 1976 the top one percent of wage earners had a pre-tax income of nine percent. In 2007 the top one percent had a pretax income of 23.5 percent. This income disparity does not create jobs, as some espouse, and no evidence is used to support that premise. Meanwhile, the median income for all other Americans declined and the poverty rate accelerated. These multiple disparities, and the incessant bickering over government's role, make it increasingly difficult to effect needed changes.

The gridlock is exacerbated by feeble congressional attempts to trim a $1.324 trillion dollar deficit (as of 2012) through cutting spending but resisting raising tax revenues. If no changes are made within a generation, Social Security is scheduled to cover only about 75% of present benefits.

Medicare is a health-services program for retirees over 65 or the qualifying disabled, and one of the largest social services programs paid for through payroll taxes. The Gallup Poll finds that 25.7% of adults get healthcare from those programs or military/veterans' benefits. In 2011 Medicare consumed 16% of the federal budget. Since it was begun in 1965, the mortality rate has increased by over five years. Together with expanded longevity, greater technological precision in diagnosing serious diseases, and greater numbers participating in the system, the program will always be a subject of budget restraint, especially as the population ages and medical costs continue to rise.

The government has often made promises it has difficulty keeping because voters have elected representatives who simultaneously campaign with slogans to reduce the deficit but not raise taxes or curtail entitlements. Medicare recipients at this writing receive far more in benefits than they paid in taxes. The American public, itself in burdened debt ($14,550 in credit card debt per household in 2011), blames government for its inability to solve the national debt problem, but still consistently refuses to have any taxes raised to ease the national financial pinch.

There are two main threats to medical solvency—the costs of medical care rise exponentially and too many Americans (about 30 million) are uninsured. Government pays more than half of the costs of Medicaid, the health program for the poor. Republicans have used the nation's legitimate concerns about the deficit to attempt to privatize government health programs. Insurance corporations would simply raise costs while discontinuing those unable to pay. The far right is not really concerned about stabilizing budgets but about realizing antipathy to government social programs.

Government reports show that about 100 million Americans, about a third of the population, lives in poverty or near it. Median household income in 2000 was $61,000. In 2011 it was $55,000. Have market forces, free enterprise, supposedly job-creating corporations, and reduction of government taxes ensured broader prosperity? No they have not, and yet government stimulus packages have been repeatedly denigrated and shot down because Republican diehards refuse to accept that government can aid in economic recovery.

One of the most successful government programs that put millions of youth to work and helped revive the economy was the Civilian Conservation Corps (CCC) first funded in March 1933. [8] Most of the then four million male enrollees served in national or state forests or parks or military reservations, planting billions of trees, reinforcing bridges, dams and building roads and trails, while getting both a formal and technical education. The CCC existed until 1942 when it ended because World War II provided military opportunities. As a cook on a Northwest mountain trail crew in 1952-53 I was fully aware of the legacy of this far-reaching program putting unemployed men to work. Ask yourself what a similar government-funded organization might do for the jump-starting of the sluggish economy today and what is preventing it from happening. [9]

Profound distrust of government is not going to solve the country's problems. Permanent congressional campaigning for elected representatives in order to secure the next election dooms easy governance. Politicians are really only hardening the existing polar opposites by appealing to ideologies un-reconcilable with economic realities. America is in a slough of despond dictated by contemporary adherents of a failed ideology.

Let's review a few of the contemporary trends that show America's torn national past. Campaign slogans are not a good barometer of elected official's subsequent actions. Once in office, elected politicians are more often influenced by the size of a donor's campaign contribution. Those running for national office have to pander to traditional southern interests—evangelical concerns like religion in public life, tough immigration policies, a strong military, no gun control, states' rights, less taxes, and limited government. There is less interest about realistic programs the nation needs to compete in a global economy. Our slave past is still hampering our plodding toward an improved American dream.

The debates and campaign topics are not usually about indispensable investments in human capital, education, technology, or energy alternatives. The conservative issues still revolve around the role of the national government and the role of the individual freedoms, impractical topics that skirt how America has plummeted even in its own image, and how it is blindsided by an internal, myopic vision of how to proceed in a volatile and complicated world. It takes America a few days to decide to go to war, but years delaying legislating on a sensible energy policy.

A country was divided by a racist past in half of its states, and dominated by cunning and fundamentalist politicians—who are most likely representative of the general population. They are applauded for playing the outrageous fool, and spoil rational discussion on the most significant national topics. Unless the nation ultimately confronts and divests itself completely of its inglorious past, it will not overcome the obstructionist obstacles and ingrained animosities toward the national government, simplistic notions about individual liberties, and discredited ideas about taxation. The Civil War is long over but the cultural divide between North and South suffuses our political narrative and impedes America's domestic progress and national unity.

For 178 years, from 1609 to 1776 at Independence and then to 1787 when the Constitution was created, settlers in America accepted the rule of a King and English Parliament with state houses dispensing local laws. For another 78 years, from the Constitution of 1787 to the war in 1860, southern states lived with legally sanctioned slavery. And for another century after that, from 1865 to 1965, southern states universally discriminated against freed slaves to promote White supremacy and ignored equality of rights and the laws that supported them. In what sense has America been united all these years?

In the more than 400 years of immigration experience and life under royal, colonial and finally experimental democracy for European immigrants and reluctantly for kidnapped and then freed slaves, Americans have salvaged few historical lessons from their struggles for personal liberty and a robust relationship with government and each other. There will always be some rebellious spirits against governmental authority. But the search for a more permanent political unity that mirrors social unity should have been finished by now. It clearly is not. Succeeding generations will show whether or not the fabric of presumed American unity, the *e pluribus unum* that referred to states and not people, will endure, or get that fragile unity ripped asunder by the same kind of extremists that brought us a war between ourselves.

Come, I will make the continent indissoluble . . . (Walt Whitman)

ENDNOTES

Preface

1. "As a result, the intense struggle between Republicans and Democrats that emerged from the Civil War and Reconstruction generally paralleled the traditional geographic divisions between free states and slave states." E. Black & M. Black. (2002). *The Rise of Southern Republicans*. (Cambridge, MA: The Belnap Press of Harvard University Press, 2002), p. 14. This book documents the political transformation and validates my premise. It concludes: "Old-fashioned sectional conflict has dissipated but sectional considerations continue to pervade national politics through the conservative agenda pursued by Republican congressional leaders from the South" (p. 404).

2. M. Potok, "The Year in Hate and Extremism." *Intelligence Report*, Spring 2011, pp. 41-67.

3. The Republican-controlled House of Representatives wanted to dismantle the Consumer Financial Protection Agency designed to protect consumers from questionable mortgage practices and credit card abuses by declaring "it had too much power." The only power any agency has is the power Congress gives it that includes developing rules to enforce the legislation. Americans have piled on the debt. As of 2012 the average credit card debt is $6,503, and the average auto loan debt if $15,370. From a credit score range from 300-850, the average American credit score is 661.

4. Banks and financial institutions, unknown except by the most savvy homeowners, bundled mortgages into various packages and pooled them into investments. A financial security was created with thousands of housing loans that were then funneled into a trust that managed the security. A loan service collected mortgage payments from homeowners and forwarded them to this trust that then sold them to investors. So who owns the mortgage? Good question, as many courts have ruled that the companies that bundled the mortgage payments do not own the mortgage lien. But this complicated sleight-of-hand financial process, and the lack of governmental regulation to question or audit it, helped create the economic catastrophe that sent the country into a tailspin. The public's lack of understanding of this sophisticated and complicated financial ruse on home mortgages caused them to turn their raw political anger about the economic downturn towards the national government, easier to hate and closer to home so to speak. Yet the banks, not the borrowers, received federal money to keep them for failing. For a comprehensive overview of how banks gamed the system see C. Ketchum, "Stop Payment, A Homeowner's Revolt Against he Banks." *Harpers*, (January 2012). 324(1940), pp. 28-36.

5. A. De Tocqueville, *Democracy in America*, (Chicago: University of Chicago Press, 2000), p. 329. On the other hand, Americans do not appear to rely on political institutions to manage problems of national unity and diversity in the U.S. See Merelman *et al.*, "Unity and Diversity in American Political Culture: An Exploratory Study of the National Conversation on American Pluralism and Identity. *Political Psychology*, 19(4), December 1998, pp. 781-807.

6. Tom Delay was convicted in federal court in 2011. Delay began the process of inviting lobbyists into the House chambers to write favorable legislation thereby corrupting Congress and the people's legislative business. Members of Congress have blown past ethical boundaries in accepting campaign contributions, a now legalized form of bribery. See R. G. Kaiser, *So Damn Much Money, The Triumph of Lobbying and the Corrosion of American Government*. (New York: Alfred A. Knopf, 2009), p. 4ff.

Chapter One Notes
1. Only one other country, tiny Denmark, has a government debt ceiling. According to Nobel economist Jospeh Stiglitz: "Regrettably, the financial markets and right-wing economists have gotten the problem exactly backwards: they believe that austerity produces confidence, and that confidence will produce growth. But austerity undermines growth, worsening the government's fiscal position, or at least yielding less improvement than austerity's advocates promise." J. E. Stiglitz, "The Ideological Crisis of Western Capitalism," *The Jakarta Post*, July 8, 2011, p. 2. During a recession the country needs a fiscal strategy as well as an economic growth strategy. By the end of 2011 it had neither because of the financial crisis created by the Bush Administration and congressional Republicans in 2000 to 2008, and the agenda of far right extremists during the Obama Administration.
2. Hofstadter, 2008, p. 29, & R. Paul, R., *The Revolution, A Manifesto*. (New York: Grand Central Publishing, 2008). But this theme also comes from Austrian economists like F. A Hayek and echoed by conservative Nobel laureates like Milton Friedman discussed in a subsequent chapter.
3. W. B. Yearns, *The Confederate Congress*. (Athens: The University of Georgia Press, 1960), p. 4.
4. For an extensive argument between these positions see Milton Friedman, *Capitalism and Freedom*, (Chicago: University of Chicago Press, 2002). According to a New York Times/CBS News Poll, 73% of Democrats and 61% of Independents believe that providing health care coverage for the poor is the government's responsibility. Only 25% of Republicans agreed.
5. A. De Tocqueville, *Democracy in America*. (Chicago: University of Chicago Press, 2000), p. 360. The empirical basis for this authoritarianism was first enunciated in *The Authoritarian Personality* (1950), one of the first studies of mass behavior that combined social science research to personality traits. Although this is groundbreaking research in prejudice and racism, it was originally intended to study anti-Semitism and fascist tendencies in individuals. Its theoretical basis was lodged in Freud, now somewhat discredited, whose conclusions of childhood effects upon personality have been bypassed with advances in genetics and the neurosciences.
6. According to the Gallup Poll, unionized workers are more likely to be Democrats than Republicans, whether they work for the government or the private sector. State workers are also more likely to be Democrats than are federal, local, or nongovernment workers, regardless of union status. By 48% to 39%, more Americans in 2011 agreed with unions than with Republican governors in state budget battles. It may surprise many stout Wisconsin Republicans—led by conservative Governor Scott Walker who sought to disband unions, that workers' compensation, unemployment insurance, workplace safety standards, and the protection of natural resources and the environment—were pioneered by Wisconsin Republicans in the early 20th century. (Cronon, 2011.) The Republican radical right defied the law about open meetings act in Wisconsin, and provoked bitter partisan divisiveness throughout the Midwest as they sought to impose doctrinaire conservative policies while having contempt for differing perspectives.
7. According to the Senate Joint Committee on Taxation, the share of federal tax revenue in 2006 was about 43%, about the same it was in 1960. Payroll taxes had risen from about 20% in 1960 to about 43% today, while corporate taxes had fallen from about 20% in 1960 to about 8% in 2006. Americans' home equity fell 35% from 2007-2009, unemployment more than doubled, and Wall Street profits rose 720%. So the real question about taxes is, why aren't corporations paying an equal share of taxes as are ordinary wage earners? Unlike ordinary Americans, corporations, to avoid higher taxes, have moved corporate offices overseas. Zug, Switzerland has over 30,000 American companies listed as headquarters, often nothing more than mailboxes. American

corporations have in essence renounced American corporate citizenship to avoid their fair share of U.S. taxes. In fairness, tax rates are universally lower by about half in most of he developed world. But $1.2 trillion dollars (the approximate cost of the Iraq war) in corporate profits are parked in overseas banks and their taxes deposited in foreign countries.

8. Figures according the Director of the Office of Management and Budget. J. Lew in "The Easy Cuts are Behind Us," *The New York Times*, February 6, 2011, p. wk9. The Office of the Comptroller of the Currency (OCC) is an obscure federal agency that reputedly oversees bank performances. It has consistently defended banks and views the new Consumer Protection Agency as a kind of financial enemy. Tax rates for the superrich from 1979 to 2009 dropped by 25%, while tax rates for the average income earner during the same period fell by only 8%.

9. http://www.creditcards.com/credit-card-news/credit-card-industry-facts-personal-debt-statistics-1276.phpconsumer debt of $2.4 trillion.

10. The financial crisis beginning in 2007 was a wide-ranging banking conspiracy of deception to clients and the public, abetted by deferential regulators and credit agencies with obvious conflicts of interest. Government rescued about 70% of all financial institutions and some auto companies. By 2011, 353 banks had failed, and housing prices had fallen nationally by 33% from 2006-2009 levels. Congress created the *Fraud Enforcement and Recovery Act* but allocated a pittance to its enforcement efforts. See "Financial Crisis: Wall Street and the Anatomy of a Financial Collapse" a report by the Senate Permanent Subcommittee on Investigations, and C. Mollenkamp and L. Rappaport, *The Wall Street Journal*, April 14, 2011, C1. David Freedman reports that the formula banks use to help with risk-taking decisions is wrong. D. H. Freedman, "A Formula for Economic Calamity," *Scientific American*, (November 2011), 305(5), 77-79.

11. The abortion topic is always combustible. The quality of a woman's life has always depended on her access to an education and the ability to control her family. According to 2011 data from the Guttmacher Institute, 30% of abortions occur to non-Hispanic Black women, 36% to non-Hispanic white women, 25% to Hispanic women and 9% to women of other races. Forty-two percent of women obtaining abortions have incomes below 100% of the poverty level. http://www.guttmacher.org/pubs/fb_induced_abortion.html. The official poverty rate in 2011 was 14.3% and growing. See also a report from the Brooking Institution about poverty becoming a part of suburbia in major cities: http://www.brookings.edu/papers/2010/0120_poverty_kneebone.aspx.

12. In 2011 the Department of Defense budget was over $739 billion, more than was spent on defense for the rest of the world combined, and larger than federal spending for Medicare, education, and interest on the debt. See "Budgetary Savings from Military Restraint," by the Cato Institute; "Restoring America's Future," the Bipartisan Policy Center; the 2010 report by the National Commission on Fiscal Responsibility; and R. Dreyfyss, "Taking Aim at the Pentagon Budget," *The Nation*, (April 11, 2011), pp. 22-26. According to a 2011 Gallup Poll, 39% of Americans thought defense spending was "too much," 35% said it was "about right," and 22% said it was "too little."

13. De Tocqueville, *Democracy in America*, 1969, p. 113.

14. The same report found numerous instances of racism and national identity. Some of the leading figures in the ultra-conservative movement were imported directly from the anti-immigrant vigilante group known as the Minutemen Project. *ResistNet* and Tea Party Patriots harbor anti-immigrants members, Nativists ("I want my country back"), and racists. The popular women of this group have sweet lips with acetylene words. This does not include conservative groups like *60 Plus* that fight for benefits to seniors. Funding for these groups comes from corporations, non-party, non-profit organizations and political action committees. See reports by the Institute for Research and Education on Human Rights.

278

15. http://www.gallup.com/poll/146708/Americans-Worries-Economy-Budget-Top-Issues.aspx.

16. The anti-union Massey, West Virginia mine blast killed 29 miners in 2010. In 2011 it was still cited for 80 safety regulations by the Mine Safety and Health Administration (MSHA).

17. D. Burghardt & L. Zeskind, 2010, & at www.irehr.org.

18. http://www.gallup.com/poll/21118/Bush-Face-Toughest-Audience-State-Union.aspx.

19. T. Frank, *The Wrecking Crew, How Conservatives Rule.* (New York: Metropolitan Books, 2008).

20. N. Klein, *The Shock Doctrine, The Rise of Disaster Capitalism.* (New York: Picador, 2007).

21. Cf. Sherwin, 1963. John Birch in 1941 was an American missionary in China who rescued Lt. Col. Jimmie Doolittle after he parachuted over China after his raid over Tokyo. Gen. Claire Chennault made Birch, who spoke Chinese, a captain and assigned him to air combat intelligence during the war. After the war Birch was assigned to the Office of Strategic Services (OSS), the predecessor of the CIA. He was on a routine patrol in north China in 1945 surveying how far the Chinese communists had penetrated when he came upon a communist force. He refused to surrender his weapon, and he was seized, shot, and bayoneted at least 15 times and his body thrown on a heap of garbage. Robert Welch selected Birch as the symbol of his anti-communist organization.

22. L. E. Panetta & P. Gall, *Bring Us Together, The Nixon Team and the Civil Rights Retreat.* (Philadelphia: J. B. Lippincott Company, 1971). (Panetta, 1971. Leon Panetta worked as Director of the Office of Civil Rights during the Nixon Administration and was fired for doing his job according to the law. Panetta later was a congressman from California (1977-1993), Director of the Office of Management and Budget, President Clinton's Chief of Staff, Director of the CIA in 2009, and Secretary of the Defense Department in 2011.

23. A. Cooke, *America Observed.* (Ed. R. A. Wells). (New York: Reinhardt Books, 1988). Discrimination exists elsewhere in the world too. But Brazil, with 200 million people, nearly the population equivalent of the U.S., is an example of a country that also had slavery. Its ethnic demographic today is 54% White and nearly 40% mulatto, or mixed race.

24. http://memory.loc.gov/cgi-bin/query/D?hlaw:1:./temp/~ammem_hVSh:: This federal legislation, clearly intended to emancipate those slaves that sought to enlist in the military, was written prior to the Constitution that, in deference to the Southern votes necessary to pass and ratify the Constitution, bypassed slavery except as property, and to parcel an arbitrary arithmetic ("three fifths of all other persons") for choosing congressional representation.

25. Mormons also wanted their own country in the late 19th century with a stretch of territory from Utah to San Diego so missionaries would have an outlet to the sea. The Union had to temper that secessionist movement too.

26. R. Berger, *Government by Judiciary, The Transformation of the Fourteenth Amendment.* (Cambridge, MA: Harvard University Press, 1977).

27. S. Mencimer, "If at First You Don't Secede." *Mother Jones Magazine,* (July/August 2010), pp. 14-15. The U.S. Supreme Court rejected Virginia's request to speed up the challenge to the health care law, *The Patient Protection and Affordable Care Act* (2010), derisively called by opponents, "Obamacare."

28. "The powers not delegated to the United States by the Constitution, nor prohibited by it to the States, are reserved to the States respectively, or to the people." The Tenth Amendment Center website provides their erroneous argument.

29. Clint Bolick, The Goldwater Institute, quoted in *The Arizona Republic,* 3/28/10, p. B13.

30. J. Gillis, J., "A Scientist, His Work and a Climate Reckoning." *The New York Times*, (December 22, 2010), A1ff. Cf. D. Demeritt, "The Construction of Global Warming and the Politics of Science, *Annals of the Association of American Geographers*, June 2001, 91(2), pp. 307-337. Cf. also M. Shermer, "What is Pseudoscience?" *Scientific American*, 305 (3), (September 2011), p. 92. For the conservative argument that climate change is a vast bogus scheme and global conspiracy, including that the inspiration for the science comes from Karl Marx, see B. Sussman, *Climategate, A Veteran Meteorologist Exposes the Global Warming Scam*. (Washington, DC: WND Books, 2010).

31. C. D. Thomas, *et al.*, "Rapid Range Shifts of Species Associated with High Levels of Climate Warming." *Science*, 333(6045), (August 19, 2011), 1024-1026. For a detailed scientific report on how climate change is now effecting Mozambique, the Mekong Delta in Vietnam, and Mexico and Central America see De Sherbinin, *et.al.*, "Casualties of Climate Change," *Scientific American*, (January 2011), 64-71, & R.A. Muller, "I Stick to the Science," *Scientific American*, (June 2011), 304(6), 84-87. Cf. also C. Mooney, "The Reality Gap," *The American Prospect*, (July/August 2011), pp. 18-25.

32. http://www.opensecrets.org/politicians/industries.php?cycle=2010&cid=N00005582. See also Inhofe's editorial defending his skepticism about global warming: J. Inhofe, "All Pain, No Gain." *USAToday*, (May 17, 2011), p. 8A.

33. http://eltahir.mit.edu/news/climate-change-6000-years-ago-sahara-desert-explained & http://www.livescience.com/10944-fish-swam-sahara-bolstering-africa-theory.html.

34. C. P. Pierce, *Idiot America, How Stupidity Became a Virtue in the Land of the Free*. (New York: Anchor Books, 2010). The overwhelming evidence favoring natural selection and evolution are also not a part of the ultra-conservative mindset. See my own "Accepting Evolution or Discarding Science." *Kappa Delta Pi Record*, (Summer 2006), v. 42(4), pp. 156-160 For fuller explanations see such works as Allan Bloom's, *The Closing of the American Mind*. (New York: Simon & Schuster, 1987), & Susan Jacoby's *The Age of American Unreason*. (New York: Pantheon, 2008).

35. S. Gandel, "Why Banks Are Still Failing Us," Time, September 25, 2011, pp. 40-45. President F.D. Roosevelt in this first legislative initiative created the *Emergency Bank Act* in 1933 to regain investor confidence in the banking system. The Justice Dept. settled a $335 million payout in December 2011 from Bank of America to Black and Hispanic homeowners who were discriminated against with higher fees than White homeowners for the same amount of mortgages.

36. H. Beirich, "Behind the Academies," *Intelligence Report*, (Montgomery: Southern Poverty Law Center, Spring 2011), pp. 12-13.

37. C. Robertson, "For Politics in South, Race Divide is Defining." *The New York Times*, (October 3, 2011), A10ff.

38. J. Sachs, *The Price of Civilization, Reawakening American Virtue and Prosperity*. (New York: Random House, 2011), p. 223-24.

Chapter Two Notes

1. The conservative argument is that many government agencies interfere with job creations by levying taxes and energy sources through costly regulations. According to research from the National Federation of Independent Business (http://www.nfib.com/) it is lack of consumer demand, not taxes or regulations that chokes the economy.

2. M. Potok, "The Year in Hate and Extremism," *Intelligence Report*, Spring 2011, pp. 41-67.

3. Jim Greer, Chair of the Florida Republican Party was "appalled" that Obama would speak to schoolchildren and spread his "socialist ideology." Glenn Beck compared Obama to Mussolini. See J. LePore, *The Whites of their Eyes, The Tea Party's Revolution and the Battle of American History*. (Princeton: Princeton University Press, 2010), p. 9. Eastman Johnson's (1824-1906) painting *Clara Hall (The Tea Party)*, depicts an upper

middle class child serving tea to her dolls. Cf. Matt Bai, "The Tea Party's Not-So Civil War." (January 15, 2012), *The New York Times Magazine*, 34-39.

4. P. Wehner, "The GOP and the Birther Trap," *The Wall Street Journal*, April 14, 2011, A17.

5. See *Ezekiel* 18:17: "This man shall not die for the iniquity of his father . . . " On immigration cf., "SB 1070 Has Been a Costly Failure," *The Arizona Republic*, April 23, 2011, B4. No one state can comprehensively address illegal immigration but its attempt by state legislators embolden the radical conservatism.

6. H. Beirich, "The Year in Nativism," *Intelligence Report*. (Montgomery: Southern Poverty Law Center, Spring 2011), pp. 35-39.

7. J Preston, "State Lawmakers Outline Plans to End Birthright Citizenship, Drawing Outcry." *The New York Times*, (January 6, 2011), A18.

8. Richard Hofstadter chronicled this persistent dumbing down trend in *Anti-Intellectualism in America*, a book that won the Pulitzer Prize in Non-Fiction in 1964. Alan Bloom's *The Closing of the American Mind* in 1987 provided a similar dispirited decline. The latest wakeup call is from is Susan Jacoby, *The Age of American Unreason*. (New York: Pantheon, 2008).

9. T. Lavin, "How the Recession Changed Us." *The Atlantic Monthly*, 307(1), (January/February 2011), 72-73. Jose Ortega y Gasset lamented the same decline in the lean capabilities of the people in *The Revolt of the Masses* (1985), p. 10.

10. S. Theokas, *Shut Out of the Military, Today's High School Education Doesn't Mean You're Ready for Today's Army*. (Washington, DC: The Education Trust, 2010).

11. R. Arum & J. Roksa, *Academically Adrift, Limited Learning on College Campuses*. (Chicago: University of Chicago Press, 2011). On the other hand, investments in social capital do pay dividends. See E.S. Smith, "The Effects of Investments in Social Capital of Youth on Political and Civic Behavior in Young Adulthood: A Longitudinal Analysis." *Political Psychology*, 20(3), September 1999, pp. 553-580.

12. *Ibid.*, p. 3.

13. M. Trinka, "Educating Americans About Their History, Through Poster-Sized Lessons." *The New York Times*, (December 7, 2010), A24.

14. *The Nation's Report Card, Civics 2006*: National Assessment of Educational Progress at Grades 4, 8 and 12. (Washington, DC: National Center for Educational Statistics, U.S. Department of Education). Less than half of all states fail at teaching the civil rights movement, one of the most significant events in the 20th century. *SPLC Report*, Winter 2011, 41(4), p. 4.

15. Arum & Roksa, *op. cit.*, p. 121.

16.Tea Party members take their name from the Boston Tea Party of 1773 and the American rebellion against British taxation. Edmund Burke noted in a 1774 speech, "Leave America, if she have taxable matter in her, to tax herself." E. Burke, *Speech of Edmund Burke, Esq. on American Taxation, April 19, 1774*. (3rd edition). (London: J. Dodsley, 1775), p. 89. Burke in his speeches on conciliation with America argued persuasively against the imposition of taxes in the colonies but his view did not prevail in Parliament.

17. C. B. Dew, *Apostles of Disunion, Southern Secession Commissioners and the Causes of the Civil War*. (Charlottesville: University Press of Virginia, 2010), p. 25. W. W. Freehling in *The Road to Disunion, (Vol. II) Secessionists Triumphant 1854-1861*. (New York: Oxford University Press, 2007) makes the case for subtle but significant differences between the border south states and the lower south.

18. C. Freeland, "The Rise of the New Global Elite." *The Atlantic*, 307(1), (January/February 2011), 44-55. Regarding taxes, *The Taxpayer Protection Pledge* (Taxpayer Protection Pledge: "I, _____, pledge to the taxpayers of the (____ district of the) state of _____ and to the American people that I will: ONE, oppose any and all

efforts to increase the marginal income tax rate for individuals and business; and TWO, oppose any net reduction or elimination of deductions and credits, unless matched dollar for dollar by further reducing tax rates) insisted on my lobbyist Grover Norquist was signed by 41 senators and 236 Republican representatives for the 112th Congress. The question is: why should lobbyists require legislators to sign documents in advance of discussion about legislation with other legislators?

19. The legislation was known as *The Emergency Economic Stabilization Act*. For an elaboration of how TARP led to the rise of the Tea Party see D. Armey, D. & M. Kibbe, *Give Us Liberty, A Tea Party Manifesto.* (New York: William Morrow, 2010).

20. D. Armey & M. Kibbe, *op. cit.*, p. 61. By implication, does this also mean that elected representatives of government fall into that category?

21. R. M. Hutchins, *Adam Smith, The Wealth of Nations*. In *Great Books of the Western World*, Vol. 39. (Chicago: Encyclopaedia Britannica, 1952), p. 401.

22. http://www.fcic.gov/report/conclusions. Even under the Hoover Administration when the Great Depression began, Roosevelt as a candidate in 1932 opposed direct relief spending by the government and both he and Hoover believed in cutting federal spending to the bone.

23. J. M. Burns, *Roosevelt: The Lion and the Fox*. (New York A Harvest/HBJ Book, 1956), p. 125.

24. J. M. Keynes, *The Collected Writings of John Maynard Keynes. Vol.VII, The General Theory of Employment, Interest and Money*. (Cambridge UK: Macmillian/St. Martin's Press, 1973). Cf. S. Nasar, *Grand Pursuit, The Story of Economic Genius*. New York: Simon & Schuster, 2011), pp. 355-56. The buildup of America's military armaments in 1941 also officially ended the depression and increased its debt, which the economic recovery after the war effectively erased. Congress assisted in paying for the war by increasing taxes and collecting revenue at the source of income.

25. J. Nichols & R. W. McChesney. "The Money and Media Election Complex." *The Nation*, (November 29, 2010), 11-17. J. Sachs, *The Price of Civilization, Reawakening American Virtue and Prosperity.* (New York: Random House, 2011). R. G. Kaiser, *So Damn Much Money, The Triumph of Lobbying and the Corrosion of American Government.* (New York: Alfred A. Knopf, 2009).

26. A. Juahsz, *The Tyranny of Oil.* (New York: William Morrow, 2008), pp. 148ff.

27. *Ibid.*, pp. 255-56.

28. http://pewresearch.org/ for January 11, 2012. The percentage is closer to three-fourths among Democrats, Blacks and among those 18-34. For a detailed look at how banks and other financial institutions gamed the system to help create the economic meltdown see M. Lewis, *The Big Short, Inside the Doomsday Machine.* (New York: W. W.Norton and Co., 2011).

29. B. Kiviat, "Below the Line. *Time*, (November 28, 2011), 35-41. The poverty line is established as $22,314 for a family of four, and that constituted 46.2 million Americans, or 15.1% of the population, who lived at or below that figure.

30. D. Alpert, & R. Hockett, N. Roubini. (October 10, 2011). *The Way Forward, Moving From the Post-Bubble, Post-Bust Economy to Renewed Growth and Competitiveness.* Washington, DC: The New America Foundation. http://newamerica.net/publications/policy/the_way_forward.

Chapter Three Notes

1. The Cato Institute in Washington DC is a non-government supported think tank, not affiliated with any political party, but devoted to limited government, free enterprise and individual liberty. "The fact is, that almost all the governments that have ever existed in the civilized world, have been, in part at least, monarchical and aristocratic. The first government constituted on principles approaching to those which Utilitarians hold, we

think, that of the United States." (Thomas Babington, Lord Macaulay in *The Westminster Review* No. XXI, Article XVI, and reprinted in *Reviews, Essays and Poems*. (London: Ward, Lock, & Co., c, 1880), p. 388.

2. N. Schachner, 1957, C. Bowers, 1967 & 1969, & F. Brodie, 1974.

3. B. Goldwater, *With No Apologies, Personal and Political Memoirs*. (New York: William Morrow and Co., 1979), p. 53.

4. L. Edwards, *Goldwater, The Man Who Made a Revolution*. (Washington, DC: Regnery Publishing, 1995), p. 231.

5. B. Goldwater, 1979, *op. cit.*, p. 192-93.

6. F. A. Hayek, *The Road to Serfdom, Texts and Documents* (Vol. 2). (Ed. B. Caldwell). (Chicago: The University of Chicago Press, 2007, 1944), p. 83. Cf. also. F. Fukuyama, "Big-Government Skeptic." *The New York Times Book Review*, May 8, 2011, 12, & J. Green, "The Tea Party's Brain." *The Atlantic Monthly*, (November 2010), pp. 98-106. See also P. Samuelson, *Economics*. (11th edition). (New York: McGraw Hill, 1980), pp. 813 & 827.

7. F.A. Hayek, *The Constitution of Liberty*. (Ed. R. Hamowy). (Chicago: The University of Chicago Press, 2011). I also consulted the earlier 1960 University of Chicago edition.

8. F.A. Hayek, *Ibid.,* 1960 edition, p. 257. Libertarian congressman Ron Paul subsumed the idea of a tyrannical government from Austrian economists who lived under the Nazis and its persecution of individual liberties and transposed that idea of government out of context to a democratic government and made it his political platform. See especially in this book Chapter 19, "Social Security," pp. 295-305 for a fuller description of Hayek's views.

9. M. Friedman, *Capitalism and Freedom*. (Chicago: University of Chicago Press, 2002), p. 13. For originating economic ideas by Adam Smith and John Maynard Keynes, among others, see my economic history section in *The Evolution of the Social Sciences*, (Landham, MD: Lexington Books, 2009), pp. 221-241. For a more conservative view see Turlock, G., A. Seldon, & G. L. Brady, *Government Failure, A Primer in Public Choice*. (Washington, DC: The Cato Institute, 2002).

10. Jeffrey Sachs, J. (2011). *The Price of Civilization, Reawakening American Virtue and Prosperity*. (New York: Random House, 2011), p. 27.

11. Three editions: A. Smith, A. (1991). *The Wealth of Nations*. (Amherst, NY: Prometheus Books, 1991), & *The Wealth of Nations*. Oxford: Oxford University Press, 1976-77, Glascow Edition), & R, M. Hutchins, Adam Smith, *An Inquiry into the Nature and Causes of the Wealth of Nations*. In *Great Books of the Western World* Vol. 39. (Chicago: Encyclopaedia Britannica, Inc., 1952).

12. D. K. Foley, *Adam's Fallacy, A Guide to Economic Theology*. (Cambridge, MA: The Belnap Press of Harvard University Press, 2006), p. 216 & p. 224. Neither Adam Smith in *The Wealth of Nations* (1776), nor David Ricardo in *On the Principles of Political Economy and Taxation* (1817) mention slavery in their discussions of property, commodities and wages. Yet surely the shirts they wore while writing their economic treatises came from the cotton produced by southern American slaves.

13. "The principal objection to all such taxes is their inequality, an inequality of the worst kind as they must frequently fall much heavier upon the poor than upon the rich." Smith in Hutchins, 1952, *op. cit.*, p. 372. And see J. Buchan, *Adam Smith and the Pursuit of Perfect Liberty*. (London: Profile Books, 2006), p. 115. For contemporary research on inequality see P. Beramendi & T. R. Cusack, "Diverse Disparities: The Politics and Economics of Wage, Market, and Disposal Income Inequalities, *Political Research Quarterly*, 62(2), June 2009, pp. 257-275. Political parties directly effect the distribution of disposable income through their choices of fiscal instruments.

14. R. Parloff, (January 17, 2011). "On History's Stage: Chief Justice John Roberts, Jr." *Fortune*, Vol. 163(1), 63-76.

15. John Stuart Mill, *On Liberty, op. cit.*, p. 1032.
16. See *Minersville School District v. Gobitis* (1940), *Engel v. Vitale* (1962), *Wisconsin v. Yoder* (1972), among others.
17. S. Chan, "The Fed? He's Not a Fan." *The New York Times*, (December 12, 2010), wk2. A Hayek contemporary Czech economist raised in Vienna, Joseph A. Schumpeter (1883-1950) did argue in favor of a centralized bank, like the Fed or the Bank of England, that are independent of the treasury. For a comprehensive study of the Federal Reserve see Samuelson, *op. cit.*, 1980, Chapter 17, pp. 295-312.
18. W. C. Wade, *The Fiery Cross, The Ku Klux Klan in America.* (New York: Oxford University Press, 1987), p. 12.
19. Based on obscure free market advocates, Paul predicted the collapse of the housing bubble. But it did not take a psychic to see that housing market bubble coming. I'm not a rocket scientist, and even I, sensing a bubble, got out of the equities market in October 2005, and still believe that government has to regulate the economy so citizens do not lose savings and the economy self-destruct.
20. R. Paul, *The Revolution, A Manifesto.* (New York: Grand Central Publishing, 2008), p. 69.
21. *Ibid.*, p. 176. The Department of Education, like any other federal agency, simply administers the laws passed by Congress, like student loans. They do not exist as separate, executive agencies independent of the congressional laws that create them.
22. *Ibid.*, p. 86.
23. The character Orren Boyle in Ayn Rand's, *Atlas Shrugged, op. cit.*, 1999, p. 45.
24. R. Paul, 2008, *op. cit.*, p. 98.
25. *Ibid.*, p. 135.
26. J. Smith & R. Lenz ((Winter 2011). "New Soldiers of the Confederacy." *Intelligence Report,* No. 144, pp. 12-14. For more on militancy movements see Chapter 14.
27. For a detailed analysis of how the two revolutions influenced each other see W. & A. Durant, *Rousseau and Revolution.* (New York: MJF Books, 1967). For how these ideas shaped educational policy see my own *Education and the U.S. Government*, (New York: St. Martin's Press, 1987). For Enlightenment dissenters to real tyranny, see my *Outcasts and Heretics*, (Lanham, MD: Lexington Books, 2007), pp. 269-86.
28. J. J. Rousseau, *The Social Contract.* (New York: Barnes & Noble Books, 1995), pp. 13-15. Of course Karl Marx wanted to do empower the proletariat to rule and proclaimed capital as the principal evil—to overturn the social contract. The Industrial Revolution did create more severe inequalities of wealth that those that exist today. His ideas, however, were stillborn when *Das Capital* was first published, and would not have received any prominence had not Vladimir Lenin used them as a basis for totalitarian rule in the USSR.
29. http://avalon.law.yale.edu/18th_century/rightsof.asp.
30. W. A. Niskanen, *Bureaucracy and Public Economics.* (Brookfield, VT: Edward Elgar Publishing Co., 1994), pp. 229ff.
31. Rousseau, *op. cit.*

Chapter Four Notes
1. John Stuart Mill, "On Liberty." (In E. A. Burtt, Ed.) *The English Philosopher from Bacon to Mill.* (New York: The Modern Library, 1939), p. 949. An earlier version of this chapter appeared in *Emeritus Voices*, Winter 2011, No. 8, pp. 37-57.
2. G. Epps, "The Constitution: A Love Story." *The American Prospect*, (11/11) 22(9), 36-40.
3. Woodrow Wilson, *The State, Elements of Historical and Practical Politics.* (Boston: D.C. Heath & Co., 1897), p. 47. In Article II of the *Articles of Confederation*: "Each state

retains its sovereignty, freedom, and independence, and every Power, Jurisdiction and right, which is not by this confederation expressly delegated to the United States, in congress assembled."

4. Washington hoped that the institution of slavery would one day disappear. His last will and testament freed his own slaves. But after his death, his nephew and great-nephew inherited Mount Vernon and brought their own slaves with them to re-populate the plantation. See S. Casper, "Rebranding Mount Vernon," *The New York Times*, February 21, 2011, A17.

5. http://memory.loc.gov/ammem/amlaw/lwjc.html.

6. S. Levinson, *Our Undemocratic Constitution, Where the Constitution Goes Wrong (And How We the People Can Correct It)*. (New York: Oxford University Press, 2006).

7. http://www.constitution.org/jl/2ndtr19.txt. For more about the 600+ slaves Jefferson owned in his lifetime and his slave mistress Sally Hemmings with whom he fathered six children see http://www.monticello.org/site/plantation-and-slavery/people-plantation.

8. Article III, Section 2, 1.

9. *Stare decisis* is the legal term court's use to reply on precedents set by previous court decisions. However, even judges like Associate Justice Clarence Thomas seek to roll back decisions to the original meaning of the Constitution. He is thus an ultra-conservative "originalist" on the U.S. Supreme Court.

10. J. LePore, *The Whites of their Eyes, The Tea Party's Revolution and the Battle of American History*. (Princeton: Princeton University Press, 2010), p. 144.

11. James Madison in C. Rossiter, (ed.) *The Federalist Papers*. (New York: Mentor Book, 1961), p. 104.

12.http://www.law.cornell.edu/supct/html/historics/USSC_CR_0030_0001_ZS.html. There have been both White and Black sovereign movements. See R. Lenz, 'Sovereign' President, *Intelligence Report*, (Fall 2011), 143, pp. 33-35, and L. Nelson, 'Sovereigns' in Black, *Intelligence Report*, (Fall 2011), 143, pp. 36-40.

13.http://www.oyez.org/cases/1792-1850/1832/1832_2. See B. Hicks, "The Holdouts," *Smithsonian*, March 2011, pp. 51-60.

14. http://www.constitution.org/cons/kent1798.htm.

15. *Ibid.*

16.http://org2.democracyinaction.org/o/6879/p/salsa/web/common/public/signup?signup _page_KEY=2946.

17. The Southern Poverty Law Center lists scores of federal and state officials linked to the covertly racist southern Council of Conservative Citizens. See the complete file at: http://www.splcenter.org/get-informed/intelligence-report/browse-all-issues/2004/fall/communing-with-the-council/see-no-evil.

18. Thomas Carlyle, *The Best of Carlyle*. (Ed. H.L. Creek). (New York: Thomas Nelson, 1939), p. 479.

19. D. Armey, D. & M. Kibbe, *Give Us Liberty, A Tea Party Manifesto*. New York: William Morrow, 2010), p. 169. Armey is a Georgia native but spent his adult life in Texas, so he is a perfect example of the southern, anti-government mentality.

20. http://memory.loc.gov/ammem/pihtml/pi027.html.

Chapter Five Notes

1. A complete international database of over 35,000 voyages, estimates and over 67,000 names exists of the Trans-Atlantic slave trade business at: http://www.slavevoyages.org/tast/index.faces. Cf. also J. Pope-Hennesy, *Sins of the Fathers, The Atlantic Slave Trade 1141-1807*. (Edison, NJ: Castle Books, 2004).

2. H. Thomas, *The Slave Trade, The History of the Atlantic Slave Trade 1440-1870*. (London: Papermac, 1998), p. 805.

3. *Extracts from the Votes and Proceedings of the American Continental Congress.* (Boston: Edes and Gill, 1774).

4. *Journals of the Continental Congress*, Vol. 26, pp. 118-119.

5. Jefferson in his will freed five children of his slave mistress of 38 years, Sally Hemmings—later freed by Jefferson's daughter—and the mother of his twelve children, including Madison and younger brother Eston. They lived with their families and mother Sally in Charlottesville, Virginia until her death in 1835. Madison and his family then moved to the free state of Ohio. Two of his sons served the Union in the Civil War.

6. *U.S. Constitution*, Article I, Section 9, and Article 4.

7. Today the National Park Service staffs the house as an historical residence.

8. S. Johnson, *Taxation No Tyranny: An Answer to the Resolutions and Address of the American Congress.* (London: T. Cadell, 1775), p. 89. I am indebted to the library and librarians at the University of Cambridge in England where I hold a Senior Visiting Fellow appointment for access to these and other original documents.

9. *Ibid.*, p. 85.

10. R. Soodalter, *Hanging Captain Gordon, The Life and Trial of an American Slave Trader.* (New York: Washington Square Press, 2006), p. 29.

11. *Ibid.*, p. 71.

12. *Ibid.*, pp. 82-83.

13. H. Laurens, *The Papers of Henry Laurens*, (Columbia: The University of South Carolina Press, 1970, V. II, p. 425.

14. J. Rakove, *Revolutionaries, A New History of the Invention of America.* (Boston: Houghton Mifflin, 2010), p. 238.

15. *Fugitive Slave Circulars*, 1876, Sommersett Circular, p. 4.

16. J. Bicknell, J. & T. Day, *The Dying Negro.* (London: W. Flexney, 1773), p. 4.

17. For Madison's personal views on slavery see: http://rediscover1812.com/?p=5.

18. Soodalter, *op cit.*

19. *Ibid.*, pp. 17-18, & 193-94.

20. See *Harper's Weekly*, March 8, 1862. Two days before Gordon's hanging, William Wallace, "Willie," Lincoln, the president's third eldest son, died, aged 11, causing Lincoln to grieve the rest of his life.

21. D. Robertson, *Denmark Vesey, The Buried Story of America's Largest Slave Rebellion and the Man Who Led it.* (New York: Vintage Books, 1999). The world's largest slave revolt was probably that of Spartacus, a Thracian slave and ex-gladiator, who gathered over 90,000 ex-slaves from throughout Rome in 73 BCE. A joint military expedition by Pompey and Crassus defeated them and crucified them all along the Via Appia stretching from Rome to Brindisi, nearly 150 miles.

22. Among them J. D. B. Debow (1820-1867), whose *Debow's Review* published in New Orleans served southern slave interests. Apologists from the South, like Nunford, (1910), Jenkins (1935), Johnson (1978) followed with favorable reviews of slavery's status.

23. G. Myrdal, *An American Dilemma: The Negro Problem and Modern Democracy.* (New York: Harper & Row, 1944), p. 441.

24. J. B. Moore, *The Works of James Buchanan.* (New York: Antiquarian Press, 1960), Vol. X, p. 66.

25. James Buchanan, Letter to George Mason, December 29, 1856.

26. E. M. Maltz, *Slavery and the Supreme Court, 1825-1861.* (Lawrence: University Press of Kansas, 2009).

27. Johnson, L. H. (1978). *Division and Reunion: America 1848-1877.* (New York: John Wiley, 1978), p. 67.

28. *Texas v. White*, 74 U.S. 700 (1869).

29. R. W. Johannsen, *Democracy on Trial, A Documentary History of American Life, 1845-1877.* (Urbana: University of Illinois Press, 1988), p. 172.

30. B. Levine, B. (2006). *Confederate Emancipation.* (New York: Oxford University Press, 2006), p. 33; C. Sandberg, *Abraham Lincoln.* (3 vols.) (New York: Dell Publishing Co., 1959), Vol. 3, p. 722.

31. For a complete list go to: http://www.homeofheroes.com/e-books/mohE_black/list.html.

32. According to an AP report on November 5, 1999, Sen. John McCain of Arizona on the Confederate flag said: "I know how be offensive to some people, but I had ancestors who fought in the Confederate army and I thought they fought honorably." But that honor is besmirched by the war's objective, which was to maintain insurrection against constitutional government and protect White supremacy and forced slavery.

33. C. M. Blow, (January 7, 2012). "The G.O.P.'s 'Black People' Platform." *The New York Times,* A19.

34. J. M. Dabbs, *The Southern Heritage.* (New York: Alfred A. Knopf, 1958).

35. G. Myrdal, 1944, op. cit., p. 451.

Chapter Six Notes

1. J. W. Burgess, *The Middle Period, 1817–1858.* (New York: Charles Scribner's Sons, 1897), p. 61ff.

2. N. E. Cunningham, *The Presidency of James Monroe.* (Lawrence: University Press of Kansas, 1996), p. 96.

3. "And be it further enacted, That, in all that territory ceded by France to the United States, under the name of Louisiana, which lies north of thirty-six degrees and thirty minutes north latitude, excepting only such part thereof as is included within the limits of the State contemplated by this act, slavery and involuntary servitude, otherwise than in the punishment of crimes whereof the party shall have been duly convicted, shall be and is hereby forever prohibited: Provided always, That any person escaping into the same, from whom labor or service is lawfully claimed in any State or Territory of the United States, such fugitive may be lawfully reclaimed, and conveyed to the person claiming his or her labor or service, as aforesaid."
http://www.historycentral.com/documents/Thomas.html

4. Monroe's foreign policy legacy was his doctrine regarding all of the Americas, known as the Monroe Doctrine. During the early part of the 19th century European powers like England, France, Spain and Russia had been overseers and political manipulators throughout North and Latin America. The United States was sympathetic to revolutionary movements seeking independence from colonial powers as America had been in the previous century. Independence from Europe and self-governance had been building in U.S. foreign policy initiatives since the conclusion of the War of 1812. Latin countries used the distraction of the Napoleonic Wars (1799–1815) in Europe to further their national independence.

5. Adams proposed in his first annual message to Congress the usual list of items of the nation's foreign and domestic concerns. The press belittled and Congress rebuked all his proposals, from torpedoing a Pan-American conference the U.S. had been invited to by Latin nations, from the improvement of road and canals, to strengthening the banks as a centralized credit authority, to refinancing the public debt, to increasing revenue for the sale of public lands. He was personally unpopular but it is unclear whether it was because of his person or his policies.

6. B. C. Clark, *John Quincy Adams.* (Boston: Little, Brown and Company, 1932), p. 353.

7. M. Cable, *Black Odyssey, the Case of the Slave Ship Amistad.* (New York: Penguin Books, 1971).

Chapter Seven Notes
1. J. Meacham, *American Lion, Andrew Jackson in the White House.* (New York: Random House, 2008).
2. The Federal Deposit Insurance Corporation has a detailed history of this first major financial crisis in the 1980s at: http://www.fdic.gov/bank/historical/s&l/.
3. For an update see "Wall Street and the Financial Crisis: Anatomy of a Financial Collapse," a report of the Permanent Subcommittee on Investigations of the U.S. Senate, April 13, 2011.
4. Here are excerpts from the *South Carolina Exposition and Protest*, a work largely by Calhoun's that outlines his argument for the sovereignty of the states and in opposition to the tariff laws of 1828. The tariff raised the tax on common manufactured goods coming from England, and made these goods more expensive in the South than the same goods made in the North. The North hoped to gain by having southerners buy more northern goods and not those from England. I quote this significant document at length because of its importance to the issue and argument that the South used and is still used today in radical conservative politics. It is a logical, political argument without legal standing. And it is instructive to know that the argument was never argued or presented before federal courts to prove its legality.
    "The General Government is one of specific powers, and it can rightfully exercise only the powers expressly granted, and those that may be necessary and proper to carry them into effect, all others being reserved expressly to the States or the people. It results, necessarily, that those who claim to exercise power under the Constitution, are bound to show that it is expressly granted, or that it is necessary and proper as a means of the granted powers. The advocates of the Tariff have offered no such proof. It is true that the third section of the first article of the Constitution authorizes Congress to lay and collect an impost duty, but it is granted as a tax power for the sole purpose of revenue, a power in its nature essentially different from that of imposing protective or prohibitory duties. Their objects are incompatible. The prohibitory system must end in destroying the revenue from imports. It has been said that the system is a violation of the spirit, and not the letter of the Constitution. The distinction is not material. The Constitution may be as grossly violated by acting against its meaning as against its letter; but it may be proper to dwell a moment on the point in order to understand more fully the real character of the acts under which the interest of this, and other States similarly situated, has been sacrificed . . . The Constitution grants to Congress the power of imposing a duty on imports for revenue, which power is abused by being converted into an instrument of rearing up the industry of one section of the country on the ruins of another. The violation, then, consists in using a power granted for one object to advance another, and that by the sacrifice of the original object . . ."
http://www.sagehistory.net/jeffersonjackson/documents/Calhoun1828.htm. Cf. also Meyerson, H. (October 2011). Foundering Fathers. *The American Prospect*, 22(8), p.16.
5. P. C. Nagel, *John Quincy Adams, A Public Life, A Private Life.* (New York: Alfred Knopf, 1997), p. 339.
6. *State Papers on Nullification.* (no author) (New York: Da Capo Press, 1970), pp. 28-29.
7. *Ibid.*, p. 77. Cf. also W. W. Freehling, *The Road to Disunion, (Vol. II) Secessionists Triumphant 1854-1861.* (New York: Oxford University Press, 2007), pp. 345-51.
8. *Ibid.*, p. 222.
9. *Ibid.*, p. 343.
10. J. C. Calhoun, (Ed. R. K. Cralle). *A Disquisition and a Discourse on the Constitution and Government of the United States.* (New York: Russell & Russell, 1968, 1856).

11. A brother served in the U.S. Congress and an uncle as Confederate Governor of South Carolina. States Rights Gist spent a year at Harvard Law School, returned to open a law office and was commissioned a Brigadier General in the Confederate Army. States Rights the person was killed in the battle of Franklin, Tennessee in 1864.

12. Calhoun, *op. cit.*, p. 119. In fact, Calhoun was describing the relationship with states prior to the Constitution during the time of the *Articles of Confederation* (1776–1787) when states were sovereign governmental entities. According to Article III of the *Articles of Confederation*: "Each state retains its sovereignty, freedom and independence . . ." But after 1791 when the Constitution was ratified by a majority of states, states lost that sovereignty—a term that smacks of medieval royal status and not democratic governance—to a national government not just a federal union. Just as Lincoln appealed to the principles embodied in the *Declaration of Independence* in the Gettysburg address, Calhoun appealed to the principles in the *Articles of Confederation* in his argument for states rights. Both sidestepped the Constitution when it was politically expedient.

13. R. V. Remini, *At the Edge of the Precipice, Henry Clay and the Compromise that Saved the Union.* (New York: Basic Books, 2010), p. 25.

14. B. Levine, *Confederate Emancipation.* (New York: Oxford University Press, 2006), p. 225.

15. Alexander Stephens, Vice President of the Confederacy, March 1861. Quoted in Levine, *Ibid.*, p. 228.

16. D. K. Sharpes, "GOP Selectively Reveres Constitution." *The Arizona Republic*, (August 29, 2011), B6.

Chapter Eight Notes

1. The United States at the time was on a gold and silver standard, but switched exclusively to gold in 1834, and in 1900 when Congress passed the *Gold Standard Act*. In 1834, the United States fixed the price of gold at $20.67 per ounce, where it remained until 1933. There is contemporary relevance to this historic banking issue. Had banks and other unregulated financial institutions not created complicated financial notes like derivatives, collateral debt obligations, and credit default swaps, essentially bets on whether stocks would rise or fall and insurance on banking notes in the 1930s and 2000s, without adequate government regulation, the national economy might not have nosedived in 2006.

2. *The Pittsburgh Mercury*, October 7, 1840.

3. Prior to the 17th Amendment to the U.S. Constitution in 1913, U.S. Senators were elected by state legislatures and continued to hold office as state legislators while serving as a U.S. Senator. In order to afford his senatorial seat, however, Tyler had to sell one of his slaves, Eliza Ann. A hundred years on, some Republican presidential candidates seek an overturning of this Amendment.

4. *Registry of Debates, 1824–1837, 21st Congress*, 1st Session, p. 433.

5. *Ibid.*, pp. 360-377.

6. J. S. Reeves, *American Diplomacy under Tyler and Polk.* (Baltimore: The Johns Hopkins Press, 1907), p. 89.

7. 49.6% to 46.1% of the popular vote.

8. W. R. Borneman, *Polk, The Man Who Transformed The Presidency and America.* (New York: Random House, 2008). Polk expanded the country in what is today the southwest and far west, and most of the states—Texas, Colorado, New Mexico, Arizona, California, Idaho, Utah, Washington and Oregon—that did not then include the Louisiana Purchase. He nearly doubled the size of the continental U.S. Because of this U.S. expansion he is usually credited as one of the top ten presidents.

9. Reeves, 1907, *op. cit.*, pp. 150ff.

10. In 1850 Congress admitted Utah as a territory and Brigham Young was sworn in as the first territorial Governor. But Mormons met secretly as a shadow state legislature to enact their own laws as the State of Deseret. Mormons wanted to govern themselves as a religious state in their frontier communities. As a state they knew that they would outnumber non-Mormons and be able to pass legislation favorable to them. Not much has changed since.
11. http://memory.loc.gov/cgi-bin/ampage.
12. The new special interests groups are corporations and SuperPacs with seemingly unlimited expenditures that gain legislative favors like mitigating regulations and minimizing taxes.

Chapter Nine Notes
1. J. LePore, *The Whites of their Eyes, The Tea Party's Revolution and the Battle of American History*. (Princeton: Princeton University Press, 2010), pp. 140-41.
2. B. Levine, *Half Slave and Half Free, The Roots of the Civil War*. (New York: Hill & Wang, 1992), pp. 21-22.
3. It was called Deparc Freres et Locoul Sugar Company. See L. Gore, *Memories of the Old Plantation Home*. (Vacherie, LA: The Zoe Company, 2007), p. 137.
4. F. Douglass, F. (2003). *Frederick Douglas on Slavery and the Civil War*. (Ed. P. S. Foner). (Mineola, NY: Dover Publications, 2003), p. 35. Cf. also Kendrick, P. & S. Kendrick, *Douglass and Lincoln, How a Revolutionary Black Leader and a Reluctant Liberator Struggled to End Slavery and Save the Union*. (New York: Walker & Co., 2008)
5. F. Douglass, (1968, 1855). *My Bondage and My Freedom*. (New York: Arno Press and The New York Times, 1968), & (New York: Miller, Orton & Mulligan, 1855), p. 64.
6. H. B. Stowe, *Uncle Tom's Cabin*. (New York: Penguin Classics, 1986), p. 60.
7. R. V. Remini, *At the Edge of the Precipice, Henry Clay and the Compromise that Saved the Union*. (New York: Basic Books, 2010). p. 5.
8. Clay had been Speaker of the House, Secretary of State, Senator and presidential contender. Trained as a lawyer in Richmond, he was mentally adroit, had a penchant for oratory, personal charm, and possessed keen negotiation skills. He was an ardent federalist, championing the War of 1812, as well as congressional support of roads, canals and transportation systems.
9.*http://memory.loc.gov/cgibin/query/r?ammem/hlaw:@field%28DOCID+@lit%28sj041 44%29%29:*
10. Among other sites at: http://www.ourdocuments.gov/doc.php?flash=true&doc=28.
"That the Constitution, and all Laws of the United States which are not locally inapplicable, shall have the same force and effect within the said Territory of Nebraska as elsewhere within the United States, except the eighth section of the act preparatory to the admission of Missouri into the Union approved March sixth, eighteen hundred and twenty, which, being inconsistent with the principle of non-intervention by Congress with slaves in the States and Territories, as recognized by the legislation of eighteen hundred and fifty, commonly called the Compromise Measures, is hereby declared inoperative and void . . ."
11. See T. Horwitz, *Midnight Rising, John Brown and the Raid That Sparked the Civil War* (New York: Henry Holt, 2011) for an extended study. Also Cf. Stephen Vincent Benet's *John Brown's Body*, a narrative epic poem of the Civil War first published in 1928.
12. Quoted in Horwitz, 2011, *op. cit.*, p. 187
13. Henry David Thoreau, on October 30, 1859, "A Plea for Captain John Brown" at http://law2.umkc.edu/faculty/projects/ftrials/johnbrown/thoreauplea.html. "For once we are lifted out of the trivialness and dust of politics into the region of truth and manhood.

No man in America has ever stood up so persistently and effectively for the dignity of human nature, knowing himself for a man, and the equal of any and all governments. In that sense he was the most American of us all. He needed no babbling lawyer, making false issues, to defend him. He was more than a match for all the judges that American voters, or office-holders of whatever grade, can create. He could not have been tried by a jury of his peers, because his peers did not exist. When a man stands up serenely against the condemnation and vengeance of mankind, rising above them literally by a whole body—even though he were of late the vilest murderer, who has settled that matter with himself- the spectacle is a sublime one- didn't ye know it, ye Liberators, ye Tribunes, ye Republicans?—and we become criminal in comparison. Do yourselves the honor to recognize him. He needs none of your respect."

14. F. Brodie, *Thaddeus Stevens, Scourge of the South.* (New York: Norton, 1959), p. 134, and a facsimile appears in Horwitz, 2011, *op. cit.*, p. 256.

15. Quoted in T. Horwitz, *Midnight Rising, John Brown and the Raid That Sparked the Civil War.* (New York: Henry Holt, 2011), p. 262.

16. Lincoln in Galena, Illinois on July 23, 1856 quoted in C. Sandberg, *Abraham Lincoln.* (3 vols.) (New York: Dell Publishing Co., 1959), Vol. 1, p. 223.

17. South Carolina remained in session until after the results of the Electoral College were known favoring Lincoln, and then voted unanimously to secede. In February 1861 Louisiana, Mississippi, Alabama, George, Florida and Texas all voted to secede, then met in a convention in Montgomery and established the Confederate States of America. Jefferson Davis, like Lincoln born near the Ohio River in Kentucky, was elected Confederate President. After the fall of Fort Sumter in Charleston Harbor, signaling that both sides would fight rather than yield, Virginia, Tennessee, Arkansas and North Carolina joined the Confederacy.

18. Peter Blow's sons, Dred Scott's childhood friends, helped pay Scott's legal costs. Peter Blow's son purchased Scott from his owners and set him free. Dred Scott died nine months later.

19. W. W. Freehling, *The Road to Disunion, (Vol. II) Secessionists Triumphant 1854-1861.* New York: Oxford University Press, 2007), p. 327.

20. A. De Tocqueville, *Democracy in America.* (Chicago: University of Chicago Press, 2000), p. 344.

Chapter Ten Notes

1. F. L. Olmsted, *A Journey in the Seaboard Slave States.* (New York: G. P. Putnams, 1904), p. 165.

2. *Ibid.*, p. 339.

3. *Ibid.*, p. 340.

4. http://www.census.gov/history/www/through_the_decades/overview/1860.html.

5. W. A. McDougall, *Throes of Democracy, The American Civil War Era 1829–1877.* (New York: HarperCollins, 2008), p. 399. By 1865 after the war the state of South Carolina lost half of its wealth, 60% of its landed value, and a third (20,000) of white males of military age. In W. W. Freehling, *The Road to Disunion, (Vol. II) Secessionists Triumphant 1854-1861.* (New York: Oxford University Press, 2007), p. 375.

6. W. B. Yearns, *The Confederate Congress.* (Athens: The University of Georgia Press, 1960), p. 3. Only about 20% of the people living in South Carolina could vote, as all slaves—60% of the total population—and women were ineligible.

7. W. T. Sherman, *Memoirs.* Vol. II. (New York: D. Appleton & Co., 1875), p. 382. Gen. Sherman was President of the Louisiana Military Seminary, later to become Louisiana State University, before the war. Only 5% of the Louisiana population of 708,002 voted for delegates to the secession convention in 1861.

8. J. H. Aughey, *The Iron Furnace, or Slavery and Secession*. (Philadelphia: William S. & Alfred Martien, 1863), p. 51.

9. John Q. Adams, in A. Koch & W. Peden, *The Selected Writings of John and John Quincy Adams*. (New York: Alfred A. Knopf. 1946), pp. 303 & 307. And in J. W. Loewen, "Getting the Civil War Right." *Teaching Tolerance*, (Fall 2011) 40, 22-28.

10. T. H. Williams, T. H. (2010, 1955). *P. G. T. Beauregard, Napoleon in Gray*. (Baton Rouge, LA: Louisiana State University Press, 2010), pp. 67-68.

11. B. H. Reid, *Robert E. Lee, Icon for a Nation*. (Amherst, NY: Prometheus Books, 2007), p. 69.

12. B. H. Reid, 2007, *op. cit.*, p. 172.

13. A. Goodheart, "The Shrug That Made History." *The New York Times Magazine*, (April 3, 2011), pp. 40ff.

14. Ben Butler had previously served in the Massachusetts state house, and would later become a congressman and a Governor of Massachusetts. George Plimpton was a direct descendant.

15. P. M. Angle, *The Lincoln Reader*. (New Brunswick, NJ: Rutgers University Press, 1947), p. 354.

16. "I do order and declare that all persons held as slaves within said designated States, and parts of States, are, and henceforward shall be free; and that the Executive government of the United States, including the military and naval authorities thereof, will recognize and maintain the freedom of said persons. And I hereby enjoin upon the people so declared to be free to abstain from all violence, unless in necessary self-defence [sic]; and I recommend to them that, in all cases when allowed, they labor faithfully for reasonable wages. And I further declare and make known, that such persons of suitable condition, will be received into the armed service of the United States to garrison forts, positions, stations, and other places, and to man vessels of all sorts in said service."

17. C. Sandberg, 1959, *op. cit.,*, p. 831.

18. http://en.wikipedia.org/wiki/New_Nationalism.

19. E. Rothstein, "The South Reinterprets Its 'Lost Cause,'" *The New York Times*, December 6, 2011, p. C1ff.

Chapter Eleven Notes

1. C. B. Dew, *Apostles of Disunion, Southern Secession Commissioners and the Causes of the Civil War*. (Charlottesville: University Press of Virginia, 2001), pp. 30ff.

2. See an address by William L. Harris, Mississippi commissioner to the general assembly of Georgia on December 17, 1860 for a typical diatribe that pulled no punches about the real cause on behalf of slavery. Dew, 2001, *op. cit.*, pp. 83ff.

3. September 3, 1783, signed by Ben Franklin, John Jay and John Adams.

4. http://www.college-cram.com/study/usgovernment/us-documents/louisiana-purchase-treaty-1803-treaty-of-cession/.

5. At the time the Vice President received the second largest number of electoral votes in a presidential election. The twelfth Amendment of 1804 resolved the issue of the election of the vice president and his duties. B. F. Melton, *Aaron Burr, Conspiracy to Treason*. (New York: John Wiley & Sons, 2002).

6. After the conspiracy collapsed, the family moved to Mississippi, and Virginia militia trashed the mansion. Blennerhassett was arrested and held until Burr was acquitted.

7. "The advising, certainly, and perhaps the procuring, is more in the nature of a conspiracy to levy war than of the actual levying of war. According to the opinion, it is not enough to be leagued in the conspiracy, and that war be levied, but it is also necessary to perform a part: that part is the act of levying war."
http://www.law.umkc.edu/faculty/projects/ftrials/burr/marshallopinion.html.

8. Take the case in 2010 of a Moroccan-born naturalized U.S. citizen, Khalid Ouzzani, 32, a used car and auto parts dealer in Kansas City who swore an oath of allegiance to Al-Qaeda, a terrorist group dedicated to killing Americans. Ouzzani was arrested for sending money to Al-Qaeda—hence aiding and abetting the enemy—for money laundering and bank fraud. He obtained a loan of $175,000 under false pretenses, purchased an apartment in the United Arab Emirates, and then sold it and gave the profits to Al-Qaeda. This case is not exactly equivalent to Burr's proposed insurrection but it does illustrate how the government is still trying to determine how to prosecute treason and terrorism.
9. B. F. Melton, 2002, *op. cit.*, p. 20.
10. The so-called 527 committees, who take their name from a section in the tax code, have direct ties to special interest groups—wealthy individuals, corporations, unions, big businesses. They can and do give unlimited funds and use that money to influence elections and laws. This is all legal but ethically questionable.
11. C. Eaton, *Jefferson Davis*. (New York: The Free Press, 1977), p. 37.
12. *Ibid.*, p. 95.
13. Although many sections of the Constitution of the Confederacy copied the U.S. Constitution—thereby saving time from the impetuous decision to collectively secede and prepare for war—Article 4, Section 1 supported slavery and made no attempt to revoke, delay of reform any action against it. "The citizens of each State shall be entitled to all the privileges and immunities of citizens in the several States; and shall have the right of transit and sojourn in any State of this Confederacy, with their slaves and other property; and the right of property in said slaves shall not be thereby impaired." http://www.usconstitution.net/csa.html#A1Sec9. Frederick Douglass had a counter-argument: "While slavery exists, and the union of these states endures, every American citizen must bear the chagrin of hearing his country branded before the world as a nation of liars and hypocrites; and behold his cherished flag pointed at with the utmost scorn and derision." (Frederick Douglass, 1855, *op. cit.*, p. 438).
14. R. Von Abele, *Alexander H. Stephens, A Biography*. (New York: Alfred A. Knopf, 1946), p. 216.
15. V. Davis, *Jefferson Davis, Ex-President of the Confederate States of America, A Memoir by His Wife*. Vol. II. (Freeport, NY: Books for Libraries Press, 1890, 1971), p. 631ff.
16. http://en.wikipedia.org/wiki/Cornerstone_Speech.
17. Von Abele, 1946, *op. cit.*, p. 104. As a lawyer Stevens defended a slave woman and convinced the jury to acquit her of a transgression, which it did.
18. A. Stephens, *A Constitutional View of the Late War Between the States, Its Causes, Character, Conduct and Results*. (Vol. I & II) (Philadelphia: National Publishing Company, 1868), p. 40.
19. *Ibid.*, Vol. 1, p. 478.
20. *Ibid.*, p. 25.
21. Dew, 2001, *op. cit.*, p. 14.
22. T. H. Williams, *P. G. T. Beauregard, Napoleon in Gray*. (Baton Rouge, LA: Louisiana State University Press, 2010), p. 266 & n.
23. *Ibid.*, pp. 269-71.

Chapter Twelve Notes
1. After the Civil War, as many as 9,000 southerners immigrated to Brazil where they are known as the *Confererados* around the cities of Americana and Santa Barbara D'Oeste in the state of Sao Paulo. (http://www.confederados.com.br/.) The spouse of one of my former doctoral students is a direct descendant of these émigrés.

2. C. V. Woodward, *Origins of the New South 1877-1913*. (Baton Rouge: Louisiana State University Press, 1951), pp. 399-400.
3. March 6, 1865, and in J. A. Stern, *Mary Chestnut's Civil War Epic*. (Chicago: The University of Chicago Press, 2010), p. 88.
4. T. S. Philpot, *Race, Republicans, & the Return of the Party of Lincoln*. (Ann Arbor: The University of Michigan Press, 2007), p. 158.
5. A Nevins & H. S. Commanger, *A Pocket History of the United States*. (New York: Simon & Schuster, 1954), p. 217.
6. *Ibid.*, p. 220.
7. F. Brodie, *Thaddeus Stevens, Scourge of the South*. (New York: Norton, 1959).
8. *Ibid.*, p. 229.
9. L. H. Johnson, *Division and Reunion: America 1848-1877*. (New York: John Wiley, 1978).
10. "All persons born or naturalized in the United States, and subject to the jurisdiction thereof, are citizens of the United States and of the state wherein they reside." (14th Amendment, 1868).
11. Vicksburg would not celebrate the 4th of July again until 1944 during World War II.
12. J. Y. Simon, *The Papers of Ulysses S. Grant*. (Carbondale, IL: Southern Illinois University Press, Vol. 25, 2003), p. 295. By 1875 the Sheriff of Vicksburg found it impossible to keep the peace as Whites were slaughtering unarmed and innocent Blacks. Cf. also N. Lemann, *Redemption, The Last Battle of the Civil War*. (New York: Farrar, Straus and Giroux, 2006), pp. 34 & 119.
13. "The predominant feeling of those lately in rebellion is that of deep-seated hatred . . . and a haughty contempt for the negro whom they cannot treat as a freedman . . . " (*Report of the Joint Committee on Reconstruction*, Part I, pp. 92, 109, & in W. L. Fleming, *Documentary History of Reconstruction, Political, Military, Social, Religious, Educational & Industrial 1865 to the Present Time*. (Vols. I & II). (Cleveland: The Arthur H. Clarke Company, 1906). p. 36-38. See also N. Lemann, *op. cit.*, 2006 that describes the horrors of Reconstruction.
14. *Ibid.*, pp. 68-71.
15. 170 U.S. 213 (1898).
16. Constitution and Ritual of The Knights of the White Camelia, 1869, in Fleming, 1906, *op. cit.*, p. 351.
17. After the Greek *kuklos*, circle, and thereafter known as the Invisible Empire of the South.
18. *Intelligence Report*, Spring 2011, No. 141, p. 44.
19. S. Glain, "Backward, Christian Soldiers," *The Nation*, February 28, 2011, pp. 15-22.
20. Fleming, 1906, *op. cit.*, p. 336.
21. *Ibid.*, pp. 375-76.
22. W. C. Wade, *The Fiery Cross, The Ku Klux Klan in America*. (New York: Oxford University Press, 1987), p. 105.
23. Fleming, *op. cit.*, 1906, pp. 128ff.
24. *Eleventh Census, 1890, Vital and Social Statistics, Part II, Statistics of Deaths, 27-425*. Cf. Woodward, 1951, *op. cit.*, p. 159. In 1871 in Mississippi, 30 Negro schools and churches were burned and 63 Blacks murdered and no one was ever indicted. Lemann, 2006, *op. cit.*, p. 49.
25. A. Hoozenboom, *The Presidency of Rutherford B. Hayes*. (Lawrence: Kansas State University Press, 1988), p. 9.
26. Holding the country hostage with purse strings is still a Republican political strategy, as the nation came disastrously close to shutting down in 2011.
27. Woodward, 1951, *op. cit.*, p. 249.
28. *Ibid.*, p. 269.

29. Woodrow Wilson, a direct descendant of Pocahontas in the ninth generation, had been a Virginia native, a political science professor at Princeton and its president before becoming U.S. President.

30. In the 1948 presidential election year the Dixiecrats, overtly racist and White supremacist in its platform and opposing civil rights for Blacks, captured all the electoral votes of the states of South Carolina, Mississippi, Alabama and Louisiana. http://en.wikipedia.org/wiki/Dixiecrat.

Chapter Thirteen Notes

1. B. Boyarsky, *Ronald Reagan, His Life and Rise to the Presidency.* (New York: Random House, 1981), p. 25. Ronald Reagan, in private correspondence with King Hussein of Jordan, wondered what kind of fish were in the Dead Sea and whether he could send some California fish to invigorate its waters. The King's response was polite, but he assured Reagan that the salty Dead Sea really was dead. This trivial anecdote passes for American diplomacy, but often reveals the ignorance and lack of understanding even American presidents have of the world.

2. R. Hofstadter, *Anti-Intellectualism in American Life.* (New York: Vintage Books, 1963), p. 431. Cf. also R. Jenkins, *Franklin Delano Roosevelt.* (New York: Times Books, Henry Holt, 2003).

3. *The Economic Conditions of the South,* Washington, DC: U.S. Government Printing Office, issued June 22, 1938.

4. J. M. Burns, *Roosevelt: The Lion and the Fox.* (New York: A Harvest/HBJ Book, 1956), p. 85. For a pictorial history of the Civilian Conservation Corps, one of the most successful of Roosevelt's government programs that put people to work see S. Cohen, *The Tree Army, A Pictorial History of the Civilian Conservation Corps, 1933-1942.* (Missoula. MT: Pictorial Histories Publishing Co., 1980).

5. S. Kennedy, *Southern Exposure.* (Garden City, NY: Doubleday & Co., 1946). In 1938 one of the houses in Washington State I lived in as a child next to the railroad tracks had no phone, no electricity (we used kerosene lamps at night), and no indoor toilet but an outhouse. The town's Blacks lived in a restricted area near the river.

6. Roosevelt's famous phrase in the 1933 inaugural address—"The only thing we have to fear is, fear itself"—was said to have come from Emerson, whom Roosevelt probably read while at Harvard. But it is also a phrase found much earlier in Seneca.

7. "I have been very much alarmed at the increased racial feeling all over the country and I am wondering if it wouldn't be well to appoint a commission to analyze the situation and have a remedy to present to Congress . . . it is going to require the inauguration of some sort of policy to prevent such happenings." Truman letter to Attorney General Tom Clark, September 20, 1946.

8. The major sections of Truman's executive order are worth reviewing. "Freedom From Fear is more fully realized in our country than in any other on the face of the earth. Yet all parts of our population are not equally free from fear. And from time to time, and in some places, this freedom has been gravely threatened. It was so after the last war, when organized groups fanned hatred and intolerance, until, at times, mob action struck fear into the hearts of men and women because of their racial origin or religious beliefs."

"Today, Freedom From Fear, and the democratic institutions which sustain it, are again under attack. In some places, from time to time, the local enforcement of law and order has broken down, and individuals -- sometimes ex-servicemen, even women -- have been killed, maimed, or intimidated.

"The preservation of civil liberties is a duty of every Government-state, Federal and local. Wherever the law enforcement measures and the authority of Federal, state, and local governments are inadequate to discharge this primary function of government, these measures and this authority should be strengthened and improved.

"The Constitutional guarantees of individual liberties and of equal protection under the laws clearly place on the Federal Government the duty to act when state or local authorities abridge or fail to protect these Constitutional rights.

"Yet in its discharge of the obligations placed on it by the Constitution, the Federal Government is hampered by inadequate civil rights statutes. The protection of our democratic institutions and the enjoyment by the people of their rights under the Constitution require that these weak and inadequate statutes should be expanded and improved. We must provide the Department of Justice with the tools to do the job . . . "

9. One life that mirrors the discrimination during the Truman era was Ollie Matson who died aged 80 in 2011, one of America's greatest athletes, as attested to by his professional coaches. He starred in football at the University of San Francisco, whose team went undefeated in 1951, but was not invited to play in a bowl game because the college had two Black players. Because it lost the bowl appearance money and had planned to play Black players, USF discontinued the football program. Matson went on to play in the NFL for 14 seasons, with one year for war duty as a soldier, and won two Olympic medals as a sprinter. He taught PE and coached football at Los Angeles High School. He ended his working life as a Special Events Coordinator for the Los Angeles Coliseum.

10. The result was a split within the Democratic Party over civil rights. South Carolina, Mississippi and Alabama had predictably defected. But Truman had taken a stand and he insisted on a workable fair employment practices program and enforcement of civil rights guaranteed by the Constitution. H. S. Truman, *Memoirs. Vol. 2, Years of Trial and Hope.* (Garden City, NY: Doubleday & Co., 1956), p. 179.

11. July 26, 1948. Also see R. Dalleck, *Harry S. Truman.* (New York: Times Books, Henry Holt, 2008). p. 81.

12. Roosevelt had issued an Executive Order establishing the Fair Employment Practices Committee that encouraged full participation in national defense programs without regard to race, religion or national origin but it expired in 1946 after the war. Truman's Committee of Civil Rights was meant to create the need for new, similar legislation.

13. M. Sherwin, *The Extremists.* (New York: St. Martin's Press, 1963), p. 173.

14. Wade, 1987, *op. cit.*, pp. 299ff.

15. J. A. G. Robinson, *The Montgomery Bus Boycott and the Women Who Started It.* (Knoxville, TN: The University of Tennessee Press, 1987).

16. R. Kennedy, *Thirteen Days, A Memoir of the Cuban Missile Crisis.* (New York: Norton, 1971).

17. Wade, 1987, *op. cit.*, pp. 317ff

18. L. B. Johnson, *Vantage Point, Perspective of the Presidency, 1963-69.* (New York: Holt, Rinehart & Winston, 1971).

19. L. E. Panetta & P. Gall (1971). *Bring Us Together, The Nixon Team and the Civil Rights Retreat.* (Philadelphia: J. B. Lippincott Company, 1971), p. 27.

20. Russell, a lifetime bachelor, was the chief sponsor of the National School Lunch Act of 1946 and a vigorous advocate for foreign and military policies. The Russell Senate Office Building is named after him.

21. http://www.ourdocuments.gov/doc.php?flash=old&doc=97.

22. H. D. Graham, "Richard Nixon and Civil Rights: Explaining an Enigma. *Presidential Studies Quarterly*, Winter 1996, 26(1), 93-106.

23. F. Brodie, *Richard Nixon, The Shaping of His Character.* (New York: W. W. Norton & Company, 1981).

24. Goldwater, 1979, *op. cit.*, p. 103. I listened as a teenager to a Nixon campaign speech in 1951 when he was running as Eisenhower's vice presidential candidate, my first attendance at a political event. I attended Nixon's inauguration on that damp, bone-chilling wintry day in Washington, and brought my young son with me. We stood on the corner of Constitution and New Jersey avenues to listen to Nixon's address. Later, I

worked for the Nixon Administration in Washington prior to Watergate and was flattered to be asked to respond to letters addressed to him on educational policy.

25. R. Murphy, R. & H. Gulliver, *The Southern Strategy*. (New York: Charles Scribner's Sons, 1971). I entered government in September 1969 just when the whole desegregation issue was exploding, though I was not officially a part of it. However, in 1972 I was responsible for funding school projects for disadvantaged students in Greenwood, Mississippi and Hayti, Missouri. I observed first-hand the difficulties school administrators had in attempting to implement desegregation laws and to satisfy parents not just unhappy but antagonistic at having any Blacks in school with White children. The project was called TREND, Targeting Resources for the Educational Needs of the Disadvantaged, a neat way of circumventing the desegregation issue to focus on poor children in schools, just as had been done during the Roosevelt Administration.

26. D. K. Sharpes, *Education and the U.S. Government*. (New York: St. Martin's Press, 1987), pp.134ff. Panetta later became a congressman from California, budget director under Carter, Chief of Staff under Clinton, and CIA director and Secretary of the Department of Defense under President Obama.

27. 396 U.S. 19, 1969.

28. C. Bernstein & B. Woodward, *All the President's Men*. (New York: Simon and Schuster, 1974); D. K. Sharpes, "Residence and Race in Education: Conflicts in Courts and Communities." *Journal of Teacher Education*, 1973, 24(4), 289-93. Cf. "Desegregation Studied by Arlington Board," (*The Washington Post*, November 22, 1969, p. E32) on my own efforts as Chair of the Arlington Community Action Program to force integration of all-Black Drew Elementary School in Arlington Virginia in 1969.

29. C. Bernstein & B. Woodward, 1974, *op. cit.*

30. The dirty tricks included bugging, following people to gather "dirt" on them, false press leaks, fake letters, canceling campaign rallies of the opposition, investigating private lives, planting spies in the opposition's offices, stealing documents, and planting provocateurs at political demonstrations. The Nixon team had over 50+ people working on such schemes. (Bernstein & Woodward, 1974, p. 135) It's safe to assume that some of these tactics are still used to disparage political opponents, just like the provocateurs that were present at town forums in the 2010 congressional campaign. The leader of the five burglars was James McCord, a former FBI and CIA employee. At the time of his arraignment he was a so-called security coordinator of the Committee for the Re-election of the President and a Lieutenant Colonel in a special reserve unit. Among the personal items found on the burglars was the name of E. Howard Hunt and a small notation "W. House" and "W.H." E. Howard Hunt was a White House employee who worked for Charles W. Colson, a special assistant to Nixon, and Hunt had been on the CIA payroll from 1949 to 1970.

31. Nixon's criminal cabinet officers, Maurice Stans (Commerce) and John Mitchell (Attorney General), and more than a dozen corrupted members of his immediate staff were convicted. John Erhlichman (1925-1999), presidential counsel, Stanford law school graduate, spent 18 months in prison, as did H. R. Haldeman (1926-1993), Nixon's Chief of Staff. Pleading guilty were Jeb McGruder, Bart Porter, Donald Segretti, Herbert Kalmbach, Nixon's lawyer, Fred LaRue, Egil Krough, and John Dean. Charles Colson, the so-called hatchet man in the White House, served seven months in prison where he got religion. Others like former Attorney General Kleindiest were indicted but not convicted for lack of evidence.

32. Wade, 1987, *op. cit.*, p. 388.

33. B. Goldwater, 1979, *op. cit.*, p. 273

34. G. Wills, *Reagan's America, Innocents at Home*. (New York: Doubleday & Co. 1987), pp. 368-69. Either because he had contempt for Carter or a standard Republican disdain for government programs, Reagan dismantled the solar panels Carter had

installed on the roof of the White House as a sign of the government's progress in reducing fossil fuel use. One of those panels is on display today in a museum in China's solar city operated entirely on solar power. China leads the U.S. in alternative energy technologies.

35. W. Kleinknecht, *The Man Who Sold the World, Ronald Reagan and the Betrayal of Main Street America.* (New York: Nation Books, 2009). Reagan's laissez-faire attitude toward cronyism and corruption resulted in the indictment, conviction or investigation of 138 members of his Administration, an unparalleled level of governmental malfeasance (p. 193).

36. http://www.museum.tv/eotvsection.php?entrycode=fairnessdoctrine. Talk radio and television—where the majority of people get their news—and with the exception of National Public Radio, has provided political entertainment instead of instruction in facts by simplifying complicated issues, usually exploiting the most uninformed position, and often ignoring facts and public records. Over 90% of radio stations are listed as conservative. The rise of fear-mongering media talk has lessened intelligent discussion of the day's most essential topics.

37. A typical National Football League game—the most watched program according to rating agencies—that has 60 minutes of actually playing time, has an average of about 45 minutes of advertising. In other words, 75% of the time of a NFL game includes ads for the major corporations like beer companies, trucks, autos, petroleum industries, electronics, fast food, retailers and other TV programs. If you add the 12+ minutes of ads during halftime, the amount of TV advertising approximately equals the amount of actual game time. The advance of corporate America did not originate with Reagan but got a substantial boost from his Administration's encouragement and release of regulations.

38. Typically a corporation borrowed money for a hostile takeover, then consolidated projects and sold off assets, including eliminating jobs, to recoup the money to pay back the loan. Thus, reaping enormous paper profits, corporations made them eligible for a similar takeover by a larger corporation. Thus was inaugurated the financial pinball machine of money chasing short-term profits benefitting only corporate titans, but not enlarging the productive economy or creating new industrial jobs. We witnessed what happened when paper profits, fueled by creative but destructive financial securities, collapsed in 2008 causing the artificial money economy to crater, having no fixed collateral to back it other than financial legerdemain. All of this was a direct result of policies Reagan initiated and that George W. Bush continued.

39. As a result of the U.S. Supreme Court's decision that in effect that elected Bush president in 2000, Blacks saw the court's decision as illegitimate reinforcing their distrust of the political system. See J. M. Avery, "Race, Partisanship, and Political Trust Following *Bush versus Gore* (2000)." *Political Behavior*, 29(3), September 2007, pp. 327-342.

40. T. Frank, *The Wrecking Crew, How Conservatives Rule.* (New York: Metropolitan Books, 2008), p. 132. The Innovation Emergency Management firm in the summer of 2005, before Katrina struck, received a million dollars to develop a plan for hurricane disaster. It came up with sensible plans that were never implemented because the government, though it had money for contractors, claimed it had no money for buying into the resources needed to make the plan work. Cf. N. Klein, *The Shock Doctrine, The Rise of Disaster Capitalism.* (New York: Picador, 2007), p. 517.

41. Braucher, J. D. Cohen, & R. M. Lawless (January 20, 2012). "Race, Attorney Influence and Bankruptcy Chapter Choice." Social Science Research Network at: http://papers.ssrn.com/sol3/papers.cfm?abstract_id=1989039 and to appear in the *Journal of Empirical Legal Studies*. Chapter 13 Bankruptcy offers less security and costs more than other bankruptcies such as Chapter 7.

Chapter Fourteen Notes

1. Because more states are allowing citizens to carry concealed weapons, manufacturers are customizing guns, and gun prices, for women's handbags, many with pink trim and handles. What could be more feminine than a woman packing? See C. Pearlman, "Purse Pistols, NYTM, March 20, 2011, p. 19.

2. M Potok, "Rage on the Right, The Year in Hate and Extremism." *Intelligence Report*, Spring 2010, 41-63. The Southern Poverty Law Center in Montgomery, Alabama regularly receives hate and death threat Emails. It has armed guards posted around its buildings, 24-hour security, metal detectors, entry barricades, and security at the homes of key personnel. It spends more than one million annually to ensure the safety of its staff and offices. See http://www.americannaziparty.com/about/index.php.

3. *Intelligence Report*, Spring 2011, Issue 141, 41ff. Neo-Nazi groups have also been accused of crimes in Germany. N. Kulish, "Neo-Nazis Suspected in Long Wave of Crimes, Including Murders, in Germany," *The New York Times*, November 14, 2011, A4.

4. Here are samples, all with multiple websites in parentheses. Ku Klux Klan (187 chapters or klaverns); Neo-Nazi groups (often includes skinheads, 161 affiliates; Anti-immigrant Nativists or White Nationalists; Christian Identity groups (37); Neo-Confederates (68); Black Separatists (121); General Hate groups (antigay (14), anti-immigration (12), holocaust denial (7); Racist music (13); Radical Traditional Catholic (13); Other (42); White Power Nationalists (122 affiliates); Patriots (512) and associated groups.

5. S. Scherr, "Going Under." *Intelligence Report*, Summer 2009, pp. 12.

6. There is a large body of evidence linking adolescent aggression to computer video games, e.g., C. A. Anderson, L. Berkowitz, E. Donnerstein, L. R. Huesmann, J. Johnson, D., Linz, *et al.* "The Influence of Media Violence on Youth." *Psychological Science in the Public Interest, 2003, 4*, 81-110. S. M. Dorman, "Video and computer games; Effect on children and implications for health education." *Journal of School Health, 1997, 67*, 133-139; J. B. Funk, Hagan, J., Schimming, J., Bullock, W. A., Buchman, D. D., & M. Myers, "Aggression and Psychopathology in Adolescents With a Preference for Violent Electronic Games." *Aggressive Behavior, 2002, 28*, 134-144.

7. There is no straight line between individual acts of murder and assassination and politically puerile rhetoric, not matter how vitriolic. Individual acts of violence can occur amid a climate of political violent talk. The unbalanced assailant is usually not a political or even socially accepted animal. Moreover, care for the mentally ill reveals systematic erosion in favor of privacy, individual freedom and civil rights. President Reagan stopped federal funding for community mental health clinics. Beginning in 2008 Republicans tried to eliminate mental health coverage in the health care legislation. The Republican controlled legislature in Arizona from 2008 to 2010 cut funding for mental health by 47%.

8. *The New York Times*, January 19, 2011, A18.

9. N. Bunkley, "Savage Militia Plotted to Kill Police, Charges Say." *The New York Times*, March 30, 2010, A1ff.

10. http://guardiansofthefreerepublics.com/guardian.html.

11. P. Carlson, "All Shook Up." *Smithsonian*, December 2010, 10-12.

Epilogue

1. "At every stage, and under all circumstances, the essence of the struggle is to equalize opportunity, destroy privilege, and give to the life and citizenship of every individual the highest possible value both to himself and to the commonwealth." See T.R. Roosevelt,

(1910). "The New Nationalism." Speech at Osawatomie, Kansas located at one site at: http://en.wikipedia.org/wiki/New_Nationalism.

2. "Exactly as the special interests of cotton and slavery threatened our political integrity before the Civil War, so now the great special business interests too often control and corrupt the men and methods of government for their own profit. We must drive the special interests out of politics."

3. "It is necessary that laws should be passed to prohibit the use of corporate funds directly or indirectly for political purposes; it is still more necessary that such laws should be thoroughly enforced."

4. "We grudge no man a fortune in civil life if it is honorably obtained and well used. It is not even enough that it should have gained without doing damage to the community. We should permit it to be gained only so long as the gaining represents benefit to the community. This, I know, implies a policy of a far more active governmental interference with social and economic conditions in this country than we have yet had, but I think we have got to face the fact that such an increase in governmental control is now necessary."

5. "Therefore, I believe in a graduated income tax on big fortunes, and in another tax which is far more easily collected and far more effective—a graduated inheritance tax on big fortunes, properly safeguarded against evasion and increasing rapidly in amount with the size of the estate."

6. H. Agar, *The Price of Union*. (Boston: Houghton Mifflin, 1950), p. 660.

7. J. Sachs, *The Price of Civilization, Reawakening American Virtue and Prosperity*. (New York: Random House, 2010).

8. S. Cohen, *The Tree Army, A Pictorial History of the Civilian Conservation Corps, 1933-1942*. (Missoula. MT: Pictorial Histories Publishing Co., 1980).

9. In 1933 the U.S. population was only 125 million, a third of what it was in 2012. So roughly 6% of unemployed men were enrolled in the nine years from 1933-42. Such a program today, if the same ratios were maintained, would enroll about 12 million, or the approximate number of all unemployed, men and women.

REFERENCES

Adams, H. (1938). *A Catalogue of the Books of John Quincy Adams*. Boston: Athenaeum.

Adorno, T. & E. Frenkel-Brunswik, D. J. Levinson, & R. N. Sanford. (1982). *The Authoritarian Personality*. New York: W. W. Norton.

Agar, H. (1950). *The Price of Union*. Boston: Houghton Mifflin.

Alpert, D., & R. Hockett, N. Roubini. (October 10, 2011). *The Way Forward, Moving From the Post-Bubble, Post-Bust Economy to Renewed Growth and Competitiveness*. Washington, DC: The New America Foundation.

Altermann, E. (March 7/11, 2011). Ronald Reagan Superstar. *The Nation*, 11.

Angle, P. M. (Ed.) (1947). *The Lincoln Reader*. New Brunswick, NJ: Rutgers University Press.

Applegate, D. (April 23, 2011). A Nation Stirs, *The New York Times Book Review*, 1

Armey, D. & M. Kibbe. (2010). *Give Us Liberty, A Tea Party Manifesto*. New York: William Morrow.

Arum, R. & J. Roksa. (2011). *Academically Adrift, Limited Learning on College Campuses*. Chicago: University of Chicago Press.

Athearn, R. G. (1956). *William Tecumseh Sherman and the Settlement of the West*. Norman: University of Oklahoma Press.

Aughey, J. H. (1863). *The Iron Furnace, or Slavery and Secession*. Philadelphia: William S. & Alfred Martien.

Aytoun, J. (1876). *How to Settle the Eastern Question*. London: Hardwicke & Bogue.

Armitage, D. (2004). John Locke, Carolina, and the Two Treatises of Government. *Political Theory*, 32(5), 602–627.

Avery, J. M. (September 2007). Race, Partisanship, and Political Trust Following *Bush versus Gore* (2000)." *Political Behavior*, 29(3), pp. 327-342.

Bai, M. (October 16, 2011). Does Anyone Have a Grip on the G.O.P.? *The New York Times Magazine*, pp. 44ff.

⸻ (January 15, 2012). The Tea Party's Not-So Civil War. *The New York Times Magazine*, 34-39.

Bailyn, B. (1992). *The Ideological Origins of the American Revolution*. Cambridge MA: Harvard University Press.

Bales, K. (1999). *Disposable People: New Slavery in the Global Economy*. Berkeley University of California Press.

Ballard, M. (2007). *The Campaign for Vicksburg*. Ft. Washington, PA: Eastern National.

Bauerlein, M. & C. Jeffery. (November/December, 2011). The Job Killers. *Mother Jones Magazine*, 36(6). 20-22.

Barker, E. (1960). *Social contract*. New York: Oxford University Press.

Barry, J. M. (January 2012). God, Government and Roger Williams' Big Idea. *Smithsonian*, pp. 72-90.

Barzun, J. (2000). *From Dawn to Decadence, 1500 to the Present*. New York: Perennial.

⸻ (1989). *The Culture We Deserve*. Middletown, CT: Wesleyan University Press.

Beirich, H. (Spring 2010). Midwifing the Militias. *Intelligence Report*, 31-35.

⸻ Behind the Academies. (Spring 2011). *Intelligence Report*, Montgomery: Southern Poverty Law Center, 12-13.

Beramendi P. & T. R. Cusack. (June 2009). Diverse Disparities: The Politics and Economics of Wage, Market, and Disposal Income Inequalities, *Political Research Quarterly*, 62(2), pp. 257-275.

Berger, R. (1977). *Government by Judiciary, The Transformation of the Fourteenth Amendment*. Cambridge, MA: Harvard University Press.

Bernstein, C. & B. Woodward. (1974). *All the President's Men*. New York: Simon and Schuster.

Bickford, C. B. & K. R. Bowling. (1989). *Birth of the Nation: The First Federal Congress 1789–1791*. Madison, WI: Madison House.

Bicknell, J. & T. Day. (1773). *The Dying Negro*. London: W. Flexney.

Birt, D. (1989). *An American in the Tower*. London: British Museum.

Black, E. & M. Black. (2002). *The Rise of Southern Republicans*. Cambridge, MA: The Belnap Press of Harvard University Press.

Bloom, A. (1987). *The Closing of the American Mind*. New York: Simon & Schuster.

Borchard, R. (1957). *John Stuart Mill, The Man*. London: Watts.

Borneman, W. R. (2008). *Polk, The Man Who Transformed The Presidency and America*. New York: Random House.

Boyle, K. (November 27, 2011). The Not-So-Invisible Empire. *The New York Times Book Review,* 34.

Boyd, J. P. (1955). *The Papers of Thomas Jefferson*. Princeton: Princeton University Press.

Bowers, C. (1969). *The Young Jefferson, 1743–1789*. Boston: Houghton Mifflin.

—— (1967). *Jefferson in Power*. Boston: Houghton Mifflin.

Boyarsky, B. (1981). *Ronald Reagan, His Life and Rise to the Presidency*. New York: Random House.

Boyd, J. P. (1955). *The Papers of Thomas Jefferson*. Princeton: Princeton University Press.

Boyd, W. (1963, 1911). *The Educational Theory of Jean Jacques Rousseau.* New York: Russell & Russell.

Brandt, I. (1965). *The Bill of Rights, Its Origin and Meaning*. Indianapolis: Bobbs Merrill.

Braucher, J. D. Cohen, & R. M. Lawless (2012). Race, Attorney Influence and Bankruptcy Chapter Choice. Social Science Research Network (http://papers.ssrn.com/sol3/papers.cfm?abstract_id=1989039) (in anticipation of publication in the *Journal of Empirical Legal Studies*.

Bressette, P. (July/August 2011). The War Within the States. *The American Prospect*, pp. 25-29.

Brodie, F. (1981). *Richard Nixon, The Shaping of His Character*. New York: W. W. Norton & Company.

—— (1974). *Thomas Jefferson, An Intimate History*. New York: W. W. Norton.

—— (1966). *No Man Knows My History: The Life of Joseph Smith, the Mormon Prophet*. New York: A.A. Knopf.

—— (1959). *Thaddeus Stevens, Scourge of the South*. New York: Norton.

Bronowski, J. & Mazlish, B. (1960). *The Western Intellectual Tradition.* New York: Harper & Brothers Publishers.

Bronowski, J. (1973). *The Ascent of Man*. Boston: Little, Brown.

Brookhiser, R. (2011). *James Madison*. New York: Basic Books.

Brown, D. (1970). *Bury My Heart at Wounded Knee*. New York: Pan Books.

Buchan, J. (2006). *Adam Smith and the Pursuit of Perfect Liberty*. London: Profile Books.

Bullock, A. (1985). *The Humanist Tradition in the West*. New York: W. W. Norton.

Bunkley, N. (March 30, 2010). Savage Militia Plotted to Kill Police, Charges Say." *The New York Times*, A1ff.

Burdtt, E. (1939) *The English Philosophers from Bacon to Mill*. New York: Modern Library.

Burgess, J. W. (1897). *The Middle Period, 1817–1858*. New York: Charles Scribner's Sons.

Burghardt, D. & L. Zeskind, (2010). *Tea Party Nationalism: A Critical Examination of the Tea Party Movement and the Size, Scope, and Focus of Its National Factions*. Kansas City, MO: Institute for Research & Education On Human Rights.

Burke, E. (1775). *Speech of Edmund Burke, Esq. on American Taxation, April 19, 1774*. (3rd edition). London: J. Dodsley.

—— (1791). *Speech of Edmund Burke, Esq., March 22, 1775*. London: J. Dodsley.

—— (1777) *A Letter from Edmund Burke, Esq. to John Farr and John Harris, Sheriffs of Bristol on the Affairs of America*. (4th. Ed.) London: J. Dodsley.

—— (1798). *The Beauties of the Late Right Hon. Edmund Burke*. (2 vols.) London: J. W. Myers.

—— (1793). *Burke's Reflections on the Revolution in France*. London: J. Parsons.

—— (1886). *Two Speeches on Conciliation with America and Two Letters on Irish Questions*. London: George Routledge and Sons.

Burns, J. M. (1956). *Roosevelt: The Lion and the Fox*. New York: A Harvest/HBJ Book.

Burns, K. (April 12, 2011). A Conflict's Acoustic Shadows. *The New York Times*, A21.

Cable, M. (1971) *Black Odyssey, the Case of the Slave Ship Amistad*. New York: Penguin Books.

Calhoun, J. C. (1968, 1856). (Ed. R. K. Cralle). *A Disquisition and a Discourse on the Constitution and Government of the United States*. New York: Russell & Russell.

Callan, E. (1997). *Creating Citizens, Political education and Liberal Democracy*. Oxford: Clarendon Press.

Carlson, P. (December 2010). All Shook Up. *Smithsonian*, 10-12.

Carlyle, T. (1939). *The Best of Carlyle*. (Ed. H.L. Creek). New York: Thomas Nelson.

Cassell, F. A. (1975). The Great Baltimore Riot of 1812. *Maryland Historical Magazine* 70(3), 241-242.

Catton, B. (1960). *The Civil War*. New York: The Fairfax Press.

Cayton, A. (July 4, 2010). To Save the Union. *The New York Times Book Review*, p. 17.

Chernow, R. (2004). *Alexander Hamilton*. New York: Penguin Books.

Cicero. (2006), *Political Speeches*. (Trans. & edited D.H. Berry). Oxford: Oxford University Press.

Cisco, W. B. (1991). *States Rights Gist, A South Carolina General of the Civil War*. Shippensburg, PA: White Mane Publishing Co.

Cobban, A. (1964). *Rousseau and the Modern State*. London: Archon Books.

Cockrell, M. F. (2003). *The Lost Account of the Battle of Corinth and Court-Martial of Gen. Van Dorn*. Wilmington, NC: Broadfoot Publishing Company.

Cohen, R. (Spring 2011). Fringe Ideas Assault Nation's Core Values. *SPLC Report*, p. 2.

Cohen, S. (1980). *The Tree Army, A Pictorial History of the Civilian Conservation Corps, 1933-1942*. Missoula. MT: Pictorial Histories Publishing Co.

Coleman, J. (1966). *Equality of Educational Opportunity*. Washington, DC: U.S. Dept. of Health, Education and Welfare.

Commager, H. S. (1962). *The American Mind, An Interpretation of American Thought and Character Since the 1880s*. New Haven: Yale University Press.

—— (1967). *Freedom and Order*. New York: George Braziller.

Cooke, A. (1988). *America Observed*. (Ed. R. A. Wells). New York: Reinhardt Books.

Corwin, E. S. (1958). *The Constitution and What it Means Today*. Princeton: Princeton University Press.

Chan, S. (December 12, 2010). The Fed? He's Not a Fan. *The New York Times*, wk2.

Chitwood, O. P. (1939). *John Tyler, Champion of the Old South*, New York: D. Appleton-Century Co.

Cotton, G. A. (2008). *Mrs. Balfour's Civil War Diary*. Vicksburg, MI: Old Court House Museum.

Clark, B. C. (1932). *John Quincy Adams*. Boston: Little, Brown and Company.

Cunningham, N. E. (1996). *The Presidency of James Monroe*. Lawrence: University Press of Kansas.

Crane, S. (1982). *The Red Badge of Courage*. New York: W. W. Norton.

Cronon, W. (March 22, 2011). Wisconsin's Radical Break. *The New York Times*, A17.

Crutchfield, J. A. (1985). *The Natchez Trace, A Pictorial History*. Franklin: TN: Territorial Press.

Dabbs, J. M. (1958). *The Southern Heritage*. New York: Alfred A. Knopf.

Dalleck, R. (2008). *Harry S. Truman*. New York: Times Books, Henry Holt.

Daniel, J. R. V. (1949). *A Handbook of Virginia History*. Richmond: Department of Conservation and Development.

Daniel, L. (1998). *The Battle of Shiloh*. FT. Washington, PA: Eastern National.

Davis, V. (1890, 1971). *Jefferson Davis, Ex-President of the Confederate States of America, A Memoir by His Wife*. Vol. II. Freeport, NY: Books for Libraries Press.

Delbanco, A. (March 27, 2011). Riven Nation. *The New York Times Book Review*, p. 12.

Demeritt, D. (June 2001). The Construction of Global Warming and the Politics of Science, *Annals of the Association of American Geographers*, 91(2), pp. 307-337.

De Sherbinin, A. & K. Warner, C. Ehrhart. (January 2011). Casualties of Climate Change. *Scientific American*, 64-71.

De Tocqueville, A. (1969). *Democracy in America*. New York: Doubleday.

—— (2000). *Democracy in America*. (Trans. & Ed. H.C. Mansfeld & D. Winthrop). Chicago: University of Chicago Press.

Dew, C. B. (2001). *Apostles of Disunion, Southern Secession Commissioners and the Causes of the Civil War*. Charlottesville: University Press of Virginia.

Dewey, J. (1944). *Democracy and Education*. New York: The Free Press.

Dickenson, T. (August 11, 2011). We're Winning. *The Guardian*, pp. 6-10.

Douglas, W. O. (1980). *The Court Years, 1939–1975, The Autobiography of William O. Douglas*. New York: Random House.

Douglas, F. (2003). *Frederick Douglas on Slavery and the Civil War*. (Ed. P. S. Foner). Mineola, NY: Dover Publications.

—— (1968, 1855). *My Bondage and My Freedom*. New York: Arno Press and The New York Times & New York: Miller, Orton & Mulligan.
D'Souza, D. (1995). *The End of Racism*. New York: The Free Press.
De Tocqueville, A. (2000). *Democracy in America*. Chicago: University of Chicago Press.
Durant, W. & A. Durant. (1967). *Rousseau and Revolution*. New York: MJF Books.
DuBois, W. E. B. (1969). *The Black North in 1901*. New York: The Arno Press.
—— (1994). *The Souls of Black Folk*. New York: Gramercy Books.
Dreyfyss, R. (April 11, 2011). Taking Aim at the Pentagon Budget. *The Nation*, pp. 22-26.
Dworkin, R. (May 13, 2010). The Decision that threatens Democracy. *The New York Review of Books*, 63–67.

Eaton, C. (1977). *Jefferson Davis*. New York: The Free Press.
Edwards, L. (1995). *Goldwater, The Man Who Made a Revolution*. Washington, DC: Regnery Publishing.
Eleventh Census, 1890, Vital and Social Statistics, Part II, Statistics of Deaths, 27-425.
Emanuel, E.J. (October 30, 2011). How Much Does Health Cost? *The New York Times*, bw5.
Epps, G. (February 7, 2011). Stealing the Constitution. *The Nation*, pp. 11-17.
—— (11/11). The Constitution: A Love Story. *The American Prospect*, 22(9), 36-40.
Extracts from the Votes and Proceedings of the American Continental Congress. (1774). Boston: Edes and Gill.

Faulkner, W. (1991, 1948). *Intruder in the Dust*. New York: Vintage.
Fenno, R. (1985). *Congress in Change, Evolution and Reform*: Washington DC: American Enterprise Institute.
Fernandez-Armesto, F. (2000). *Civilizations*. London: Macmillan.
Finley, M. I. (1960). *Slavery in Classical Antiquity*. Cambridge: W. Heffer and Sons.
Finn, C. (1977). *Education and the Presidency*. Lexington, MA: Lexington Books.
Feldstein, M. S. (October 13, 2011). How to Stop the Drop in Home Values. *The New York Times, A25*.
Ferguson, J. H. & D. E. McHenry. (1950). The American Federal Government. New York: McGraw Hill.
Fleming, W. L. (1906). *Documentary History of Reconstruction, Political, Military, Social, Religious, Educational & Industrial 1865 to the Present Time*. (Vols. I & II). Cleveland: The Arthur H. Clarke Company.
Foley, D. K. (2006). *Adam's Fallacy, A Guide to Economic Theology*. Cambridge, MA: The Belnap Press of Harvard University Press.
Foner, E. (1976). *Tom Paine and Revolutionary America*. New York: Oxford University Press.
Ford, R. T. (October 28, 2011). Moving Beyond Civil Rights. *The New York Times, A23*.
Fox-Genovese, E., & Genovese, E. D. (2005) *The Mind of the Master Class, History and Faith in the Southern Slaveholders' Worldview*. New York: Cambridge University Press.
Frank, T. (2008). *The Wrecking Crew, How Conservatives Rule*. New York: Metropolitan Books.

Freedman, D. H. (November 2011). A Formula for Economic Calamity. *Scientific American*, 305(5), 77-79.

Freehling, W. W. (2007). *The Road to Disunion, (Vol. II) Secessionists Triumphant 1854-1861.* New York: Oxford University Press.

Freeland, C. (January/February 2011). The Rise of the New Global Elite. *The Atlantic*, 307(1), 44-55.

Freeman, D. S. (1993). *Washington.* New York: Charles Scribner's Sons.

Freeman, K. (1952). *God, Man and State, Greek Concepts.* Boston: Beacon Press.

Freeman, C. (2003). *The Closing of the Western Mind, The Rise of Faith and The Fall of Reason.* New York: Knopf.

Fredrickson, G. M. (1988). *The Arrogance of Race, Historical Perspectives on Slavery, Racism, and Social Inequality.* Middletown, CT: Wesleyan University Press.

Friedman, M. (2002). *Capitalism and Freedom.* Chicago: University of Chicago Press.

Fugitive Slave Circulars. (1876). London: Stanford.

Fugitive Slave Circulars. (1876). London: Stanford (Sommersett circular).

Fukuyama, F. (May 8, 2011). Big-Government Skeptic. *The New York Times Book Review*, 12.

Furgurson, E. B. (2001). *Not War But Murder, Cold Harbor 1864.* New York: Vintage Books.

Furnas, J. C. (1969). *The Americans, A Social History of the United States, 1587–1914.* New York: G. P. Putnam's Sons.

Galbraith, J. K. (1996). *The Good Society, The Human Agenda.* Boston: Houghton Mifflin.

Gasset, J. O. (1985). *The Revolt of the Masses.* Notre Dame: University of Notre Dame Press.

Gaustad, E. S. (2005). *Roger Williams.* New York: Oxford University Press.

Gilje, P. A. (Summer 1980). "The Baltimore Riots of 1812 and the Breakdown of the Anglo-American Mob Tradition." *Journal of Social History*, Vol. 13, No. 4, 547–564.

Gillette, W. (1979). *Retreat from Reconstruction.* Baton Rouge: Louisiana State University Press.

Gillis, J. (December 22, 2010). A Scientist, His Work and a Climate Reckoning. *The New York Times*, A1ff.

Ginsburg, E. (1934). *The House of Adam Smith.* New York: Columbia University Press.

Goldman, R. & D. Gallen. (1992). *Thurgood Marshall, Justice for All.* New York: Carroll & Graff.

Goldwater, B. (1979). *With No Apologies, Personal and Political Memoirs.* New York: William Morrow and Co.

—— (1990). *The Conscience of a Conservative*: Washington, DC: Regnery Gateway.

Goodheart, A. (February 6, 2011). Violence and Retribution, A History of a Slave Revolt in Louisiana Illuminates the White Fear of Black Insurrection. *The New York Times Book Review*, 24.

—— (April 3, 2011). The Shrug That Made History. *The New York Times Magazine*, pp. 40ff.

Gore, L. L. (2007). *Memories of the Old Plantation Home.* Vacherie, LA: The Zoe Company.

Gandel, S. (September 25, 2011). Why Banks Are Still Failing Use, *Time*, pp. 40-45.

Graham, H. D. (Winter 1996). Richard Nixon and Civil Rights: Explaining an Enigma. *Presidential Studies Quarterly*, 26(1), 93-106.

Graham, R. (May 1966). Causes for the Abolition of Negro Slavery in Brazil: An Interpretive Essay. *The Hispanic American Historical Review*. 46(2), 123-137.

Granholm, J. M. (2011). *A Governor's Story, The Fight for Jobs and America's Economic Future*. New York: PublicAffairs.

Granieri, R. J. (July/August 2011). Judging Henry Clay. *The American Interest*, VI (6), 102-107.

Grant, U. S. (1886). *Personal Memoirs*. London: Simpson Low, Marston, Searle & Rivington.

Green, J. (November 2010). The Tea Party's Brain. *The Atlantic Monthly*, 98-106.
——— (January/February 2011). Strict Obstructionist. *The Atlantic Monthly*, 307(1), 64-70.

Hacker, A. (1992). *Two Nations, Black and White, Separate, Hostile and Unequal*. New York: Charles Scribner's Sons.

Hamer, P. M. (1970). *The Papers of Henry Laurens*. (16 vols.) Columbia: University of South Carolina Press.

Hamilton, A., J. Madison, & J. Jay (1961). *The Federalist Papers*. New York: New American Library.

Hamilton, E. (1993, 1930). *Many Thousand Gone, African Americans from Slavery to Freedom*. New York: Alfred E. Knopf.

Harris, J. W. (2009). *The Hanging of Thomas Jeremiah, A Free Black Man's Encounter with Liberty*. New Haven: Yale University Press.

Harris-Perry, M. (December 13, 2010). The Misunderestimation of Sarah Palin. *The Nation*, p. 10.

Harrison, M & S. Gilbert. (1993). *Thomas Jefferson, Word for Word*. La Jolla: Excellent Books.

Hayek, F. A. (2007, 1944). *The Road to Serfdom, Texts and Documents* (Vol. 2). (Ed. B. Caldwell). Chicago: The University of Chicago Press.
—— (2011). *The Constitution of Liberty*. (Ed. R. Hamowy). Chicago: The University of Chicago Press.
—— (1960). *The Constitution of Liberty*. Chicago: The University of Chicago Press.
—— (1979). *The Political Order of a Free People*. Chicago: The University of Chicago Press.

Heater, D. (1990). *Citizenship, the Civic Ideal in World History, Politics and Education*. London: Longmans.

Herrnstein, R. J. & C. Murray. (1994). *The Bell Curve, Intelligence and Class Structure in American Life*. New York: The Free Press.

Hicks, B. (March 2011). The Holdouts. *Smithsonian*, 51-60.

Hobbes, T. (1962, 1651). *Leviathan*. London: J. M. Dent & Sons.

Hofstadter, R. (1963). *Anti-Intellectualism in American Life*. New York: Vintage Books.
—— (1976, 1948). *The American Political Tradition*. New York: Vintage Books.
—— (2008, 1952). *The Paranoid Style in American Politics and Other Essays*. New York. Vintage Books.

Hoover, H. (1952). *The Memoirs of Herbert Hoover*. (Vol. II) New York: Macmillan.

Hoozenboom, A. (1988). *The Presidency of Rutherford B. Hayes*. Lawrence: Kansas State University Press.

Horwitz, T. (2011). *Midnight Rising, John Brown and the Raid That Sparked the Civil War.* New York: Henry Holt.
Hume, D. (1967). *A Treatise of Human Nature.* (Ed. L. A. Selby Bigge). Oxford: The Clarendon Press.
—— (1990, 1799). *Dialogues Concerning Natural Religion.* New York: Penguin.
—— (1967). *On Human nature and the Understanding.* New York: Collier Books.
Hutchins, R. M. (1952). *Adam Smith.* In *Great Books of the Western World* Vol. 39. Chicago: Encyclopaedia Britannica, Inc.

Inhofe, J. (May 17, 2011). All Pain, No Gain. *USAToday*, p. 8A.
Intelligence Report (Summer 2010). Montgomery: Southern Poverty Law Center.
Isaacs, H. (1972). *Idols of the Tribe, Group Identity and Political Change.* Cambridge, MA: Harvard University Press.

Jacoby, S. (2008). *The Age of American Unreason.* New York: Pantheon.
Jefferson, T. (1972). *Notes on the State of Virginia.* New York: W.W. Norton.
—— (1905). *The Writings of Thomas Jefferson.* Washington DC: Thomas Jefferson Memorial Foundation.
Jencks, C. (1973). *Inequality, A Reassessment of the Effect of Family and Schooling in America.* New York: Harper & Row.
Jenkins, R. (2003). *Franklin Delano Roosevelt.* New York: Times Books, Henry Holt.
Jenkins, W. D. (1935). *Pro-Slavery Thought in the Old South.* Chapel Hill: The University of North Carolina Press.
Johannsen, R. W. (1988). *Democracy on Trial, A Documentary History of American Life, 1845-1877.* Urbana: University of Illinois Press.
Johnson, L. B. (1971). *Vantage Point, Perspective of the Presidency, 1963-69.* New York: Holt, Rinehart & Winston.
Johnson, B. R. (June 24, 2009). *Testimony, Office of Intelligence and Analysis before the House Committee on Homeland Security, Subcommittee on Intelligence, Information Sharing, and Terrorism Risk Assessment.* Washington, DC: Department of Homeland Security.
Johnson, S. (1775). *Taxation No Tyranny: An Answer to the Resolutions and Address of the American Congress.* London: T. Cadell.
Johnson, L. H. (1978). *Division and Reunion: America 1848-1877.* New York: John Wiley.
Jones, A. H. M. (1956). Slavery in the Ancient World. *The Economic History Review*, 9, 185–199.
Jones, J. (1999). *A Social History of the Laboring Classes from Colonial Times to the Present.* Oxford: Blackwell.
Judson, B. (2009). *It Could Happen Here, America on the Brink.* New York: Harper.
Juahsz, A. (2008). *The Tyranny of Oil.* New York: William Morrow.

Kaiser, R. G. (2009). *So Damn Much Money, The Triumph of Lobbying and the Corrosion of American Government.* New York: Alfred A. Knopf.
Keller, L. (Fall 2009). The Second Wave, Return of the Militias. *Intelligence Report,* 31-39.
Kendrick, P. & Kendrick, S. (2008). *Douglass and Lincoln, How a Revolutionary Black Leader and a Reluctant Liberator Struggled to End Slavery and Save the Union.* New York: Walker & Co.

Kennedy, R. (1971). *Thirteen Days, A Memoir of the Cuban Missile Crisis.* New York: Norton.

Kennedy, S. (1946). *Southern Exposure.* Garden City, NY: Doubleday & Co.

Ketchum, C. (January 2012). Stop Payment, A Homeowner's Revolt Against the Banks. *Harpers*, 324(1940), pp. 28-36.

Keynes, J. M. (1973). *The Collected Writings of John Maynard Keynes. Vol. VII, The General Theory of Employment, Interest and Money.* Cambridge, UK: Macmillian/St. Martin's Press.

Kim, R. (November 22, 2010). Tea Party Takeaways. *The Nation*, pp. 5-6.

Kiviat, B. (November 28, 2011). Below the Line. *Time*, 35-41.

Klein, N. (2007). *The Shock Doctrine, The Rise of Disaster Capitalism.* New York: Picador.

Kleinknecht, W. (2009). *The Man Who Sold the World, Ronald Reagan and the Betrayal of Main Street America.* New York: Nation Books.

Koch, A. (1973). *Jefferson and Madison, The Great Collaboration.* London: Oxford University Press.

Koch, A. & W. Peden. (1946). *The Selected Writings of John and John Quincy Adams.* New York: Alfred A. Knopf.

Kolchin, P. (1992). The Tragic Era? Interpreting Southern Reconstruction in Comparative Perspective. (In F. McGlynn & S. Dresher, Eds.) *The Meaning of Freedom: Economics, Politics and Culture After Slavery.* Pittsburgh: University of Pittsburgh Press.

Kocienniewski, D. (March 25, 2011). G.E. Turns the Tax Man Away Empty-Handed. *The New York Times*, A1ff.

Kucera, J. (Summer 2010). The Seeds of Discontent. *U.S. News and World Report*, 40–41.

Kulish, N. (November 14, 2011). Neo-Nazis Suspected in Long Wave of Crimes, Including Murders, in Germany," *The New York Times*, A4.

Laurens, H. (1970). *The Papers of Henry Laurens.* Columbia: The University of South Carolina Press.

Lavin, T. (January/February 2011). How the Recession Changed Us. *The Atlantic Monthly*, 307(1), 72-73.

Lee, H. (2010), *To Kill a Mockingbird.* London: Arrow Books.

Lekachman, R. (1966). *The Age of Keynes.* New York: Random House.

Lenz, R. (Fall 2011). 'Sovereign' President, *Intelligence Report*, 143, pp. 33-35

Lemann, N. (2006). *Redemption, The Last Battle of the Civil War.* New York: Farrar, Straus and Giroux.

LePore, J. (2010). *The Whites of their Eyes, The Tea Party's Revolution and the Battle of American History.* Princeton: Princeton University Press.

—— (April 24, 2011). Poor Jane's Almanac. *The New York Times*, wk8.

Levine, B. (2006). *Confederate Emancipation.* New York: Oxford University Press.

—— (1992). *Half Slave and Half Free, The Roots of the Civil War.* New York: Hill & Wang.

Levinson, S. (2006). *Our Undemocratic Constitution, Where the Constitution Goes Wrong (And How We the People Can Correct It).* New York: Oxford University Press.

Levy, L. (1969). *Essay on the Making of the Constitution.* New York: Oxford University Press.

Lew, J. (February 5, 2011). The Easy Cuts are Behind Us. *The New York Times*, p. wk9.

Lewis, M. (2011). *The Big Short, Inside the Doomsday Machine*. New York: W. W. Norton and Co.

Leibovich, M. (October 3, 2010). "Being Glenn Beck." *The New York Times Magazine*, pp. 34ff.

Lilla, M. (May 27, 2010). The Tea Party Jacobins. *The New York Review of Books*, 53–56.

Liptak, A. (December 19, 2010). Justice Offer Receptive Ear to Business Interests. *The New York Times*, A1ff.

Locke, J. (1824). *The Works of John Locke*. London: C. Baldwin.

—— (1961). *An Essay Concerning Human Understanding*. New York. E. P. Putnam.

Loewen, J. W. (Fall 2011). Getting the Civil War Right. *Teaching Tolerance*, 40, 22-28.

Lukacs, J. (2007). *George Kennan, A Study of Character*. New Haven: Yale University Press.

Madison, J. (1893). *Journal of the Constitutional Convention*. Chicago: Scott, Foresman & Co.

Madrick, J. (2009). *The Case for Big Government*. Princeton: Princeton University Press.

Mahoney, J. & D. Rueschemeyer (2003). *Comparative Historical Analysis in the Social Sciences*. New York: Cambridge University Press.

Malbin, M. (1980). *Unelected Representatives: Congressional Staff and the Future of Representative Government*. New York: Basic Books.

—— (ed.) (1961). *The Federalist Papers*. New York: New American Library.

Maltz, E. M. (2009). *Slavery and the Supreme Court, 1825-1861*. Lawrence: University Press of Kansas.

Macaulay, T. B. (c. 1880). *Reviews, Essays and Poems*. London: Ward, Lock, & Co.

McCulloch v Maryland, March 6, 1819.

McDonald, F. (1985). *Novus Ordo Seculorum, The Intellectual Origins of the Constitution*. Lawrence, KS: University Press of Kansas.

McDougall, W. A. (2008). *Throes of Democracy, The American Civil War Era 1829–1877*. New York: HarperCollins.

McNeil, N. (1989). The First Congress, Translating the Constitution. *Constitution*, 1(4), 52–61.

Meacham, J. (2008). *American Lion, Andrew Jackson in the White House*. New York: Random House.

Meet the 'Patriots'. *Intelligence Report*, Montgomery, AL: Southern Poverty Law Center, pp. 12-31.

Melton, B. F. (2002). *Aaron Burr, Conspiracy to Treason*. New York: John Wiley & Sons.

Meltzer, M. (1984). *The Black Americans, A History in Their Own Words*. New York: Harper & Row.

Menand, L. (2001). *The Metaphysical Club*. New York: Farrar, Straus & Giroux.

Mencimer, S. (July/August 2010). If at First you Don't Secede. *Mother Jones Magazine*, pp. 14-15.

Merelman R.M., G. Streich, & P. Martin. (December 1998). Unity and Diversity in American Political Culture: An Exploratory Study of the National Conversation on American Pluralism and Identity. *Political Psychology*, 19(4), December 1998, pp. 781-807.

Meyerson, H. (October 2011). Foundering Fathers. *The American Prospect*, 22(8), pp. 12-16.

Mill, J. S. (1969). *Autobiography*. (Ed. J. Stillinger). Boston: Houghton Mifflin.

—— (1977). *Essays on Politics and Society*. Toronto: University of Toronto Press.

—— (1939). *Utilitarianism*. (In E. A. Burtt, Ed.) *The English Philosopher from Bacon to Mill*. New York: The Modern Library.

—— (1939). On Liberty. (In E. A. Burtt, Ed.) *The English Philosopher from Bacon to Mill*. New York: The Modern Library.

—— (1965). *Principles of Political Economy, with Some of Their Applications to Social Philosophy*. Toronto: University of Toronto Press.

Miniter, R. (1999). The False Promise of Slave Redemption. *Atlantic Monthly*, 284(1), 63–70.

Mitchell, M. (1973, 1936). *Gone With The Wind*. New York: Avon Books.

Mitchell, W. (April 4, 2011.) Beyond Austerity. *The Nation*, 11-17.

Mollenkamp, C. & L. Rappaport, (April 14, 2011). Financial Crisis, *The Wall Street Journal*, C1.

Mooney, C. (July/August 2011). The Reality Gap. *The American Prospect*, pp. 18-25.

Moore, J. B. (1960). *The Works of James Buchanan*. New York: Antiquarian Press.

Morgan, E. S. (1988.) *Inventing the People, The Rise of Popular Sovereignty in England and America*. New York: W. W. Norton.

Morris, C. R. (1959). *Locke, Berkeley, Hume*. Oxford: Oxford University Press.

Morrison, S. L. (1972, 1923). *Sources and Documents Illustrating the American Revolution, 1794–1788 and the Formation of the Federal Constitution*. London: Oxford University Press.

Muller, R.A. (June 2011). I Stick to the Science. *Scientific American*, 304(6), 84-87.

Munford, B. B. (1910). *Virginia's Attitude Toward Slavery and Secession*. New York: Longmans, Green and Co.

Murphy, R. & H. Gulliver. (1971). *The Southern Strategy*. New York: Charles Scribner's Sons.

Myrdal, G. (1944). *An American Dilemma: The Negro Problem and Modern Democracy*. New York: Harper & Row.

Nagel, P. C. (1997). *John Quincy Adams, A Public Life, A Private Life*. New York: Alfred Knopf.

Nasar, S. (2011). *Grand Pursuit, The Story of Economic Genius*. New York: Simon & Schuster.

Nation's Report Card, The, Civics 2006: National Assessment of Educational Progress at Grades 4, 8 and 12. Washington, DC: National Center for Educational Statistics, U.S. Department of Education.

Neely, M.E. (2002). *The Union Divided, Party Conflict in the Civil War North*. Cambridge, MA: Harvard University Press.

Nelson, L. (Fall 2011) 'Sovereigns' in Black, *Intelligence Report*, 143, pp. 36-40.

Nichols, J. & R. W. McChesney. (November 29, 2010). The Money and Media Election Complex. *The Nation*, 11-17.

Niskanen, W. A. (1994). *Bureaucracy and Public Economics*. Brookfield, VT: Edward Elgar Publishing Co.

Noonan, P. (May1-2, 2010). The Big Alienation. *The Wall Street Journal*, A13.

Olmsted, F. L. (1904). *A Journey in the Seaboard Slave States*. New York: G. P. Putnams.

Olson, R. G. (2004). *Science and Religion, 1450–1900, From Copernicus to Darwin*. Baltimore: The Johns Hopkins University Press.

—— (1993). *The Emergence of the Social Sciences, 1642–1792*. New York: Twayne Publishers.

Overstreet, H. & B. (1964). *The Strange Tactics of Extremism*. New York: W. W. Norton.

Padover, S. K. (1967). *The Washington Papers*. New York: Grosset and Dunlap.

Paine, T. (1993). *The Age of Reason, Being an Investigation of True and Fabulous Theology*. New York: Gramercy Books.

—— (1995). *Collected Writings*. (ed. E. Foner). (New York: The Library of America.

Palast, G. (2004). *The Best Democracy Money Can Buy*. New York: A Plume Book.

Panetta, L. E. & P. Gall (1971). *Bring Us Together, The Nixon Team and the Civil Rights Retreat*. Philadelphia: J. B. Lippincott Company.

Parloff, R. (January 17, 2011). On History's Stage: Chief Justice John Roberts, Jr. *Fortune*, Vol. 163(1), 63-76.

Partridge, A. R. (December 2010). Building a 21st Century Democracy. *The ASU Magazine*, 14(2), 24-33.

Paul, R. (2008). *The Revolution, A Manifesto*. New York: Grand Central Publishing.

Perry, L. (1989*). Intellectual Life in America, A History*. Chicago: University of Chicago Press.

Philpot, T. S. (2007). *Race, Republicans, & the Return of the Party of Lincoln*. Ann Arbor: The University of Michigan Press.

Pierce, C. P. (2010). *Idiot America, How Stupidity Became a Virtue in the Land of the Free*. New York: Anchor Books.

Plato. (1956). *Protagoras*. (Ed. I. Edman). New York: The Modern Library.

—— (1956). *Theaetetus*. (Ed. I. Edman). New York: The Modern Library.

—— (1944). *The Republic* (Trans. B. Jowett). New York: The Heritage Press.

—— (1961). *The Collected Dialogues*. Princeton: Princeton University Press.

—— (1994). *Symposium* (Tr. R. Waterfield). Oxford: Oxford University Press.

—— (1956). *The Works of Plato* (Ed. I. Edman). New York: Modern Library.

Plessey v Ferguson. (1896). 163, U.S. 537.

Plyler v. Doe (1982). 457 U.S. 202.

Pole, J. R. (1966). *Political Representation in England and the Origins of the American Republic*. London: Macmillan.

Pope-Hennesy, J. (2004). *Sins of the Fathers, The Atlantic Slave Trade 1141-1807*. Edison, NJ: Castle Books.

Potok, M. (Spring 2010). Rage on the Right, The Year in Hate and Extremism. *Intelligence Report*, 41-63.

—— (2009). *Terror From the Right*. Montgomery, AL: Southern Poverty Law Center.

—— (Spring 2011). The Year in Hate and Extremism. *Intelligence Report*, 41-67.

Preston, J. (January 6, 2011). State Lawmakers Outline Plans to End Birthright Citizenship, Drawing Outcry. *The New York Times*, A18.

Rakove, J. (2010). *Revolutionaries, A New History of the Invention of America*. Boston: Houghton Mifflin.

Rand, A. (1999). *Atlas Shrugged*. New York: A Plume Book.

Rasmussen, D. (2011). *American Uprising, The Untold Story of America's Largest Slave Revolt*. New York: HarperCollins.

Rasmussen, S. & D. Schoen. (2010). *Mad as Hell, How the Tea Party Movement is Fundamentally Remaking Our Two-Party System*. New York: Harper.

Rayner, B. L. (1834). *Life of Thomas Jefferson*. Boston: Tilly, Colman and Holden.

Reeves, J. S. (1907). *American Diplomacy under Tyler and Polk*. Baltimore: The Johns Hopkins Press.

Reich, R. (September 4, 2011). The Limping Middle Class. *The New York Times*, bw6.

Reid, B. H. (2007). *Robert E. Lee, Icon for a Nation.* Amherst, NY: Prometheus Books.

Registry of Debates, 1824–1837, 21st Congress, 1st Session, pp. 360-377.

Remini, R. V. (2010). *At the Edge of the Precipice, Henry Clay and the Compromise that Saved the Union.* New York: Basic Books.

Report of the Financial Crisis Inquiry Commission (2011). Washington, DC: Financial Crisis Inquiry Commission.

Report to the President on the Economic Conditions in the South. (1938). Washington DC: National Emergency Council.

Reynolds, D. S. (2010, April 18). Tocqueville: The Life. *New York Times Book Review*, p. 19.

—— (October 3, 2010). Learning to be Lincoln. *The New York Times Book Review*, p. 20.

Rhodes, T. (2000). *Republicans in the South, Voting for the State House, Voting for the White House.* Westport, CN: Praeger.

Riegle, D. (1972). *O Congress.* New York: Doubleday.

Robertson, C. (November 7, 2010) White Democrats Lose More Ground in the South. *The New York Times*, 22.

—— (February 21, 2011). Making a Stand for the Confederacy, 150 Years Later. *The New York Times*, A10.

____ (October 3, 2011). For Politics in South, Race Divide is Defining. *The New York Times*, A10ff.

Robertson, D. (1999). *Denmark Vesey, The Buried Story of America's Largest Slave Rebellion and the Man Who Led it.* New York: Vintage Books.

Robinson, J.A. G. (1987). *The Montgomery Bus Boycott and the Women Who Started It.* Knoxville, TN: The University of Tennessee Press.

Rockefeller, J. D. (1973). *The Second American Revolution.* New York: Harper & Row.

Roosevelt, T. R. (1910). The New Nationalism. Speech at Osawatomie, KS at: http://en.wikipedia.org/wiki/New_Nationalism.

Roosevelt, F. D. (1944). *Rendezvous With Destiny.* (Ed. J.B.S. Hardman). New York: The Dryden Press.

Rosenblatt, R. (January 5, 1981). Reagan, Man of the Year. *Time Magazine*, 11-23.

Ross, D. (1991). *The Origins of American Social Science.* New York: Cambridge University Press.

Rossiter, C. (ed.) (1961). *The Federalist Papers.* New York. Mentor Book.

Rousseau, J. J. (1979). *Emile.* New York: Basic Books.

—— (1964, 1768). *Emile, Julie and other writings.* Woodbury, NY: Barrons Educational Series, Inc.

—— (1995, 1762). *The Social Contract.* New York: Barnes & Noble Books.

Rude, G. (1988). *The French Revolution.* London: Phoenix Giant.

Rutenberg, J. & S. F. Kovalski. (December 26, 2011). Paul Disowns Extremists' Views But Doesn't Disavow Support. *The New York Times*, A1ff.

Rutland, R. A. (1987). *James Madison, The Founding Father.* New York: Macmillan.

____ (1977). *The Federalist Papers of James Madison.* (Vol. 10). Chicago: University of Chicago Press.

Sachs, J. (2011). *The Price of Civilization, Reawakening American Virtue and Prosperity.* New York: Random House.

Samuelson, P. (1980). *Economics.* (11th edition). New York: McGraw Hill.

Sandberg, C. (1959). *Abraham Lincoln.* (3 vols.) New York: Dell Publishing Co.

Sandel, M. J. (1996). *Democracy's Discontent, America in Search of a Public Philosophy*. Cambridge: Harvard University Press.
Scherr, S. (Summer 2009). Going Under. *Intelligence Report*, pp. 12-19.
Schachner, N. (1957). *Thomas Jefferson*. New York: Thomas Yosloff.
Schlesinger, A. (1992). *The Disuniting of America, Reflections on a Multicultural Society*. New York: W.W. Norton.
Schraad-Tischler, D & N. Azahaf. (2011). *Social Justice in the OECD—How Do Member States Compare?* Paris: OECD.
Seelye, K. Q. (November 30, 2010). Celebrating Secession Without the Slaves. *The New York Times*, A19.
Sen, A. (1992). *Inequality Reexamined*. Cambridge: Harvard University Press.
────── (2002). Rationality and Freedom. Cambridge: The Belnap Press of Harvard University Press.
Settle, M. L. (2001). *I, Roger Williams, A Fragment of Autobiography*. New York: W. W. Norton.
Severson, K. & R. Brown. (November 3, 2011). Georgia Men Held in Plot to Attack Government. *The New York Times*, A17.
Sharpes, D. K. (1987). *Education and the U.S. Government*. New York: St. Martin's Press.
────── (1973). Residence and Race in Education: Conflicts in Courts and Communities. *Journal of Teacher Education*, 24(4), (1973), 289-93.
────── (August 29, 2011). GOP Selectively Reveres Constitution. *The Arizona Republic*, B6.
────── (2007). *Outcasts and Heretics, Profiles in Independent Thought and Courage*. Landham, MD: Lexington Books.
────── (2009). *The Evolution of the Social Sciences*. Lanham, MD: Lexington Books.
────── (Summer 2006). Accepting Evolution or Discarding Science. *Kappa Delta Pi Record*, v. 42(4), pp. 156-160.
Sherman, W. T. (1875). *Memoirs*. Vol. II. New York: D. Appleton & Co.
Shermer, M. (September 2011). What is Pseudoscience? *Scientific American*, 305 (3), p. 92.
Sherwin, M. (1963). *The Extremists*. New York: St. Martin's Press.
Siegel, L. (January 15, 2012). What's Race Got To Do With It? *The New York Times*, BW SR9/.
Silberman, C. E. (1964). *Crisis in Black and White*. New York: Vintage Books.
Simon, J. Y. (2003). *The Papers of Ulysses S. Grant*. Carbondale, ILL: Southern Illinois University Press. (Vol. 25).
Sloan, A. & T. Newmyer (November 1, 2010). Why Can't Washington Magically Fix the Economy? *Fortune*, pp. 96-108.
Sloan, A. (September 5, 2011). Relief from Economic Turmoil. *Fortune*, 164(4), 56-61.
Smith, A. (1991). *The Wealth of Nations*. Amherst, NY: Prometheus Books.
────── (1976-77). *The Wealth of Nations*. Oxford: Oxford University Press (Glascow Edition).
Smith, J. & R. Lenz ((Winter 2011). New Soldiers of the Confederacy. *Intelligence Report,* No. 144. pp. 12-14.
Smith, R. N. (February 11, 2011). The Reagan Revelation. *Time*, pp. 30-33.
Smith, E. S., (September 1999). The Effects of Investments in Social Capital of Youth on Political and Civic Behavior in Young Adulthood: A Longitudinal Analysis." *Political Psychology*, 20(3), pp. 553-580.
Snyder, T. D. (2010). *Mini-Digest of Education Statistics*. Washington DC: National Center for Education Statistics, Institute of Education Science, U.S. Department of Education.

Soodalter, R. (2006). *Hanging Captain Gordon, The Life and Trial of an American Slave Trader.* New York: Washington Square Press.

Spencer, H. (1906, 1861). *Education, Intellectual, Moral and Physical.* London: Watts & Co.

—— (1870). *First Principles.* London: Williams and Norgate.

—— (1972). *On Social Evolution.* (Ed. J.D.Y. Peel) Chicago: The University of Chicago Press.

—— (1969). *Principles of Sociology.* Hamden, CN: Archon Books.

Stanley, A. (February 5, 2011). The Reagan We May Never Know. *The New York Times*, C1.

Starobin, P. (July 4, 2010). What If America Broke Apart? *The Arizona Republic*, B11-B12.

State of Metropolitan America (2010). Washington, DC: The Brooking Institution.

State Papers on Nullification. (no author) (1970). New York: Da Capo Press. (And 1834, Boston: Dutton and Wentworth)

Stephens, A. (1868). *A Constitutional View of the Late War Between the States, Its Causes, Character, Conduct and Results.* (Vol. I & II) Philadelphia: National Publishing Company.

Stephenson, W. H. (1938). *Isaac Franklin, Slave Trader and Planter of the Old South.* Baton Rouge: Louisiana State University Press.

Stern, J. A. (2010). *Mary Chestnut's Civil War Epic.* Chicago: The University of Chicago Press.

St. John, J. (1987). *Constitutional Journal.* Ottawa, IL: Jameson Books.

Stiglitz, J. E. (July 8, 2011). The Ideological Crisis of Western Capitalism. *The Jakarta Post*, p. 2.

Stone, I. (1956). *Men to Match My Mountains, The Opening of the Far West, 1840-1900.* Garden City, N.Y., Doubleday.

Stowe, H. B. (1986). *Uncle Tom's Cabin.* New York: Penguin Classics.

Strober, D. H., & G.S. Strober. (1998). *Reagan, The Man and His Presidency.* Boston: Houghton Mifflin.

Sussman, B. (2010). *Climategate, A Veteran Meteorologist Exposes the Global Warming Scam.* Washington, DC: WND Books.

Swann v Charlotte-Mechlenberg (1971). 402, US 1.

Tanenhaus, S. (May 23, 2010). The Textbook Libertarian. *The New York Times*, wk3.

—— (January 15, 2012). History vs. the Tea Party. *The New York Times*, bw8.

Tarnas, R. (1991). *The Passion of the Western Mind, Understanding the Ideas That Have Shaped our World View.* New York: Ballantine.

Terkel, S. (1992). *How Blacks and Whites Think and Feel About the American Obsession.* New York: Doubleday.

Theokas, S. (2010). *Shut Out of the Military, Today's High School Education Doesn't Mean You're Ready for Today's Army.* Washington, DC: The Education Trust.

The Nation's Report Card, Civics 2006: National Assessment of Educational Progress at Grades 4, 8 and 12. Washington, DC: National Center for Educational Statistics, U.S. Department of Education.

Thomas, H. (1998). *The Slave Trade, The History of the Atlantic Slave Trade 1440-1870.* London: Papermac.

Thomas, C. D. (August 19, 2011). Rapid Range Shifts of Species Associated with High Levels of Climate Warming. *Science*, 333(6045), 1024-1026.

Thoreau, H.D. (October 30, 1859). A Plea for Captain John Brown. http://law2.umkc.edu/faculty/projects/ftrials/johnbrown/thoreauplea.html.

Thucydides (1831). *The Peloponnesian War*. London: A. J. Valpy.
Turgot, A–R–J. (1963). *Reflections on the Formation and the Distribution of Riches*. New York: Augustus. M. Kelley.
Trade and Development Report, 2011, Overview. United Nations: Geneva.
Trinka, M. (December 7, 2010). Educating Americans About Their History, Through Poster-Sized Lessons. *The New York Times*, A24.
Truman, H. S. (1956). *Memoirs. Vol. 2, Years of Trial and Hope*. Garden City, NY: Doubleday & Co.
Truth, S. (1968). *Narrative of Sojourner Truth, A Bondswoman of Olden Time*. New York: Arno Press.
Turlock, G., & A. Seldon, G. L. Brady. (2002). *Government Failure, A Primer in Public Choice*. Washington, DC: The Cato Institute.
Tylor, E. B. (1958). *Religion in Primitive Culture*. New York: Harper & Bros.
—— (1865). *Researches into the Early History of Mankind and the Development of Civilization*. London: John Murray.
—— (1958). *The Origins of Culture*. New York: Harper & Brothers Publishers.

United States v Cruickshank et al. 92 U.S. 542 (1876).

Van Deusen, G. G. (1937). *The Life of Henry Clay*. Boston: Little, Brown & Co.
Von Abele, R. (1946). *Alexander H. Stephens, A Biography*. New York: Alfred A. Knopf.
Van Doren, C. (1991). *A History of Knowledge, The Pivotal Events, People, and Achievements of World History*. New York: Ballantine.
Von Drehle, D. (April 18, 2011). Why We're Still Fighting he Civil War. *Time*, 40–51.

Wade, W.C. (1987). *The Fiery Cross, The Ku Klux Klan in America*. New York: Oxford University Press.
Walsh, M.W. (October 23, 2011). The Little State With a Big Mess. *The New York Times*, bu1ff.
Ward, A. (2008). *The Slaves' War, The Civil War in the Words of Former Slaves*. Boston: Houghton Mifflin Company.
Washington, B. T. (1968*). Up From Slavery*. New York: Magnum Books.
Weber, M. (1949). *The Methodology of the Social Sciences* (Trans. & Ed. E. A. Shils & H. A. Finch) New York: The Free Press.
—— (1994). *Sociological Writings*. (Ed. W. Heydebrand). New York: Continuum.
—— (1958). *The Protestant Ethic and the Spirit of Capitalism*. New York: Charles Scribner's Sons.
Wehner, P. (April 14, 2011). The GOP and the Birther Trap. *The Wall Street Journal*, A17.
Whitman, W. (1923). *Leaves of Grass* (3 vols. in one) New York: D. Appleton and Co.
Whose Legal Right? (December 2011). *American Prospect*, 22(10), 7-11.
Williams, T. H. (2010, 1955). *P. G. T. Beauregard, Napoleon in Gray*. Baton Rouge, LA: Louisiana State University Press.
Williams, C. R. (1928). *The Life of Rutherford B. Hayes*. (Vol. II). Columbus: Ohio State Archaeological and Historical Society. (pp. 33-68).
Wills, G. (1978). *Inventing America*. New York: Doubleday.
—— (1981). *Explaining America: The Federalist*. New York: Doubleday.
—— (1992). *Lincoln at Gettysburg, The Words That Remade America*. New York: Simon & Schuster.
—— (1987). *Reagan's America, Innocents at Home*. New York: Doubleday.

Wilson, W. (1897). *The State, Elements of Historical and Practical Politics.* Boston: D.C. Heath & Co.

Wilson, J. K. (1996). *New Gingrich, Capitol Crimes and Misdemeanors.* Monroe, Maine: Common Courage Press.

Whitford, D. (January 16, 2012). Romney Means Business. *Fortune*, 17-18.

Wiltse, C. M. (1944). *John C. Calhoun, Nationalist*, 1782–1828. New York: The Bobbs-Merrill Co.

Winch, P. (1958). *The Idea of a Social Science.* London: Routledge & Kegan Paul.

Wittenberg, E. J. (2002). *Little Phil, A Reassessment of the Civil War Leadership of Gen. Philip H. Sheridan.* Washington DC: Brassey's, Inc.

Woodward, C. V. (1951). *Origins of the New South 1877-1913.* Baton Rouge: Louisiana State University Press.

Woodward, C. (October 30, 2011). The Great Divide. *The Arizona Republic*, B11.

—— (1956). *Reunion and Reaction, The Compromise of 1877 and the End of Reconstruction.* Garden City, NY: Doubleday Anchor Books.

Woodward, B. & C. Bernstein. (1976). *The Final Days.* New York: Avon.

Wright, W. A. (1993). *African Americans in the Early Republic, 1789–1831.* Wheeling, IL: Harlan Davidson.

X, M. (1965). *The Autobiography of Malcolm X.* New York: Grove Press.

Yearns, W. B. (1960). *The Confederate Congress.* Athens: The University of Georgia Press.

Zaitchik, A. (Fall 2010). Patriot Paranoia. *Intelligence Report*, Issue139, Montgomery, AL:: Southern Poverty Law Center, pp. 27-34.

Zernike, K. (December 20, 2010). Proposed Amendment Would Enable States to Repeal Federal Law. *The New York Times*, A13.

INDEX

327

Donald K. Sharpes, Ph.D. is Senior Visiting Fellow at Cambridge University, and Professor in the Emeritus College at Arizona State University, a former research associate at Stanford University and technical division director in the U.S. Department of Education in Washington DC. He has taught at the universities of Maryland, Maine, Virginia, Virginia Tech, Utah State, Weber State and Arizona State. He did postdoctoral studies at the University of Sussex, was a Visiting Scholar at Oxford University in 1998–1999, and has lived and worked in Asia and the Middle East. He has authored 20 books and over 240 articles in the social and behavioral sciences, humanities, and teacher education. He has been a foreign correspondent for *The Salt Lake Tribune*, and a contributor to several newspapers, and been published in the U.S., England, Finland, Norway, Germany (in German), India, Malaysia, China (in Chinese), Hong Kong, and Denmark (in Danish). He has been awarded four Fulbright scholarships, one each to Malaysia, Cyprus, Denmark and Indonesia, and been sponsored by the governments of Malaysia, China, South Africa, Mongolia, Kazakhstan, Uzbekistan, and universities throughout the world. He was Distinguished Visiting Professor at Qinghai Normal University from 1988-94, and the first American inducted as a Fellow in the China Senior Professors Association. He is past President of International Studies of the American Educational Research Association that in 2008 awarded him a Lifetime Achievement Award.

www.ingramcontent.com/pod-product-compliance
Lightning Source LLC
LaVergne TN
LVHW051452080426
835509LV00017B/1747